Lessons in Critical Reading and Writing

Lessons in Critical Reading and Writing

Three Masters of Russian Fiction

Jean Sisk

Harcourt Brace Jovanovich, Inc.
New York   Chicago   San Francisco   Atlanta   Dallas

Copyright © 1970 by Harcourt Brace Jovanovich, Inc.

All rights reserved. No part of this publication may be reproduced or transmitted in any form or by any means, electronic or mechanical, including photocopy, recording, or any information storage and retrieval system, without permission in writing from the publisher.

PRINTED IN THE UNITED STATES OF AMERICA

ISBN 0-15-335402-X

To the Reader

Americans are great readers of fiction, perhaps because American writers are great writers of fiction. Hawthorne, Melville, Crane, Twain, Hemingway, Faulkner, Steinbeck — all have won admirers in all corners of the reading world; all have been translated into a number of other languages, the Russian language among them. It is paradoxical that Russian readers may be more aware of American writers and American fiction of certain periods than American readers are of great Russian novelists and writers of short stories. The major purpose of this book is to encourage a reciprocity of enjoyment — to open, for American readers, the door to one of the greatest of literary worlds, the world of fiction written by three of Russia's universally acclaimed writers — Turgenev, Tolstoy, and Dostoevsky.

When one opens a door, one takes a first look, making a visual survey of what lies beyond. Tempted by the initial view, one enters a room to become acquainted in a more leisurely way with its contents. If the browsing proves interesting, then one's curiosity is aroused by what is beyond the *next* door, and the next, and . . . The fictional worlds of the three Russian masters presented in this book are so vast that we can provide in these pages only a glimpse, an exploration of an anteroom or — more accurately — a small gallery of portraits, places, and subjects whose purpose is to display samples of the kinds of resources the museum holds.

In this book you will find several stories by each of the three writers. These particular stories were chosen, first of all, because they are enjoyable in themselves and because they have something "relevant" to say to contemporary Americans, even though most of them were written over fifty years ago. They have also been selected because they deal with themes, introduce characters, picture landscapes and social settings, and narrate situations that are typical of each writer's major works — their long novels. If these stories whet your appetite for more, or if you study the longer works of Turgenev, Tolstoy, and Dostoevsky at a later time, you should find that the doors to enjoyment and understanding will then open a little more easily to reveal not unfamiliar contents.

To increase your understanding of the close tie between Russian writers and the historical and social contexts of Russian society, each section in this book offers additional material about that society and the role of Russian writers as the conscience of their culture and the voice of the oppressed. To add a dimension of greater depth to your appreciation of the literary excellence of these men, critical comments about their work, as they clarify stories and themes, are also provided. In addition, there are suggestions for discussion and writing that may be used as they prove helpful to you.

We hope that you have time to read and discuss all the selections in the book; but if you don't, choose those of most interest and save the rest for more leisurely reading.

JEAN SISK

CONTENTS

PART ONE   Introduction

Russian Life and Literature   3

PART TWO   Ivan Turgenev

Ivan Turgenev: Introduction   17
    Ivan Turgenev by Henry James   18

I. Reading Literature
    Tales from *A Sportsman's Notebook*   24
        Bezhin Lea   25
        Meeting   45
        The Reformer and the Russian German   55

II. The Reader as Critic
    Talking and Writing About Literature:
        Art as a Means or as an End in Itself   68
    The Russian Critics and "Art for Art's Sake"   69
    Turgenev Responds   72
    Putting Yourself in the Critic's Place   74

III. The Reader as Writer:
    Putting Yourself in the Author's Place   76

PART THREE Leo Tolstoy

Leo Tolstoy: Introduction 85
   Leo Tolstoy by Prince D. S. Mirsky 85
Gorky on Tolstoy
   Leo Tolstoy Is Dead by Maxim Gorky 92

I. Reading Literature
   War
      The Raid 104
      After the Ball 130
   Peasants
      Alyosha 143
      Elias and *A Grain as Big as a Hen's Egg* 151

II. The Reader as Critic
   Talking and Writing About Literature:
      Art as Transmission of Feeling 162
   Tolstoy's Theories of Literature 163
   Tolstoy's Definition of Art 163
   "Good" Art and "Bad" Art 164
   The Universality of Art 165
   Your Own Theories 166

III. The Reader as Writer: "External" Characterization 169
   Tolstoy's Technique:
      Revealing the Internal Through External Description 170
   Tolstoy's Technique: Repetition of Detail 171
   Writing a Characterization from an "External" Point of View 173

PART FOUR   Theodore Dostoevsky

Theodore Dostoevsky: Introduction   177
  Dostoevsky by Marc Slonim   177

I. Reading Literature
   Terror
     Followers of Petrashevsky by Yevgeny Yevtushenko   185
     Dostoevsky's Account of Prison: A Letter to His Brother   188
     The Peasant Marey   194
   The Russians
     The Crocodile   202
   The Meek Ones
     An Honest Thief   240

II. The Reader as Critic
    Art as the "Higher Realism"   259
    Varieties of Realism and Reality   261
    Dostoevsky's "Realism"   263
    Another Point of View: Art as Symbol   266

III. The Reader as Writer: Writing "Dramatic" Dialogue   267
     Dostoevsky's Method of Working   268
     Dostoevsky's Narrative Method   271
     Writing a Dramatic Dialogue or Monologue   273

A Concluding Portrait
   Dostoevsky: The Making of a Novelist by Ernest Simmons   273

PART FIVE   Variations on a Theme:
         The "Negative Hero" in Russian Literature

   The "Negative Hero" in Russian Literature: Introduction   281
       Oblomov: The Prototype of the "Negative Hero"   282
       The Diary of a Superfluous Man by Ivan Turgenev   285
       The Memoirs of a Madman by Leo Tolstoy   332
       The Dream of a Ridiculous Man by Theodore Dostoevsky   349
       A Moscow Hamlet by Anton Chekhov   372

PART SIX   On Translation

       The Impossibilities of Translation   383
       The Russian Language   387
       Kinds of Translations   391
       Putting Yourself in the Translator's Place   398
       Reproducing Speech in Writing   405

Lessons in Critical
Reading and Writing

PART ONE

Introduction

RUSSIAN LIFE AND LITERATURE

A poet in Russia is more than a poet.
There the fate of being born a poet
falls only on those stirred by the pride of belonging,
who have no comfort, and no peace.

There the poet is his century's image,
and the visionary symbol of the future.
Without shyness, the poet summing up
the total, all that has happened before him.[1]

These words by a contemporary Russian writer are the key to an appreciation and understanding of the stories you will read in this book. All these stories but one were written in the last century by three writers of fiction acknowledged to be among the greatest in the world—Ivan Turgenev (1818–1883), Leo Tolstoy (1828–1910), and Theodore Dostoevsky (1821–1881). In a sense, all writers "sum up the total" of the nation they live in, but the Russian writer, perhaps more than the writers of any other country, represented to his own country and to the world the experiences, feelings, problems, and triumphs of the typically Russian culture.

Probably there is greater similarity between men of different nations at a given time than between men of the same nation in different centuries, more in common between an American and a Russian of 1964 than between a Russian of 1664 and of today. And yet, though Englishmen, Americans, Russians may not exist in the abstract, they do, without question, look on life in somewhat different ways, and these ways are embodied in their literary tradition perhaps even more surely than in their institutions. For "it is in literature," as Alfred North Whitehead has said, "that the concrete outlook of humanity receives its expression. Accordingly, it is to literature that we must look if we hope to discover the inward thoughts of a generation." Now, the inward thoughts of a people are more fundamental and more complex than the way it acts, the way it dresses, and the way it builds its houses—though these outward signs, the labels by which an age is recognized, are

---

[1] From the Prologue "Prayer Before the Poem" from *Bratsk Station and Other New Poems* by Yevgeny Yevtushenko, copyright 1966 by Sun Books Pty. Ltd. Reprinted by permission of Doubleday & Company, Inc.

often clear reflections of the deeper, hidden thoughts, just as, for example, in the landscape architecture of the eighteenth century, passing from the patterned classical garden to the wild and profuse "English" garden, was expressed the change in dominant ideas and tastes from the ordered design of rationalist systems to the unrestraint and abundance of romanticism.

Through the work of its many artists is built the artistic tradition of a nation. It expresses its culture, which is not some mystic quality that in an inexplicable way makes human beings of one land essentially different and of necessity forever alien to those of other lands, but an involved combination of attitudes and feelings that develop through the circumstances of history. The way a people responds to the events with which it must contend is determined by the nature of the events and is formed by the tradition built up through a series of such responses over a long period of time, rather than by some predetermined, innate qualities of character. And a people's art is a record of how its attitudes and feelings are shaped in the historic process. No simple explanation can be given for a matter so complex.[1] [*Helen Muchnic*]

Even though no "simple" explanations can be offered for the above, there are understandable reasons why Russian writers became the spokesmen for their society. For one thing, the writers and literary critics were practically the only educated group who stood outside the serf class or the governing nobility either by birth or by choice. Turgenev and Tolstoy were members of the hereditary landed gentry (major or minor nobility). Both these writers, though they remained aristocrats by right and by taste, castigated their own class for perpetuating the evils of serfdom and the brutal corporal and capital punishment that degraded both the peasantry and the violators of the autocratic civil and military codes.

During the nineteenth century, when these literary giants were writing, Russia was governed by a succession of Romanov kings with absolute power over the people—Alexander I (1801–1825), Nicholas I (1825–1855), Alexander II (1855–1881), and Alexander III (1881–1894). The society over which they ruled was roughly divided into three classes —the gentry, the clergy, and the peasantry. In addition, there were certain types of "town dwellers" of ambiguous station in life—tradesman, artisans, and "burghers." Membership in the gentry was hereditary, but the Russian practice of dividing property equally among male heirs,

---

[1] From the book *An Introduction to Russian Literature* by Helen Muchnic, copyright, 1947, ©, 1964, by Helen Muchnic. Reprinted by permission of E. P. Dutton & Co., Inc.

instead of leaving entire estates to the oldest son, tended to proliferate the number of minor nobility with small landholdings who, nevertheless, enjoyed all the privileges accorded to the gentry—freedom from taxation and from military conscription.

The peasants were actually serfs owned by landowners and factory owners. They were freed by Alexander II's Emancipation Decree of 1861, just two years before our own Emancipation Proclamation freed the Negro slaves, to whom the Russian serfs have frequently been compared. At the time of their emancipation, there were approximately 50 million peasants—over four fifths of the entire population of Russia at that time. Only half of these, however, were actually in total bondage to a landowner. A great number of the serfs worked on state-owned land, and others were fortunate enough to have owners who allowed them to pay an annual fee for the land they farmed instead of exacting from them three days of labor per week, as was the custom with some gentry. Enterprising peasants who paid this annual fee were often able to amass some property of their own, become fairly prosperous, and eventually acquire their freedom.

The 1897 census revealed that thirty-six years after the emancipation about 80 percent of the rural population was illiterate. And even then, at the end of the nineteenth century, the gentry and clergy together made up only 2 percent of the total population of Russia, with the military comprising only a little more than 6 percent, the peasantry over 80 percent and the town dwellers about 9 percent.

In this situation, the writers and literary critics became the conscience of their country. Perhaps no critic has better expressed the Russian writer's mission than V. G. Belinsky—with N. G. Chernyshevsky and N. A. Dobrolyubov, one of the three greatest nineteenth-century Russian critics. Belinsky, along with other liberals who wished to "Westernize" or reform Russian life, was shocked by the publication of Gogol's "Select Passages from Correspondence with Friends," in which the famous novelist

> hailed despotism and blind obedience to the Church and asserted that literacy was harmful to the people; that serfdom was a wholesome, patriarchal institution; that capital and corporal punishments were excellent; that fear was the best foundation for family life; that no reforms in the administration of justice were necessary, and so on.[1] [*Marc Slonim*]

[1] From *The Epic of Russian Literature: From Its Origins Through Tolstoy* by Marc Slonim, copyright 1950 by Oxford University Press, Inc. Reprinted by permission of the publisher.

In his "Letter to N. V. Gogol," published in 1847, Belinsky described the conditions in Russia to which he believed the dedicated writer should address himself:

> ... you failed to realize that Russia sees her salvation not in mysticism, or asceticism, or pietism, but in the successes of civilization, enlightenment, and humanity. What she needs is not sermons (she has heard enough of them!) or prayers (she has repeated them too often!), but the awakening in the people of a sense of their human dignity lost for so many centuries amid dirt and refuse; she needs rights and laws conforming not to the preaching of the church but to common sense and justice, and their strictest possible observance. Instead of which she presents the dire spectacle of a country where men traffic in men, without even having the excuse so insidiously exploited by the American plantation owners who claim that the Negro is not a man; a country where people call themselves not by names but by nicknames such as Vanka, Vaska, Steshka, Palashka; a country where there are not only no guarantees for individuality, honor, and property, but even no police order, and where there is nothing but vast corporations of official thieves and robbers of various description. The most vital national problems in Russia today are the abolition of serfdom and corporal punishment and the strictest possible observance of at least those laws that already exist. This is even realized by the government itself (which is well aware of how the landowners treat their peasants and how many of the former are annually done away with by the latter), as is proved by its timid and abortive half-measures for the relief of the white Negroes and the comical substitution of the single lash knout by a cat-o'-three tails. Such are the problems that prey on the mind of Russia in her apathetic slumber....
>
> ... you do not properly understand the Russian public. Its character is determined by the condition of Russian society in which fresh forces are seething and struggling for expression, and finding no outlet, they induce merely dejection, weariness, and apathy. Only literature, despite the Tartar censorship, shows signs of life and progressive movement. That is why the title of writer is held in such esteem among us; that is why literary success is easy among us even for a writer of little talent. The title of poet and writer has long since eclipsed the tinsel of epaulets and gaudy uniforms ... and here the public is right, for it looks upon Russian writers as its only leaders, defenders, and saviors against Russian

autocracy, orthodoxy, and nationality, and therefore, while always prepared to forgive a writer a bad book, will never forgive him a pernicious book.[1] [*V. G. Belinsky*]

The most difficult obstacle in the way of the writers' freedom to criticize the existing condition, however, was the censor, to whom Belinsky referred in his letter. All the writers whose stories you will read in this book were, at one time or another, involved with these guardians of czarist restrictions on free speech. Turgenev, the first author represented in this book, echoed Belinsky's concerns both with the conditions of society and with the restrictions placed on his work by the censors:

> I often went to see him [Belinsky] in the afternoon to pour out all my troubles to him. He had rented an apartment on the ground floor on the Fontanka Embankment, not far from Anichkin Bridge, consisting of several somber and rather damp rooms. I can't help saying it again: we had been going through very difficult times just then. Our young men today have never had to experience anything like it. Let the reader judge for himself: in the morning you may have got back your proofs from the censor, all mangled and mutilated and stained with red ink as though with blood; you may even have had to pay a personal call on the censor and after offering all sorts of useless and humiliating explanations and justifications, listen to him delivering his all too often sneering sentence from which there was no appeal. . . .[2]
>
> . . . In the street you probably ran across Mr. Bulgarin or his friend Mr. Grech; or some general, any general, not even your civil service chief, who snubbed or, what is worse, praised you. . . . You looked round: bribery was rampant, serfdom remained as firm as a rock, the barracks were in the forefront of everything, no courts of justice, rumors about the impending closure of the universities, the number of admissions to which were soon to be reduced to three hundred, journeys abroad were becoming impossible, no decent book could be ordered from abroad, a sort of

---

[1] From the book *Belinsky, Chernyshevsky and Dobrolyubov: Selected Criticism,* translated and edited by Ralph E. Matlaw, copyright, ©, 1962, by E. P. Dutton & Co., Inc. Reprinted by permission of the publisher.

[2] The censor F. was particularly distinguished for his humor at such interviews. "Good Lord," he used to say, "I don't want to cross out a single letter of your article. All I want is to destroy its spirit." He said to me one day looking with feeling into my eyes: "You don't want me to cross anything out. But just think: if I don't cross anything out, I may lose 300 rubles a year, and if I do—who cares? There were a few words before and now there aren't any more—what does it matter? How then can you expect me not to cross out? Really, young man!" [Turgenev's note].

> dark cloud was constantly hanging over the whole of the so-called department of learning and literature and, to cap it all, denunciations whispered and spread on all sides; no common bond among the younger generation, no common interests, everyone afraid and groveling—you might as well give it up! Well, you went to see Belinsky, somebody else came along, too, you started talking and—you felt better. The subjects of our talks were mostly of such a nature that no censor would in those days have passed them in print, but actually we never discussed politics: the utter uselessness of such discussions was clear to anyone.[1] [*Ivan Turgenev*]

American students are, unfortunately, not well acquainted with the great Russian writers. This perhaps may be because translations are never too satisfactory, perhaps because Russian writing is thought of as being ponderous, or perhaps because the "cold war" of recent decades has tinted American perceptions of even Russian *literature* of the past with negatively red, rather than rose-colored, prejudices. This is indeed a loss for the American student, a loss that this collection of stories and criticism attempts, in small part, to remedy.

The noted critic William Lyon Phelps, in trying to transmit his own enthusiasm for Russian masters of fiction to the reading public of 1911, explained the characteristics of Russian fiction that make it seem both like and unlike American literature:

> At the start, we notice a rather curious fact, which sharply differentiates Russian literature from the literature of England, France, Spain, Italy, and even from that of Germany. Russia is old; her literature is new. Russian history goes back to the ninth century; Russian literature, so far as it interests the world, begins in the nineteenth. Russian literature and American literature are twins. But there is this strong contrast, caused partly by the difference in age of the two nations. In the early years of the nineteenth century, American literature sounds like a child learning to talk, and then aping its elders; Russian literature is the voice of a giant, waking from a long sleep and becoming articulate. It is as though the world had watched this giant's deep slumber for a long time, wondering what he would say when he awakened. And what he has said has been well worth the thousand years of waiting. . . .
> The immense size of the country produces an element of large-

---

[1] From *Turgenev's Literary Reminiscences*, edited by David Magarshack, copyright © 1958 by Farrar, Straus & Cudahy, Inc. Reprinted by permission of Farrar, Straus & Giroux, Inc.

ness in Russian character that one feels not only in their novels, but almost invariably in personal contact and conversation with a more or less educated Russian. This is not imaginary and fantastic; it is a definite sensation, and immediately apparent. Bigness in early environment often produces a certain comfortable largeness of mental vision. One has only to compare in this particular a man from Russia with a man from Holland, or still better, a man from Texas with a man from Connecticut. The difference is easy to see, and easier to feel. It is possible that the man from the smaller district may be more subtle, or he may have had better educational advantages; but he is likely to be more narrow. A Texan told me once that it was eighteen miles from his front door to his front gate; now I was born in a city block, with no front yard at all. I had surely missed something.

Russians are molded on a large scale, and their novels are as wide in interest as the world itself. There is a refreshing breadth of vision in the Russian character, which is often as healthful to a foreigner as the wind that sweeps across the vast prairies. This largeness of character partly accounts for the impression of vastness that their books produce on Occidental eyes.

... The good Russian women seem immensely superior to the men in their instant perception and recognition of moral values, which gives them a chart and compass in life. Possibly, too, the women are stiffened in will by a natural reaction in finding their husbands and brothers so stuffed with inconclusive theories. "The Russian hero is always silly and stupid, he is always sick of something; always thinking of something that cannot be understood, and is himself so miserable, so m–i–serable! He will think, think, then talk, then he will go and make a declaration of love, and after that he thinks, and thinks again, till he marries. ... And when he is married, he talks all sorts of nonsense to his wife, and then abandons her."[1] One is appalled by the prodigious amount of nonsense that Russian wives and daughters are forced to hear from their talkative and ineffective heads of houses. It must be worse than the metaphysical discussion between Adam and the angel, while Eve waited on table, and supplied the windy debaters with something really useful.

... The amount of space given in Russian novels to philosophical introspection and debate is a truthful portrayal of the subtle Russian mind. Russians love to talk; they are strenuous in con-

---

[1] This is a quotation from I. A. Goncharov's *Oblomov*. See also page 281.

versation, and forget their meals and sleep. I have known some Russians who will sit up all night, engaged in the discussion of a purely abstract topic, totally oblivious to the passage of time. . . . The Anglo-Saxon is content to allow ideas that are inconsistent and irreconcilable to get along together as best they may in his mind, in order that he may somehow get something done. Not so the Russian.

. . . Finally, in reading the works of Tolstoy, Turgenev, Dostoevsky, Gorky, Chekhov, Andreyev, and others, what is the general impression produced on the mind of a foreigner? It is one of intense gloom. Of all the dark books in fiction, no works sound such depths of suffering and despair as are fathomed by the Russians. Many English readers used to say that the novels of George Eliot were "profoundly sad,"—it became almost a hackneyed phrase. Her stories are rollicking comedies compared with the awful shadow cast by the literature of the Slavs. Suffering is the heritage of the Russian race; their history is steeped in blood and tears, their present condition seems intolerably painful, and the future is an impenetrable cloud. In the life of the peasants there is, of course, fun and laughter, as there is in every human life; but at the root there is suffering, not the loud protest of the Anglo-Saxon laborer, whose very loudness is a witness to his vitality—but passive, fatalistic, apathetic misery. Life has been often defined, but never in a more depressing fashion than by the peasant in Gorky's novel, who asks quietly: "What does the word life mean to us? A feast? No. Work? No. A battle? Oh, no!! For us life is something merely tiresome, dull—a kind of heavy burden. In carrying it we sigh with weariness and complain of its weight. Do we really love life! The love of life! The very words sound strange to our ears! We love only our dreams of the future—and this love is with no hope of fruition." Suffering is the cornerstone of Russian life, as it is of Russian fiction.[1] [*William Lyon Phelps*]

Phelps sums up the greatness of Russian literature in this way:

> Extreme sensitiveness to impression is what has led the Russian literary genius into realism; and it is what has produced the greatest realists that the history of the novel has seen. The Russian mind is like a sensitive plate; it reproduces faithfully. It has

---

[1] From *Essays on Russian Novelists* by William Lyon Phelps, copyright 1911 by The Macmillan Company; renewed 1940 by William Lyon Phelps. Reprinted by permission of The Macmillan Company.

no more partiality, nor more prejudice, than a camera film; it reflects everything that reaches its surface. A Russian novelist, with a pen in his hand, is the most truthful being on earth.[1] [*William Lyon Phelps*]

The Russian "truthfulness" took the form of realism in writing; all the writers you will study in this book were realists of one kind or another. But Russian realism is not to be confined to the usual connotation of the literary movement that attempted to represent only the material or surface aspects of life "as it is" rather than as we would wish it to be. Russian realism is, instead, a manner of looking at life in a serious way, an honest attempt to get at the various kinds of truths in individual lives and in society—the truths of social and political kinds, the psychological truths, the philosophical realities. Consequently, realism in Russian writing is not always "objective" and impersonal; rather, it represents a point of view that is typically Russian, as well as a Russian contribution to world literature.

It seems that the Russians were naturally endowed with the possibility of conceiving of everyday things in a serious vein; that a classicistic aesthetics which excludes a literary category of "the low" from serious treatment could never gain a firm foothold in Russia. Then too, as we think of Russian realism, remembering that it came into its own only during the nineteenth century and indeed only during the second half of it, we cannot escape the observation that it is based on a Christian and traditionally patriarchal concept of the creatural dignity of every human individual regardless of social rank and position, and hence that it is fundamentally related rather to old Christian than to modern occidental realism. The enlightened, active bourgeoisie, with its assumption of economic and intellectual leadership, which everywhere else underlay modern culture in general and modern realism in particular, seems to have scarcely existed in Russia. At least it cannot be found in the novels, not even in Tolstoy or Dostoevsky. There are in the realistic novels members of the higher aristocracy, noble landowners of various ranks and degrees of wealth, there are hierarchies of civil servants and of the clergy; then there are petty bourgeois and peasants, that is, the people in its most living multiplicity. But what lies between, the wealthy upper bourgeoisie and the merchant class, is still generally split up into guilds and in any case is completely patriarchal in atti-

[1]*Ibid.*

tudes and forms of life. . . . This sort of thing has nothing whatever in common with the enlightened bourgeoisie of central and western Europe. The reformers, rebels, and conspirators — of whom there are many — come from the most varied classes, and the manner of their revolt, however different it may be in the individual instances, still everywhere shows a close connection with the Christian and traditionally patriarchal world from which they manage to break away only through painful violence.

Another characteristic feature which strikes the western reader of Russian literature is the uniformity of the population and its life in that vast country, an obviously spontaneous or at least very long-established unity of all that is Russian, so that it often seems superfluous to state in what particular region the action takes place. Even the character of the landscape is much more homogeneous than in any other European country. With the exception of the two principal cities, Moscow and Saint Petersburg, whose distinctly different characteristics are clearly to be recognized from literary sources, it is a rare occurrence if a city, hamlet, or province is identified. . . .

. . . The landowners, civil servants, merchants, clergymen, petty bourgeois, and peasants seem everywhere to be "Russian" in much the same way. . . .

Now, within this great and homogeneous national family (which is differentiated from contemporary European society above all by the fact that an enlightened bourgeoisie, conscious of its value and working toward a definite end, has scarcely begun to exist) all through the nineteenth century an inner movement of the most powerful nature prevails. This is unmistakably recognized in the literary output of the time. Considerable movement prevails in the other European literatures of this period too, especially in French literature; but it is a different kind of movement. The most essential characteristic of the inner movement documented in Russian realism is the unqualified, unlimited, and passionate intensity of experience in the characters portrayed. That is the strongest impression which the western reader receives, before and above all else, especially in Dostoevsky but also in Tolstoy and the others. It seems that the Russians have preserved an immediacy of experience which had become a rare phenomenon in western civilization of the nineteenth century. A strong practical, ethical, or intellectual shock immediately arouses them in the depths of their instincts, and in a moment they pass from a quiet and almost vegetative existence to the most monstrous excesses both in practical and spiritual matters. The pendulum of their vitality, of their actions, thoughts, and emotions seems to oscillate farther than elsewhere in Europe. . . . There is something truly monstrous—especially in Dostoevsky but elsewhere too—in the change from love to hatred, from humble devotion to animal brutality, from a passionate love of truth to the most vulgar lust for pleasure, from pious simplicity to the most cruel cynicism. Such changes often occur in one person—almost without transition—in tremendous and unpredictable oscillations. And each time the person spends himself completely, so that his words and acts reveal chaotic instinctive depths of a kind which to be sure were not unknown in the countries of the west but which scientific detachment, sense of form, and respect for social proprieties prevented the writers there from expressing without restraint. When the great Russians, especially Dostoevsky, became known in central and western Europe, the immense spiritual potential and the directness of expression which their amazed readers encountered in their works seemed like a revelation of how the mixture of realism and tragedy might at last attain its true fulfillment.[1] [*Erich Auerbach*]

In view of what you may know of today's strictures on freedom in Russia, it may seem strange that the great Russian writers of the nineteenth century were obsessed with truths and freedoms of all kinds. Perhaps, though, after you have read the stories that follow—and after you have, in future years, explored the longer works of Tolstoy, Turgenev, and Dostoevsky to which these short selections introduce you—you will agree with a contemporary American critic, Irving Howe:

> It is hard to resist the feeling that Russian literature, especially the fiction of the nineteenth century, is somehow "special." It glows with a humane exaltation, it burns with a sense of irreducible tragedy; and together these qualities make the other literatures of Europe seem affairs of mere surface, vanity, and passing worldliness.[2] [*Irving Howe*]

[1] From *Mimesis: The Representation of Reality in Western Literature* by Erich Auerbach, translated by Willard R. Trask (Princeton University Press, 1953; Princeton Paperback, 1968). Reprinted by permission of the publisher.

[2] From "The Continuity of Russian Voices" by Irving Howe, copyright © 1967, by Harper's Magazine, Inc. Reprinted from the January, 1968 issue of *Harper's Magazine* by permission of the author.

PART TWO

Ivan Turgenev

IVAN TURGENEV

The Russian novelist who was best known to his contemporaries in Western Europe and America was Ivan Sergeyevich Turgenev, an aristocrat by birth and taste. It is perhaps ironic that readers outside Russia learned of that country through the writings of the one Russian literary giant who lived most of his life in Western Europe and who was, indeed, considered a "Westerner" by his great fellow artists Tolstoy and Dostoevsky. Turgenev later explained in his *Literary Reminiscences* the reasons for his leaving Russia:

> So far as I am concerned, I can truthfully say that personally I realized very well all the disadvantages of being cut off from my native soil and of such a violent interruption of all the links and connections that bound me to the environment in which I had grown up.... But there was nothing to be done about it. That mode of life, that kind of environment, and particularly, the social stratum, if one may put it that way, to which I belonged — the landowning and serf-owning stratum of society — did not represent anything that could hold me back. On the contrary, almost everything I saw around me aroused in me a feeling of embarrassment and indignation and, finally, disgust. There could be no question of any hesitation on my part. I had either to submit and follow meekly the well-trodden track, go along the well-beaten path, or turn away from it without a moment's hesitation and renounce everyone and everything, even at the risk of losing much that was near and dear to my heart. I chose the latter.... I plunged headlong into "the German Sea" which was to purify and regenerate me, and when I finally emerged from its waves, I discovered myself to be a "Westerner," and I have remained one ever since.[1]
> [*Ivan Turgenev*]

Another expatriate writer, Henry James, had left his country, the United States, and had settled in Europe, where he became acquainted with Turgenev. The short essay that follows is James's tribute to the Russian writer whose artistic credo had the greatest influence on his own work.

---

[1] From *Turgenev's Literary Reminiscences*, edited by David Magarshack, copyright © 1958 by Farrar, Straus & Cudahy, Inc. Reprinted by permission of Farrar, Straus, & Giroux, Inc.

Ivan Turgenev

HENRY JAMES

There is perhaps no novelist of alien race who more naturally than Ivan Turgenev inherits a niche in a library for English readers; and this not because of any advance or concession that in his peculiar artistic independence he ever made, or could dream of making, such readers, but because it was one of the effects of his peculiar genius to give him, even in his lifetime, a special place in the regard of foreign publics. His position is in this respect singular; for it is his Russian savor that as much as anything has helped generally to domesticate him.

Born in 1818, at Orel in the heart of Russia, and dying in 1883, at Bougival near Paris, he had spent in Germany and France the latter half of his life; and had incurred in his own country in some degree the reprobation that is apt to attach to the absent—the penalty they pay for such extension or such beguilement as they may have happened to find over the border. He belonged to the class of large rural proprietors of land and of serfs; and with his ample patrimony, offered one of the few examples of literary labor achieved in high independence of the question of gain—a character that he shares with his illustrious contemporary Tolstoy, who is of a type in other respects so different. It may give us an idea of his primary situation to imagine some large Virginian or Carolinian slaveholder, during the first half of the century, inclining to "Northern" views; and becoming (though not predominantly under pressure of these, but rather by the operation of an exquisite genius) the great American novelist—one of the great novelists of the world. Born under a social and political order sternly repressive, all Turgenev's deep instincts, all his moral passion, placed him on the liberal side; with the consequence that early in life, after a period spent at a German university, he found himself, through the accident of a trifling public utterance, under such suspicion in high places as to be sentenced to a term of tempered exile—confinement to his own estate. It was partly under these circumstances perhaps that he gathered material for the work from the appearance of which his reputation dates—*A Sportsman's Sketches,* published in two volumes in 1852. This admirable collection of impressions of homely country life, as the old state of servitude had made it, is often spoken of as having borne to the great decree of Alexander II the relation borne by Mrs. Beecher Stowe's famous novel to the emancipation

From *Library of the World's Best Literature,* edited by Charles Dudley Warner. New York: International Society, 1897.

of the Southern slaves. Incontestably, at any rate, Turgenev's rustic studies sounded, like *Uncle Tom's Cabin,* a particular hour: with the difference, however, of not having at the time produced an agitation — of having rather presented the case with an art too insidious for instant recognition, an art that stirred the depths more than the surface.

The author was designated promptly enough, at any rate, for such influence as might best be exercised at a distance: he traveled, he lived abroad; early in the sixties he was settled in Germany; he acquired property at Baden-Baden, and spent there the last years of the prosperous period — in the history of the place — of which the Franco-Prussian War was to mark the violent term. He cast in his lot after that event mainly with the victims of the lost cause; setting up a fresh home in Paris — near which city he had, on the Seine, a charming alternate residence — and passing in it, and in the country, save for brief revisitations, the remainder of his days. His friendships, his attachments, in the world of art and of letters, were numerous and distinguished; he never married; he produced, as the years went on, without precipitation or frequency; and these were the years during which his reputation gradually established itself as, according to the phrase, European — a phrase denoting in this case, perhaps, a public more alert in the United States even than elsewhere.

Tolstoy, his junior by ten years, had meanwhile come to fruition; though, as in fact happened, it was not till after Turgenev's death that the greater fame of *War and Peace* and of *Anna Karenina* began to be blown about the world. One of the last acts of the elder writer, performed on his deathbed, was to address to the other (from whom for a considerable term he had been estranged by circumstances needless to reproduce) an appeal to return to the exercise of the genius that Tolstoy had already so lamentably, so monstrously forsworn. "I am on my deathbed; there is no possibility of my recovery. I write you expressly to tell you how happy I have been to be your contemporary, and to utter my last, my urgent prayer. Come back, my friend, to your literary labors. That gift came to you from the source from which all comes to us. Ah, how happy I should be could I think you would listen to my entreaty! My friend, great writer of our Russian land, respond to it, obey it!" These words, among the most touching surely ever addressed by one great spirit to another, throw an indirect light — perhaps I may even say a direct one — upon the nature and quality of Turgenev's artistic temperament; so much so that I regret being without opportunity, in this place, to gather such aid for a portrait of him as might be supplied by following out the unlikeness between the pair. It would be too easy to say that Tolstoy was, from the Russian point of view, for home consumption, and Turgenev for foreign: *War and Peace* has probably had more readers in Europe and America than *A House of Gentlefolk* or *On the Eve* or *Smoke* — a circumstance less detrimental than it may appear to my claim of our having, in the Western world, supremely adopted the author of the latter works. Turgenev is in a peculiar degree what I may call the novelists' novelist — an artistic influence extraordinarily valuable and ineradicably established. The perusal of Tolstoy — a wonderful mass of life — is an immense event, a kind of splendid accident, for each of us: his name represents nevertheless no such eternal spell of method, no such quiet irresistibility of presentation, as shines, close to us and lighting our possible steps, in that of his precursor. Tolstoy is a reflector as vast as a natural lake; a monster harnessed to his great subject — all human life! — as an elephant might be harnessed, for purposes of traction, not to a carriage, but to a coach-house. His own case is prodigious, but his example for others dire: disciples not elephantine he can only mislead and betray.

One by one, for thirty years, with a firm, deliberate hand, with intervals and patiences and waits, Turgenev pricked in his sharp outlines. His great external mark is probably his concision: an ideal he never threw over — it shines most perhaps even when he is least brief — and that he often applied with a rare felicity. He has masterpieces of a few pages; his perfect things are sometimes his least prolonged. He abounds in short tales, episodes clipped as by the scissors of Atropos[1]; but for a direct translation of the whole we have still to wait — depending meanwhile upon the French and German versions, which have been, instead of the original text (thanks to the paucity among us of readers of Russian), the source of several published in English. For the novels and *A Sportsman's Sketches* we depend upon the nine volumes (1897) of Mrs. Garnett.[2] We touch here upon the remarkable side, to our vision, of the writer's fortune — the anomaly of his having constrained to intimacy even those who are shut out from the enjoyment of his medium, for whom that question is positively prevented from existing. Putting aside extrinsic intimations, it is impossible to read him without the conviction of his being, in the vividness of his own tongue, of the strong type of those made to bring home to us the happy truth of the unity, in a generous talent, of material and form — of their being inevitable faces of the same medal; the type of those, in a word, whose example deals death to the

[1]*Atropos:* In Greek mythology, the eldest of the three Fates, who was responsible for cutting the thread of life.
[2]*Mrs. Garnett:* Mrs. Constance Garnett (1862–1946), a well-known translator of Russian literature into English.

perpetual clumsy assumption that subject and style are—aesthetically speaking, or in the living work—different and separable things. We are conscious, reading him in a language not his own, of not being reached by his personal tone, his individual accent.

It is a testimony therefore to the intensity of his presence, that so much of his particular charm does reach us; that the mask turned to us has, even without his expression, still so much beauty. It is the beauty (since we must try to formulate) of the finest presentation of the familiar. His vision is of the world of character and feeling, the world of the relations life throws up at every hour and on every spot; he deals little, on the whole, in the miracles of chance—the hours and spots over the edge of time and space; his air is that of the great central region of passion and motive, of the usual, the inevitable, the intimate—the intimate for weal or woe. No theme that he ever chooses but strikes us as full; yet with all have we the sense that their animation comes from within, and is not pinned to their backs like the pricking objects used of old in the horse-races of the Roman carnival, to make the animals run. Without a patch of "plot" to draw blood, the story he mainly tells us, the situation he mainly gives, runs as if for dear life. His first book was practically full evidence of what, if we have to specify, is finest in him—the effect, for the commonest truth, of an exquisite envelope of poetry. In this medium of feeling—full, as it were, of all the echoes and shocks of the universal danger and need—everything in him goes on; the sense of fate and folly and pity and wonder and beauty. The tenderness, the humor, the variety of *A Sportsman's Sketches* revealed on the spot an observer with a rare imagination. These faculties had attached themselves, together, to small things and to great: to the misery, the simplicity, the piety, the patience, of the unemancipated peasant; to all the natural wonderful life of earth and air and winter and summer and field and forest; to queer apparitions of country neighbors, of strange local eccentrics; to old world practices and superstitions; to secrets gathered and types disinterred and impressions absorbed in the long, close contacts with man and nature involved in the passionate pursuit of game. Magnificent in stature and original vigor, Turgenev, with his love of the chase, or rather perhaps of the inspiration he found in it, would have been the model of the mighty hunter, had not such an image been a little at variance with his natural mildness, the softness that often accompanies the sense of an extraordinary reach of limb and play of muscle. He was in person the model rather of the strong man at rest: massive and towering, with the voice of innocence and the smile almost of childhood. What seemed still more of a contradiction to so much of him, however, was that his work was all delicacy and fancy, penetration and compression. . . .

Character, character expressed and exposed, is . . . what we inveterately find. Turgenev's sense of it was the great light that artistically guided him; the simplest account of him is to say that the mere play of it constitutes in every case his sufficient drama. No one has had a closer vision, or a hand at once more ironic and more tender, for the individual figure. He sees it with its minutest signs and tricks — all its heredity of idiosyncrasies, all its particulars of weakness and strength, of ugliness and beauty, of oddity and charm; and yet it is of his essence that he sees it in the general flood of life, steeped in its relations and contacts, struggling or submerged, a hurried particle in the stream. This gives him, with his quiet method, his extraordinary breadth; dissociates his rare power to particularize from dryness or hardness, from any peril of caricature. He understands so much that we almost wonder he can express anything; and his expression is indeed wholly in absolute projection, in illustration, in giving of everything the unexplained and irresponsible specimen. He is of a spirit so human that we almost wonder at his control of his matter; of a pity so deep and so general that we almost wonder at his curiosity. The element of poetry in him is constant, and yet reality stares through it without the loss of a wrinkle. No one has more of that sign of the born novelist which resides in a respect unconditioned for the freedom and vitality, the absoluteness when summoned, of the creatures he invokes; or is more superior to the strange and second-rate policy of explaining or presenting them by reprobation or apology — of taking the short cuts and anticipating the emotions and judgments about them that should be left, at the best, to the perhaps not most intelligent reader. And yet his system, as it may summarily be called, of the mere particularized report, has a lucidity beyond the virtue of the cruder moralist.

If character, as I say, is what he gives us at every turn, I should speedily add that he offers it not in the least as a synonym, in our Western sense, of resolution and prosperity. It wears the form of the almost helpless detachment of the short-sighted individual soul; and the perfection of his exhibition of it is in truth too often but the intensity of what, for success, it just does not produce. What works in him most is the question of the will; and the most constant induction, he suggests, bears upon the sad figure that principle seems mainly to make among his countrymen. He had seen — he suggests to us — its collapse in a thousand quarters; and the most general tragedy, to his view, is that of its desperate adventures and disasters, its inevitable abdication and defeat. But if the men, for the most part, let it go, it takes refuge in the other sex; many of the representatives of which, in his pages, are supremely strong

—in wonderful addition, in various cases, to being otherwise admirable. This is true of such a number—the younger women, the girls, the "heroines" in especial—that they form in themselves, on the ground of moral beauty, of the finest distinction of soul, one of the most striking groups the modern novel has given us. They are heroines to the letter, and of a heroism obscure and undecorated: it is almost they alone who have the energy to determine and to act. Elena, Lisa, Tatyana, Gemma, Marianna —we can write their names and call up their images, but I lack space to take them in turn. It is by a succession of the finest and tenderest touches that they live; and this, in all Turgenev's work, is the process by which he persuades and succeeds.

It was his own view of his main danger that he sacrificed too much to detail; was wanting in composition, in the gift that conduces to unity of impression. But no novelist is closer and more cumulative; in none does distinction spring from a quality of truth more independent of everything but the subject, but the idea itself. This idea, this subject, moreover—a spark kindled by the innermost friction of things—is always as interesting as an unopened telegram. The genial freedom—with its exquisite delicacy—of his approach to this "innermost" world, the world of our finer consciousness, has in short a side that I can only describe and commemorate as nobly disinterested; a side that makes too many of his rivals appear to hold us in comparison by violent means, and introduce us in comparison to vulgar things.

FOR WRITING OR DISCUSSION

1. To what former American social class does James compare the class to which Turgenev belonged? What are the bases of the comparison in historical period, cultural similarities, and financial security?

2. How does James justify classifying Turgenev as a "liberal"? In what ways was Turgenev liberal in relation to his own times?

3. Turgenev has often been called a "Europeanized Russian." What biographical details in James's essay relate literally to this idea? In what ways was Turgenev "Westernized" in his ideas as well as in his actual choice of places to live?

4. James calls Turgenev the "novelists' novelist." How does he develop this generalization? What qualities of Turgenev's writing does he mention in the two paragraphs that follow this phrase?

5. If you had never read one of Turgenev's stories before, would James's essay lead you to expect stories of excitement and adventure in which plot interest is high, or tales of a quieter kind? In what element of fiction does James believe Turgenev's major talent lies?

I. Reading Literature

Tales from *A Sportsman's Notebook*

The three stories that follow—"Bezhin Lea," "Meeting," and "The Reformer and the Russian German"—appeared in 1852 in a collection of stories variously translated as *A Sportsman's Notebook, A Sportsman's Sketches, The Hunting Sketches,* and *Sketches from a Hunter's Album.* The Russian title, *Zapiski okhoknika,* means literally "Notes of a Hunter." Most of the stories had appeared in a literary magazine, *The Contemporary,* prior to the publication of the book.

As James remarked in the essay you have just read, material for the sketches was gathered at Spasskoye, Turgenev's country estate in Russia. The stories were written, however, between 1848 and 1851 in Europe, where Turgenev had gone as a young man to be educated in German universities and where he returned after his year-and-a-half exile at Spasskoye (May 1852–December 1853). He had been sent into exile for circumventing the censors by the publication of his obituary in praise of Gogol. As you read these sketches of Russian country life, remember that they are written from the point of view of a liberal landowning aristocrat who wrote about peasants prior to their emancipation. Try to imagine the state of the nation and the rigid censorship that occasioned the criticism of the *Sketches* because they were disrespectful of the gentry. Consider also what aspects of these very quiet, seemingly uncritical tales were thought of as being as influential in freeing the Russian serf from bondage as *Uncle Tom's Cabin,* which appeared in the same year as the *Sketches,* was in helping to free the Negro slave.

"Bezhin Lea" (Bezhin Meadows), which follows, is probably the best known of the stories from *A Sportsman's Notebook:* Turgenev, in the role of the aristocratic landowner who is the narrator of the tale, describes a group of young peasant boys who have been sent to keep watch over the horses during a summer night's pasturage. Notice, as you read, how the reader assumes the role of the observer and is gradually drawn into the circle around the campfire.

Bezhin Lea

It was a beautiful July day, one of those days which occur only when the weather has been unchanged for a long time. From early morning the sky is clear and the sunrise does not so much flare up like a fire as spread like a mild pinkness. The sun—not fiery, not molten, as it is during a period of torrid drought, not murkily crimson as it is before a storm, but bright and invitingly radiant—peacefully drifts up beneath a long, thin cloud, sends fresh gleams through it and is immersed in its lilac haze. The delicate upper edge of the long line of cloud erupts in snaky glints of light: their gleam resembles the gleam of beaten silver. But then again the playful rays break out—and as if taking wing the mighty sun rises gaily and magnificently. About midday a mass of high round clouds appear, golden-gray, with soft white edges. They move hardly at all, like islands cast down on the infinite expanses of a flooding river which flows around them in deeply pellucid streams of level blue; away toward the horizon they cluster together and merge so that there is no blue sky to be seen between them; but they have themselves become as azure colored as the sky and are pervaded through and through with light and warmth. The light, pale-lilac color of the heavens remains the same throughout the day and in all parts of the sky; there is no darkening anywhere, no thickening as for a storm, though here and there pale-blue columns may stretch downward, bringing a hardly noticeable sprinkling of rain. Toward evening these clouds disappear. The last of them, darkling and vague as smoke, lie down in rosy mistiness before the sinking sun. At the point where the sun has set just as calmly as it rose into the sky, a crimson glow lingers for a short time over the darkened earth, and, softly winking, the evening star burns upon the glow like a carefully carried candle. On such days all the colors are softened; they are bright without being gaudy; everything bears the mark of some poignant timidity. On such days the heat is sometimes very strong and occasionally even "simmers" along the slopes of the fields. But the wind drives away and disperses the accumulated heat, and whirling dust storms—a sure sign of settled weather—travel in tall white columns along roads through the plowland. The dry pure air is scented with wormwood, harvested rye, and buckwheat. Even an hour before nightfall you can feel no dampness. It is just such weather that the farmer wants for harvesting his grain.

"Bezhin Lea" from *Sketches From a Hunter's Album* by Ivan Turgenev, translated by Richard Freeborn. Published in England by Penguin Books Ltd. and reprinted with their permission.

It was on precisely such a day that I once went out grouse-shooting in Chernsk county in the province of Tula. I found, and bagged, a fair number of birds. My full game-pouch cut mercilessly at my shoulder. But I did not finally decide to make my way home until the evening glow had already died away and chill shadows began to thicken and proliferate in air that was still bright, though no longer illumined by the rays of the sunset. With brisk steps I crossed a long "plaza" of bushy undergrowth, clambered up a hillock, and, instead of the expected familiar moor with a little oak wood to the right of it and a low-walled white church in the distance, I saw completely different places which were unknown to me. At my feet there stretched a narrow valley; directly ahead of me rose, like a steep wall, a dense aspen wood. I stopped in bewilderment and looked around. "Ah-ha!" I thought. "I'm certainly not where I should be: I've swerved too much to the right"—and, surprised at my mistake, I quickly descended from the hillock. I was at once surrounded by an unpleasant, motionless damp, just as if I had entered a cellar. The tall, thick grass on the floor of the valley was all wet and shone white like a smooth tablecloth; it felt clammy and horrible to walk through. As quickly as possible I scrambled across to the other side and, keeping to the left, made my way along beside the aspen wood. Bats already flitted above its sleeping treetops, mysteriously circling and quivering against the dull paleness of the sky; a young hawk, out late, flew by high up, taking a direct, keen course in hurrying back to its nest. "Now then, as soon as I reach that corner," I said to myself, "that's where the road'll be, so what I've done is to make a detour of about three quarters of a mile!"

I made my way finally to the corner of the wood, but there was no road there, only some low, unkempt bushes spread out widely in front of me and beyond them, in the far distance, an expanse of deserted field. Again I stopped. "What's all this about? Where am I?" I tried to recall where I had been during the day. "Ah, those must be the Parakhin bushes!" I exclaimed eventually. "That's it! And that must be the Sindeyev wood.... How on earth did I get as far as this? It's very odd! Now I must go to the right again."

I turned to the right, through the bushes. Meanwhile, night was approaching and rose around me like a thunder cloud; it was as if, in company with the evening mists, darkness rose on every side and even poured down from the sky. I discovered a rough, overgrown track and followed it, carefully peering ahead of me. Everything quickly grew silent and dark; only quail gave occasional cries. A small night bird, which hurried low and soundlessly along on its soft wings, almost collided with me and plunged off in terror. I emerged from the bushes and wandered along the boundary of a field. It was only with difficulty that I could make out distant objects. All around me the field glimmered faintly; beyond it, coming closer each moment, the sullen murk loomed in huge clouds. My footsteps sounded muffled in the thickening air. The sky, which had earlier grown pale, once again began to shine blue, but it was the blue of the night. Tiny stars began to flicker and shimmer.

What I thought was a wood had turned out to be a dark, round knoll. "Where on earth am I?" I repeated again out loud, stopping for a third time and looking questioningly at my yellow English piebald, Diana, who was by far the most intelligent of all four-legged creatures. But this most intelligent of four-legged creatures only wagged her small tail, dejectedly blinked her tired little eyes, and offered me no practical help. I felt ill at ease in front of her and strode wildly forward, as if I had suddenly realized which way to go, circled the knoll, and found myself in a shallow hollow which had been plowed over. A strange feeling took possession of me. The hollow had the almost exact appearance of a cauldron with sloping sides. Several large upright stones stood in the floor of the hollow—it seemed as if they had crept down to that spot for some mysterious consultation—and the hollow itself was so still and silent, the sky above it so flat and dismal that my heart shrank within me. A small animal of some kind or other squeaked weakly and piteously among the stones. I hurried to climb back on to the knoll. Up to that point I had not given up hope of finding a way home, but now I was at last convinced that I had completely lost my way and, no longer making any effort to recognize my surroundings, which were almost totally obliterated by the darkness, I walked straight ahead of me, following the stars and hoping for the best.... For about half an hour I walked on in this way, with difficulty, dragging one foot after another. Never in my life, it seemed, had I been in such waste places: not a single light burned anywhere, not a single sound could be heard: one low hillock followed another, field stretched after endless field and bushes suddenly rose out of the earth under my very nose. I went on walking and was on the point of finding a place to lie down until morning, when suddenly I reached the edge of a fearful abyss.

I hastily drew back my outstretched leg and, through the barely transparent nighttime murk, saw far below me an enormous plain. A broad river skirted it, curving away from me in a semicircle; steely gleams of water, sparkling with occasional faint flashes, denoted its course. The hill on which I was standing fell away sharply like an almost vertical precipice. Its vast outlines could be distinguished by their blackness from the blue emptiness of the air, and directly below me, in the angle formed by the precipice and the plain, beside the river, which at that point was a dark, unmoving mirror, under the steep rise of the hill, two fires smoked and flared redly side by side. Figures clustered round them, shadows flickered, and now and then the front half of a small curly head would appear in the bright light.

At least I knew the place I had reached. This meadowland is known in our region as Bezhin Lea. There was now no chance of returning home, especially at night; moreover, my legs were collapsing under me from fatigue. I decided to make my way down to the fires and to await the dawn in the company of the people below me, whom I took to be drovers. I made my descent safely, but had hardly let go of my last handhold when suddenly two large, ragged, white dogs hurled themselves at me with angry barks. Shrill childish voices came from the fires and two or three boys jumped up. I answered their shouted questions. They ran toward me, at once calling off the dogs who had been astonished by the appearance of my Diana, and I walked toward them.

I had been mistaken in assuming that the people sitting round the fires were drovers. They were simply peasant boys from the neighboring villages keeping guard over the horses. During hot summer weather it is customary in our region to drive the horses out at night to graze in the field, for by day the flies would give them no peace. Driving the horses out before nightfall and back again at first light is a great treat for the peasant boys. Barheaded, dressed in tattered sheepskin jackets, and riding the friskiest ponies, they race out with gay whoops and shouts, their arms and legs flapping as they bob up and down on the horses' backs and roar with laughter. Clouds of fine sandy dust are churned up along the roadway; a steady beating of hooves spreads far and wide as the horses prick up their ears and start running; and in front of them all, with tail high and continuously changing his pace, gallops a shaggy chestnut stallion with burrs in his untidy mane.

I told the boys that I had lost my way, and sat down among them. They asked me where I was from and fell silent for a while in awe of me. We talked a little about this and that. I lay down beside a bush from which all the foliage had been nibbled and looked around me. It was a marvelous sight: a reddish circular reflection throbbed around the fires and seemed to fade as it leaned against the darkness; a flame, in flaring up, would occasionally cast rapid flashes of light beyond the limit of the reflection; a fine tongue of light would lick the bare boughs of the willows and instantly vanish; and long sharp shadows, momentarily breaking in, would rush right up to the fires as if the darkness were at war with the light. Sometimes, when the flames grew weaker and the circle of light contracted, there would suddenly emerge from the encroaching dark the head of a horse, reddish brown, with sinuous markings, or completely white, and regard us attentively and gravely, while rapidly chewing some long grass and then, when again lowered, would at once disappear. All that was left was the sound as it continued to chew and snort. From the area of the light it was difficult to discern what was happening in the outer darkness, and therefore at close quarters, everything seemed to be screened from view by an almost totally black curtain; but off toward the horizon, hills and woods were faintly visible, like long blurs. The immaculate dark sky rose solemnly and endlessly high above us in all its mysterious magnificence. My lungs melted with the sweet pleasure of inhaling that special, languorous, and fresh perfume which is the scent of a Russian summer night. Hardly a sound was audible around us.... Now and then a large fish would make a resounding splash in the nearby river and the reeds by the bank would faintly echo the noise as they were stirred by the outspreading waves.... Now and then the fires would emit a soft crackling.

Around the fires sat the boys, as did the two dogs who had been so keen to eat me. They were still unreconciled to my presence and, while sleepily narrowing their eyes and glancing towards the fire, would sometimes growl with a special sense of their personal dignity; to start with, these were only growls, but later they became faint yelps, as if the dogs regretted their inability to satisfy their appetite for me. There were five boys in all: Fedya, Pavlusha, Ilyusha, Kostya, and Vanya. (I learned their names from their conversation and I now intend to acquaint the reader with each of them.)

The first of them, Fedya, the eldest, would probably have been fourteen. He was a sturdy boy, with handsome and delicate, slightly shallow features, curly fair hair, bright eyes, and a permanent smile which was a mixture of gaiety and absent-mindedness. To judge from his appearance, he belonged to a well-off family and had ridden out into the fields not from necessity but simply for the fun of it. He was dressed in a colorful cotton shirt with yellow edging; a small cloth overcoat, recently made, hung open somewhat precariously on his small narrow shoulders, and a comb hung from his pale-blue belt. His ankle-high boots were his own, not his father's. The second boy, Pavlusha, had disheveled black hair, gray eyes, broad cheekbones, a pale, pock-marked complexion, a large but well-formed mouth, an enormous head—as big as a barrel, as they say—and a thick-set, ungainly body. Hardly a prepossessing figure—there's no denying that!—but I nonetheless took a liking to him: he had direct, very intelligent eyes and a voice with the ring of strength in it. His clothes gave him no chance of showing off: they consisted of no more than a simple linen shirt and much-patched trousers. The face of the third boy, Ilyusha, was not very striking: hook-nosed, long, myopic, it wore an expression of obtuse, morbid anxiety. His tightly closed lips never moved, his frowning brows never relaxed; all the while he screwed up his eyes at the fire. His yellow, almost white, hair stuck out in sharp little tufts from under the small felt cap which he was continually pressing down about his ears with both hands. He had new bast[1] shoes and foot cloths; a thick rope wound three times around his waist drew smartly tight his neat black topcoat. Both he and Pavlusha appeared to be no more than twelve years old. The fourth, Kostya, a boy of about ten, aroused my curiosity by his sad and meditative gaze. His face was small, thin and freckled, and pointed like a squirrel's; one could hardly see his lips. His large, dark, moistly glittering eyes produced a strange impression, as if they wanted to convey something which no tongue—at least not his tongue—had the power to express. He was small in stature, of puny build, and rather badly dressed. The last boy, Vanya, I hardly noticed at first: he lay on the ground quietly curled up under some angular matting and only rarely poked out from under it his head of curly brown hair. This boy was only seven.

So it was that I lay down apart from them, beside the bush, and from time to time looked in their direction. A small pot hung over one of the fires, in which "taters" were being cooked. Pavlusha looked after them and, kneeling down, poked the bubbling water with a small sliver of wood. Fedya lay, leaning on one elbow, his sheepskin spread round him. Ilyusha sat next to Kostya and continually, in his tense way, screwed up his eyes. Kostya, with his head slightly lowered, stared off somewhere into the distance. Vanya did not stir beneath his matting. I pretended to be asleep. After a short while the boys renewed their talk.

To start with, they gossiped about this and that—tomorrow's work or the horses. But suddenly Fedya turned to Ilyusha and, as if taking up from where they had left off their interrupted conversation, asked him:

"So you actually did see one of them little people, did you?"

"No, I didn't see him, and you can't really see him at all," answered Ilyusha in a weak, croaky voice which exactly suited the expression on his face, "but I heard him, I did. And I wasn't the only one."

"Then where does he live around your parts?" asked Pavlusha.

---

[1] *bast:* the fibrous inner bark of trees, used for making cord and, here, composition soles for shoes.

"In the old rolling-room."[1]

"D'you mean you work in the factory?"

"Of course we do. Me and Avdyushka, my brother, we work as glazers."

"Cor! So you're factory workers!"

"Well, so how did you hear him?" asked Fedya.

"It was this way. My brother, see, Avdyushka, and Fyodor Mikheyevsky, and Ivashka Kosoy, and the other Ivashka from Redwold, and Ivashka Sukhorukov as well, and there were some other kids as well, about ten of us in all, the whole shift, see — well, so we had to spend the whole night in the rolling-room, or it wasn't that we had to, but that Nazarov, the overseer, he wouldn't let us off, he said: 'Seeing as you've got a lot of work here tomorrow, my lads, you'd best stay here; there's no point in the lot o'you traipsing off home.' Well, so we stayed and all lay down together, and then Avdyushka started up saying something about 'Well, boys, suppose that goblin comes?' and he didn't have a chance, Avdey didn't, to go on saying anything when all of a sudden over our heads someone comes in, but we were lying down below, see, and he was up there, by the wheel. We listen, and there he goes walking about, and the floorboards really bending under him and really creaking. Then he walked right over our heads and the water all of a sudden starts rushing, rushing through the wheel, and the wheel goes clatter, clatter and starts turning, but them gates of the Keep[2] are all lowered. So we start wondering who'd raised them so as to let the water through. Yet the wheel turned and turned, and then stopped. Whoever he was, he went back to the door upstairs and began coming down the stairway, and down he came, taking his time about it, and the stairs under him really groaning from his weight.... Well, so he came right up to our door, and then waited, and then waited a bit more — and then that door suddenly burst open, it did. Our eyes were poppin' out of our heads, and we watch — and there's nothing there.... And suddenly at one of the tubs the form[3] started moving, rose, dipped itself and went to and fro just like that in the air like someone was using it for swilling, and then back again it went to its place. Then at another tub the hook was lifted from its nail and put back on the nail again. Then it was as if someone moved to the

---

[1]*rolling-room:* "Rolling-room" and "dipping-room" are terms used in paper factories to describe the place where the papers are baled out in the vats. It is situated right by the mill, under the mill wheel.

[2]*the Keep:* the name used in Turgenev's region for the place where the water runs over the wheel.

[3]*the form:* the net with which the paper is scooped out.

door and started to cough all suddenlike, like he'd got a tickle, and it sounded just like a sheep bleating. . . . We all fell flat on the floor at that and tried to climb under each other—bloody terrified we were at that moment!"

"Cor!" said Pavlusha. "And why did he cough like that?"

"Search me. Maybe it was the damp."

They all fell silent.

"Are them 'taters done yet?" Fedya asked.

Pavlusha felt them.

"Nope, they're not done yet. . . . Cor, that one splashed," he added, turning his face towards the river, "likely it was a pike. . . . And see that little falling star up there."

"No, mates, I've really got something to tell you," Kostya began in a reedy voice. "Just you listen to what my dad was talkin' about when I was there."

"Well, so we're listening," said Fedya with a condescending air.

"You know that Gavrila, the carpenter in the settlement?"

"Sure we know him."

"But d'you know why he's always so gloomy, why he never says nothing, d'you know that? Well, here's why. He went out once, my dad said—he went out, mates, into the forest to find some nuts. So he'd gone into the forest after nuts and he lost his way. He got somewhere, but God knows where it was. He'd been walkin', mates, and no! he couldn't find a road of any kind, and already it was night all around. So he sat down under a tree and said to himself he'd wait there till mornin'—and he sat down and started to snooze. So he was snoozin' and suddenly he hears someone callin' him. He looks around—there's no one there. Again he snoozes off—and again they're callin' him. So he looks and looks, and then he sees right in front of him a water-fairy sittin' on a branch, swingin' on it she is and callin' to him, and she's just killin' herself laughin'. . . . Then that moon shines real strong, so strong and obvious the moon shines it shows up everythin', mates. So there she is callin' his name, and she herself's all shiny, sittin' there all white on the branch, like she was some little minnow or gudgeon, or maybe like a carp that's all whitish all over, all silver. . . . And Gavrila the carpenter was just frightened to death, mates, and she went on laughin' at him, you know, and wavin' to him to come closer. Gavrila was just goin' to get up and obey the water-fairy, when, mates, the Lord God gave him the idea to cross hisself. . . . An' it was terrible difficult, mates, he said it was terrible difficult to make the sign of the cross 'cos his arm was like stone, he said, and wouldn't move, the darned thing wouldn't! But soon as he'd managed to cross hisself, mates, that water-fairy stopped laughin' and started in to cry.... An' she cried, mates, an' wiped her eyes with her hair that was green and heavy as hemp. So Gavrila kept on lookin' and lookin' at her, and then he started askin' her, 'What's it you're cryin' for, you forest hussy, you?' And that water-fairy starts sayin' to him, 'If you hadn't crossed yourself, human being that you are, you could've lived with me in joy and happiness to the end of your days, an' I'm cryin' and dyin' of grief over what that you crossed yourself, an' it isn't only me that'll be dyin' of grief, but you'll also waste away with grievin' till the end of your born days.' Then, mates, she vanished, and Gavrila at once comprehended-like—how to get out of the wood, that is; but from that day on he goes around everywhere all gloomy."

"Phew!" exclaimed Fedya after a short silence. "But how could that evil forest spirit infect a Christian soul—you said he didn't obey her, didn't you?"

"You wouldn't believe it, but that's how it was!" said Kostya. "Gavrila claimed she had a tiny, tiny voice, thin and croaky like a toad's."

"Your father told that himself?" Fedya continued.

"He did. I was lyin' on my bunk an' I heard it all."

"What a fantastic business! But why's he got to be gloomy? She must've liked him, because she called to him."

"Of course she liked him!" Ilyusha interrupted. "Why not? She wanted to start tickling him, that's what she wanted. That's what they do, those water fairies."

"Surely there'll be water fairies here," Fedya remarked.

"No," Kostya answered, "this is a clean place here, it's free. 'Cept the river's close."

They all grew quiet. Suddenly, somewhere in the distance, a protracted, resonant, almost wailing sound broke the silence—one of those incomprehensible nocturnal sounds which arise in the deep surrounding hush, fly up, hang in the air and slowly disperse at last as if dying away. You listen intently—it's as though there's nothing there, but it still goes on ringing. This time it seemed that someone gave a series of long, loud shouts on the very horizon and someone else answered him from the forest with sharp high-pitched laughter and a thin, hissing whistle which sped across the river. The boys looked at each other and shuddered.

"The power of the holy cross be with us!" whispered Ilyusha.

"Oh, you idiots!" Pavlusha cried. "What's got into you? Look, the 'taters are done," (They all drew close to the little pot and began to eat the steaming potatoes; Vanya was the only one who made no move.) "What's wrong with you?" Pavlusha asked.

But Vanya did not crawl out from beneath his matting. The little pot was soon completely empty.

"Boys, have you heard," Ilyusha began saying, "what happened to us in Varnavitsy just recently?"

"On that dam, you mean?" Fedya asked.

"Ay, on that dam, the one that's broken. That's a real unclean place, real nasty and empty it is. Round there is all them gullies and ravines, and in the ravines there's masses of snakes."

"Well, what happened? Let's hear."

"This is what happened. Maybe you don't know it, Fedya, but that's the place where one of our drowned men is buried. And he drowned a long time back when the pond was still deep. Now only his gravestone can be seen, only there's not much of it—it's just a small mound.... Anyhow, a day or so ago, the bailiff calls Yermil the dog-keeper and says to him: 'Off with you and fetch the mail.' Yermil's always the one who goes to fetch the mail 'cos he's done all his dogs in—they just don't somehow seem to live when he's around, and never did have much of a life nohow, though he's a good man with dogs and took to it in every way. Anyhow, Yermil went for the mail, and then he mucked about in the town and set off home real drunk. And it's nighttime, a bright night, with the moon shining.... So he's riding back across the dam, 'cos that's where his route came out. And he's riding along, this dog-keeper Yermil, and he sees a little lamb on the drowned man's grave, all white and curly and pretty, and it's walking about, and Yermil thinks: 'I'll pick it up, I will, 'cos there's no point in letting it get lost here,' and so he gets off his horse and picks it up in his arms—and the lamb doesn't turn a hair. So Yermil walks back to the horse, but the horse backs away from him, snorts and shakes its head. So when he's quieted it, he sits on it with the lamb and starts off again holding the lamb in front of him. He looks at the lamb, he does, and the lamb looks right back at him right in the eyes. Then that Yermil the dog-keeper got frightened: 'I don't recall,' he thought, 'no lambs looking me in the eye like that afore.' Anyhow, it didn't seem nothing, so he starts stroking its wool and saying 'Sssh, there, sssh!' And that lamb bares its teeth at him suddenlike and says back to him. 'Sssh, there, sssh!...'"

The narrator had hardly uttered this last sound when the dogs sprang up and with convulsive barks dashed from the fire, disappearing into the night. The boys were terrified. Vanya even jumped out from beneath his mat. Shouting, Pavlusha followed in hot pursuit of the dogs. Their barking quickly retreated into the distance. There was a noisy and restless scurrying of hooves among the startled horses. Pavlusha gave loud calls:

"Gray! Beetle!" After a few seconds the barking ceased and Pavlusha's voice sounded far away. There followed another short pause, while the boys exchanged puzzled looks as if anticipating something new. Suddenly a horse could be heard racing toward them: it stopped sharply at the edge of the fire and Pavlusha, clutching hold by the reins, sprang agilely from its back. Both dogs also leapt into the circle of light and at once sat down, their red tongues hanging out.

"What's there? What is it?" the boys asked.

"Nothing," Pavlusha answered waving away the horse. "The dogs caught a scent. I thought," he added in a casual tone of voice, his chest heaving rapidly, "it might have been a wolf."

I found myself full of admiration for Pavlusha. He was very fine at that moment. His very ordinary face, enlivened by the swift ride, shone with bold courageousness and a resolute firmness. Without a stick in his hand to control the horse and in total darkness, without even so much as blinking an eye, he had galloped all by himself after a wolf. . . . "What a marvelous boy!" was my thought, as I looked at him.

"And you saw them, did you, those wolves?" asked the cowardly Kostya.

"There's plenty of them round here," answered Pavlusha, "but they're only on the prowl in the winter."

He again settled himself in front of the fire. As he sat down he let a hand fall on the shaggy neck of one of the dogs, and the delighted animal kept its head still for a long while as it directed sideward looks of grateful pride at Pavlusha.

Vanya once again disappeared under his mat.

"What a lot of horrible things you've been telling us, Ilyusha," Fedya began. As the son of a rich peasant, it was incumbent upon him to play the role of leader (though for his own part he talked little, as if for fear of losing face). "And it could've been some darned thing of the sort that started the dogs barking. . . . But it's true, so I've heard, that you've got unclean spirits where you live."

"In Varnavitsy, you mean? That's for sure! It's a really creepy place! More than once they say they've seen there the old squire, the one who's dead. They say he goes about in a coat hanging down to his heels, and all the time he makes a groaning sound, like he's searching for something on the earth. Once grandfather Trofimych met him and asked him: "What's it you are searching for on the earth, good master Ivan Ivanych?' "

"He actually asked him that?" broke in the astonished Fedya.

"He asked him that."

"Well, good for Trofimych after that! So what did the other say?"

" 'Split-grass,' he says. 'That's what I'm looking for.' And he talks in such a hollow, hoarse voice: 'Split-grass. And what, good master Ivan Ivanych, do you want split-grass for?' 'Oh, my grave weighs so heavy,' he says, 'weighs so heavy on me, Trofimych, and I want to get out, I want to get away....' "

"So that's what it was!" Fedya said. "He'd had too short a life, that means."

"Cor, stone me!" Kostya pronounced. "I thought you could only see dead people on Parents' Sunday."

"You can see dead people at any time," Ilyusha declared with confidence. So far as I could judge, he was better versed in village lore than the others. "But on Parents' Sunday you can also see the people who're going to die that year. All you've got to do is to sit down at night in the porch of the church and keep your eyes on the road. They'll all go past you along the road—them who're going to die that year, I mean. Last year, grandma Ulyana went to the church porch in our village."

"Well, did she see anyone?" Kostya asked him with curiosity.

"Sure she did. To start with she just sat there a long, long time, and didn't see no one and didn't hear nothing. Only there was all the time a sound like a dog starting to bark somewhere. Then suddenly she sees there's someone coming along the road—it's a little boy in nothing but a shirt. She looked closer and she saw it was Ivashka Fedoseyev walking along."

"Is that the boy who died in the spring!" Fedya broke in.

"That's the one. He walks along and doesn't even raise his head. But Ulyana recognized him. But then she looks again and sees a woman walking along, and she peers and peers and—God help us!—it's she herself, Ulyana herself, walking along."

"Was it really her?" asked Fedya.

"God's truth. It was her."

"But she hasn't died yet, has she?"

"No, but the year's not over yet either. You take a close look at her and then ask yourself what sort of a body she's got to carry her soul around in."

Again they all grew quiet. Pavlusha threw a handful of dry sticks on the fire. They blackened in sharp outline against the instantly leaping flames, and began to crackle and smoke and bend, curling up their burned tips. The reflections from the light, shuddering convulsively, struck out in all directions but particularly upward. Suddenly, from God knows where, a small white pigeon flew directly into the reflections, fluttered around in terror, bathed by the fierce light, and then vanished with a clapping of its wings.

"Likely it's lost its way home," Pavlusha remarked. "Now it'll fly until it meets up with something, and when it finds it, that's where it'll spend the night till dawn."

"Look, Pavlusha," said Kostya, "mightn't that be the soul of some good person flying up to heaven, eh?"

Pavlusha threw another handful of sticks on the fire.

"Maybe," he said after a pause.

"Pavlusha, tell us, will you," Fedya began, "were you able to see that heavenly foreboding[1] in Shalamavo?"

"You mean, when you couldn't see the sun that time? Sure."

"Didn't you get frightened, then?"

"Sure, and we weren't the only ones. Our squire, tho' he lets us know beforehand that 'Well, there'll be a foreboding for you,' but soon as it gets dark they say he got real scared. And in the servants' hut, that old granny, the cook, well—soon as it's dark, listen, she ups and smashes all the pots in the oven with a pair of tongs. 'Who's going to need to eat now it's the end of the world,' she says. The cabbage soup ran out all over everywhere. And, boy! What rumors there were going about in our village, such as there'd be white wolves and birds of prey coming to eat people, and there'd be Trishka[2] himself for all to see."

"What's this Trishka?" asked Kostya.

"Don't you know about Trishka?" Ilyusha started up heatedly. "You're a dumb cluck, mate, if you don't know who Trishka is. It's just dunces you've got in your village, nothing but dunces! Trishka—he'll be a real astonishing person, who'll be coming, and he'll be coming when the last times are near. And he'll be the sort of astonishing person you won't be able to catch hold of, you won't be able to do nothing to him: that's the sort of astonishing person he'll be. The peasants, say, will want to try to catch him, and they'll go out after him with sticks and surround him, but what he'll do is lead their eyes astray—he'll lead their eyes astray so that they start beating each other. Say they put him in prison and he asks for some water in a ladle; they'll bring him the ladle and he'll jump right into it and vanish clean away, all trace of him. Say they put chains on him, he'll just clap his palms together and they'll fall right off him. So then this Trishka'll go walking through the villages and the towns; and this smart fellow, this Trishka, he'll tempt all Christian

---

[1] *heavenly foreboding:* the name given by the local peasants to an eclipse of the sun.
[2] *Trishka:* The superstition about "Trishka" probably contains an echo of the legend about Antichrist, who, in Christian belief, represents the powers of evil by opposing Christ.

folk ... but there won't be a thing you can do to him.... That's the sort of astonishing, real cunning person he'll be."

"Yes, that's the one," Pavlusha continued in his unhurried way. "He was the one that we were all waiting for. The old men said that soon as the heavenly foreboding begins, Trishka'll be coming. So the foreboding began, and everyone poured out into the street and into the field to see what'll happen. As you know, our place is high up and open so you can see all around. Everyone's looking—and suddenly down from the settlement on the mountain there's a man coming, strange-looking, with an astonishing big head.... Everyone starts shouting: 'Oy, oy, it's Trishka coming! Oy, oy, it's Trishka!' and they all raced for hiding, this way and that! The elder of our village, he crawled into a ditch and his wife got stuck in a gate and let out such a howling noise that she fair terrified her own watchdog, and it broke its chain, rushed through the fence and into the wood. And Kuzka's father, Dorofeyich, jumped in among the oats, squatted down there and began to make cries like a quail, all 'cos he thought to himself: 'For sure that soul-destroying enemy of mankind'll spare a poor wee birdie!' Such a commotion they were all in! ... But all the time that man who was coming was simply our barrel-maker Vavila, who'd bought himself a new can and was walking along with that empty can perched on his head."

All the boys burst out laughing and then once again fell quiet for an instant, as people talking out in the open air frequently do. I looked around me: the night stood guard in solemn majesty; the raw freshness of late evening had been replaced by midnight's dry mildness, and it still had a long time to lie like a soft quilt over the dreaming fields; there was still a long time to wait until the first murmur, the first rustlings and stirrings of morning, the first dew-beads of dawn. There was no moon in the sky: at that season it rose late. Myriads of golden stars, it seemed, were all quietly flowing in glittering rivalry along the Milky Way, and in truth, while looking at them, one sensed vaguely the unwavering, unstoppable racing of the earth beneath....

A strange, sharp, sickening cry resounded twice in quick succession across the river, and, after a few moments, was repeated farther off....

Kostya shuddered: "What was that?"

"That was a heron's cry," Pavlusha answered calmly.

"A heron," Kostya repeated. "Then what was it, Pavlusha, I heard yesterday evening?" he added after a brief pause. "Perhaps you know."

"What did you hear?"

"This is what I heard. I was walkin' from Stone Ridge to Shashkino, and at first I went all the way along by our nut trees, but afterward I went through that meadow—you know, by the place where it comes out like a narrow file,[1] where there's a tarn.[2] You know it, the one that's all overgrown with reeds. So, mates, I walked past this tarn an' suddenly someone starts makin' a groanin' sound from right inside it, so piteous, piteous, like: Oooh—oooh ... oooh—oooh! I was terrified, mates. It was late an' that voice sounded like somebody really sick. It was like I was goin' to start cryin' myself.... What would that have been, eh?"

"In the summer before last, thieves drowned Akim the forester in that tarn," Pavlusha remarked. "So it may have been his soul complaining."

"Well, it might be that, mates," rejoined Kostya, widening his already enormous eyes. "I didn't know that Akim had been drowned in that tarn. If I'd known, I wouldn't have got so terrified."

"But they do say," continued Pavlusha, "there's a kind of little frog makes a piteous noise like that."

"Frogs? No, that wasn't frogs ... what sort of ..." (The heron again gave it's cry over the river.) "Listen to it!" Kostya could not refrain from saying. "It makes a noise like a wood-demon."

"Wood-demons don't make a cry, they're dumb," Ilyusha inserted. "They just clap their hands and chatter...."

"So you've seen one of them, a wood-demon, have you?" Fedya interrupted him scornfully.

"No, I haven't, and God preserve that I should see one. But other people have seen one. Just a few days ago one such overtook one of our peasants and was leading him all over the place through the wood and around and around some clearing or other.... He only just managed to get home before it was light."

"Well, did he see him?"

"He saw him. Big as big he was, he said, and dark, all wrapped up, just like he was behind a tree so you couldn't see him clearly, or like he was hiding from the moon, and looking all the time, peering with his wicked eyes, and winking them, winking...."

"That's enough!" exclaimed Fedya, shuddering slightly and convulsively hunching his shoulders. "Phew!"

"Why should this devilish thing be around in the world?" commented Pavlusha. "I don't understand it at all!"

"Don't you scold it! It'll hear you, you'll see," Ilyusha said.

Again a silence ensued.

"Look up there, look up there, all of you!" the childish voice of Vanya

---

[1] *narrow file:* a sharp turn in a ravine.
[2] *tarn:* a deep hole filled with spring water remaining after the spring torrents, which does not dry up even in summer.

suddenly cried. "Look at the little stars of God, all swarming like bees!"

He had stuck his small, fresh-complexioned face out from beneath the matting, was leaning on one little fist and slowly looking up with his large, placid eyes. The boys all raised their eyes to the sky, and did not lower them until quite a while had passed.

"Tell me, Vanya," Fedya began to say in a gentle voice, "is your sister Anyutka well?"

"She's well," Vanya answered, with a faint lisp.

"You tell her she ought to come and see us. Why doesn't she?"

"I don't know."

"Tell her that she ought to come."

"I'll tell her."

"Tell her that I'll give her a present."

"And you'll give one to me, too?"

"I'll give one to you, too."

Vanya sighed. "No, there's no need to give me one. Better you give it to her, she's so good to us."

And once more Vanya laid his head on the ground. Pavlusha rose and picked up the little pot, now empty.

"Where are you going?" Fedya asked him.

"To the river, to get some water. I'd like a drink."

The dogs got up and followed him.

"See you don't fall in the river!" Ilyusha called after him.

"Why should he fall?" asked Fedya. "He'll be careful."

"All right, so he'll be careful. Anything can happen, though. Say he bends down, starting to dip up the water, but then a water-sprite grabs him by the hand and pulls him down below. They'll start saying afterward that, poor boy, he fell in the water. . . . But what sort of a fall is that? Listen, listen, he's in the reeds," he added, pricking up his ears.

The reeds were in fact moving, "hushing," as they say in our parts.

"Is it true," asked Kostya, "that that ugly woman, Akulina, has been wrong in the head ever since she went in the water?"

"Ever since then. . . . And look at her now! They say she used to be real good-looking before. The water-sprite did for her. Likely he didn't expect they'd drag her out so soon. He corrupted her down there, down in his own place at the bottom of the water."

(I had come across this Akulina more than once. Covered with tatters, fearsomely thin, with a face as black as coal, a vacant gaze and permanently bared teeth, she used to stamp about on the same spot for hours at a time, at some point on the road, firmly hugging her bony hands to her breast and slowly shifting her weight from one foot to the other just like a wild animal in a cage. She would give no sign of understanding, no matter what was said to her, save that from time to time she would break into convulsions of laughter.)

"They do say," Kostya went on, "that Akulina threw herself in the river because her lover deceived her."

"Because of that very thing."

"But do you remember Vasya?" Kostya added sadly.

"What Vasya?" asked Fedya.

"The one who drowned," Kostya answered, "in this very river. He was a grand lad, a really grand lad! That mother of his, Feklista, how she loved him, how she used to love Vasya! And she sort of sensed, Feklista did, that ruin would come to him on account of water. That Vasya used to come with us boys in the summer when we went down to the river to bathe—and she'd be all bothered, his mother would. The other women wouldn't care, going waddling by with their washtubs, but Feklista would put her tub down on the ground and start calling to him: 'Come back, come back, light of my life! O come back, my little falcon!' And how he came to drown, God alone knows. He was playing on the bank, and his mother was there, raking hay, and suddenly she heard a sound like someone blowing bubbles in the water—she looks, and there's nothing there 'cept Vasya's little cap floating on the water. From then on, you know, Feklista's been out of her mind: she goes and lies down at that place where he drowned, and she lies down, mates, and starts singing this song—you remember the song Vasya used to sing all the time— that's the one she sings, plaintivelike, and she cries and cries, and complains bitterly to God...."

"Here's Pavlusha coming," Fedya said.

Pavlusha came up to the fire with a full pot in his hand.

"Well, boys," he began after a pause, "things aren't good."

"What's happened?" Kostya quickly asked.

"I heard Vasya's voice."

They all shuddered.

"What's that you're saying? What's it all about?" Kostya babbled.

"It's God's truth. I was just bending down to the water and suddenly I hear someone calling me in Vasya's voice, and it was just like it was coming from under the water: "Pavlusha, hey, Pavlusha!' I listen, and again it calls: 'Pavlusha, come down here!' I came away. But I managed to get some water."

"God preserve us! God preserve us!" the boys said, crossing themselves.

"It was a water-sprite for sure calling you, Pavlusha," Fedya added.

'And we were only just talking about him, about that Vasya.'

"Oh, it's a real bad omen," said Ilyusha, giving due weight to each word.

"It's nothing, forget it!" Pavlusha declared resolutely and again sat down. "Your own fate you can't escape."

The boys grew quiet. It was clear that Pavlusha's words had made a profound impression on them. They began to lie down before the fire, as if preparing to go to sleep.

"What was that?" Kostya suddenly asked, raising his head.

Pavlusha listened.

"It's some snipe in flight, whistling as they fly."

"Where would they be flying?"

"To a place where there's never any winter, that's what they say."

"There isn't such a land, is there?"

"There is."

"Is it far away?"

"Far, far away, on the other side of the warm seas."

Kostya sighed and closed his eyes.

More than three hours had already flowed by since I joined the boys. Eventually the moon rose. I failed to notice it immediately because it was so small and thin. This faintly moonlit night, it seemed, was just as magnificent as it had been previously. But many stars which had only recently stood high in the sky were beginning to tilt toward its dark edge; all around absolute quiet descended, as usually happens only just before morning: everything slept the deep, still sleep of the predawn hours. The air was not so strongly scented, and once again it seemed to be permeated with a raw dampness. O brief summer nights! The boys' talk died away along with the dying of the fires. Even the dogs dozed: and the horses, so far as I could make out by the vaguely glittering, feeble flux of the starlight, were also lying down with their heads bowed. A sweet oblivion descended on me and I fell into a doze.

A current of fresh air brushed my face. I opened my eyes to see that morning was beginning. As yet there was no sign of dawn's pinkness, but in the east it had begun to grow light. The surrounding scene became visible, if only dimly. The pale-gray sky shone bright and cold and tinged with blue; stars either winked their faint light or faded; the ground was damp and leaves were covered with the sweat of dew, here and there sounds of life, voices, could be heard, and a faint, light wind of early morning began its wandering and fleet-footed journey across the earth. My body responded to it with a mild, joyful shivering. I got briskly to my feet and walked over to the boys. They slept the sleep of the dead about the embers of the fire; only Pavlusha raised himself halfway and glanced intently at me.

I nodded my head at him and set off to find my way home along the bank of the river, shrouded with smoky mist. I had hardly gone more than a mile when sunlight streamed all around me down the length of the wide damp lea, and ahead of me across the freshly green hills, from forest to woodland, and behind me along the far, dusty track, over the glistening blood-red bushes and across the river which now shone a modest blue under the thinning mist, flowed torrents of young, hot sunlight, crimson at first and later brilliantly red, brilliantly golden. Everything began quivering into life, awakening, singing, resounding, chattering. Everywhere, large drops of dew began to glow like radiant diamonds. There carried to me, pure and crystal clear as if also washed clean by the freshness of the morning's atmosphere, the sound of a bell. And suddenly I was overtaken by the racing drove of horses, refreshed after the night, and chased along by my acquaintances, the boys.

I have, unfortunately, to add that in that same year Pavlusha died. He did not drown; he was killed in falling from a horse. A pity, for he was a fine lad!

FOR WRITING OR DISCUSSION

1. What happens in the story? Summarize the events of the night in one or two sentences. Does this story support James's comment that Turgenev's stories are "without a patch of 'plot' to draw blood"? What elements of fiction hold the reader's attention?

2. James refers in his essay to Turgenev's use of "old-world practices and superstitions" as sources for his stories. What superstitions are overheard by the narrator as the boys encircle their campfire? Do you think these tales constitute a kind of "plot" for the story? Explain your answer.

3. Who are the characters in the sketch? Name and suggest one or two adjectives to summarize your impression of each boy. Why does the reader tend to think of the boys as a group? What is distinctive about each boy? How are they alike?

4. Would you say that the boys in the story are attractive people? If so, how can it be said that the story itself may have drawn an accurate picture of the peasant's life, a picture that, taken along with the other sketches in the collection, drew public attention to hardships and inequities in the lives of the serfs?

5. Does the story seem like the kind of "socially significant" fiction

you are accustomed to expect from certain American writers or essayists? Why or why not?

6. Why do you suppose the title of this story refers to a place? What is the importance of the setting in the story? Locate passages that indicate the passing of time in the same place. Then point out one or two paragraphs that seem to you especially beautiful and detailed descriptions and read them aloud to the class.

7. What colors predominate in the descriptions of nature? How do these colors change as night and day succeed each other?

8. What is "poetic" about this story?

REACTING TO CRITICISM

Identify passages in the story that may have contributed to the following statements by critics of Russian literature. Then participate in a class discussion in which you support or refute either or both of these two statements:

> In several ways this story might be taken as a symbol of all Turgenev's work: in the narrator's position as eavesdropper, in his unsympathetic interest in all that is dreamy and superstitious in the Russian people, in his respect for the rational, and in the dismal feeling that what is hopeful for Russia will not survive. We have here, in short, an author who is an analytic onlooker, never identified with his subject.[1] [*Helen Muchnic*]

> The realism of Turgenev's manner, whether it be taken as respect for the observed fact or, in a more special sense, as the ability to focus the lens of his writer's eye with such precision that the subject acquires a dramatic immediacy, is admirably illustrated by "Bezhin Lea." The opening description of the July day is an example of Turgenev at his most brilliant. A special magic haunts the picture that Turgenev offers us and suggests that such beautiful July days are a part of innocence, of boyhood, clothed in the magic of recollection. The reality, then, is the night in which Turgenev encounters the peasant boys around their fires, hears their stories of hauntings and darkenings of the sun. Serfdom here is not represented as a problem of social relationships; it is a presence, like the darkness surrounding and enclosing the boys' lives. The drama of flickering firelight and darkness has a quality of sorcery that illuminates the darkness and light in the boys' minds, dramatically

---

[1] From the book *An Introduction to Russian Literature* by Helen Muchnic, copyright, 1947, ©, 1964, by Helen Muchnic. Reprinted by permission of E. P. Dutton & Co., Inc.

holds them in the writer's eye, photographs them forever in the reader's gaze. Then after the mystery of the night's experience, comes the splendor of the morning and Turgenev's always clear-minded insistence of the ephemerality of life with the announcement that Pavlusha has been killed in falling from a horse. The color words, the visual richness, the simplicity of the anecdote so magnificently recreated and the finely etched characterization of the boys leave residue of wonder.[1] [*Richard Freeborn*]

Meeting

You will recall that Henry James praised Turgenev's remarkable sensitivity to women and remarked on his tendency to contrast strong women to weak men. James's statement referred principally to the aristocratic, intellectual, liberal women of Turgenev's famous novels, but in this charming little sketch, observe how Turgenev's understanding of feminine psychology and his awareness of women's physical attractions extend even to the simple peasant girl who is at once the heroine and the victim of the tale.

Meeting

I was sitting in a birch wood one autumn, about the middle of September. From early morning there had been occasional drizzle, succeeded from time to time by periods of warm sunny radiance; a season of changeable weather. The sky was either covered with crumbling white clouds or suddenly clear for an instant in a few places, and then, from behind the parted clouds, blue sky would appear, lucid and smiling, like a beautiful eye. I sat and looked around me and listened. The leaves scarcely rustled above my head; by their very noise one could know what time of year it was. It was not the happy, laughing *tremolo* of spring, not the soft murmuration and long-winded talkativeness of summer, not the shy and chill babblings of late autumn, but a hardly audible dreamy chattering. A faint wind ever so slightly moved through the treetops. The interior of the wood, damp from the rain, was continually changing, depending on whether the sun was shining or whether it was covered by cloud; the interior was either flooded with light, just as if everything in it had suddenly smiled: the delicate trunks of the not-too-

---

[1]From Introduction to *Sketches From a Hunter's Album*.

"Meeting" from *Sketches From a Hunter's Album* by Ivan Turgenev, translated by Richard Freeborn. Published in England by Penguin Books Ltd. and reprinted with their permission.

numerous birches would suddenly acquire the soft sheen of white silk, the wafer-thin leaves which lay on the ground would suddenly grow multicolored and burn with crimson and gold, while the beautiful stems of tall curly bracken, already embellished with their autumn coloring which resembles the color of overripe grapes, would stand there shot through with light, endlessly entangling and crisscrossing before one's eyes; or suddenly one would again be surrounded by a bluish dusk: the bright colors would instantly be extinguished and the birches would all stand there white, without a gleam on them, white as snow that has only just fallen and has not yet been touched by the chilly sparkling rays of the winter sun; and secretively, slyly, thinly drizzling rain would begin to filter and whisper through the wood.

The foliage on the birches was still almost completely green, although it had noticeably faded; only here and there stood a young tree all decked out in red or gold, and one could not help watching how brightly it flared up when the sun's rays broke, gliding and scintillating, through the myriad network of fine branches only just washed by glittering rain. There was not a single bird to be heard: all had taken cover and fallen silent; only the mocking little voice of the tomtit tinkled occasionally like a little steel bell.

Before I had stopped in this little birch wood, I had gone with my dog through a grove of tall aspens. I confess that I am not particularly fond of that tree — the aspen — with its pale-mauve trunk and gray-green, metallic foliage which it raises as high as possible and spreads out in the air like a quivering fan; nor do I like the continual flutterings of its round untidy leaves which are so awkwardly attached to their long stalks. It acquires beauty only on certain summer evenings when, rising on high in isolation among low bushy undergrowth, it meets the challenge of the ebbing rays of the sunset and gleams and trembles, suffused from its topmost branches to its roots by a uniform yellow and puple light; or when, on a clear windy day, it is all noisily streaming and babbling against the blue sky, and every leaf, seized by the wind's ardor, appears to want to tear itself free, fly away and hurry off into the distance. But in general I dislike this tree and therefore, without stopping to rest in the aspen grove, I made my way to the little birch wood, settled myself under a tree whose branches began close to the ground and were able, in consequence, to shelter me from the rain, and, having gazed admiringly at the surrounding view, fell into the kind of untroubled and mild sleep familiar only to hunters.

I cannot say how long I was asleep, but when I opened my eyes the entire interior of the wood was filled with sunlight, and in all directions through the jubilantly rustling foliage a bright blue sky peered and seemed to sparkle; the clouds had vanished, dispersed by the wind that had sprung up; the weather had cleared, and in the air could be felt that special dry freshness which, imbuing the heart with a feeling of elation, almost always means a peaceful and clear evening after a rainy day.

I was on the point of rising and again trying my luck, when suddenly my eyes lighted on a motionless human form. I looked closely and saw that it was a young peasant girl. She was sitting twenty paces from me, her head lowered in thought and both hands dropped on her knees; in the half-open palm of one of them lay a thick bunch of wild flowers and at each breath she took, the bunch slipped quietly down on to her checked skirt. A clean white blouse, buttoned at the neck and at the wrists, gathered in short soft folds about her waist; two rows of large yellow beads fell from her neck on to her bosom. She was very pretty in her own way. Her thick fair hair of a beautiful ash color was parted into two carefully styled semicircles below a narrow crimson ribbon drawn almost down to her temples, which were white as ivory; the rest of her face was faintly sunburned to that golden hue which is only acquired by a delicate skin. I could not see her eyes because she did not raise them; but clearly saw her fine, high eyebrows and long eyelashes, which were damp, and on one of her cheeks I saw the dried traces of a tear that had come to rest at the edge of her slightly pale lips and glittered in the sunlight. The whole appearance of her head was very charming; even the slightly thick and rounded nose did nothing to spoil it. I particularly liked the expression on her face for the way in which it was so artless and gentle, so melancholy and full of childish bewilderment at her own grief.

She was evidently waiting for someone. Something crackled faintly in the wood and she at once raised her head and looked round; in the transparent shade her large eyes, bright and frightened, flashed quickly before me like the eyes of a doe. She listened for a few moments without taking her wide-open eyes from the place where the faint sound had been made, then heaved a sigh, turned her head calmly back, bent still farther down and began slowly to finger the flowers. Her eyelids reddened, her lips gave a quiver of bitterness and another tear slipped from beneath her thick lashes, coming to rest on her cheek where it glittered radiantly. Some time passed in this way, and the poor girl did not move save to make a few regretful gestures with her hands and to go on listening and listening. Again something made a noise in the wood and she was instantly alerted. The noise continued, grew louder as it approached, and finally could be heard the noise of rapid, decisive footsteps. She straightened herself and appeared to be overcome with shyness; her attentive features began to quiver and burn with expectation. The figure of a man could be glimpsed through the thicket. She peered in that direction, blushed suddenly, gave a joyful and happy smile, got ready to stand up and once again suddenly lowered her head, growing pale and confused— and she only raised her faltering, almost imploring gaze to the newcomer when he had stopped beside her.

I examined him with curiosity from my hiding-place. I confess that he produced an unpleasant impression on me. To all appearances he was the pampered valet of some rich young master. His clothes displayed pretensions to good taste and dandified casualness: they consisted of a short, bronze-colored topcoat buttoned up to the neck and inherited, more than likely, from his master, a little rose-tinted necktie with mauve tips, and a black velvet cap with gold lace edging worn pulled down over the eyebrows. The rounded collar of his white shirt pressed unmercifully up against his ears and bit into his cheek, while his starched cuffs covered his hands right down to the red and crooked fingers which were embellished with gold and silver rings containing turquoise forget-me-nots. His face—ruddy, fresh complexioned and impudent—belonged to the category of faces which, so far as I have been able to judge, almost invariably annoy men and, unfortunately, are very often pleasing to women. He clearly made an effort to endow his rather coarse features with an expression of superciliousness and boredom; he endlessly screwed up his already tiny milk-gray eyes, frowned, let his mouth droop at the edges, gave forced yawns and with a casual, though not entirely skilled, air of abandon either patted the reddish, artfully coiled hair on his temples or twiddled the little yellow hairs that stuck out on his fat upper lip—in a word, he showed off insufferably. He began to show off as soon as he saw the young peasant girl waiting for him; he slowly approached her at a lounging pace, came to a stop, shrugged his shoulders, stuck both hands into the pockets of his topcoat and, with hardly more than a fleeting and indifferent glance at the poor girl, lowered himself to the ground.

"Well," he began, still looking away to one side, swinging his leg and yawning, "have you been here long?"

The girl was unable to answer him immediately.

"A long time, sir, Victor Alexandrych," she said eventually in a scarcely audible voice.

"Ah!" He removed his cap, grandly drew his hand through his thick, tightly coiled hair, which began almost at his eyebrows, and, glancing round with dignity, once more carefully covered his priceless head. "And I'd almost completely forgotten. After all, look how it rained!" He yawned once more. "There's a mass of things to be done, what with everything to be got ready and the master swearing as well. Tomorrow we'll be off. . . ."

"Tomorrow?" the girl said and directed at him a look of fright.

"That's right—tomorrow. Now, now, now, please," he added hastily and with annoyance, seeing that she had begun to tremble all over and was quietly lowering her head, "please, Akulina, no crying. You know I can't stand crying." And he puckered up his snub nose. "If you start, I'll leave at once. What silliness—blubbering!"

"No, I won't, I won't," Akulina uttered hurriedly, making herself swallow her tears. "So you're leaving tomorrow?" she added after a brief pause. "When will God bring you back to see me again, Victor Alexandrych?"

"We'll meet again, we'll meet again. If not next year, then later. It seems the master wants to enter government service in St. Petersburg," he continued, speaking the words casually and slightly through the nose, "and maybe we'll go abroad."

"You'll forget me, Victor Alexandrych," Akulina said sadly.

"No, why should I? I won't forget you. Only you've got to be sensible, not start playing up, obey your father . . . I'll not forget you—no-o-o." And he calmly stretched himself and again yawned.

"You mustn't forget me, Victor Alexandrych," she continued in an imploring voice. "I've loved you so much, it seems, and it seems I've done everything for you. . . . You tell me to listen to my father, Victor Alexandrych. . . . There's no point in listening to my father. . . ."

"Why not?" He uttered these words as it were from his stomach, lying on his back with his arms behind his head.

"There's no point, Victor Alexandrych. You know that yourself. . . ."

She said nothing. Victor played with the steel chain of his watch.

"You're not a fool, Akulina," he started saying at last, "so don't talk nonsense. I want what's best for you, do you understand me? Of course, you're not stupid, you're not a complete peasant girl, so to speak; and your mother also wasn't always a peasant girl. But you're without any education, so you've got to listen when people tell you things."

"I'm frightened, Victor Alexandrych."

"Hey, there, that's a lot of nonsense, my dear. What's there to be frightened of! What's that you've got there," he added, turning to her, "flowers?"

"Flowers," answered Akulina despondently. "They're some field tansies I've picked," she continued, brightening slightly, "and they're good for calves. And these are marigolds, they help against scrofula. Just look what a lovely little flower it is! I've never seen such a lovely little flower before in all my born days. Then there are some forget-me-nots, here are some violets. But these I got for you," she added, taking out from beneath the yellow tansies a small bunch of blue cornflowers tied together with a fine skein of grass, "would you like them?"

Victor languidly stretched out his hand, took the bunch, casually sniffed the flowers and began to twiddle them in his fingers, gazing up in the air from time to time with thoughtful self-importance. Akulina looked at him and her sad gaze contained such tender devotion, such worshipful humility and love. Yet she was also afraid of him, and fearful of crying; and taking her own leave of him and doting on him for the last time; but he lay there in the lounging pose of a sultan and endured her worship of him with magnanimous patience and condescension. I confess that his red face vexed me with its pretentiously disdainful indifference through which could be discerned a replete and self-satisfied vanity. Akulina was so fine at that moment, for her whole heart was trustfully and passionately laid open before him, craving him and yearning to be loved, but he . . . he simply let the cornflowers drop on the grass, took a round glass in a bronze frame out of the side pocket of his topcoat and started trying to fix it in place over his eye; but no matter how hard he tried to keep it in place with a puckered brow, a raised cheek and even with his nose, the little eyeglass kept on falling out and dropping into his hand.

"What's that?" Akulina asked finally in astonishment.

"A lorgnette," he answered self-importantly.

"What's it for?"

"So as to see better."

"Show it me."

Victor frowned, but he gave her the eyeglass.

"Don't break it, mind."

"You needn't worry, I won't." She raised it timidly to her eye. "I don't see anything," she said artlessly.

"It's your eye, you've got to screw up your eye," he retorted in the voice of a dissatisfied mentor. She screwed up the eye before which she was holding the little glass. "Not that one, not that one, idiot! The other one!" exclaimed Victor and, giving her no chance to correct her mistake, took the lorgnette from her.

Akulina reddened, gave a nervous laugh and turned away.

"It's obviously not for the likes of me," she murmured.

"That's for sure!"

The poor girl was silent and let fall a deep sigh.

"Oh, Victor Alexandrych, what'll I do without you?" she suddenly said.

Victor wiped the lorgnette with the edge of his coat and put it back in his pocket.

"Yes, yes," he said eventually, "it sure will be hard for you, to start with." He gave her several condescending pats on the shoulder; she ever so quietly lifted his hand from her shoulder and timidly kissed it. "Well, all right, all right, you're a good kid," he went on, giving a self-satisfied smile, "but what can I do about it? Judge for yourself! The master and I can't stay here; it'll be winter soon now and to spend the winter in the country — you know this yourself — is just horrible. But it's another matter in St. Petersburg! There are simply such wonderful things there, such as you, stupid, wouldn't be able to imagine even in your wildest dreams! What houses and streets, and the so*chi*ety, the culture — it's simply stupendous!" Akulina listened to him with greedy interest, her lips slightly parted like a child's. "Anyhow," he added, turning over, "why am I telling you all this? You won't be able to understand it."

"Why say that, Victor Alexandrych? I've understood it, I've understood everything."

"What a bright one you are!"

Akulina lowered her head.

"You never used to talk to me like that before, Victor Alexandrych," she said without raising her eyes.

"Didn't I before? Before! You're a one! Before indeed!" he commented, pretending to be indignant.

Both were silent for a while.

"However, it's time for me to be going," said Victor, on the point of raising himself on one elbow.

"Stay a bit longer," Akulina declared in an imploring voice.

"What's there to wait for? I've already said good-by to you."

"Stay a bit," Akulina repeated.

Victor again lay back and started whistling. Akulina never took her eyes off him. I could tell that she was slowly working herself into a state of agitation: her lips were working and her pale cheeks were faintly crimsoning.

"Victor Alexandrych," she said at last in a breaking voice, "It's sinful of you ... sinful of you, Victor Alexandrych, in God's name it is!"

"What's sinful?" he asked, knitting his brows, and he raised himself slightly and turned his head toward her.

"It's sinful, Victor Alexandrych. If you'd only say one kind word to me now you're leaving, just say one word to me, wretched little orphan that I am...."

"But what should I say to you?"

"I don't know. You should know that better than me, Victor Alexandrych. Now you're going away, and if only you'd say word.... Why should I deserve this?"

"What a strange girl you are! What can I say?"

"Just say one word...."

"Well, you've certainly gone on and on about the same thing," he said in disgruntlement and stood up.

"Don't be angry, Victor Alexandrych," she added quickly, hardly restraining her tears.

"I'm not angry, it's only that you're stupid.... What do you want? You know I can't marry you, don't you? Surely you know I can't? So what's it you want? What is it?" He stuck his face forward in expectation of her answer and opened wide his fingers.

"I don't want anything ... anything," she answered, stammering and scarcely daring to stretch her trembling hands out towards him, "only if you'd just say one word in farewell...."

And tears streamed from her eyes.

"Well, so there it is, you've started crying," Victor said callously, tipping his cap forward over his eyes.

"I don't want anything," she went on, swallowing her tears and covering her face with both hands, "but what'll it be like for me in the family, what'll there be for me? And what's going to happen to me, what's going to become of me, wretch that I am! They'll give their orphan girl away to someone who doesn't love her ... O poor me, poor me!"

"Moan away, moan away!" muttered Victor under his breath, shifting from one foot to the other.

"If only he'd say one little word, just one word.... Such as, Akulina, I ... I ..."

Sudden heart-rending sobs prevented her from finishing what she was saying. She flopped on her face in the grass and burst into bitter, bitter tears. Her whole body shook convulsively, the nape of her neck rising and falling. Her long-restrained grief finally poured forth in torrents. Victor stood for a moment or so above her, shrugged his shoulders, turned and walked away with big strides.

Several moments passed. She grew quiet, raised her head, jumped up, looked about her and wrung her hands; she was on the point of rushing after him, but her legs collapsed under her and she fell on her knees. I could not hold myself back and rushed towards her, but she had hardly had time to look at me before she found the strength from somewhere to raise herself with a faint cry and vanish through the trees, leaving her flowers scattered on the ground.

I stopped there a moment, picked up the bunch of cornflowers and walked out of the wood into a field. The sun was low in the pale clear sky and its rays had, as it were, lost their color and grown cold; they did not shine so much as flow out in an even, almost watery, light. No more than half an hour remained until evening, but the sunset was only just beginning to crimson the sky. A flurrying wind raced towards me across the dry, yellow stubble; hastily spinning before it, little shriveled leaves streamed past me across the track and along the edge of the wood; the side which faced on to the field like a wall shuddered all over and glistened with a faint sparkling, distinctly though not brightly; on the red-tinted grass, on separate blades of grass, on pieces of straw, everywhere innumerable strands of autumn cobwebs glittered and rippled. I stopped, and a feeling of melancholy stole over me, for it seemed to me that the somber terror associated with the approaching winter was breaking through the cheerless, though fresh, smile of nature at this time of withering. High above me, ponderously and sharply sundering the air with its wings, a vigilant raven flew by, turned its head, looked sideward at me, took wing and disappeared beyond the wood with strident cawings; a large flock of pigeons rose smartly from a place where there had been threshing and after suddenly making a huge wheeling turn in the air settled busily on to the field—a sure sign of autumn! Someone rode by on the other side of a bare hillock, his empty cart clattering noisily....

I returned home; but the image of the poor Akulina took a long time to fade from my mind, and her cornflowers, which have long since withered, remain with me to this day....

FOR WRITING OR DISCUSSION

1. Contrast the setting of this story with the setting of "Bezhin Lea" as to place, season of the year, and mood.

2. When does the reader first learn the peasant girl's name? Are the names of the characters in the story of any significance to the development of characterization? Or might the author have referred to the characters throughout his tale as "the peasant girl" and "the valet" or "her lover"?

3. Henry James often adopted in his own stories the point of view of a narrator who sees the action as if through the "camera's eye." In what

way is "Meeting" told from a similar viewpoint? If you were preparing a scenario for a short film or TV show, what successive "scenes" would you have your cameraman focus upon? Which would be distance shots and which close-ups?

4. Do you feel *with* the peasant girl, from the inside—or *for* her, as a sympathetic outside observer? What does your answer indicate about Turgenev's realistic technique and its relation to the "seeing eye of the camera"?

5. When does the narrator himself become involved in the story? How is his role as a character similar to or different from the narrator's role in "Bezhin Lea"?

6. Contrast the narrator's reactions to nature and to people. Which does he describe more subjectively, with more emotional overtones? How do you explain this difference? In what way is there a touch of "romanticism" in Turgenev's attitude toward nature?

REACTING TO CRITICISM

1. In what way does the story illustrate these statements from Henry James's essay?

 a. "No one has had a closer vision, or a hand at once more ironic and more tender, for the individual figure."

 b. "His vision is of the world of character and feeling, the world of the relations life throws up at every hour and on every spot; he deals little, on the whole, in the miracles of change—the hours and spots over the edge of time and space; his air is that of the great central region of passion and motive, of the usual, the inevitable, the intimate. . . ."

 c. ". . . all the natural wonderful life of earth and air and winter and summer and field and forest. . . ."

2. Another critic commenting on this story says:

"Meeting" deals explicitly with an emotional problem and is the only attempt Turgenev made in his *Sketches* to describe such emotions among the peasantry. The glitter of the natural scene at the beginning reflects and sets in relief the expectations of the peasant girl awaiting her lover, just as the final breath of autumn is an orchestration of her tears, but for once the touch is a shade too sentimental, the artlessness betrays a shade too much of the artifice that contributed to its making.[1] [*Richard Freeborn*]

[1]From the Introduction to *Sketches From a Hunter's Album.*

Do you think that the abandoned peasant girl in "Meeting" is sentimentalized, or do you find the author's attitude merely "tender," the word Henry James used to describe Turgenev's more sympathetic reactions to his own characters? Cite examples from the story to prove your points.

The Reformer and the Russian German

This sketch is one of two fragments published after Turgenev's death — it was not, in fact, published until 1964. Editors believe that probably it was intended to criticize one of two types of tyrannical landlords. The story is a good illustration of the way in which humor was used for the censor's benefit to cloak the true intention of the author. As you read, consider the way in which the landlord's "Western" traits are satirized and yet how the "Russian" qualities of his peasants present an equally dismal view of the "Russianized," or Slavophile," position.

The Reformer and the Russian German

I was sitting in the so-called clean room of a wayside inn on the main Kursk road and asking the innkeeper, a stout man with wavy gray hair, bulging eyes and sagging stomach, about the number of hunters who had recently visited the Telegin marsh, when the door was suddenly flung wide open and a traveler entered the room, a tall, graceful gentleman in a stylish traveling coat. He removed his cap.

"Yevgeny Alexandrych!" I cried. "What luck, eh?"

"Ah, ***!" he exclaimed in his turn.

We shook each other's hands. "How pleased I am, how pleased," we both babbled, not without a certain tenseness.

"Where in God's name are you going?" I asked at last.

"To Kursk. . . . I've come into an inheritance."

"Has your aunt died?" I asked with a modest show of sympathy.

"She's died," he answered with a faint sigh. "Innkeeper!" he added in a loud voice, "the samovar[1] — and quick about it! Yes," he continued, turning to me again, "she died. I'm just now on my way to receive what she's left me."

Yevgeny Alexandrych's servant came in, a young man with reddish-colored hair and dressed in the manner of a *chasseur*.[2]

[1]*samovar:* a metal urn used to heat water for tea.
[2]*chausseur:* hunter.

"The Reformer and the Russian German" from *Sketches From a Hunter's Album* by Ivan Turgenev, translated by Richard Freeborn. Published in England by Penguin Books Ltd. and reprinted with their permission.

"Hans!" my acquaintance declared. *"Geben Sie mir eine Pfeife."*[1]

Hans went out.

"Is your valet a German?" I asked.

"No, he's—er—a Finn," answered Yevgeny Alexandrych, leaving intervals between the words. "But he understands German."

"And he speaks Russian?"

Yevgeny Alexandrych paused briefly before saying: "Oh, yes, he speaks it!"

Hans returned, respectfully set the pipe directly between his master's lips, placed a square-shaped scrap of white paper on the bowl and touched a match to it. His master began to smoke, taking the pipe with the side of his mouth, and contorting his lips over the amber stem like a dog seizing a hedgehog. The innkeeper brought in a hissing and bubbling samovar. I took a seat beside Yevgeny Alexandrych and struck up a conversation with him.

I had known Yevgeny Alexandrych Ladygin in St. Petersburg. He was a tall, personable man with large bright eyes, an aquiline nose and a resolute expression of the face. All who knew him, and many who did not, spoke of him as a "practical" man. He expressed himself without grandiloquence, but powerfully; while listening to others, he used to clench his jaws in impatience and let his cheek twitch; he was self-assured in his speeches and he would walk about the streets at a brisk pace without moving either his arms or his head, darting his eyes rapidly from side to side. Seeing him, more than one passer-by no doubt exclaimed despite himself: "Phew, there's a man for you, by God! Where's that fellow off to?" But Yevgeny Alexandrych was simply on his way to dinner.

Rising from the table, he used to button his coat right up to the neck with such chill and concentrated resoluteness that he might have been setting off at that very moment to fight a duel, having just put his signature to his will. And yet, despite this, there was not a trace of boastfulness to be discerned in him; he was a stubborn man, one-sided and insistent in his opinions, but no fool, not malicious, looking everyone straight in the eye and fond of justice. ... True, he would have found it much pleasanter to punish oppressors than alleviate the lot of the oppressed, but there can be no accounting for people's tastes. He did four years or so of service in a guards regiment, and the remainder of his life was fearfully busy—with what? you may ask. ... With nothing save various futile matters, which he always set about in a fever of activity and with systematic stubbornness. He was a type of Russian pedant—Russian,

---

[1] *"Geben ... Pfeife.":* "Give me a pipe."

take note, not Little Russian.[1] There is an enormous difference between the two, to which attention should be paid more than ever now that, since Gogol's time, these two related, but opposed, nationalities have often been confused.

"Are you going to spend a long time in the country?" I asked Ladygin.

"I don't now—perhaps it'll be a long time," he answered me with concentrated energy and glanced away indifferently, like a man of strong character who has taken an irrevocable decision but is ready, notwithstanding, to take account of that fact.

"You must have a host of plans in mind?" I remarked.

"Plans? It depends what you call plans. You don't think, do you," he added with a grin, "that I belong to the school of young landowners who find difficulty in telling the difference between oats and buckwheat and dream of English winnowing machines, threshing machines, rotation of crops, sugar-beet factories and brick huts with little gardens facing onto the street? I can assure you that I have nothing in common with those gentlemen. I'm a practical man. But I do have a number of ideas in mind ... I don't know whether I'll succeed in doing everything I intend doing," he added with modest arrogance, "but, in any case, I'll try."

"It's like this, you see," he continued, transferring his pipe with dignity from his right hand to his left and grandly emitting smoke through his whiskers, "it's time for us landowners to start using our brains. It's time to look into the way our peasants live and, having once understood what their needs are, to lead them firmly along a new road toward a chosen aim...." He fell into a reverential silence in the presence of his own phrase. "That's my basic idea for you," he started up again: "Russia in general must have—and consequently the way of life of the Russian peasant must have—its own indigenous, characteristic, so to speak, aim for the future. Isn't that true? It must, mustn't it? In that case you must strive to perceive it and then act in accordance with its spirit. It's a difficult task, but nothing is given us for nothing. I will gladly devote myself to it ... I'm free to do it and I sense in myself a certain firmness of character. I have no preconceived system: I'm not a Slavophile and I'm not a devotee of the West ... I, though I say it again, I am a practical man—and I know ... I know how to get things done!"

"That's all very fine," I protested. "You—if I may be so bold as to say so—you want to be a little Peter the Great of your own village."

"You're laughing at me!" Yevgeny Alexandrych said animatedly.

[1] *Little Russian:* Ukrainian. At that time, the Muscovite state (i.e., Russia) denied the name "Russian" to inhabitants of the Ukrainian states.

"Though," he added after a short pause, "what you've said has an element of truth in it."

"I wish you every possible success," I remarked.

"Thank you for wishing. . . ."

Yevgeny Alexandrych's servant entered the room.

"*Sind die Pferde angespannt, Hans?*"[1] my acquaintance asked.

"*Ja . . . Sie sind.*[2] They're ready, sir," Hans answered.

Yevgeny Alexandrych hastily finished his tea, rose and drew on his overcoat.

"I don't dare to invite you to stay with me," he declared. "It's more than seventy miles to my village. However, if it should occur to you to . . ."

I thanked him. We said good-by. He drove off.

For the space of a whole year I heard nothing of my St. Petersburg friend. Once only, I recall, at a dinner given by the Marshal of Nobility a certain eloquent landowner, a retired chief of the fire brigade called Sheptunovich, referred in my presence (between swigs of Madeira) to Yevgeny Alexandrych as a member of the nobility given to daydreaming and a man readily carried away by his own ideas. The majority of the guests at once expressed agreement with the fire-brigade chief, but one of them, a stout man with a purplish face and unusually wide teeth, who vaguely reminded one of some sort of healthy root vegetable, added for his own part that he, Ladygin, had something wrong with him up there (indicating his temples) — and gave regretful shakes of his own remarkable head. Apart from this instance, no one even so much as uttered Yevgeny Alexandrych's name in my presence. But on one occasion, in the autumn, it happened to me, while traveling from marsh to marsh, to land up a long way from home. A fearful thunderstorm caught me out on the open road. Happily, a village could be seen not far off. With difficulty we reached the outskirts of the village. My driver turned toward the gates of the nearest hut and shouted for the hut's owner. The man, an upstanding peasant of about forty, let us in. His hut was not remarkable for its neatness, but it was warm inside and not smoky. In the entranceway a woman was frantically chopping up cabbage.

I seated myself on a bench and asked for a jug of milk and some bread. The woman set off to get the milk.

"Who is your master?" I asked the peasant.

"Ladygin, Yevgeny Alexandrych."

"Ladygin? Are we already in Kursk Province here?"

---

[1] "*Sind . . . Hans?*": Are the horses hitched up?
[2] "*Ja . . . sind.*": "Yes, they are."

"Kursk, of course. From Khudyshkin it's all Kursk."

The woman entered with a jug, produced a wooden spoon that was new and had a strong smell of lamp-oil attaching to it, and pronounced:

"Eat, my dear sir, to your heart's content," and went out, clattering in her bast[1] shoes. The peasant was on the point of going out behind her, but I stopped him. Little by little we started talking. Peasants for the most part are not too willing to chat with their lords and masters, particularly when things are not right with them; but I have noticed that some peasants, when things are going really badly, speak out unusually calmly and coldly to every passing "master" on the subject that is close to their heart, just as if they were talking about someone else's problem — save that they may occasionally shrug a shoulder or suddenly drop their eyes. From the second word the peasant uttered I guessed that Yevgeny Alexandrych's wretched peasants made a poor living.

"So you're not satisfied with your master?" I asked.

"We're not satisfied," the peasant answered resolutely.

"How so? Does he oppress you, is that it?"

"Fagged us right out, worked us to the bone, that's what he's done."

"How's he done it?"

"This is how. The lord knows what sort of a master he is! Not even the old men in the village can remember such a master. It isn't that he's ruined the peasants; he's even reduced the quitrent[2] of those who pay it. But things don't go no better, God forbid. He came to us last autumn, at the Feast of the Savior — arrived at night, he did. The next morning, just as soon as the sun'd started to show, he'd jumped out of bed and — dressed, he had, real lively — and he came running from house to house. He's a one for dashing here and there; dreadful fluttery he is, like he's got a fever shaking him. And so he went from house to house. 'Fellow,' he says, 'all your family in here!' An' he stands there in the very middle of the hut, not shifting at all and holding a little book in his hands, and looks around him, he does, like a hawk. Fine eyes he's got, bright ones. An' he asks the man o' the house: 'What's your name? How old are you?' Well, the peasant answers, of course, and he notes it down in his book. 'And what's your wife's name? Children's names? How many horses have you? Sheep? Pigs? Sucking-pigs? Chickens? Geese? Carts? Plows and harrows? Are the oats in? the rye? How much flour? Give me some of your *kvass*[3] to try! Show me your horse collars! Have you got boots? How many jugs? basins? spoons? How many

[1] *bast:* the fibrous inner bark of trees, used for making cord and, here, composition soles for shoes.
[2] *quitrent:* a fixed rent due from peasants to their master.
[3] *kvass:* a mildly fermented drink usually made in the home.

sheepskin coats? How many shirts?' By God, yes, he even asked about shirts! An' he notes everything down, just like he was making an investigation. 'What d'you trade in?' he asks. 'D'you go into town? Often? Precisely how many times each month? Are you fond of drinking? D'you beat your wife? D'you also beat your children? What's your heart set on?' Yes, twice, by God he asked that," the peasant added, in response to my involuntary smile.

"And he went round all the yards, all the huts, he did. He quite wore out Tit, the elder, and Tit even fell on to his knees in front of him and said: 'Good master, have mercy on me! If I've done something wrong in your eyes, then I'd rather you ordered me to be flogged!' The next day, again before it was light, he got up and ordered all the peasants there are here to come to an assembly. So we all came. It was in the yard of his house. He came out on to the porch, greeted us and started talking. Talk, he did, talk and talk. The strange thing was we didn't understand what he was saying though he seemed to be talking Russian. 'Everything,' he said, 'is wrong, you're doing everything the wrong way. I'm going to lead,' he said, 'in a different way, though I don't want at all to have to force you. But,' he said, 'you're my peasants. You fulfill all your obligations,' he added. 'If you fulfill them, fine; if you don't, I shan't leave a stone unturned.' But God knows what he wanted done!"

" 'Well,' he said, 'now you've understood me. Go back to your homes. My way's going to start from tomorrow.' So we went home. We walked back to the village. We looked at each other and looked at each other — and wandered back to our huts."

FOR WRITING OR DISCUSSION

1. How does the beginning of the story differ from the initial paragraphs of "Bezhin Lea" and of "Meeting"? Would you say that, from beginning to end, this sketch moves more or less quickly than the others? Does the fact that it is actually an unfinished fragment of what was to be a longer work explain the difference in narrative movement? Why or why not?

2. Is the setting more or less important in this story than in the other two you have read? What *is* the setting at the beginning of the story and at the end?

3. How is the point of view used in this fragment different from the "camera's eye" technique of the two preceding stories? Is the story more unified or less unified than the other two stories?

4. What is the significance of Yevgeny's being called a Russian Ger-

man? How is his statement that he is neither a Slavophile nor a Westerner borne out or denied by his actions or speech?

5. Do you think that there is any evidence that Turgenev, who considered himself a "Westernized" Russian, was poking fun at himself in the story? Explain.

6. Describe the various types of humor in this story. Cite passages in which the humor is simply good-natured fun, caricature, satire, or irony. Is there any progression in the kind of humor used?

7. Are the peasants in this story more or less attractive than those in "Bezhin Lea" and "Meeting"? Explain your answer.

8. What does an American reader learn from this story about life in nineteenth-century rural Russia?

RELATING THE STORY TO HISTORICAL AND SOCIAL CRITICISM

1. In what way does this story illustrate in a humorous manner the differences between Slavophiles and Westerners that are briefly described in the following passages? In what ways is Ladygin both a Slavophile and a Westerner?

> While the issue of Byzantine[1] culture was debated ... another foreign influence, that of Western Europe, was infiltrating into Russia to become dominant there in the next century. From the time of Ivan the Terrible, foreign artists, soldiers, and craftsmen were invited to enter Russia, and when Russian ambassadors were sent abroad they were instructed to observe with care the ways of foreign courts. They returned with delighted accounts of what they had seen and took over what they found, in the true manner of barbarians. One prince, for example, was so enchanted with clocks that he filled his rooms with them; another built a coach "upholstered in gold brocade, lined with costly sable, and hooped in pure silver in place of iron." The government hired German soldiers, placed the army under the instruction of German officers, obtained equipment from Holland and England, invited German actors and German scholars to enter the Imperial Service, and, imbued with zeal for education, formed an Academy of Sciences near Moscow, setting up a school in the Kremlin in 1667 for the imparting of "cunning in letters and the Slavonic, Greek, and Latin tongues, and other free teachings." During the time of Ivan the Terrible there were enough Germans in Moscow

[1]*Byzantine:* relating to the Eastern Roman Empire (330–1453), which was greatly influenced by the culture of the Middle East.

to form a community of their own, which was called the German Quarter; and Peter the Great continued to borrow soldiers and technicians from Europe. What Russia took from the West was useful knowledge and practical schemes to make life safer and more comfortable. Western influence was, therefore, primarily secular; and, as regards its effect on the people, the reverse of the churchly Byzantine. The West introduced new political concepts, new ideas of civic relations, new provinces of knowledge, and changes in customs, manners, and beliefs. It affected the day-to-day existence of men in all spheres of life, but did not provide a universal language of formal theories and observances. And so, whereas the Byzantine Church (Russian Orthodox) embraced the entire community but hardly touched the lives of individuals, the Westernized state affected the individual but not the community as a whole. These two conflicting tendencies — the churchly East, representing nationalism and tradition, the old, the native, a unique Holy Russia; and the secular West, standing for intellectual enterprise, social progress, and the promotion of political organizations along European lines — are the root of the intellectual debate which in the nineteenth century evolved into the controversy between the Slavophiles and the Westerners and which down to the twentieth century dominated Russian thought. These two foreign influences (i.e., the Byzantine-Oriental and the Western) were grafted on an indigenous civilization which neither of them expressed, and the cultivation of native modes within the orbit of those consciously acquired shapes the character of Russian literature.[1] [*Helen Muchnic*]

The average Slavophile was simply a fanatic of absolute rule and the Orthodox Church, to which feelings he usually added a sort of sentimental attachment to the "good old time," by which he understood all sorts of things: patriarchal habits of the times of serfdom, manners of country life, folk songs, traditions, and folk dress. At a time when the real history of Russia had hardly begun to be deciphered, they did not even suspect that the federalist principle had prevailed in Russia down to the Mongol invasion; that the authority of the Moscow Czars was of relatively late creation. . . . Few of them realized also that the religion of the great mass of the Russian people was *not* the religion which is professed by the official "Orthodox" church, but a thousand va-

---

[1]From *An Introduction to Russian Literature*.

rieties of "Dissent." They thus imagined that they represented the ideals of the Russian *State,* and the Moscow *Church,* which are of mixed Byzantine, Latin, and Mongolian origin. With the aid of the fogs of German metaphysics which were in great vogue at the time, and with that love of abstract terminology which prevailed in the first half of the nineteenth century, discussion upon such themes could evidently last for years without coming to a definite conclusion.[1] [*Prince Kropotkin*]

2. The following passage gives a fuller picture than Turgenev does of the quality of Russian peasant life. Where in "The Reformer and the Russian German" does Turgenev hint in understated fashion at the essential nature of peasant life?

Physically active as the Russian peasant was during his five or six months in the field, he was not among the more efficient farmers of Europe. This was due less to lack of strength and intelligence than to other causes. Primitive methods and primitive implements were still in use at the end of the century. The traditional light, wheelless plow called *sokha* was still being widely employed, though it cut too shallow a furrow. The three-field system of cropping, the most common technique, involved putting one field down to winter corn and another to spring corn, while a third was left fallow, the crops being then rotated. A peasant household would hold a narrow strip in each of the three fields and often several strips in each field, the different strips being frequently far separated both from each other and from the cultivator's hut, with consequent waste of time in getting from one to the other. The narrowness of the strips, sometimes as little as two yards across, precluded cross-plowing, and resulted in land going to waste on providing boundaries.

Then again, individual farmers were discouraged from improving their land because of the communal system of land-tenure, according to which, in most of the Great Russian area of European Russia, the arable land was liable to repartition every so often. Manure was in short supply owing to the neglect of animal husbandry, and why both manure and clear land when you were going to lose it anyway just as soon as the next repartition occurred? Then there were the unsuitable soil and climatic conditions—the bogs and infertile soils of central Russia and the in-

---

[1]From *Ideals and Realities in Russian Literature* by Prince Kropotkin. Reprinted by permission of the publisher, Alfred A. Knopf, Inc.

sufficient rainfall of the black earth region, immensely fertile as it was in potential. The difficulty of transporting produce owing to poor communications was another handicap.

To the above must be added the traditional "go-slow" attitude bred in the peasants by centuries of oppression. Their attitude to the squire, who owned the peasants themselves along with the land before emancipation, was one of deep suspicion which continued long after the peasants had become free men and had perhaps begun to work for the local landowner as hired laborers. Well-meaning landowners might sincerely propose generous innovations of benefit to the peasantry ... but the peasants remained stubbornly convinced that there must be some snag even if they could not see what it was. This attitude made things difficult for those landlords who wished to improve farming methods by mechanization. The peasants often refused to use the new machinery, and would break it, accidentally or on purpose.[1]

[*Ronald Hingley*]

SUMMARY DISCUSSION OF SELECTIONS FROM *A SPORTSMAN'S NOTEBOOK*

1. Now that you have read a sampling of the twenty-five stories in *A Sportsman's Notebook,* discuss your reactions to them as pieces of "social" literature. How might these sketches have been instrumental in freeing the serfs? Relate your comments to Turgenev's statement, below, regarding the circumstances surrounding the writing of these sketches:

> It has never entered my head to condemn those of my contemporaries who by a different, a less negative, way attained that freedom and that awareness I had striven for. All I want to say is that *I* saw no other way before me. I could not breathe the same air as those who stood for the things I hated so much; I could not remain at their side. I expect I had not the necessary stamina, the necessary strength of character, for that. I had to put a certain distance between myself and my enemy so as to be able to attack him more effectively from the distance that separated us. In my eyes this enemy had a clearly defined form and bore a well-known name: this enemy was — serfdom. Under this name I gathered and concentrated everything against which I had made up my mind to fight to the very end, which I had sworn never to be reconciled to.

[1]From *Russian Writers and Society* by Ronald Hingley, © Ronald Hingley 1967. Reprinted by permission of McGraw-Hill Book Company.

... That was my Hannibal oath; and I was not the only one to take it in those days. The reason I went to Western Europe was to be able to carry it out the better. And I do not think that the fact that I am a Westerner deprived me of any sympathy with Russian life or of any understanding of its idiosyncrasies and needs. *A Sportsman's Sketches*, those studies which were so new at the time and which have been long out-stripped since, I wrote abroad; some of them at difficult moments of my life when I was undecided whether to return to my country or not. It might be objected that the bit of the Russian spirit that can be detected in them was preserved not because of my Western ideas, but in spite of those ideas and against my own will. It is difficult to argue about such a thing. All I know is that I should, of course, not have written those studies if I had stayed in Russia.[1] [*Ivan Turgenev*]

2. Now read the judgment of one of our foremost critics and historians of Russian literature, Marc Slonim, on both the social and the literary merits of *A Sportsman's Notebook:*

Their social impact was comparable to that of *Uncle Tom's Cabin*, but, unlike the American abolitionist, the Russian avoided any save an oblique attack on serfdom and refused to emphasize scenes of abuse, cruelty, or violence. With his usual sense of proportion he simply portrayed various characters among the peasants and landowners he met during his hunting trips.

There was no unity of plot in the twenty-one sketches (twenty-five in the edition of 1880), but a general idea ran through every one of them. Turgenev's object was to give a realistic picture of the peasants, to show them as human beings endowed with the same feelings of dignity, love, and courage, with the same aspirations that were usually attributed to only the upper classes. . . .

Turgenev never stressed the evils of serfdom. He simply made the human dignity of the peasants stand out against the background of social injustice. Such a confrontation was in itself an indictment; it was reinforced by the lively and often ironic portraits of landowners. Here again Turgenev did not introduce monsters or ogres; he intimated rather than accused. Penochkin, the aristocratic slaveowner in "The Steward," is one of the most cultured squires in the county, his French is faultless, his manners

---

[1]From *Turgenev's Literary Reminiscences.*

refined, but when at one of his delightful dinners the red wine is not served at the right temperature he merely whispers an order: "See about Fedor"—which means that the unfortunate flunky is to be thoroughly flogged. Another Turgenev hero, the kind, talkative, and hospitable Stegunov, listens with an angelic smile to the swishing of a whip and jovially imitates the knouting: "Chuki-chuki-chuk!"

Another group of landowners betrays the economic and moral degradation of the class that enjoyed the privilege of owning souls. Their portrayal aroused the concern of the authorities under Nicholas I: in the secret report on the *Hunting Sketches* their author was charged with "ridiculing the landowners, presenting them in a light derogatory to their honor, and in general propagating opinions detrimental to the respect due to the nobility from the other classes." Lvov, the censor who passed the book, was ousted from his post, while Turgenev himself was arrested, jailed, and subsequently confined for more than a year on his estate, under the pretext that he had published an article on Gogol's death "in disregard of censorship regulations."

Turgenev, who had become fully familiar with the horrors of serfdom in a childhood spent at Spasskoye, his mother's estate, and whose liberal leanings, strengthened by his friendship with Belinsky, Herzen, Nekrassov, Granovsky, and other idealists, had taken his Hannibal's oath to fight relentlessly against serfdom. His *Hunting Sketches* fulfilled this youthful pledge: they served as an eloquent defense of the oppressed and an objective and efficient plea for their liberation. Their impact was enormous, the social implications being enhanced by the lack of any tendentiousness. Their success was not due merely to their appearance at the right moment, when the best part of educated society was engaged in a crusade against serfdom; it was also a literary novelty in being a sober, realistic description of life, done in a detached, objective manner, without any indications of the author's sympathies or aversions—except for his tone and certain vague intimations—and with no sentimentality or patronizing of the underdog. . . .

. . . The landscapes of central Russia, with its unencompassable fields of wheat, its forests and rivers, forming the background of each sketch, not only are appropriate to the structure of the stories but also assume an independent stylistic value.

The plot of each sketch usually consisted of some individual episode, its main interest lying in psychological portraiture and in the pictures of nature which conveyed, in a slightly wistful, delicate manner, the very atmosphere of the Russian land.[1] [*Marc Slonim*]

Do you agree with Marc Slonim's view that Turgenev's objective method of "intimating" the evils of serfdom, though perhaps devised as a way of evading censorship, is more effective both for purposes of social reform *and* artistic merit than a more direct way of "accusing" landowners and autocrats? Explain your answer.

[1] From *The Epic of Russian Literature: From Its Origins Through Tolstoy* by Marc Slonim, copyright 1950 by Oxford University Press, Inc. Reprinted by permission of the publishers.

II. The Reader as Critic

Talking and Writing About Literature:
Art as a Means or as an End in Itself

One of the perennial arguments that critics, writers, and readers engage in concerns the purpose of literature. The literary critic will, for example, discuss questions such as: What is the value of art to the individual and to society? Is art necessary to human life as a means of enjoyment and expression, or is it merely a way the artist must express himself, whether or not his expression has some value for others? Must all art be "understandable" to the majority of people? What is good art? Must art be true to life, or has it a truth of its own?

The writer, too, addresses himself to these questions, but from the viewpoint of the artist. He asks: What is my relation to my "public" — prophet, entertainer, representative? How can I convey my personal view of human experience to others? Is my view of value to others?; if so, what is its value? Is my talent equal to my need to give form to human feelings and thoughts? Is my artistic expression a value in itself, or must it be of some practical use to others?

You may not have considered yourself, as a general reader, a part of this controversy about the purposes of art, yet any time you pick up a book or any other printed material, you have some purpose in doing so — usually a rather well-defined one in the case of newspapers, periodicals, encyclopedias, dictionaries, and other sources of information. But perhaps reading a novel or a poem is merely a school assignment imposed by the teacher, a "practical" necessity along the road to the diploma. When you read for your own pleasure, though, do you read just for escape from life, or do you sometimes find your reading a way of learning about life, a valuable experience for its own sake? Do you ask yourself questions about the characters? Do you become involved in the ideas expressed? Do you feel as if the story had happened to you?

And how many times have you felt yourself in the place of the reader, described by Turgenev, who "always feels ill at ease"? Such a reader

> is easily bewildered and even aggrieved if an author treats his
> imaginary character like a living person, that is to say, if he sees

and displays his good as well as his bad sides, and, above all, if he does not show unmistakable signs of sympathy or antipathy for his own child. The reader feels like getting angry: he is asked not to follow a well-beaten path, but to tread his own path. "Why should I take the trouble?" he can't help thinking. "Books exist for entertainment and not for racking one's brains. And, besides, would it have been too much to ask the author to tell me what to think of such and such a character or what he thinks of him himself?" But it is even worse if the author's attitude toward that character is itself rather vague and undefined, if the author himself does not know whether or not he loves the character he has created. . . . The reader is ready to ascribe to the author all sorts of nonexistent sympathies or antipathies, provided he can escape from the feeling of unpleasant "vagueness."[1] [*Ivan Turgenev*]

The Russian Critics and "Art for Art's Sake"

The question of the uses of art was a live issue in Turgenev's day, not only to the critics and writers united against the censors who scissored passages that disagreed with official points of view, but also to the intellectuals and to the educated gentry and artisans who considered the writer and the artist their only spokesmen in the struggle against autocracy. It is easy to understand how practically Russian writers have served their own country if one understands their importance in nineteenth-century social reform. The Soviet censorship that exists today has replaced the censorship of the czars, and though recent attempts to liberalize the rights of artists to express themselves without necessarily expressing the Soviet position are a hopeful sign for the freedom of Russian artists, still many Russian writers voluntarily dedicate their talents to the service of the state.

Try to imagine yourself as a reader in nineteenth-century Russia trying to decide whether you agree with the critics who say that art should be "utilitarian" (that is, that it should serve some socially useful purposes by dealing with content and ideas relevant to the problems of the times) or with writers like Turgenev who believed that art is an end in itself (that the "how" of art, the form of the work of art itself, is more important than the "what," the content or subject matter) because it is the author's ability to put ideas into a certain form that enables the reader to understand and enjoy the content. First, let Turgenev's critic-friend V. G. Belinsky, speak:

[1] From *Turgenev's Literary Reminiscences*.

The French read, say, Rabelais or Pascal, writers of the sixteenth and seventeenth centuries. There is nothing surprising in this, because these writers are still read by people of all educated nations. The language of these writers, especially Rabelais, has become old; but the *content* of their works will always possess a vital interest because it is closely connected with the idea and significance of an entire historical epoch. This testifies to the fact that only *content* — not language, not style — can save a writer from oblivion in the face of changes in the language, customs, and the ideas of society.[1] [*V. G. Belinsky*]

Another critic, N. G. Chernyshevsky, much more "utilitarian" in his views, is not satisfied with the assumption that the subject matter of art is of more lasting value than the form of a particular work. He wants content to concern itself with social problems needing reform.

It is better not to raise a man than to raise him without the influence of ideas on civic affairs, without the influence of that sense that rouses participation in them. If ideas and impulses that have social utility as their goal are excluded from the sphere of my observations and of the activities in which I indulge, that is, if civic motives are excluded, what will be left for me to observe? There will remain the troubled bustling of separate individuals with their personal narrow worries about their own pocketbook, their own bellies, or their own distractions. If I observe people as they are when the feeling of participation in civic activity has been removed from them, what kind of ideas will I form about people and about life....

Think what conversation becomes in any society when it ceases to deal with civic affairs. No matter how intelligent and noble the conversationalists may be, they begin to gossip and prattle if they do not talk about civic matters....

... He who lives in a society that has no interests except petty day-to-day calculations cannot help being imbued with a pettiness of will.... We are so smart that we try to convince ourselves that we fear everything that we do only because we have no strength for anything exalted; we try to convince ourselves that that's all nonsense, that in reality there is nothing like that and will not be anything like it.

[1]From the book *Belinsky, Chernyshevsky and Dobrolyubov: Selected Criticism*, translated and edited by Ralph E. Matlaw, copyright, ©, 1962, by E. P. Dutton & Co., Inc. Reprinted by permission of the publisher.

But if there is? Well, then the same thing will happen to us that happened to our Romeo in Mr. Turgenev's tale. He too did not foresee anything and did not want to foresee it. He too closed both his eyes and drew back, and when the time came — well, your elbow is near but you can't bite it.[1] [*N. G. Chernyshevsky*]

A third influential critic, N. A. Dobrolyubov, agrees that the content of a work is of fundamental importance, and he stresses the writer's duty to use his talent to describe the kinds of characters and actions the Russian nation needed in order to become truly enlightened and free. He takes issue with the kinds of critics and readers who are satisfied with the "prettiness" of literature or with the romantic sentimentalizing over nature:

> Aesthetic criticism has now become the hobby of sentimental young ladies. In conversation with them the devotees of pure art may hear many subtle and true observations, and then they can sit down and write a review in the following style: "Here is the content of Mr. Turgenev's novel" (there follows a summary of the story). "This pale sketch is enough to show how much life and poetry, of the freshest and most fragrant kind, is to be found in this novel. But only by reading the novel itself can one obtain a true idea of that feeling for the most subtle poetical shades of life, of that keen psychological analysis, of that profound understanding of the hidden streams and currents of public thought, and of that friendly and yet bold attitude toward reality that constitute the distinguishing features of Mr. Turgenev's talent. See, for example, how subtly he has noted these psychological features" (then comes a repetition of a part of this summary, followed by an excerpt from the novel); "recall this poetical living picture" (excerpt), "or this lofty and bold delineation" (excerpt). "Does not this penetrate to the depths of your soul, compel your human dignity and the great, eternal significance of the sacred ideas of truth, goodness, and beauty! *Comme c'est joli, comme c'est délicieux!*"[2] [*N. A. Dobrolyubov*]

Here we disagree with the advocates of so-called art for art's sake, who believe that the excellent delineation of a tree leaf is as important, say, as the excellent delineation of a human character. Subjectively, this may be right: two artists may possess talent as

---

[1] *Ibid.*
[2] *Ibid.*

such to an equal degree and only their spheres of activity may be different.

But we shall never agree that a poet who wastes his talent on exemplary descriptions of leaf buds and brooks can be as important as an artist who is able with equal talent to reproduce, say, the phenomena of public life. We think that for literary criticism, for literature, and for society itself, the question of what the talent of an artist is spent on, of how it is expressed, is far more important than that of the degree and quality of the talent he possesses in himself, in the abstract, as a potentiality.[1] [*N. A. Dobrolyubov*]

All three of the critics quoted above praised Turgenev for his marvelous powers of description, for his awareness of social change, and for his courage in presenting aspects of life that were, to say the least, unflattering to the rulers. But Dobrolyubov in particular felt that Turgenev had a duty to make his revolutionary "heroes," like Bazarov in *Fathers and Sons* and Insarov in *On the Eve,* more heroic men of action, more exemplary of what the Russian liberal *should* be.

Turgenev Responds

In his responses to the critics, made on different occasions, Turgenev enunciated the artistic credo that has been accepted by most modern writers of America and Europe:

> The critics, generally speaking, have not got quite the right idea of what is taking place in the mind of an author or of what exactly his joys and sorrows, his aims, his successes and failures are ... they refuse to believe that to reproduce truth and the reality of life correctly and powerfully is the greatest happiness for an author, even if this truth does not coincide with his own sympathies.[2] [*Ivan Turgenev*]

> Every writer *who does not lack talent* (that, of course, is the indispensable condition), every writer, I say, tries his best to give a vivid and true reproduction of the impressions he has obtained from his own life and from the life of others, and every reader has the right to judge how far he has succeeded in this and where he has gone wrong; but who has the right to tell him which impressions are of any use in literature and which aren't? If he is truthful, he is right; if he has no talent, no amount of "objectivity" will

[1]*Ibid.*
[2]From *Turgenev's Literary Reminiscences.*

be of any help to him. We have now a multiplicity of writers who consider themselves to be "unconscious creative artists" and who choose only "vital" subjects; and yet it is they who are most of all imbued with this disastrous "tendentiousness." Everyone knows the saying: *a poet thinks in images;* this saying is absolutely incontestable and true; but on what ground do you, his critic and judge, permit him to reproduce an imaginative picture of nature, be it something out of the life of the common people or a character who is true to himself (another stock phrase!), and yet as soon as he touches something vague, something that is psychologically complex or even morbid, something that has emerged from the very depth of our social life and is not just some particular case, you shout: Stop! This is no good at all! This is ratiocination, this is a preconceived idea, this is politics, this is journalism! You maintain that the journalist and the poet have different objects in view.... No! Their objects can be the same, absolutely the same, except that the journalist looks at them with the eyes of the journalist and the poet with the eyes of the poet. In art the question: how? is more important than the question: what? If all that you repudiate appears as an *image*—note: as an *image*—in the writer's mind, what right have you to suspect his intentions, why do you push him out of the temple where the priests of "unconscious" art sit in state on bedecked altars before which rises the incense all too often kindled by the hands of those selfsame priests? Believe me, no man of real talent ever serves aims other than his own and he finds satisfaction in himself alone; the life that surrounds him provides him with the contents of his works; he is its *concentrated reflection;* but he is as incapable of writing a panegyric as a lampoon.... When all is said and done—that is beneath him. Only those who can do no better submit to a given theme or carry out a program.[1] [*Ivan Turgenev*]

I shall say briefly that I am, above all, a realist and chiefly interested in the living truth of the human race; to everything supernatural I am indifferent, and I do not believe in absolutes and systems; I love freedom more than anything else, and so far as I can judge I am sensitive to poetry. Everything human is dear to me, Slavophilism is alien, and so is all manner of orthodoxy.[2] [*Ivan Turgenev*]

[1]*Ibid.*
[2]*Ibid.*

Putting Yourself in the Critic's Place

Turgenev's assumption that in art the question "how?" is more important than the question "what?" is open to challenge, as you have learned from reading the statements of critics who believed that content and social value are more worthwhile than technique and style. But perhaps you should consider now the relation of content and style, what the modern critic refers to as the "unity of subject and form." The question is this: Does the author's style have to be so deliberately and obviously aimed at getting a "message" across that the social implications of his work are inescapable to the reader? Or does the author's attempt to render life around him in an objective way, using images that impress themselves on the mind and sense of the reader, result in getting a "message" across more subtly and therefore more effectively?

You will recall that in his essay on Turgenev (pages 18–23), James compared the effect of *A Sportsman's Notebook* on the freeing of the Russian serf to the effect of *Uncle Tom's Cabin* on the emancipation of the American Negro slave; yet the two works are completely different in style and tone. Harriet Beecher Stowe's oversentimentalized and heavy-handed moralizing leaves no doubt in the reader's mind that her purpose in writing the book was to dramatize the plight of the Negro, and her characters are all overdrawn—almost caricatures of the "real." Turgenev's characters are, in contrast, underdrawn, and his style more objective and understated. It may be precisely *because* Turgenev was writing "from a distance" in Western Europe, with a cooler pen and less didactic intent, that his pictures of the social types in nineteenth-century Russia conveyed a truthfulness and authenticity that is more convincing than straight documentary journalism *or* Harriet Beecher Stowe's effusions.

To prepare yourself to write about Turgenev's success in letting the "how" of art convey the "what" of subject matter, follow these procedures:

1. Estimate the knowledge of Russian life among the farm peasants, house serfs, landed gentry, civic officials of villages and towns, intellectuals, and aristocrats that you gained from reading the selections from *A Sportsman's Notebook*.

2. Select *one* of these social groups and note on the following chart the impressions you have of that particular group. To support each impression, cite as many sources as possible from Turgenev's stories and from any of the critical commentaries. Be sure to jot down the title of the story or commentary, the page, and the paragraph from which each impression comes.

Social Class: _____

Work	Amusements	Physical Appearance	Desires, Ambitions	Education	Other

3. Compare this "journalistic" summary of facts to some of the passages in the stories and commentaries from which you cited details. Discuss differences that the two kinds of style achieve in terms of interest, effective portraiture, memorability, enjoyment to the reader, and faithfulness to reality.

4. Finally, write a short theme in which you incorporate some of the material you gathered during the preceding activities as support for any of the following statements:

> The *Sketches* do, assuredly, qualify as an attack on serfdom—not a head-on one, of course, but rather in the manner of the Trojan Horse.[1] [*Bernard Guerney*]

> it is impossible to read him without the conviction of his being ... of the strong type of those made to bring home to us the happy truth of the unity, in a generous talent, of material and form—of their being inevitable faces of the same medal. . . . [*Henry James*]

> by giving life portraits of sensible, reasoning, and loving beings, bent down under the yoke of serfdom, together with life pictures of the shallowness and meanness of the life of the serf-owners—even the best of them—he awakened the consciousness of the wrong done by the system.[2] [*Prince Kropotkin*]

> And I do not think that the fact that I am a Westerner deprived me of any sympathy with Russian life or of any understanding of its idiosyncrasies and needs.[3] [*Ivan Turgenev*]

[1]From *The Hunting Sketches* by Ivan Turgenev, translated by Bernard Guilbert Guerney, copyright © 1962 by Bernard Guilbert Guerney. Reprinted by permission of The New American Library, Inc., New York.
[2]From *Ideals and Realities of Russian Literature*.
[3]From *Turgenev's Literary Reminiscences*.

III. The Reader as Writer

Putting Yourself in the Author's Place

Henry James called Turgenev "the novelists' novelist," perhaps because Turgenev became a master of style for many other writers, among them James himself. The American writer Ernest Hemingway advised young writers to read all of Turgenev. Critics of Turgenev's own day—even those who thought his writing should be more instrumental in reforming society—considered him a master craftsman.

Now put yourself in a writer's place, a writer for whom the "how" of art is more basic than the "what." You have attempted a sketch or two that somehow seem to miss, not to ring true. So you follow Hemingway's advice and turn to the Russian master. What do you observe that can help you in your own writing? Since you are a novice, let Edmund Wilson, one of America's most respected novelists and critics, point out some characteristics of Turgenev's art:

> The material of Turgenev is all his own, and his handling of it is masterly. The detail is always amusing, always characteristic; every word, every reference, every touch of description has naturalness as well as point; the minor characters, the landscapes, the milieux are all given a full succulent flavor.
>
> The weather is never the same; the descriptions of the countryside are quite concrete, and full, like Tennyson's, of exact observation of how cloud and sunlight and snow and rain, trees, flowers, insects, birds and wild animals, dogs, horses and cats behave, yet they are also stained by the mood of the person who is made to perceive them.[1] [*Edmund Wilson*]

Analyze the first paragraph and the three paragraphs before the last paragraph of "Bezhin Lea" and the first three paragraphs of "Meeting" for specific examples of the characteristics Wilson enumerates above.

---

[1]From *Turgenev's Literary Reminiscences*. Introductory essay by Edmund Wilson, originally appeared as an article in *The New Yorker* in a somewhat abridged form; © 1957 by Edmund Wilson. Reprinted by permission of Farrar, Straus & Giroux, Inc.

Then skim one of the stories you have read from *A Sportsman's Notebook* for examples of Turgenev's technique of describing characters from the viewpoint of a "detached observer," as discussed in the following quotation.

> ... in observation Turgenev is always extremely strong. He is the expert detached observer rather than the searching psychologist of the phenomena of Russian life, and when he tries to go inside his characters he is likely to be less satisfactory than when he is telling you merely what they say and do, how they look and what one feels about them. It is curious, in view of this, that he should so much complain, in his criticism of Tolstoy, of the ineptitude of the latter's account of what is going on in his character's minds. It was surely one of Tolstoy's most conspicuous gifts that he could put himself in the place of other people; it seems scarcely even a question of "psychology" but a matter of living in another's skin....
>
> ... His [Turgenev's] characters perhaps come out best when they are presenting themselves to other people—as in such masterpieces of irony as *A Correspondence* and *Faust,* in which the two ignoble men, in their letters, unconsciously reveal to the reader what they do not know about themselves.
>
> What people show themselves to be in relation to other people is Turgenev's particular forte, and he is for this reason especially successful in the invention of social types.[1] [*Edmund Wilson*]

Because Turgenev was especially skillful in describing natural scenes and characters from an "objective," realistic point of view, you should begin your apprenticeship to this novelist by selecting a particular scene that is quite familiar to you—a place or person that evokes either pleasant or unpleasant emotions in you. Try jotting down from memory a few of the details about the scene or person that you recall vividly, and then write a rough draft of a paragraph in which you attempt to reconstruct the *appearance* of the setting or character.

Read your paragraph aloud to a few friends—at least one of whom knows and one of whom does not know the place or person you are describing. Can your "public" feel their way into the scene with all their senses, as if they were actually there themselves? Are they able to see the character closely, but through the eyes of a "detached observer"? If not, then perhaps you need to study more carefully the method Turge-

[1] *Ibid.*

nev used to bring his audience to a sense of identification with a setting or a character.

Turgenev's critic-friend, Belinsky, recorded his own impressions of Turgenev's way of dealing with reality:

> He can depict scenes of reality that he has observed or studied; he can, if you wish, create, but only out of material that is ready at hand, provided by actual life. This is not simply copying from real life; the latter does not provide the author with ideas, but as it were, suggests them to him, puts him in their way. He reworks the ready-made substance according to his ideal and gives us a scene, more alive, more eloquent and full of meaning than the actual incident that prompted him to write the scene.... The chief characteristic feature of his talent lies in the fact that he would hardly be able faithfully to portray a character whose likeness he had not met in actual life. He must always keep his feet on the soil of reality. For that kind of art he has been endowed by nature with ample means: the gift of observation, and the ability swiftly and faithfully to grasp and appreciate any phenomenon.[1]
> [V. G. Belinsky]

But the best source of help for you is, as you might expect, from the writer himself:

> I have heard it said and read it in critical articles not once but many times that in my works I always "started with an idea" or "developed an idea." Some people praised me for it, others, on the contrary, censured me; for my part, I must confess that I never attempted to "create a character" unless I had for my departing point not an idea but a living person to whom the appropriate elements were later on gradually attached and added. Not possessing a great amount of free inventive powers, I always felt the need of some firm ground on which I could plant my feet.
>
> I just want to say a few parting words to my young contemporaries, my colleagues who enter upon the slippery career of literature.... It is only talent that gives one the power for this "grasping," this "clutching hold" of life (referring to Goethe's poem in which he says one must "put your hand right into the very depth of human life. Everyone lives by it, but few know it, and wherever you grasp it, there it is interesting!") and one cannot acquire talent; but talent alone is not enough. What one needs is the con-

---

[1] From *Belinsky, Chernyshevsky and Dobrolyubov: Selected Criticism.*

stant communion with the environment one undertakes to reproduce; what one needs is truthfulness, a truthfulness that is inexorable in relation to one's own feelings; what one needs is freedom, absolute freedom of opinions and ideas, and finally, what one needs is education, what one needs is knowledge.[1] [*Ivan Turgenev*]

Let us begin with Turgenev's advice to seek "firm ground" in reality and to add to the powers of observation the ingredients of truthfulness and freedom. Revisit the scene you described in your trial draft (or observe anew the person you attempted to create in words). Select a time of day that seems to reinforce the mood that the setting evokes in you, or a moment when you can observe your character unobserved. Take a good, long look. Then close your eyes and listen for a while. Set your senses of touch and smell and even taste free of their everyday routine uses, so that you can fully "observe" the setting or character. Then turn away and jot down in brief phrases just two or three visual details that seem to sum up the general impression the place or person has evoked. Next, add to this group of visual details a few phrases that express the way other sensory impressions contribute to the total unity of tone or mood. Before beginning a second draft based on actual observation, check the accuracy of your own senses. And, finally, group your "truthful" details freely, in a sequence that seems to reconstruct the scene so that the final impression conveys the mood you wish to establish for the reader.

After writing your second draft, ask the same "public" who read your first draft to comment on this one. Do they feel that your second draft is more accurate? more "truthful"? Does your description produce any emotional response in them? Is it the one you were trying to produce?

Perhaps you will be satisfied with your results, but if you wish to go one step further, recall what Turgenev said about the writer's primary method for recreating a sense of reality in the reader: ". . . *a poet thinks in images*; this saying is absolutely incontestable and true. . . ." According to the dictionary, an image can be a number of things—a "graven idol" or "portrait or likeness"—but in the sense Turgenev used the word, it means a "picture or impression in the mind." The writer's problem, after he has observed and given order to his observations, is to express the mental image in words. There are a number of ways to do this —through using words that carry sensory connotations, through direct statements about the literal appearance of things, through comparisons

[1]*Ibid*.

embodied in figures of speech such as metaphors and similes. Look again at the opening paragraphs of "Meeting" and observe how Turgenev frequently combines all three methods:

> "I sat and looked around me and listened"—the reader knows that the succeeding details will be mainly visual and auditory. "The leaves scarcely rustled above my head; by their very noise one could know what time of year it was. It was not the happy, laughing *tremolo* of spring, not the soft murmuration of long-winded talkativeness of summer, not the shy and chill babblings of late autumn, but a hardly audible dreamy chattering."

Notice the words that carry sound images—"rustled," *"tremolo,"* "murmuration," "long-winded talkativeness," "babbling," "chattering" —and notice, too, that these words are usually associated with human speech, so that a comparison of the trees to persons is implied. Observe that words like "soft" and "chill" carry also a sense of touch to reinforce the sounds they describe.

A few phrases will often carry a number of sensory images conveyed by direct statement, word connotations, and implied or explicit comparisons:

> ...and the birches would all stand there white, without a gleam on them, white as snow that has only just fallen and has not yet been touched by the chilly sparkling rays of the winter sun; and secretively, slyly, thinly drizzling rain would begin to filter and whisper through the wood.

"Bezhin Lea" is famous for its descriptive techniques, so let us look at one or two examples from this story:

> But the wind drives away and disperses the accumulated heat, and whirling dust storms—a sure sign of settled weather—travel in tall white columns along roads through the plowland. The dry pure air is scented with wormwood, harvested rye, and buckwheat. Even an hour before nightfall you feel no dampness.

Which images are created by direct statement, by word connotations, by comparisons?

Look, too, at this little scene, created in a few sentences:

> Pavlusha threw a handful of dry sticks on the fire. They blackened in sharp outline against the instantly leaping flames, and began to crackle and smoke and bend, curling up their burned tips. The reflections from the light, shuddering convulsively,

struck out in all directions, but particularly upward. Suddenly, from God knows where, a small white pigeon flew directly into the reflections, fluttered around in terror, bathed by the fierce light, and then vanished with a clapping of its wings.

As Turgenev remarked, talent is an indispensable condition of professional writing. But every amateur—that is, most of us—can learn to write with more ease, greater accuracy, and occasional grace if we begin with the life that surrounds us, observe it accurately, record our observations truthfully, and use our freedom of creative choice to reconstruct our observations in an artful way.

PART THREE

Leo Tolstoy

LEO TOLSTOY

No other name in Russian literature is as well known to Americans as the name of Leo Tolstoy. He was, in the opinion of many Russian and European critics, the greatest novelist the world has ever produced—a writer who is to the novel what Shakespeare is to drama and poetry. In the essay you are about to read, Prince Mirsky, a Russian aristocrat and man of letters, discusses Tolstoy as a fellow-Russian nobleman and writer. As you read this account, try to form some opinion about the relation of Tolstoy's own experience and thought to the literature he wrote. Was he a writer who wrote objectively, "from a distance," as Turgenev did, or was he dependent upon first-hand experience and continuing contact with Russian life?

Leo Tolstoy

PRINCE D. S. MIRSKY

Count Leo Nikolaevich Tolstoy was born at Yasnaya Polyana, ... on August 28, 1828. Nicholas Rostov (that is, Tolstoy) and Marie Bolkonsky (that is, Volkonsky) of *War and Peace* are roughly his father and mother. His education was strictly aristocratic, and he did not come in touch with the intellectuals before he went to the University. There and in subsequent life he never mixed with them. In all his books the "peasant and peer" standpoint is consistently maintained. The middle classes are absent from them. Of all the great writers of his generation he was, with the exception of Fet,[1] the least a man of letters: he was just a gentleman. His idiosyncrasies prevented him from being a man of the world; but he was most himself when, after his marriage, he spent eighteen years on his estates, farming, rearing cattle, and providing for the future welfare of his numerous children, seeing but a few relations and friends of his own class, much interested in his peasants, and writing long epics about noble families. He was a whimsical and somewhat uncouth country gentleman, but for all that a country gentleman to his fingertips. The interests of the literary profession did not exist for him, and he had no friends in the literary world (his quarrel with Turgenev is no-

---

[1]*Fet:* Afanasi Afanasievich Fet (1820?–1892), Russian poet best known for his nature poetry and love lyrics; friend of Tolstoy and Turgenev.

"Leo Tolstoy" from *Modern Russian Literature* by Prince D. S. Mirsky, published in 1925 by The Clarendon Press, Oxford. Reprinted by permission of the publisher.

torious) except Fet, who was primarily a country neighbor, and Strakhov, who had a turn of thought in tune with Tolstoy's, and was for a long time the only critic to do anything like justice to his novels. When after his "conversion" Tolstoy cast aside all his earthly interests, he still did not become a littérateur or a journalist—he became a prophet, something much more like Buddha than like Voltaire or Rousseau. The patriarchal and intensely aristocratic figure of Tolstoy is in violent contrast to the general plebeian groundwork of Russian literary life.... It is one of the principal elements of his unique position, and must not be lost sight of. It developed in him that proud individualism which is so curiously inconsistent with his anti-individual yearnings. It was Nature, of course, that made him great; but the full development of his gigantic nature was favored by his wealth and high social standing. The greatness of Tolstoy, like the greatness of Job, is primarily a moral greatness; but this moral greatness found favorable conditions for its development in the social and economic independence of those two rich men....

But to return to the facts of Tolstoy's life. In 1848, he went down from Kazan University without taking a degree, and intended to settle at his now famous estate of Yasnaya Polyana, and to engage in farming. But this at the time proved a failure, and after a period of rather wild life at Moscow he joined the army as an ensign and went to the Caucasus, where a long-drawn-out war was being waged against the mountaineers. Before he had been long in the army he completed his first story, *Childhood,* and sent it to Nekrasov, the editor of the most influential magazine of the day. Nekrasov received it with enthusiasm, and it was immediately printed over the signature L. T. (1852). Tolstoy had early begun writing diaries and the like, in which he had exercised and refined his innate genius for psychological analysis and the observation of minute facts of the inner life. He was, and always remained, an ardent admirer of Rousseau. In *Childhood* this kinship with Rousseau is very apparent. Equally apparent is a highly developed power of analysis. The story is a masterpiece which remained unsurpassed by the author for many years. In *Childhood* (and in its sequel *Boyhood,* but to a much lesser extent in *Youth*) he displayed already that wonderful power of creating the illusion of absolute truth, of absolute fidelity to life, which marks him off from all, even the greatest. It gives an impression of transcending art, of not only representing, but *being* life. It is easy to understand that it created a sensation and gave the impression that a new power was entering literature, but this sensation was at first limited to the inner circles of literature. Even after *War and Peace* Tolstoy's fame was largely confined to those inner circles and to the upper classes of whose life he had drawn such an attractive picture. It did not become universal till later. But *Childhood* was not followed up by masterpieces of superior or even equal quality. The next years were a period of transition. In the stories written between 1852 to 1862 he is not the same supreme master of psychological realism. For he was learning, and, partly under the influence of Stendhal, deepening and perfecting his methods of analysis. Personal experience had also given an edge to his analytical powers, for there are no more powerful revealers of natural man than war and its following—discomfort and danger. Fear is a great "developer." It is precisely in the treatment of fear that Tolstoy achieves his first triumphs in analysis. As a consequence the works of this period, of which the *Sevastopol* sketches may be taken as typical, are somewhat misshapen: they are exercises in analysis rather than works of art. These exercises enhanced his power of expression, but they had to be mellowed before it attained to its full maturity.

In these early stories Tolstoy is already a preacher. He preaches a gospel of return to nature and of trust in the "natural man," a developed form of the teachings of Rousseau. In Tolstoy's case it had been largely favored by intercourse with "primitive" types of Cossacks and mountaineers in the Caucasus.

In a series of stories written after 1855 Tolstoy is still a preacher. Owing to his immaturity these stories with a purpose are often even more openly didactic than those he wrote after his conversion. Such, for instance, are *Lucerne* and *Three Deaths*. This was only a transient stage. He was working hard and striving after more perfect forms of expression. The stories that mark the end of this period are again works of conscious and mature art. In *The Cossacks* (1853–61) he finds an adequate expression for his ideal of the natural man in the primitive Cossacks of the Terek, especially in the heathen and pantheist huntsman Uncle Yeroshka. In *Kholstomer, the History of a Horse* (1861), he goes one better and applies his perfected methods of analysis to the feelings of a dumb animal. *Kholstomer* thus marks the farthest limit, both in his endeavor to reach unadulterated "nature" and in the audacious expansion of his analytical methods over new and untrodden fields.

After serving for two years on the Caucasian front, Tolstoy volunteered, in 1854, to join the garrison of Sevastopol, and from there sent his three famous sketches which were published before the siege had ended, and so had all the interest of actuality. They produced a profound impression by their daring analysis and consciously unromantic representation of the great romantic stock-subject—war. After the war Tolstoy came to St. Petersburg. He was received as an equal by the greatest writers of the day, but, though by no means insensitive to popularity, he disliked the atmosphere of literary St. Petersburg. He left the army, traveled abroad, and settled in Yasnaya Polyana. There he took to the education of village children, and startled and scandalized his liberal and progressive contemporaries by declaring that the peasants had nothing to learn from "us," but on the contrary it was "we" who had to learn from the village children. In 1861 he fell in love with Sophie Bers. At first he was sure that being old (34) and ugly he had no chance of being loved by her, and under this impression wrote *Family Happiness,* the least remarkable of all his imaginative works. But in 1862 he married her and settled down to the quiet and prosperous family life of a rich country gentleman. This life continued till the beginning of his religious crisis. It saw the making of his greatest works, *War and Peace* and *Anna Karenina*—his *Iliad* and *Odyssey.*

Although for Russians the work of Pushkin is a more essential and indispensable fact of national civilization, it is probable that to the world at large these two novels are Russia's most important contribution to literature. They have been pronounced to be the greatest novels in the world, and whether this be true or not, they certainly occupy a unique place among the world's novels. That which distinguishes them from the rest is not a question of degree or quantity, but a question of presence and absence. If this peculiar Tolstoyan quality be taken as a standard of excellence, the other novelists are simply equal in their inferiority; they have not a grain of it. It is the peculiar power of creating men and women who have a convincing roundness and a vividness which makes us classify them with real men and women. In Tolstoy's characters the absolutely universal is combined with absolutely unique features in such a way that they are at once recognized not as types, nor as creations of an imagination, but as individuals. . . .

Tolstoy's philosophy at this time, best expressed in *War and Peace,* and somewhat less distinctly in *Anna Karenina,* is a philosophy of complete submission to life and to the subconscious wisdom of the race. It subordinates reason to the irrational. But Tolstoy, greatest of rationalists, who had carried the light of analysis into the deepest recesses of the animal spirit, could not remain satisfied with such an irrational solution. He felt the necessity of finding a rational explanation of life. The horror of inevitable death must be rationally justified. At the time of the completion of *Anna Karenina* the initial energy of his family happiness was spent, and the approaching age of fifty made the shadow of death an ever more menacing reality. In the years that followed the completion of *Anna Karenina,* Tolstoy underwent a crisis which, after a period of almost hopeless despair, led him to adopt a philosophy which has come to be known as Tolstoyism, and the propaganda of which filled the last thirty years of his life.

It is not my task here to describe the genesis or the essence of Tolstoyism.... It identified itself with Christianity, but of all the teaching of Christ it took "Thou shalt not oppose evil with violence" as the central point. It was, in fact, a purely negative doctrine, more akin to Buddhism than to Christianity. It involved, among other things, the negation of all modern civilization as tending to increase the inequality of men. It is profoundly rationalistic. It rejects for purely rationalistic motives the doctrine of future life and all the sacramental teaching of the Church. But, like all rationalism, it was doomed to leave an unexplained residue. Tolstoy was aware of this residue, but he did his utmost to keep his eyes away from it. His rationalism went "thus far and no farther." Under its surface there remained the irrational man. He had been well bridled, and there is scarcely a trace of him in most of Tolstoy's writings after 1880. But he is unmistakably present in the fragment called *Memoirs of a Madman,* and we catch more than one glimpse of him in the wonderful reminiscences of Gorky. Tolstoy's teaching, for reasons which it would be out of place to discuss here, attained enormous popularity, and in a few years he became the best-known writer in the world, and Yasnaya Polyana the Mecca of a new cult. Tolstoy's obvious greatness was so great that the Russian Government, who had little to like in his activities, left him unmolested, and never so much as touched a hair of his head.[1] It contented itself with pursuing his less illustrious followers.

After his conversion his literary activity did not cease, nor did it on the whole lose in quality; but it assumed a very different character, becoming a consistent and rigidly thought-out propaganda of his new doctrines. The new period of Tolstoy's literary work opens with the *Confession,* written in 1879 and published in 1882....

After his conversion Tolstoy condemned all his previous imaginative writings. But he did not condemn himself to producing no more. He wrote a quantity of plays... and stories. These stories do not possess the charm of *War and Peace;* only a few passages from *Resurrection* (1899, the youth of Katyusha Maslova) and *Hajji Murat* (written in 1903, published 1911) have the particular flavor his readers had grown accustomed to. But as his work lost the free unfettered charm of *War*

---

[1] The excommunication of Tolstoy by the Holy Synod in 1902 was a perfectly justifiable and abundantly provoked act. It did not, as is often imagined, lay a curse on him, but merely registered the fact that he had separated himself from the Church, a fact he had explicitly recognized more than once.

and Peace and *Anna Karenina,* it acquired other qualities which are also of a high artistic order, qualities of economy, construction, and concentration. The didactic and philosophical stories of this period are on the whole superior to the "tendentious" stories of his youth, like *Lucerne* or *Three Deaths*. These stories are of two kinds—stories written for the educated reader and stories intended for the "people." In the former Tolstoy continues his method of detailed description and minute analysis. But he gives it a new edge, and concentrates his forces more decidedly towards a distinct end. The first of these is *The Death of Ivan Ilyich* (1882), a counterpart of *Confession,* a piece of extraordinarily penetrating analysis and, unlike his earlier works, of powerful synthesis, constructed, like *Confession,* with the supreme art which may be qualified as "musical" or "lyrical." It was followed by *The Kreutzer Sonata* (1888), *Master and Man* (1895), *Resurrection* (1899), *Hajji Murat, The Devil,* and *Father Sergius*....

The stories written for the people reject all the paraphernalia of the realistic novel—descriptive detail and emotional analysis. They acquire a classical neatness of outline, a reticence and a conciseness which Tolstoy towards the end of his life valued above all artistic qualities. This change of artistic standards explains his later dislike for *War and Peace* and *Anna Karenina*. He chose for his model the stories of the book of Genesis; he held the story of Joseph to be the best thing in all narrative literature. His stories for the "people" are admirable for these qualities, which, again, could hardly be suspected in the Tolstoy one knew before 1880. Many of these stories are universally familiar. They are essentially parables. Most of them are very short and all of them are packed with narrative interest.... So after all, in his last period Tolstoy did not bury his talent—he only directed it toward new ways....

Meanwhile Tolstoy continued living in Yasnaya, at his house in Moscow, or in the Crimea, surrounded by the devoted attention of his wife and family and the admiring importunity of pilgrims from all parts of the world. A group of fervent Tolstoyans, chief among whom was the ex-Horse-Guardsman V. G. Chertkov, began to play an ever-increasing part in his life. The contradiction between his ascetic doctrine and the comfortable life at Yasnaya gradually came to weigh heavily on Tolstoy. He had renounced all his possessions, but they had passed to his wife who had no wish to leave her numerous children unprovided for. Tolstoy's house gradually became the field of a permanent war between Countess Tolstoy and Chertkov. Life at Yasnaya became a hell. Tolstoy more and more began to feel the incongruity of his position at home; and finally decided to leave it. At the end of October 1910 he left his house in the company of his doctor and his daughter Alexandra, the only one of his children who had adopted his doctrines. He first went to see his sister who was a nun at a convent near Optina, then he traveled farther without any destination. The state of his health forced him to stop at Astapovo Junction; ... there in the station-master's house he died on November 9, 1910. He was buried at Yasnaya. There was an enormous attendance at the burial, but over his grave no Christian prayers were said.

FOR WRITING OR DISCUSSION

1. Using information from the essay you have just read, compare Tolstoy to Turgenev in these respects: social position and wealth, dedication to literature, manner in which love of country was manifested, interest in peasants, and relation of artistic output to actual experience.

2. What two classes of Russian society were portrayed in Tolstoy's fiction? Why do you suppose the middle-class tradesmen and the intellectuals were of little interest to Tolstoy?

3. How did Tolstoy attempt to repudiate his aristocratic nature? According to Mirsky, was he ever really successful? Explain.

4. Is there any indication in the essay that Prince Mirsky's own aristocratic background prejudiced his reaction to Tolstoy's effort to identify himself with the peasants? Explain your answer.

5. What facts does Mirsky provide to develop his characterization of Tolstoy as a "whimsical and somewhat uncouth country gentleman," a "prophet," "patriarchal and intensely aristocratic," and a man of "moral greatness."

6. The name of Tolstoy's home, Yasnaya Polyana, is generally translated as Bright Meadows. How does Turgenev's story "Bezhin Lea" (Bezhin Meadows) help you supply some of the details about Tolstoy's family life on a large country estate that Mirsky does not (or cannot) include in this brief sketch of Tolstoy's life.

7. What quality of Tolstoy's art does Prince Mirsky believe most conclusively marks Tolstoy for greatness? What experiences of Tolstoy's life made it possible for him to write about war, the nobleman and peasant in rural Russia, love and domestic happiness or tragedy, and education and religious conversion with the truthfulness that Mirsky so admires?

8. How does Mirsky explain and develop the idea of the polarity in Tolstoy's life between the preacher-teacher and the great artist?

9. On what two novels does Tolstoy's worldwide reputation rest? What is Mirsky's opinion of their virtues and weaknesses?

10. What do you learn about "Tolstoyism" in this essay? How did Tolstoy's religious conversion conflict with his continuing production of great literature during the last thirty years of his life?

GORKY ON TOLSTOY

Mirsky saw Tolstoy from the viewpoint of a fellow aristocrat. He extolled Tolstoy's artistic truthfulness and his ability to convey the universal through the unique, but he looked askance at Tolstoy's abortive efforts to repudiate his noble birthright in order to live as a "godly" peasant. Mirsky's summary of the "external" facts of Tolstoy's life can help us understand the close tie between Tolstoy's own experience and the experiences he wrote about, but the essay does not convey the effect of Tolstoy's personality, his presence, on the scores of Russians—writers, political and religious leaders, and ordinary citizens—who idealized and often idolized this greatest of writers. Whether or not Mirsky's statement that Tolstoy was not interested in the intellectuals is accurate, there is no doubt that the writers and intellectuals of his day—in Europe as in Russia—were interested in him. Turgenev considered him a genius, as did Anton Chekhov and many other men of letters. He was the mentor of young artists, the guide of seekers after truth. But perhaps no other writer revered him more than Maxim Gorky, a lower-class (proletariat) writer who was a young man when Tolstoy was an aging seer. The account that follows is a section from Gorky's *Reminiscences of Tolstoy, Chekhov, and Andreyev* in which he describes his reactions upon learning of Tolstoy's death. As you read, contrast Mirsky's comment that Tolstoy was "just a gentleman" (page 104) with the final words of Gorky's tribute: "This man is godlike."

Leo Tolstoy Is Dead

MAXIM GORKY

A telegram came containing the commonest of words: "is dead."

It struck me to the heart: I cried with pain and anger, and now, half crazy, I imagine him as I know and saw him; I am tormented by a desire

From "An Unfinished Letter," translated by S. S. Koteliansky and Leonard Woolf, from *Reminiscences of Tolstoy, Chekov and Andreyev* by Maxim Gorky; copyright 1920 by The Freeman, Inc., 1920, 1921 by B. W. Huebsch, Inc., renewed 1948, 1949 by S. S. Koteliansky and Leonard Woolf. Reprinted by permission of The Viking Press, Inc.

to speak with him. I imagine him in his coffin; he lies like a smooth stone at the bottom of a stream, and in his gray beard, I am sure, is quietly hidden that aloof, mysterious little smile. And at last his hands are folded peacefully; they have finished their hard task.

I remember his keen eyes—they saw everything through and through—and the movements of his fingers, as though they were perpetually modeling something out of the air, his talk, his jokes, his favorite peasant words, his elusive voice. And I see what a vast amount of life was embodied in the man, how inhumanly clever he was, how terrifying.

I once saw him as, perhaps, no one has ever seen him. I was walking over to him at Gaspra along the coast, and behind Yussupor's estate, on the shore among the stones I saw his smallish angular figure in a gray, crumpled, ragged suit and crumpled hat. He was sitting with his head on his hands, the wind blowing the silvery hairs of his beard through his fingers: he was looking into the distance out to sea, and the little greenish waves rolled up obediently to his feet and fondled them as if they were telling something about themselves to the old magician. It was a day of sun and cloud, and the shadows of the clouds glided over the stones, and with the stones the old man grew now bright and now dark. The boulders were large, riven by cracks and covered with smelly seaweed; there had been a high tide. He, too, seemed to me like an old stone come to life, who knows all the beginnings and the ends of things, who considers when and what will be the end of the stone, of the grasses of the earth, of the waters of the sea, and of the whole universe from the pebble to the sun. And the sea is part of his soul, and everything around him comes from him, out of him. In the musing motionlessness of the old man I felt something fateful, magical, something which went down into the darkness beneath him and stretched up like a searchlight into the blue emptiness above the earth; as though it were he, his concentrated will, which was drawing the waves to him and repelling them, which was ruling the movements of cloud and shadow, which was stirring the stones to life. Suddenly, in a moment of madness, I felt, "It is possible, he will get up, wave his hand, and the sea will become solid and glassy, the stones will begin to move and cry out, everything around him will come to life, acquire a voice, and speak in their different voices of themselves, of him, against him." I cannot express in words what I felt rather than thought at that moment; in my soul there was joy and fear, and then everything blended in one happy thought: "I am not an orphan on the earth, so long as this man lives on it."

Then I walked on tiptoe away, in order that the pebbles might not scrunch under my feet, not wishing to distract his thoughts. And now I feel I am an orphan, I cry as I write—never before have I cried so inconsolably and in such bitter despair. I do not know whether I loved him; but does it matter, love of him or hatred? He always roused in me sensations and agitations which were enormous, fantastic; even the unpleasant and hostile feelings which he roused were of a kind not to oppress but rather to explode the soul; they made it more sensitive and capacious. He was grand when, with his boots scraping over the ground, as though he were imperiously smoothing its unevenness, he suddenly appeared from somewhere, from behind a door or out of some corner, and came toward you with the short, light, quick step of a man accustomed to walk a great deal on the earth. With his thumbs in his belt he would stop for a second, looking round quickly with a comprehensive glance, a glance which at once took in anything new and instantly absorbed the meaning of everything.

"How do you do?"

I always translated these words into: "How do you do? There's pleasure for me, and for you there's not much sense in it; but still, how do you do?"

He would come out looking rather small, and immediately everyone round him would become smaller than he. A peasant's beard, rough but extraordinary hands, simple clothes; all this external, comfortable democratism deceived many people, and I often saw how Russians who judge people by their clothes—an old Slavic habit—began to pour out a stream of their odious "frankness," which is more properly called "the familiarity of the pigsty."

"Ah, you are one of us! That's what you are. At last, by God's grace, I am face to face with the greatest son of our native land. Hail forever! I now bow to you."

That is a sample of Muscovite Russian, simple and hearty, and here is another but "free-thinkerish": "Leo Nikolaevich, though I disagree with your religious-philosophical views, I deeply respect in your person the greatest of artists."

And suddenly, under his peasant's beard, under his democratic crumpled blouse, there would rise the old Russian *barin,* the grand aristocrat; then the noses of the simple-hearted visitors, educated and all the rest, instantly became blue with intolerable cold. It was pleasant to see this creature of the purest blood, to watch the noble grace of his gestures, the proud reserve of his speech, to hear the exquisite pointedness of his murderous words. He showed just as much of the *barin* as was needed for these serfs, and when they called out the *barin* in Tolstoy, it appeared naturally and easily, and crushed them so that they shriveled up and whined.

One day I was returning from Yasnaya Polyana to Moscow with one of these "simple-hearted" Russians, a Moscow man, and for a long time he could not recover his breath, but kept on smiling woefully and repeating in astonishment: "Well, well, that was a cold bath. He's severe . . . pooh!"

And in the middle of it all, he exclaimed apparently with regret: "And I thought he was really an anarchist. Everyone keeps on saying 'anarchist, anarchist,' and I believe it. . . ."

The man was a large, rich manufacturer, with a great belly and a face the color of raw meat; why did he want Tolstoy to be an anarchist? One of the "profound mysteries" of the Russian soul!

When Leo Nikolaevich wished to please, he could do so more easily than a clever and beautiful woman. Imagine a company of people of all kinds sitting in his room; the Grand Duke Nikolai Mikhailovich, the house-painter Ilya, a social-democrat from Yalta, the stundist[1] Patzuk, a musician, a German, the manager of the estates of Countess Kleinmichel, the poet Bulgakov; and all look at him with the same enamored eyes. He explains to them the teaching of Lao-Tse, and he seems to me an extraordinary man-orchestra, possessing the faculty of playing several instruments at the same time, a brass trumpet, a drum, harmonium, and flute. I used to look at him just as the others did. And now I long to see him once more — and I shall never see him again.

Journalists have come asserting that a telegram has been received in Rome "denying the rumor of Tolstoy's death." They bustled and chattered, redundantly expressing their sympathy with Russia. The Russian newspapers leave no room for doubt.

To lie to him, even out of pity, was impossible; even when he was seriously ill, one could not pity him. It would be banal to pity a man like him. They ought to be taken care of, cherished, not loaded with the wordy dust of wornout, soulless words.

He used to ask: "You don't like me?" and one had to answer: "No, I don't."

"You don't love me?" — "No, today I don't love you."

In his questions he was merciless, in his answers reserved, as becomes a wise man.

He used to speak with amazing beauty of the past, and particularly of

---

[1] *stundist:* member of a Russian denomination of Protestants formed about 1860.

Turgenev; of Fet[1] always with a good-natured smile and always something amusing; of Nekrasov[2] coldly and skeptically; but of all writers exactly as if they were his children and he, the father, knew all their faults, and—there you are!

He would point out their faults before their merits, and every time he blamed someone it seemed to me that he was giving alms to his listeners because of their poverty; to listen to him then made one feel awkward; one's eyes fell before his sharp little smile and—nothing remained in one's memory.

Once he argued fiercely that G. Y. Uspensky wrote in the Tula dialect, and had no talent at all. And later I heard him say to Anton Pavlovich Chekhov: "He [Uspensky] is a writer! In the power of his sincerity he recalls Dostoevsky, only Dostoevsky went in for politics and coquetted while Uspensky is more simple and sincere. If he had believed in God, he would have been a sectarian."

"But you said he was a Tula writer and had no talent."

He drew his shaggy brows down over his eyes and said, "He wrote badly. What kind of language does he use? There are more punctuation marks than words. Talent is love. One who loves is talented. Look at lovers, they are all talented."

Of Dostoevsky he spoke reluctantly, constrainedly, evading or repressing something: "He ought to have made himself acquainted with the teaching of Confucius or the Buddhists; they would have calmed him down. The main point to realize is that he was a man of rebellious flesh; angry bumps would suddenly rise on his bald head, and his ears would move. He felt a great deal, but he thought poorly; it is from the Fourierists,[3] from Butashevich and the others, that he learned to think, and afterward all his life long he hated them. . . . He was suspicious without reason, ambitious, heavy, and unfortunate. It is curious that he is so much read. I can't understand why. It is all painful and useless, because all those Idiots, Adolescents, Raskolnikovs,[4] and the rest of them, they are not real; it is all much simpler, more understandable. It's a pity people don't read Lieskov, he's a real writer—have you read him?"

"Yes, I like him very much, especially his language."

"He knew the language marvelously, even the tricks. Strange that you

[1] *Fet:* Afanasai Afanasievich (1820?–1892), Russian poet and friend of Tolstoy and Turgenev.

[2] *Nekrasov:* Nikolai Alekseyevich Nekrasov (1821–1877), Russian poet and editor of influential magazine.

[3] *Fourierists:* followers of the social and economic ideas of François Fourier (1772–1837), a French socialist.

[4] *Idiots . . . Raskolnikovs:* people reminiscent of main characters in three of Dostoevsky's novels.

should like him; somehow you are not Russian, your thoughts are not Russian—is it all right, you're not hurt at my saying that? I am an old man, and, perhaps, I can no longer understand modern literature, but it seems to me that it is all not Russian. They begin to write a curious kind of verse; I don't know what these poems are or what they mean. One has to learn to write poetry from Pushkin, Tiutchev, Fet. Now you"—he turned to Chekhov—"you are Russian. Yes, very, very Russian."

And smiling affectionately, he put his hand on Chekhov's shoulder; and the latter became uncomfortable and began in a low voice to mutter something about his bungalow and the Tartars.

He loved Chekhov and when he looked at him his eyes were tender and seemed almost to stroke Anton Pavlovich's face. Once, when Anton Pavlovich was walking on the lawn with Alexandra Lvovna, Tolstoy, who at the time was still ill and was sitting in a chair on the terrace, seemed to stretch toward them, saying in a whisper: "Ah, what a beautiful, magnificent man; modest and quiet like a girl. He's simply wonderful."

One evening, in the twilight, half closing his eyes and moving his brows, he read a variant of the scene in "Father Sergius"[1] where the woman goes to seduce the hermit: he read it through to the end, and then, raising his head and shutting his eyes, said distinctly: "The old man wrote it well, well."

It came out with such amazing simplicity, his pleasure in its beauty was so sincere, that I shall never forget the delight which it gave me at the time, a delight which I could not, did not know how to express, but which I could suppress only by a tremendous effort. My heart stopped beating for a moment, and then everything around me seemed to become fresh and revivified.

One must have heard him speak in order to understand the extraordinary, indefinable beauty of his speech; it was, in a sense, incorrect, abounding in repetitions of the same word, saturated with village simplicity. The effect of his words did not come only from the intonation and the expression of his face, but from the play and light in his eyes, the most eloquent eyes I have ever seen. In his two eyes Leo Nikolaevich possessed a thousand eyes.

Once Suler, Sergei Lvovich, Chekhov, and someone else were sitting in the park and talking about women: he listened in silence for a long time and then suddenly said: "And I will tell the truth about women, when I have one foot in the grave. I shall tell it, jump into my coffin, pull the lid over me, and say, 'Do what you like now.'" The look he gave

---

[1]*"Father Sergius":* a story by Leo Tolstoy, finished in 1898.

us was so wild, so terrifying that we all fell silent for a while....

The old magician stands before me, alien to all, a solitary traveler through all the deserts of thought in search of an all-embracing truth which he has not found—I look at him and, although I feel sorrow for the loss, I feel pride at having seen the man, and that pride alleviates my pain and grief.

It was curious to see Leo Nikolaevich among "Tolstoyans"; there stands a noble belfry and its bell sounds untiringly over the whole world, while round about run tiny, timorous dogs whining at the bell and distrustfully looking askance at one another as though to say, "Who howled best?" I always thought that these people infected the Yasnaya Polyana house, as well as the great house of Countess Panin, with a spirit of hypocrisy, cowardice, mercenary and self-seeking pettiness and legacy-hunting. The "Tolstoyans" have something in common with those friars who wander in all the dark corners of Russia, carrying with them dogs' bones and passing them off as relics, selling "Egyptian darkness" and the "little tears of Our Lady." One of these apostles, I remember, at Yasnaya Polyana refused to eat eggs so as not to wrong the hens; but at Tula railway station he greedily devoured meat, saying: "The old fellow does exaggerate." Nearly all of them like to moan and kiss one another; they all have boneless perspiring hands and lying eyes. At the same time they are practical fellows and manage their earthly affairs cleverly.

Leo Nikolaevich, of course, well understood the value of the "Tolstoyans," and so did Sulerzhizky, whom Tolstoy loved tenderly and whom he always spoke of with a kind of youthful ardor and fervor. Once one of these "Tolstoyans" at Yasnaya Polyana explained eloquently how happy his life had become and how pure his soul, after he accepted Tolstoy's teaching. Leo Nikolaevich leaned over and said to me in a low voice: "He's lying all the time, the rogue, but he does it to please me...."

Many tried to please him, but I did not observe that they did it well or with any skill. He rarely spoke to me on his usual subjects of universal forgiveness, loving one's neighbor, the Gospels, and Buddhism, evidently because he realized at once that all that would not go down with me. I greatly appreciated this

... [Tolstoy] began asking me about my life, what I was studying, and what I read.

"I am told that you are very well read; is that true? Is Korolenko[1] a musician?"

"I believe not; but I'm not sure."

[1]*Korolenko:* Vladimir Korolenko (1853–1921), Russian novelist and short-story writer.

"You don't know? Do you like his stories?"

"I do, very much."

"It is by contrast. He is lyrical and you haven't got that. Have you read Weltmann?"

"Yes."

"Isn't he a good writer, clear, exact, and with no exaggeration? He is sometimes better than Gogol. He knew Balzac. And Gogol imitated Marlinsky."

When I said that Gogol was probably influenced by Hoffmann, Sterne, and perhaps Dickens, he glanced at me and asked: "Have you read that somewhere? No? It isn't true. Gogol hardly knew Dickens. But you must clearly have read a great deal; now look here, it's dangerous. Kolzov ruined himself by it."

When he accompanied me to the door, he embraced and kissed me and said: "You are real muzhik.[1] You will find it difficult to live among writers, but never mind, don't be afraid, always say what you feel even if it be rude; it doesn't matter. Sensible people will understand."

I had two impressions from this first meeting: I was glad and proud to have seen Tolstoy, but his conversation reminded me a little of an examination, and in a sense I did not see in him the author of *Cossacks, Kholstomier, War and Peace,* but a *barin* who, making allowances for me, considered it necessary to speak to me in the common language, the language of the street and marketplace. That upset my idea of him, an idea which was deeply rooted and had become dear to me.

It was at Yasnaya Polyana that I saw him again. It was an overcast, autumn day with a drizzle of rain, and he put on a heavy overcoat and high leather boots and took me for a walk in the birch wood. He jumped the ditches and pools like a boy, shook the raindrops off the branches, and gave me a superb account of how Fet had explained Schopenhauer to him in this wood. He stroked the damp, satin trunks of the birches lovingly with his hand and said: "Lately I read a poem,

> The mushrooms are gone, but in the hollows
> Is the heavy smell of mushroom dampness...

Very good, very true."

Suddenly a hare got up under our feet. Leo Nikolaevich started up, excited, his face lit up, and he whooped like a real old sportsman. Then, looking at me with a curious little smile, he broke into a sensible, human laugh. He was wonderfully charming at that moment.

Another time he was looking at a hawk in the park; it was hovering

---

[1] *muzhik:* Russian peasant.

over the cattle-shed, making wide circles suspended in the air, moving its wings very slightly as if undecided whether or not the moment to strike had come. Leo Nikolaevich stood up, shading his eyes with his hand, and murmured with excitement: "The rogue is going for our chickens. Now, now . . . it's coming. . . . Oh, he's afraid. The groom is there, isn't he? I'll call the groom. . . ."

And he shouted to the groom. When he shouted, the hawk was scared, swept upward, swung away, and disappeared. Leo Nikolaevich sighed, apparently reproaching himself, and said: "I should not have shouted; he would have struck all the same. . . ."

He often pointed out exaggerations in my stories, which I admitted but once. Speaking of *Dead Souls,* he said, smiling good-naturedly: "We are all of us terrible inventors. I myself, when I write, suddenly feel pity for some character, and then I give him some good quality or take a good quality away from someone else, so that in comparison with the others he may not appear too black." And then in the stern tones of an inexorable judge: "That's why I say that art is a lie, an arbitrary sham, harmful for people. One writes not what real life is, but what one thinks of life oneself. What good is that to anyone, how I see that tower or sea or Tartar—what interest or use is there in it?"

Once I was walking with him on the lower road from Dulbet to Ai-Todor; he was walking with the light step of a young man, when he said to me more nervously than was usual with him: "The flesh should be the obedient dog of the spirit, running to do its bidding; but we—how do we live? The flesh rages and riots, and the spirit follows it helpless and miserable."

He rubbed his chest hard over the heart, raised his eyebrows, and then, remembering something, went on: "One autumn in Moscow in an alley near the Sukhariot Gate I once saw a drunken woman lying in the gutter. A stream of filthy water flowed from the yard of the house right under her neck and back. She lay in that cold liquid, muttering, shivering, wriggling her body in the wet, but she could not get up."

He shuddered, half closed his eyes, shook his head, and went on gently: "Let's sit down here. . . . It's the most horrible and disgusting thing, a drunken woman. I wanted to help her get up, but I couldn't; I felt such a loathing; she was so slippery and slimy I felt that if I'd touched her, I could not have washed my hands clean for a month—horrible! And on the curb sat a bright, gray-eyed boy, the tears running down his cheeks: he was sobbing and repeating wearily and helplessly: 'Mu-um . . . mu-um-my . . . do get up.' She would move her arms, grunt, lift her head, and again—back went her neck into the filth."

He was silent, and then, looking around, he repeated almost in a whisper: "Yes, yes, horrible! You've seen many drunken women? Many—my God! You must not write about that, you mustn't."

"Why?"

He looked straight into my eyes and, smiling, repeated: "Why?" Then thoughtfully and slowly he said: "I don't know: It just slipped out . . . it's a shame to write about filth. But yet why not write about it? Yes, it's necessary to write all about everything, everything."

Tears came into his eyes. He wiped them away, and smiling he looked at his handkerchief, while the tears again ran down his wrinkles. "I am crying," he said. "I am an old man. It cuts me to the heart when I remember something horrible."

And, very gently touching me with his elbow, he said: "You too—you will have lived your life and everything will remain exactly as it was, and then you too will cry worse than I, more 'streamingly,' as the peasant women say. And everything must be written about, everything; otherwise that bright little boy might be hurt, he might reproach us—'It's untrue, it's not the whole truth,' he will say. He's strict for the truth."

Suddenly he gave himself a shake and said in a kind voice: "Now, tell me a story; you tell them well. Something about a child, about your childhood. It's not easy to believe that you were once a child. You are a strange creature, exactly as if you were born grown up. In your ideas there is a good deal of the childlike and the immature, but you know more than enough of life—and one can not ask for more. Well, tell me a story. . . ."

He lay down comfortably upon the bare roots of a pine tree and watched the ants moving busily among the gray spines.

In the South, which, with its self-asserting luxuriance and flaunting, unbridled vegetation, seems so strangely incongruous to a man from the North, he, Leo Tolstoy—even his name speaks of his inner power—seemed a small man, but knitted and knotted out of very strong roots deep in the earth; in the flaunting scenery of the Crimea, I say, he was at once both out of place and in his place. He seemed a very ancient man, master of all his surroundings; a master builder who after centuries of absence has arrived in the mansion built by him. He has forgotten a great deal which it contains; much is new to him: everything is as it should be, and yet not entirely so, and he has at once to find out what is amiss and why it is amiss.

He walked the roads and paths with the businesslike, quick step of the skilled explorer of the earth; and with sharp eyes, from which neither a single pebble nor a single thought could hide itself, he looked, measured, tested, compared. And he scattered about him the living seeds of indomitable thoughts. He said to Suler once: "You, Liovushka, read nothing, which is not good, out of self-conceit; while Gorky reads a lot, which is not good, because he distrusts himself. I write much, which is not good, because of an old man's ambition, a desire that all should think as I do. Of course, I think it is good, and Gorky thinks it is not good, and you think nothing at all; you simply blink and watch what you may clutch. One day you will clutch something which does not belong to you —it has happened to you before. You will put your claws into it, hold on for a bit, and when it begins to get loose, you won't try to stop it. Chekhov has a superb story 'The Darling'—you are rather like her."

"In what?" asked Suler, laughing.

"You can love well, but to choose—no, you can't, and you will waste yourself on trifles."

"Is everyone like that?"

"Everyone?" Leo Nikolaevich repeated. "No, not everyone."

And suddenly he asked me, exactly as if he were dealing me a blow: "Why don't you believe in God?"

"I have no faith, Leo Nikolaevich."

"It is not true. By nature you are a believer and you cannot get on without God. You will realize it one day. Your disbelief comes from obstinacy, because you have been hurt: the world is not what you would like it to be. There are also some people who do not believe, out of shyness; it happens with young people; they adore some woman, but don't want to show it for fear that she won't understand, and also from lack of courage. Faith, like love, requires courage and daring. One has to say to oneself, 'I believe'—and everything will come right, everything will appear as you want it, it will explain itself to you and attract you. Now, you love much, and faith is only a greater love; you must love still more and then your love will turn to faith. When one loves a woman, she is unfailingly the best woman on earth, and each loves the best woman; and that is faith. A nonbeliever cannot love: today he falls in love with one woman, and next year with another. The souls of such men are tramps living barren lives—that is not good. But you were born a believer and it is no use thwarting yourself. Well, you may say, beauty— and what is beauty? The highest and most perfect is God."

He hardly ever spoke to me on this subject, and its seriousness and the suddenness of it rather overwhelmed me. I was silent.

He was sitting on the couch with his legs drawn up under him, and, breaking into a triumphant little smile and shaking his finger at me, he said: "You won't get out of this by silence, no."

And I, who do not believe in God, looked at him for some reason very cautiously and a little timidly. I looked and I thought: "This man is godlike."

FOR WRITING OR DISCUSSION

1. On what aspects of Tolstoy's character do the aristocratic Mirsky and the proletariat Gorky agree? Which writer gives you the most convincing proof of Tolstoy's true greatness? What seems ironic about this?

2. How does the fact that Mirsky's essay on Tolstoy is part of a larger work by a scholar-critic and that Gorky's tribute is an excerpt from a series of personal memoirs by a writer of fiction account for some of the differences in content, point of view, and style of the two selections?

3. Gorky compares Tolstoy to several natural phenomena or objects. What are these comparisons? What impression do they convey? How do the comparisons indicate Gorky's reverential awe of Tolstoy?

4. Were you surprised to learn that Tolstoy was "smallish" in appearance? What physical attributes and personal characteristics account for the fact that when Tolstoy appeared, "everyone round him would become smaller than he"?

5. Why does Gorky say that even when Tolstoy was ill, "one could not pity him"?

6. Do you notice a difference between Mirsky's and Gorky's attitudes toward Tolstoy? Does Mirsky's "patriarch" become a more humane "father" in Gorky's account? Explain your answer.

7. What is Gorky's opinion of the "Tolstoyans" who surrounded the aged writer after his conversion?

8. Though Tolstoy was noted for his realistic portrayal of life, what limitations on his ability or desire to portray the ugly side of reality did he confess to Gorky? What did he feel other writers should do as regards exposing the sordid aspects of life?

9. Does it seem unusual that a nonbeliever like Gorky should be so impressed by the "godlike" qualities in Tolstoy and that a peasant-proletariat should admire the true "nobility" of his aristocratic idol? Explain.

I. Reading Literature

WAR: *The Raid*

"The Raid," like most of Tolstoy's fiction, is based on actual experience. Dissatisfied with his life in Moscow, where, as he reported in his diary, he "lived a very irregular life, without a job in the service, without anything to do, without a goal," Tolstoy decided to go to the Caucasus, where his brother Nikolai was an army officer engaged in fighting the hill tribes. He remained there for two years (1851–53), serving as a volunteer and later as a cadet in an artillery battery. At the same time he was pursuing his writing career. During his stay in the Crimea, he completed his autobiographical novel, *Childhood,* and wrote a number of sketches and stories, among which was "The Raid," which was published in *The Contemporary* magazine in 1853. Though it is one of Tolstoy's earliest stories of war, "The Raid" contains the germs of ideas that were later to be expanded and reexamined in his long masterwork, *War and Peace.* The Tolstoyan mixture of idealism, of adherence to spiritual values, with an uncompromisingly realistic probing and objectivity of observation, is nowhere as apparent as in Tolstoy's treatment of war and the military life, which was often romantically glorified by his social and literary colleagues. As you read "The Raid," put yourself in the place of the young observer and ask yourself the questions he poses at the beginning of the story. What answers do you have by the time you have finished reading the story? Do you detect a still youthful love of adventure in war on the part of the narrator, even though his views have been modified? How is his attitude contrasted with that of the professional soldiers?

The Raid

1

War has always fascinated me. I don't mean the tactical maneuvering of whole armies by famous generals — movements of such magnitude are quite beyond my imagination. I have in mind the real essence of war —

"The Raid" from *The Cossacks and The Raid* by Leo Tolstoy, translated by Andrew R. MacAndrew, copyright © 1961 by Andrew R. MacAndrew. Reprinted by permission of The New American Library, Inc., New York.

the killing. I was less interested in the deployment of the armies at Austerlitz and Borodino than in how a soldier kills and what makes him do it.

The time had long since passed when I used to pace my room alone, waving my arms and fancying myself as the inventor of the best way to slaughter thousands of men in an instant, a feat which would make me a general and earn me eternal glory. Now all that interested me was the state of mind that pushes a man, without apparent advantage to himself, to expose himself to danger and, what is even more puzzling, to kill his fellow man. I always wanted to believe that soldiers kill in anger; since I could not imagine them continually angry, I had to fall back on the instinct of self-preservation and a sense of duty.

I wondered too about courage—that quality respected by men throughout history. Why is courage a good thing? Why is it, unlike other virtues, often met in otherwise quite despicable persons? Could it be that the capacity to face danger calmly is a purely physical one, and that people admire it just as they admire physical size and muscular strength?

Is it courage that makes a horse hurl itself off a cliff because it fears the whip? Is it courage that drives a child expecting punishment to run off into the woods and become lost? Is it an act of courage for a woman, fearing shame, to kill her newborn child and risk facing prosecution? And is it a display of courage when a man, out of sheer vanity, risks his own life in order to kill a fellow creature?

Danger always involves a choice. What then determines this choice—a noble feeling or a base one? And shouldn't it be called either courage or cowardice accordingly?

These were the thoughts and doubts that preoccupied me. I decided to resolve them by taking part in combat as soon as the opportunity arose.

In the summer of 1845 I was at a small fortified post in the Caucasus. On July 12, Captain Khlopov appeared at the low entrance of my hut. He was in dress uniform—epaulets, sword and all. Since my arrival I'd never seen him in that attire. He must have seen my surprise for he explained: "I've come straight from the colonel. Our battalion is to march tomorrow."

"Any idea where?"

"To Fort N——. That's the assembly point."

"And from there, will there be a raid, do you think?"

"Probably."

"Which direction?"

"All I can tell you is that last night a mounted Tartar arrived with orders from the general for the battalion to move out and to take along two days' rations. Why, where, for how long—don't ask me. We've been given our orders and that's it."

"But if they've ordered you to take only two days' rations, that must mean the troops aren't expected to be on the march more than two days—"

"It means nothing."

"What do you mean?" I asked, surprised.

"Just what I say. When we went to Dargi, we took along rations for a week, but we were gone almost a whole month."

"May I come along?"

"Surely, but if you want my advice, don't. Why run the risk?"

"If you don't mind, I'll not take your advice. I've been here a whole month just waiting for an opportunity to see action. And now you want me to miss my chance."

"All right, come along, though I'm sure it'd be better if you waited for us here. You could get in some hunting while we do the job—that'd make the most sense."

He said it so convincingly that at first I was almost persuaded. Nevertheless, I finally decided to go.

"But what's there for you to see?" he asked, still trying to dissuade me. "If you want to know what a battle looks like, read Mikhailovsky's *Scenes of War,* or something. It's a good book and it gives the whole story. It notes the position of every army corps, and you'll get a good idea of how battles are fought."

"Look," I said, "those are just the things that *don't* interest me."

"What are you after, then? Simply to watch how people die? If so, I'll tell you. In 1832 there was another civilian here with us—some kind of Spaniard, I believe. He came with us on two raids, and I even remember that he wore some sort of blue cloak. Well, it's not hard to imagine how it all ended. He got killed. You see, anything may happen."

Although I felt shamed at the way he put it, I didn't try to make excuses.

"Would you say he was a brave man?" I asked.

"God knows, though I must say he always rode out in front, and wherever there was firing, he was sure to be there."

"So he was brave, then?"

"Well, it doesn't necessarily follow that a man's brave just because he pokes his nose into other people's business."

"What would you call being brave?"

"Brave. Brave?" the captain repeated, as though the question had never occurred to him before. "A brave man is a man who does what he has to do," he said after some reflection.

I remembered Plato's definition of bravery as the knowledge of what should and what should not be feared. Now, despite the generality and vagueness of the captain's definition, I felt he wasn't so far from Plato and that, if anything, his definition was more accurate than that of the Greek philosopher. Had he been as articulate as Plato, he might have said that brave is the man who fears not what should not be feared and fears what should.

I wanted to explain this thought to the captain.

"I think," I said, "that a man faced by danger must make a choice—and if his decision is determined by a sense of duty, it is courage, but if it's determined by a base motive, it is cowardice. So a man who risks his life out of vanity, curiosity, or greed is not brave, and, conversely, a man who avoids danger out of an honest feeling of family obligation or even simple conviction is no coward."

As I talked, the captain looked at me with an odd expression.

"That," he said, starting to fill his pipe, "I wouldn't want to have to prove. But we have a young second lieutenant here who likes to philosophize. You should talk to him about it. He even writes poetry, you know."

I had heard of Captain Khlopov back home in Russia, though I'd only met him here in the Caucasus. His mother owned a small piece of land within two miles of my estate. Before leaving for the Caucasus, I went to see her, and the old lady was very happy that I was going to see her Petey (that's the way she referred to the gray-haired Captain Peter Khlopov) and that I, a "living letter," would tell him about her and take him a small package. She fed me some excellent smoked goose and pie, then went to her bedroom and returned with a largish icon in a black bag with a black silk ribbon attached to it.

"This is Our Lady of the Burning Bush," she said. She made the sign of the cross over the icon, kissed it, and handed it to me. "Please give it to him. You see, when he left for the Caucasus, I said a prayer for him and promised that if he stayed alive and safe I would have this icon of the Mother of God made. And the Holy Mother and the Saints have looked after him; he has taken part in every imaginable battle without once being wounded. Michael, who spent some time with him, told me things that made my hair stand on end. You see, I only hear about him second hand—my son never writes me about his campaigns. The dear boy doesn't want to frighten me."

(Later in the Caucasus I learned from others that Captain Khlopov had been seriously wounded four times. He clearly had never told his mother about his wounds or about his campaigns.)

"So," Mrs. Khlopov went on, "I want him to wear this holy image, which I send him with my blessing. The Mother of God will intercede for him. I want him to wear the icon, especially in battle. You tell him. Just tell him his mother wanted him to."

I promised to carry out her instructions without fail.

"I'm sure you'll like my Petey very much," she went on. "He's such a nice person! You know, a year never goes by without his sending me and my daughter Annie some money. And, mind you, all he has is his army pay! Yes, I thank God with all my heart for having sent me such a son!" she concluded, tears in her eyes.

"Does he write you often?" I asked.

"Seldom, very seldom. Maybe once a year, and usually only to accompany the money. Even then, he doesn't always write. He says that when he doesn't write it means everything's fine, because if something happens, God forbid, they'd let me know soon enough anyhow."

When I gave the captain his mother's present—he had come to my room on this occasion—he asked me for some paper, carefully wrapped up the icon, and put it away. I spoke to him at length about his mother, and during the whole time he remained silent. He went to the far corner of the room and spent what seemed to me an extraordinarily long time filling his pipe.

"She's a nice old thing," he said in a somewhat muffled voice from his retreat. "I wonder if God will ever let me see her again."

There was love and sadness in those simple words.

"Why must you stay out here?" I asked. "Why not ask to be transferred, so you'd be closer to her?"

"I have to serve in the army anyhow, and here I get double pay—quite a difference to a poor man."

The captain lived carefully. He never gambled, seldom went on sprees, and smoked only the cheapest tobacco.

I liked him. He had a simple, quiet Russian face. It was easy and pleasant to look him straight in the eye. And after our conversation I felt great respect for him.

2

At four the next morning, the captain came to get me. He wore an old, threadbare tunic without epaulets, wide Caucasian trousers, a sheepskin cap once white but now yellowish and mangy, and a cheap saber. He rode a small, whitish horse, which ambled along in short strides, hanging its head and swishing its thin tail. The captain certainly was not handsome and there was nothing martial about him, but everything in him expressed such calm indifference that somehow he inspired respect.

I didn't keep him waiting. I immediately mounted and we rode together out the fort gate.

The battalion, some six hundred yards ahead of us, looked like a swaying black mass. One could tell only that they were infantry by the bayonets that pointed into the air like needles, by the drums, and by the rhythm of the soldiers' singing that reached us from time to time, led by a magnificent tenor voice from the Sixth Company I'd often admired at the fort. The road led through the middle of a deep, wide ravine, and along a small river now in flood. Flocks of wild doves whirled over it, landing on its rocky banks, taking off, swooping down in circles, vanishing from sight. The sun had not yet come up, although the top of the right slope of the ravine was beginning to brighten. The gray and whitish rocks, the yellow-green moss, the dew-covered bushes of dogberry and dwarf elm stood out very clearly against the transparent-gold background of the morning light. But the opposite side of the ravine, still wrapped in thick mist that floated in smoky, uneven layers, was damp and gloomy and presented a wide range of shades—lilac, black, white, and dark green. Right in front of us, sharp against the dark azure of the horizon, the gleaming white snowy mountains rose with amazing clarity, their shadows uncanny and yet harmonious in every detail. Crickets, grasshoppers, and thousands of other insects woke up in the tall grass and filled the air with their varied and continual noises. It seemed as if thousands of little bells were ringing inside our very ears. The air smelled of water, grass, and fog—the smell of a beautiful summer morning. The captain lit his pipe, and I found the smell of his cheap tobacco mingling with that of the tinder extraordinarily pleasant.

In order to catch up quickly with the infantry, we left the road. The captain appeared absorbed in his thoughts and never once took his short pipe out of his mouth. At every step, he prodded his horse with his heels. Rolling from side to side, it left a hardly perceptible train in the tall, wet grass. Once, from under its very feet, a pheasant rose letting out a cry and making a noise with its wings that would have set the spine of a hunter tingling; then it began to rise. The captain paid no attention whatsoever.

We had almost caught up with the battalion when we heard behind us a galloping horse, and a young, good-looking officer in a tall, white sheepskin cap overtook us. As he passed, he smiled, made a friendly sign to the captain, and flourished his whip. I only had time to notice his graceful way of sitting on his horse and holding the reins, his dark handsome eyes, his fine nose, and thin, youthful black mustache. What I liked especially about him was that he could not resist smiling when he realized that we were admiring him. From his smile alone, one could tell he was still quite young.

"What's he in such a hurry about?" the captain muttered gruffly, without removing his pipe.

"Who is he?"

"Alanin, one of my second lieutenants. He's just a month out of military school."

"I suppose this will be his first time in action?"

"Yes, that's what he's so pleased about," the captain said, slowly shaking his head. "Ah, that's youth for you!"

"How can he help being pleased? I can imagine how interesting it must be for a young officer."

The captain said nothing for a couple of minutes.

"That's just what I meant—youth," he said in a deep voice. "How else can one be pleased about something one has never experienced? And after you've seen it often, you aren't so happy about it any more. Take today, for instance—about twenty officers will take part in this expedition, and the odds are that at least one of them will be killed or wounded. No doubt about it. Today, it may be my turn, tomorrow his, the next time somebody else's. What's there to be happy about?"

3

The bright sun rose above the mountains, lighting up the valley we were following. The wavy clouds of mist scattered and it grew hot. The soldiers, loaded down with equipment and rifles, trudged heavily along the dusty road. From time to time laughter and snatches of Ukrainian reached us. Some old-timers in white tunics—most of them noncommissioned officers—walked in a group by the roadside. They smoked their pipes and talked quietly. Heavily laden carts, each drawn by three horses, moved laboriously forward, raising a thick cloud of dust that stayed suspended over the road. The officers, on horseback, rode in front. Some of them were putting their horses through their paces: they made them jump, sprint, and come to a dead stop; others were directing the regimental chorus, which, despite the heat and stuffiness, sang one song after another.

A couple of hundred yards ahead of the infantry rode some Tartar[1]

---
[1] *Tartar:* a native of Tartary, a region of Asia and eastern Europe.

horsemen. With them, riding on a large white horse and dressed in Caucasian costume, was a tall, handsome officer. Throughout the regiment he had a reputation for reckless courage and for not hesitating to tell anyone what he thought of him. His soft, black Oriental boots were trimmed with gold braid as was his black tunic under which he wore a yellow silk Circassian[1] shirt. The tall sheepskin hat on his head was pushed back carelessly. A powder flask and a pistol were fastened to silver straps across his chest and back. Another pistol and a silver-mounted dagger hung from his belt next to a saber in a red leather sheath. A rifle in a black holster was slung over his shoulder. From his dress, his style of riding, all his movements, it was obvious that he wanted to look like a Tartar. He was even saying something to the Tartars in a language I couldn't understand. But then, judging by the bewildered, amused looks they exchanged with one another, I guessed they couldn't understand him either.

He was one of those dashing, wild young officers who attempt to model themselves on the heroes of Lermontov and Marlinsky. These officers saw the Caucasus only through such romantic prisms, and in everything they were guided solely by the instincts and tastes of their models.

This lieutenant could surely have enjoyed the company of fashionable women and important men—generals, colonels, aides-de-camp. In fact, I'm certain he was eager to associate with them, being extremely vain. But somehow he felt he had to show such people his rough side, to be rude to them, although quite mildly so. When some lady appeared at the fort, he felt bound to walk under her windows with his pals, wearing a red shirt and slippers and talking and swearing loudly. But this wasn't done so much to offend as to show her by his supreme casualness how easy it would be to fall madly in love with him were he to display the slightest interest.

He also liked to go into the hills at night accompanied by a couple of friendly Tartars, lie in ambush for hostile hillmen, and take pot shots at them. Although in his heart he felt there was nothing particularly heroic about it, he persuaded himself that he had to inflict pain on hostile Tartars, people who had somehow let him down and whom he pretended to loathe and despise.

There were two things that were always with him: a rather large icon around his neck and a dagger fastened to his shirt, which he retained even when sleeping. He had convinced himself that he had enemies, and

---

[1] *Circassian:* relating to the region on the northeast coast of the Black Sea, known as Circassia.

the idea that he had to avenge himself against someone, wash off some imaginary insult with blood, was very pleasant to him. He was sure that hatred, revenge, and scorn for men in general were refined, romantic feelings.

However, his Circassian mistress, whom I got to know later, told me that he was really a very kind and gentle man and that every evening, after he'd written saturnine thoughts in his diary, he would carefully draw up his accounts on ruled paper, and then get down on his knees and pray to God. And yet this man went to so much trouble to appear as one of his heroes, if only to himself. As to his brother officers and the soldiers, they never saw him in such a light anyway.

Once, on one of his nighttime sorties, he shot a hostile Tartar in the leg and brought him back a prisoner. He kept the Tartar in his house for seven weeks, nursing him and looking after him as though he were his dearest friend. Then, when the prisoner recovered, he gave him all sorts of presents and set him free. Later, during a raid, he was fighting a rear-guard action, firing back at attacking Tartars, when he heard his name called from the enemy ranks and saw his former prisoner ride forward, signaling to him to do the same. The lieutenant complied and they shook hands. The mountaineers remained at a distance and did not fire. But as soon as the lieutenant turned his back, several shots were fired from their side, and a bullet grazed the lower part of his back.

On another occasion when I was present myself, a fire broke out in the fort. Two companies of soldiers were detailed to put it out. Suddenly, lit by the red glow of the flames, there appeared among the crowd a tall man on a black horse. Pushing people out of his way, the rider rode right up to the flames, jumped off his horse, and entered the burning house. Five minutes later the lieutenant reappeared. His hair had been singed and his forearm was badly burnt when he emerged carrying two pigeons clutched to his breast.

His name was Rosenkranz. He often spoke of his ancestry, which he traced back to the Varangians—the Scandinavian princes who were invited to rule over the Slavs in the earliest era of Russian history. He wanted it clearly understood that he and his ancestors were pure Russians.

4

The sun was midway across the sky. Its hot rays, piercing the incandescent air, beat down upon the dry earth. Overhead, the dark blue sky was completely clear, although the base of the snowy mountains was already draped in white and lilac clouds. The air was motionless and seemed to be impregnated with a sort of transparent dust. The heat was becoming unbearable.

When we were about halfway to our destination, we halted by a stream. The soldiers stacked their rifles and rushed toward the gurgling water. The battalion commander picked a shady spot where he sat himself on a drum. His whole bearing showed that he was constantly aware of his rank and importance, as he waited to have something to eat with a number of the officers. Captain Khlopov lay on the grass under his company's cart. Lieutenant Rosenkranz and a few other young officers arranged themselves on their outspread cloaks. To judge from the bottles and flasks placed among them, they intended to have a good time. The regimental singers formed a semicircle around them and sang a song of the Caucasus army.

> Recently Shamil decided
> That against us he could rise
> But, of course, he was misguided
> And quite soon we'll make him wise. . . .

Also among these officers was Second Lieutenant Alanin, the youngster who'd overtaken us during the morning. He was very amusing; his eyes sparkled, his words became garbled. He wanted to hug everyone and say how much he liked them. Unfortunately, far from making others like him, his naive warmth provoked nothing but sarcasm. Nor did he realize how touching he looked when at last, hot and exhausted, he threw himself down on his cloak, pushed his thick, black hair out of his eyes, and rested on his bent arm.

Two officers sat in the shade of a wagon playing cards.

I listened with interest to the conversations among the men and among the officers; I kept observing their expressions. In none could I discover the slightest trace of the anxiety that I myself felt; their jokes, their laughter, the stories they told, all expressed a complete lack of concern for imminent danger. It never seemed to occur to any one of them that he might no longer be around when we passed this very spot on our return.

5

It was past six in the evening when, tired and covered with dust, we gained entrance to Fort N——. The declining sun cast its slanting reddish rays on the picturesque little cannon, on the poplar groves around the fort, on the yellow fields, and on the white clouds which, huddled together near the snowy mountains, formed another range just as snowy, fantastic, and beautiful. The new moon hung above the horizon like a small transparent cloud. In the Tartar village, the faithful were being summoned to prayer from the rooftop of a hut. Our singing soldiers, filled with renewed enthusiasm and energy, were giving their all.

After a brief rest, I cleaned up and went over to see an aide I knew. I wanted him to obtain the general's consent for my plans. Walking to the fort from the outlying village where I had my quarters, I had time to notice around Fort N—— things I never expected to find there. I was passed by a pretty two-seater carriage, within which flashed a fashionable lady's hat, while my ear caught snatches of French. Then, going by under the windows of the commandant's house, I heard the measures of a polka played on a piano that needed tuning. After, in a café, I saw some clerks sitting before glasses of wine and I heard one of them say:

"No, my dear chap, speaking of politics, I must insist that Maria Gregorievna is the first among our ladies. . . ."

Further on, a stooped, threadbare, sickly looking Jew dragged along a screeching, broken-down barrel organ, and the whole street resounded with the finale of *Lucia*. Two ladies in rustling dresses, silk kerchiefs on their heads and bright umbrellas in their hands, floated gracefully past me on the planked sidewalk, while two bareheaded women, one in blue, the other in pink, stood by the porch of a small house giggling loudly, obviously to attract the attention of the officers swaggering up and down the street in new tunics with flashing epaulets and white gloves.

I found my friend the aide on the lower floor of the house occupied by the general. I had just time to tell him what I wanted and to hear that he was sure it could be arranged when the pretty carriage I'd noticed earlier rattled past the window and stopped. A tall, straight-backed infantry major got out and entered the house.

"Excuse me," the aide said, "I must go and report to the general—"

"Who is it?" I asked.

"The countess," he said, buttoning his tunic and hurrying upstairs.

A few moments later, a short, very handsome man in a tunic without epaulets but with a white cross in his buttonhole appeared on the porch. He was followed by a major, the aide, and two other officers. From the way the general moved and from his voice, one could tell he did not value lightly his exalted position.

"Bon soir, madame la comtesse," he said, thrusting his hand through the carriage window.

A small hand in a kid glove pressed his, and a pretty, smiling face appeared under a yellow hat.

Of their entire conversation, I only heard the smiling general say as I passed:

"You know, Countess, that I have sworn to fight infidels. Do please be careful—I want no infidelity in you. ..."

Laughter came from the carriage.

"*Adieu donc, cher général.*"

"*Non, au revoir,*" the general said, walking up the steps, "and please don't forget that I've invited myself to your tea party tomorrow."

The carriage rattled away.

"There's a man," I thought on my way home, "who has everything anyone could want—rank, wealth, and fame. And now, on the eve of a battle in which no one knows how many lives may be lost, this man is off flirting and promising to take tea tomorrow."

I thought then of the remark I'd heard a Tartar make: only a poor man can be brave. "When you become rich," he said, "you become a coward." But then, the general had much more to lose than most people, and, even among the Tartars, I'd never seen such elegant indifference in the face of possible doom. This thoroughly confused my theories about courage.

Later, in the house of the same aide, I met a young man who surprised me even more. He was a young lieutenant from another regiment, a man of almost feminine docility and shyness. He had approached the aide to complain indignantly against some people who, he said, had conspired to leave him behind during the coming operation. He said it was disgusting to act that way, that it was poor camaraderie, that he'd always remember it, etc. I watched his face carefully and listened to his voice, and I was fully convinced that he was not putting on an act—he was honestly indignant and depressed because they wouldn't let him fire at Tartars and be exposed in turn to their fire. He felt like a child unjustly spanked. To me, none of it made any sense.

6

The troops were to move out at 10 P.M. At eight-thirty, I mounted and rode over to see the general. But then I decided that both the general and the aide must be busy, so I tied my horse to a fence and sat down on the doorstep where I would catch the general as he was leaving.

The cool of evening replaced the heat. The glaring sun had gone, and in its place the crescent moon formed a pale silvery semicircle in the dark starry sky. It was beginning to set. Lights appeared in the houses and earthen huts and shone through the cracks in the shutters. Beyond the moonlit, whitewashed huts, the tall, slender poplars looked even taller and darker.

The long shadows of the houses, trees, and fences lay in beautiful patterns on the white, dusty road. From the river came the strangely reverberating croaking of the frogs. In the streets, one heard hurried steps, voices, and hoofbeats. From the outlying village came the sounds of the barrel organ playing some aria from an opera and then a waltz.

I won't go into my thoughts, mostly because I'm ashamed of the gloom that pervaded me amid the joyful excitement of the others and also because they have nothing to do with this story. Still, I was so deeply immersed that I never noticed the town clock strike eleven and the general and his retinue pass by.

I hastily jumped on my horse and hurried to catch up with the detachment.

The rearguard was still inside the fort, and I had difficulty making my way across the bridge which was cluttered with gun carriages, ammunition wagons, the supply carts of various companies, and, in the midst of it all, officers shouting orders.

Finally, I managed to get past the gates. I had to ride in the darkness past the detachment, which stretched over almost a mile, before I caught up with the general.

As I was passing by the guns drawn out in single file with officers riding between, I was shocked at the discord wrought in the quiet harmony of the night by a harsh voice shouting with a German accent:

"Hey, you—give us a light!"

This was followed by the eager voice of a soldier:

"Shevchenko, the lieutenant wishes a light."

The sky gradually became overcast with long, gray clouds which left but a few scattered gaps for the stars. The moon had disappeared behind the black mountains on the nearby horizon to our right; but the peaks were bathed in its pale, quivering light while the foothills were plunged in deep black shadows. The air was warm and so strangely still that not the smallest cloud, no blade of grass, stirred. It was so dark that one could not recognize objects even close at hand. On the sides of the road, I kept seeing crags, animals, strange people, and I realized they were bushes only by their faint rustle and the freshness rising from the dew with which they were spinkled. In front of me I saw an uninterrupted wall sinking and rising, followed by a few moving shapes—the mounted vanguard and the general with his retinue. Behind me another dark but shorter mass was swaying—the infantry.

The troops were so silent that one could hear clearly all the mysterious sounds of the night: the sad wail of a faraway jackal, now desperate sobs, now mad guffaws; the ringing, monotonous sounds of crickets, frogs, and quail; a curious approaching rumbling for which I could not account; and all the nocturnal, hardly audible sounds of nature which can be neither understood nor explained. All blended into that harmony one refers to as the stillness of night. The dull thudding of hoofs and the rustling of the tall grass given forth by the slowly moving force dissipated into this harmony.

Only now and then could the rumbling of a heavy gun carriage, the clang of bayonets, a few brief words, the snorting of a horse be distinguished.

Nature breathed out peace and strength.

Was it possible that there was no place for men in this beautiful world under this immense starry sky—that hatred, vengeance, and the passion for destruction could lurk in the hearts of men amid such natural beauty? Surely all these evil instincts should vanish in contact with nature—the most direct expression of beauty and goodness.

7

We had been riding for more than two hours. I was drowsy and shivering. In the darkness I kept seeing the same vague objects: a way off a black wall and moving shapes; near me the crupper of a white horse, its swishing tail and widespread hind legs, and a back in a white Circassian coat, crossed by the black line of a swaying rifle and the white handle of a pistol in an embroidered holster. The glow of a cigarette threw light on a blond mustache, a beaver collar, and a hand in a kid glove.

I'd let my head droop toward the horse's neck, close my eyes, and forget myself for a few moments. Then, I'd be jolted awake by the familiar tramping and rustling; I'd look around and feel that I was standing still while the black wall was moving toward me or that the wall remained fixed and I was about to smash into it. On one of these occasions I was struck by the increase in the rumbling which I'd been unable to account for. And now it dawned on me that it was the sound of water. We were entering a deep gorge and approaching a mountain stream in flood. The rumbling became louder, the damp grass grew thicker, there were more and more bushes, and the horizon narrowed. Now and then bright lights flared up at various points, then vanished immediately.

"Do you know what those lights are?" I whispered to one of our Tartars who was riding next to me.

"You really don't know?"

"I do not."

"The enemy. They tie straw to poles, fire them, and wave them about," he said.

"Why do they do that?"

"To tell everyone Russians are coming. There's a little running around going on in that village over there," the Tartar said and laughed. "Everybody's grabbing his belongings and going down into the ravine...."

"How do they know, off in the mountains, when a detachment's on the way?"

"How can they not know? They always know. That's the kind of people we Tartars are."

"Then their leader Shamil must be getting ready to fight?" I asked.

"No," he said, shaking his head. "Shamil won't take part in the fighting himself. He'll send his aides to lead the fight while he watches the battle through a spyglass."

"Where's his home, do you know? Far away?"

"No, not far. About eight miles over there to the left."

"How do you know? Have you ever been there?"

"I've been there. All of us have been in the mountains."

"Have you ever seen Shamil?"

"No, one doesn't see Shamil that easily! There are a hundred, three hundred, maybe a thousand guards circling around him and he's always in the center," the Tartar said with obvious admiration.

Above, the sky, now clear, was growing lighter in the east. The Pleiades were sinking below the horizon. But the ravine through which we moved remained damp and dark.

Suddenly, a little way ahead of us, there were several flashes, and a moment later bullets whistled past. The silence was pierced by shots fired close by and shrill cries. The advance patrol of enemy Tartars whooped, fired at random, and scattered.

All become quiet again. The general summoned his interpreter. The white-clad Tartar rode up to him and for a long time whispered and gesticulated. Then the general issued an order.

"Colonel Khasanov, have the men deployed in open order," he said in a quiet but clear drawl.

The detachment reached the river. By daybreak the black mountains and the gorges had been left behind. The sky, strewn with pale stars, looked higher. The east was a glowing red; a cool, penetrating breeze came from the west; and a white mist floated like smoke above the river.

8

A native guide led us to a ford. The cavalry vanguard started across. The general and his retinue followed. The horses were up to their chests in water, which gushed violently between protruding, whitish rocks, foaming and rushing around the animals' legs. The horses, bewildered by the noise of the water, kept lifting their heads and pricking up their ears, but they made their way smoothly and carefully over the uneven riverbed. The riders pulled up their feet and their weapons. The foot soldiers stripped down to their shirts and tied their clothes in bundles to the end of their rifles. Then, carrying their rifles above their heads, each holding onto the man in front, they entered the river in groups of twenty. The physical effort required to withstand the current could be seen on their faces. The artillerymen, shouting loudly, drove their horses into the river at a trot. Water splashed over the guns and the green ammunition cases. Wheels rang against the stony bottom. The heavy horses pulled determinedly, and, with water foaming around their wet tails and manes, finally clambered up onto the opposite bank.

The crossing completed, the general's expression became thoughtful and serious. He turned his horse, and followed by the cavalry, he rode off at a trot through a glade that opened out before us. Cossack patrols were dispatched around the outskirts of the forest.

Suddenly, among the trees, we saw a man on foot wearing a Circassian shirt and a tall sheepskin cap. Another followed, then another. . . . I heard one of the officers say:

"Tartars. . . ."

A puff of smoke appeared from behind a tree. . . . Then the sound of a shot, followed by another. The noise of our fire drowned out that of the enemy. But now and then, a bullet would zoom by like a bee, as if to prove that we were not doing all the shooting. The infantry raced to take their positions. The gun carriages moved at a trot to their chosen emplacements. Then came the booming report of the guns, followed by the metallic sound of flying grapeshot, the hissing of rockets, and the crackle of rifle fire. Cavalry, infantry, and artillery scattered all over the vast clearing. The puffs of smoke from the cannon, rifles, and rockets fused with the dewy greenness and the mist. Colonel Khasanov arrived at full gallop and stopped his horse abruptly in front of the general. He saluted and said:

"Shall I order the cavalry charge, sir? They're carrying their banners. ..." He pointed with his riding whip at a mounted detachment of enemy Tartars led by two men on white horses. The men had long poles in their hands, with bits of red and blue material tied to them; these the hillmen use as banners, though any chieftain can make himself such an emblem and carry it around.

"All right," the general answered. "Good luck."

The colonel whirled his horse about, drew his saber, and shouted: "Hurrah!"

"Hurrah! Hurrah! Hurrah!" came from the ranks as the cavalry followed.

Everyone watched tensely. There was one banner, then another, another, and yet another. . . .

Without waiting for the attack, the enemy fled, disappearing into the forests and then opening fire. Bullets continued to whistle through the air.

"A beautiful sight," the general remarked, bouncing gracefully up and down in the saddle, on his thin-legged black horse.

Striking his horse, a major rode up to the general and said with an affected lisp: "It is indeed beautiful, sir. War in such beautiful surroundings is a delight."

"*Et surtout en bonne compagnie,*"[1] the general said with an amiable smile.

The major bowed.

At that moment, the sharp, unpleasant hissing of an enemy cannon ball sounded above our heads. It hit somewhere behind us, and there was a cry. A soldier had been wounded.

This cry affected me in a strange way. The battle scene immediately lost what beauty it may have had for me. But no one else seemed particularly concerned: the major, whose conversation was punctuated with laughter, seemed to laugh even louder; another officer in the middle of explaining something repeated the last few words, fearing his audience might have missed them. The general didn't even glance in the direction from which the cry had come; looking elsewhere, he said something in French.

The officer in charge of the artillery rode up, saluted, and asked: "Shall we give'em a taste of their own medicine, sir?"

---

[1] "*Et . . . compagnie*": "And especially in good company."

"All right, give'em a scare," the general said nonchalantly, lighting a cigar.

The battery took up its position and the barrage began. The earth groaned, there were constant flashes of light, and the smoke, which almost completely hid the gun crews, stung our eyes.

The village was being bombarded. Then Colonel Khasanov reported to the general again and was ordered to lead the cavalry to the village. With warlike hurrahs, the cavalry disappeared in its own cloud of dust.

The show may have been really impressive to an initiate. But to me, an outsider, the whole thing was spoiled by the fact that all this commotion, enthusiasm, and shouting seemed rather pointless. It made me think of a man violently swinging an ax and hitting nothing but air.

9

When the general and his retinue, to which I had attached myself, reached the village, it had already been occupied by our troops, and all its inhabitants had disappeared.

The neat, oblong huts, with their flat, earthen roofs and picturesque chimneys, were scattered over irregular rocky ground. Between hills flowed a small river. On one side of the village were green orchards of large pear and plum trees while, on the other, strange shadows thrown by the perpendicular gravestones of a cemetery and the long poles surmounted by multicolored balls and pennants marked the graves of warriors.

The troops were assembled by the village gate.

"Well," the general said, "what do you say, Colonel, shall we let them do a bit of looting? These fellows here look as though they wouldn't mind at all," he added with a smile, pointing at the Cossacks.

I was struck by the contrast between the flippant tone of the general's words and their grim implication.

A minute later, a stream of Cossacks, dragoons, and foot soldiers was pouring with obvious delight along the winding lanes of the empty village, bringing it to life. Then, a roof collapsed somewhere; an ax resounded against a heavy wooden door; a stack of hay, a fence, a whole hut — went up in flames; a Cossack came running, dragging a bag of flour and a carpet; a soldier, beaming with pleasure, emerged from a hut with a tin basin and some bright piece of material; another, with outstretched arms, tried to corner a couple of chickens which, cackling madly, rushed up and down along a fence in a panic; another soldier found an enormous jug of milk, drank some of it, and, laughing loudly, threw it on the ground.

The battalion with which I had come from Fort N—— had also entered the Tartar village. Captain Khlpov had installed himself comfortably on top of a flat roof and was puffing thin whiffs of cheap tobacco smoke from his short pipe with such detached equanimity that the very sight of him made me forget that I was in a conquered village and made me feel completely at home.

"Ah, there you are," he said, seeing me.

Rosenkranz's tall figure kept appearing and disappearing in various parts of the village. He kept issuing orders and looked very busy and preoccupied. At one point I noticed his triumphant air as he emerged from a hut followed by two soldiers leading a tied-up Tartar. The Tartar was very old and wore only a tattered shirt and a pair of patched, threadbare trousers. He was so frail that his arms, tightly bound behind his hunched, bony back, seemed barely attached to his shoulders. He could hardly lift his deformed, bare feet. His face and even a part of his shaven head were covered with deep furrows and his twisted, toothless mouth, set between a cropped mustache and beard, kept opening and closing as though he were trying to chew something. But in his red, lashless eyes, there was a stubborn spark indicating an old man's indifference to life.

Through the interpreter, Rosenkranz inquired why he hadn't left with the rest.

"Where could I go?" the old man asked, calmly looking away.

"Where the others have gone."

"The warriors went to fight the Russians, and I'm an old man."

"Aren't you afraid of the Russians?"

"What can they do to me? I'm an old man," he said tonelessly, looking at the circle of men that had formed around him.

Later, I saw this same old man jolting along tied behind a Cossack's saddle. And he continued to look around with the same detached expression. They needed him to exchange for Russian prisoners.

I climbed onto the roof of the hut where the captain was and sat down next to him.

"There don't seem to be many of the enemy around," I said, in the hope of finding out what he thought about the battle that had taken place.

"Enemy? There aren't any," he said, surprised at my question. "You haven't seen the enemy yet. Wait until evening; there'll be plenty of 'em to see us off over there." He pointed with his pipe toward the woods we had crossed in the morning.

"What's going on?" I interrupted the captain, pointing to a group of Don Cossacks clustered together.

From the center of the group I heard something that sounded like the cry of a child and the words: "Stop it, don't flash your saber that way, they may see you over there. . . . Hey, Evstigneich—got a knife?"

"They're up to something, those swine," the captain said calmly.

At that moment, young Second Lieutenant Alanin, his face flushed and horrified, rushed toward the Cossacks from around a corner.

"Leave him alone! Don't hurt him!" he shouted in a boyish voice.

Seeing the officer, the Cossacks stepped aside, and one of them let loose a little white goat. The second lieutenant stepped in front of the men overcome with embarrassment. Then, seeing the captain and me on the roof, he turned even redder and ran toward us.

"I thought they were killing a child," he said with an awkward smile.

10

The general and the cavalry left the village first. Our battalion formed the rearguard. Khlopov's and Rosenkranz's companies were to move out together.

Captain Khlopov's prediction proved correct. No sooner had we reached the narrow woods than enemy Tartars, both on horseback and on foot, started popping up all around us, so close that at times I could clearly see some of them darting from one tree to another, their backs bent very low, their rifles clutched in both hands.

The captain removed his cap and crossed himself. Some old soldiers did the same. From among the trees came the high-pitched shouts of the enemy baiting our men. There was a succession of dry, crackling rifle shots; bullets whizzed by from both directions. Our men fired back in silence, except for a few muttered remarks that the enemy had it easy among the trees and what the devil was the artillery waiting for.

And soon the artillery did join in. The cannon spat grapeshot into the forest. This seemed to weaken the enemy. But no sooner had our troops gone a few more yards than the enemy fire again increased, along with the war cries and the baiting.

Before we were even half a mile from the village, enemy cannon balls started screaming over our heads. I saw one of them kill a soldier. . . . But why dwell on that horrible scene which I myself would give anything to forget? Lieutenant Rosenkranz, firing his own rifle, kept galloping from one end of the line to the other, shouting instructions to his men in a hoarse voice. He was somewhat pale, and this pallor seemed to suit his well-formed, manly face.

Second Lieutenant Alanin was in ecstasy: his handsome dark eyes shone with daring, his mouth was slightly twisted into a smile. Several times he rode up to the captain to ask permission to charge.

"We'll stop 'em," he pleaded. "I'm sure, sir, we'll throw 'em back."

"No need for it," the captain answered tersely. "All we're to do is cover our withdrawal."

Khlopov's company was holding a sector at the edge of the forest. The men were lying on the ground, firing at the enemy. The captain, in his threadbare tunic and shabby sheepskin cap, sat on his dirty-white horse, the reins loose in his hands, his knees sharply bent in the short stirrups. He sat there immobile, saying nothing; his soldiers knew their business and there was no need to order them around. Only now and then did he shout sharp reminders to some to keep their heads low.

There was nothing very martial about Captain Khlopov's appearance, but its directness and simplicity struck me. "Here's one who's really brave," I felt instinctively.

He was the same as ever; the same quiet movements, the same even voice, the same lack of affectation on his plain, straightforward face. Possibly, though, his eyes were somewhat more intent as a result of his total concentration; he looked like a man quietly and efficiently going about his business.

Yes, he was just as he always was—whereas in the others I could detect at least some difference from their everyday behavior: some wanted to appear calmer, others more determined, still others more cheerful than they'd have been under ordinary circumstances. But from the captain's face it was obvious that it had never even occurred to him that he might need to disguise his feelings.

The Frenchman during the battle of Waterloo who said, *"La garde meurt mais ne se rend pas,"*[1] and other heroes, often French, who coined such historic phrases were really brave and may have actually made their memorable statements. The main difference, however, between their courage and the captain's is that even if resounding words stirred inside his heart, he'd never have uttered them, because for him they'd have spoiled a great deed. And the captain must have felt that when a man senses within himself the strength to perform a great deed, words become superfluous. This, I believe, is a peculiarity of Russian bravery. And how can a Russian not be offended when he hears Russian

---

[1] *La ... pas":* "The guardsman dies but does not surrender."

officers spouting French clichés in imitation of obsolete concepts of French chivalry?

Suddenly from the platoon under Second Lieutenant Alanin there came a rather uncoordinated and subdued "hurrah." I looked that way and saw a score or so of soldiers, their rifles in their hands and their equipment on their backs, running with difficulty across the plowed field. They stumbled again and again but kept going, shouting as they ran. The young second lieutenant rode at their head, holding his unsheathed saber high in the air.

Then they all vanished into the forest. . . .

After a few minutes of whooping and crackling, a frightened horse emerged from the trees. Then I saw some soldiers carrying the dead and wounded. Among the latter was their young officer, Second Lieutenant Alanin. Two soldiers held him under the arms. His pretty-boy face was ashen, and bore only a faint trace of the enthusiasm that had animated it a minute earlier. His head was unnaturally pulled in between his shoulders and hung down on his chest. Under his unbuttoned tunic, a small bloody stain showed on his white shirt.

"Ah! What a shame!" I said, involuntarily turning away from the sight.

"Sure, it's a pity," an old soldier next to me, leaning on his rifle, said gloomily. "That kid wasn't afraid of anything. And it doesn't make sense, does it?" He looked intently at the wounded youngster. "Still, he was stupid, and now he's paid for it."

"And what about you, are you afraid?" I asked him.

"What do you think?" he asked.

11

Four soldiers were carrying the second lieutenant on a stretcher. Behind them, a medical orderly led a thin, old horse loaded with two green cases obtaining medical supplies. They waited for the doctor. Officers kept riding up to the stretcher, trying to comfort the wounded youngster.

"Well, Alanin, old man, it'll be a while now before you can dance again," Rosenkranz said to him with a smile.

He must have assumed that these words would cheer up Alanin. But Alanin's cold, sad look showed that they'd not produced the desired effect.

Captain Khlopov rode up. He looked closely at the wounded man, and his usually cold, indifferent face expressed honest sorrow.

"Well, dear boy," he said, with a warmth I hadn't expected of him, "looks like it was God's will that it should happen this way."

The wounded man turned toward him. A sad smile brought his pale features to life.

"Yes. I disobeyed you, sir."

"You'd better say it was God's will," the captain said again.

The doctor arrived. He took bandages, a probe, and some other instrument from the medical orderly, rolled up his sleeves, and, smiling cheerfully, approached the wounded man.

"Looks like they drilled a neat little hole in you," he said in a light, casual tone. "Let me have a look at it."

The young man complied. He looked at the doctor with a reproachful surprise that passed unnoticed. The doctor started to examine the wound, pressing so hard all around it that the young man, at the limit of his endurance, pushed his hand away with a moan:

"Leave me alone," he said in a hardly audible voice. "I'll die anyway."

Then he fell back. Five minutes later, when I passed by him again, I asked a soldier:

"How's the second lieutenant?"

"He's dying," the man said.

12

It was late when the detachment approached the fort in a wide column. The soldiers were singing.

The general rode in front and, to judge by his satisfied expression, the raid must have been a success. And indeed it had been; for the first time the Russians had succeeded in setting foot in the village of Mukay — and had achieved this at the cost of very few lives.

Rosenkranz silently thought back over the day's action. Captain Khlopov, deep in thought, walked with his company, leading his little whitish horse by its bridle.

The sun sank behind the snowy chain of mountains, casting its last reddish beams on a long thin cloud that hung motionless in the clear, translucent air above the horizon. The snowy mountains began to vanish in the violet mist, and only their upper reaches stood out with uncanny clarity in the crimson glow. The moon had already risen and was beginning to whiten and detach itself from the darkening azure of the sky. The green of the leaves and grass turned slowly to black and became wet with dew. The dark masses of moving soldiers produced rhythmical waves among the rich green meadows. Drums, tambourines and songs resounded over everything. The chorus leader of the Sixth Company sounded forth in full voice, and the notes of his pure, vibrating tenor, filled with feeling and power, floated through the clear evening air.

FOR WRITING OR DISCUSSION

1. The theme of this story is posed in a series of questions that the narrator asks at the beginning of his war experience. What are these questions? What are the answers he makes to each question by the end of the raid?

2. Who are the main characters in the story? What attributes of "ideal" and "real" soldiers does each represent?

3. To which of the characters in the story does each of these definitions of bravery apply?

　　a. "the knowledge of what should and what should not be feared"
　　b. "self-preservation and a sense of duty"
　　c. "a purely physical capacity"
　　d. "sheer vanity"
　　e. "doing what one has to do"

Locate other definitions of bravery scattered through the story. How is each definition or statement related to a characterization?

4. Contrast the narrator's mood with that of the soldiers who were actually facing death? What is ironic about the contrast?

5. In the absence of much plot in this story, Tolstoy poses a series of questions that gradually become answers, questions about the nature of courage. But he also unifies his story by giving descriptions of nature at different places and times of the day. What are the successive descriptions of setting? How is color used to reflect mood? Compare Tolstoy's method of description to Turgenev's in "Bezhin Lea."

6. What attitudes toward war are explored? Which attitudes do you think are Tolstoy's own?

7. How are the reactions to war expressed in "The Raid" heightened or expanded by these excerpts from "Sevastopol in May," Tolstoy's account of the siege of Sevastopol, which he witnessed during a return to the Crimea shortly after his Caucasian journey?[1]

　　a. "But Kalugin was ambitious and blessed with nerves of oak—in a word, he was what is called brave."
　　b. "Kalugin did not realize that whereas he had spent some fifty hours

---

[1]The following excerpts are from "Sevastopol in May" from *Leo Tolstoy's Short Stories*, Vol. 1, edited by Ernest Simmons. Translation by Louise and Aylmer Maude; reprinted by permission of Oxford University Press.

all in all at different times on the bastions, the captain had lived there for six months. Kalugin was still actuated by vanity, the wish to shine, the hope of rewards, of gaining a reputation, and the charm of running risks. But the captain had already lived through all that. . . . He fulfilled his duty exactly, but quite understanding how much the chances of life were against him after six months at the bastions, he no longer ran risks without serious need."

c. "When Mikhaylov dropped to the ground on seeing the bomb, he too, like Praskukhin, lived through an infinitude of thoughts and feelings in the two seconds that elapsed before the bomb burst. He prayed mentally and repeated, 'Thy will be done.' And at the same time he thought, 'Why did I enter the army? And why did I join the infantry to take part in this campaign?'"

d. "The main theme of their conversation, as usual in such cases, was not the affair itself, but the part each of the speakers had taken in it. Their faces and the tone of their voices were serious, almost sorrowful, as if the losses of the night had touched and saddened them all. But to tell the truth, as none of them had lost anyone very dear to him, this sorrowful expression was only an official one they considered it their duty to exhibit."

8. At the end of his account of war in "Sevastopol in May," Tolstoy describes the valley where the corpses lie. As you read this account, contrast its tone with the tone of "The Raid." Which is more serious? more ironic? Explain.

> But enough.
> Let us rather look at this ten-year-old boy in cap (probably his father's), with shoes on his stockingless feet and nankeen trousers held up by one brace. At the very beginning of the truce he came over the entrenchments, and has been walking about the valley ever since, looking with dull curiosity at the French and at the corpses that lie on the ground and gathering the blue flowers with which the valley is strewn. Returning home with a large bunch of flowers he holds his nose to escape the smell that is borne towards him by the wind, and stopping near a heap of corpses gazes for a long time at a terrible headless body that lies nearest to him. After standing there some time he draws nearer and touches with his foot the stiff outstretched arm of the corpse. The arm trembles a little. He touches it again more boldly; it moves and falls back to its old position. The boy gives a sudden scream, hides his face in his flowers, and runs towards the fortifications as fast as his legs can carry him.

Yes, there are white flags on the bastions and the trenches but the flowery valley is covered with dead bodies. The glorious sun is sinking toward the blue sea, and the undulating blue sea glitters in the golden light. Thousands of people crowd together, look at, speak to, and smile at one another. And these people—Christians professing the one great law of love and self-sacrifice—on seeing what they have done do not at once fall repentant on their knees before him who has given them life and laid in the soul of each a fear of death and a love of the good and the beautiful, and do not embrace like brothers with tears of joy and gladness.

The white flags are lowered, the engines of death and suffering are sounding again, innocent blood is flowing and the air is filled with moans and curses.

There, I have said what I wished to say this time. But I am seized by an oppressive doubt. Perhaps I ought to have left it unsaid. What I have said perhaps belongs to that class of evil truths that lie unconsciously hidden in the soul of each man and should not be uttered lest they become harmful, as the dregs in a bottle must not be disturbed for fear of spoiling the wine....

Where in this tale is the evil that should be avoided, and where the good that should be imitated? Who is the villain and who the hero of the story? All are good and all are bad.

Not Kalugin, with his brilliant courage—*bravoure de gentilhomme*—and the vanity that influences all his actions, not Praskukhin, the empty harmless fellow (though he fell in battle for faith, throne, and fatherland), not Mikhaylov with his shyness, nor Pesth, a child without firm principles or convictions, can be either the villain or the hero of the tale.

The hero of my tale—whom I love with all the power of my soul, whom I have tried to portray in all his beauty, who has been, is, and will be beautiful—is Truth.[1] [*Leo Tolstoy*]

9. The very end of the Sevastopol sketch has become famous as a summary of Tolstoy's entire artistic purpose: "Who is the villain and who the hero of the story? All are good and all are bad.... The hero of my tale—whom I love with all the power of my soul, whom I have tried to portray in all his beauty, who has been, is, and will be beautiful—is Truth." What are the "truths" about human courage and war that Tolstoy has expressed in "The Raid" and in the excerpts from "Sevastopol in May"? What is "realistic" about his method of dramatizing these truths?

[1]*Ibid.*

10. In an edition of Tolstoy's stories selected and edited by the American scholar Ernest Simmons, passages deleted by the Russian censors of 1853 are inserted and marked off from the censored text by brackets. Here is one such passage from the first chapter of "The Raid." The passage was originally inserted near the end of the chapter where the narrator asks the captain why he has not requested a transfer in order to be nearer his mother. Why do you think the censor objected to the passage in brackets?

"I have to serve in the army anyhow, and here I get double pay — quite a difference to a poor man."

["You should transfer to Russia. You would then be nearer to her."

"To Russia? To Russia?" repeated the captain, dubiously swaying his head and smiling mournfully. "Here I am still of some use, but there I should be the least of the officers. And besides, the double pay we get here also means something to a poor man."

"Can it be, Pavel Ivanovich, that living as you do the ordinary pay would not suffice?"

"And does the double pay suffice?" interjected the captain. "Look at our officers! Have any of them a brass farthing? They all go on tick at the sutler's, and are all up to their ears in debt. You say 'living as I do'. . . . Do you really think that living as I do I have anything over out of my salary? Not a farthing! You don't yet know what prices are like here; everything is three times dearer. . . ."][1]

WAR: *After the Ball*

Tolstoy was only twenty-four years old when he wrote "The Raid." At that time his attitude toward war, his interest in the difference between an imagined or romanticized ideal and actuality was apparent. "After the Ball," which follows, was written in 1903, when Tolstoy was seventy-five. Though it is not a report of a military action, it is a comment on the morality of the military — indeed, on the morality of the governing class. Like the earlier tale, "After the Ball" has an autobiographical source.

[1] *Ibid.*

After the Ball

"So you contend a man cannot judge independently of what is good and what is bad, that it is all a matter of environment. But I contend it is all a matter of chance. And here is what I can say about myself. . . ."

This is what our respected friend Ivan Vasilyevich said at the conclusion of a discussion we had been having about the necessity of changing the environment, the conditions in which men live, before there could be any talk about the improvement of the individual. As a matter of fact, no one had said it was impossible to judge independently of the good and the bad, but Ivan Vasilyevich had a habit of answering thoughts of his own stimulated by a discussion, and recounting experiences from his own life suggested by these thoughts. Often he became so absorbed in the story that he forgot his reason for telling it, especially since he always spoke with great fervor and sincerity. That is precisely what happened in the present case.

"At least I can make this claim with regard to myself. My own life has been molded in that way and no other—not by environment, but by something quite different."

"By what?" we asked.

"That is a long story. If you are to understand, I must tell it all to you."

"Then do."

Ivan Vasilyevich considered a moment and shook his head.

"Yes," he said, "my whole life was changed by a single night, or rather, a morning."

"Why? What happened?"

"It happened that I was deeply in love. I had often been in love before, but never so deeply. It took place a long time ago—her daughters are married women by this time. Her name was B., Varenka B. She was still strikingly beautiful at fifty, but in her youth, when she was eighteen, she was a dream: tall, slender, graceful, and majestic—yes, majestic. She always held herself as erect as if she were unable to bend, with her head tipped slightly backward; this, combined with her beauty and height, even though she was so thin as to be almost bony, gave her a queenly air that would have been intimidating if it had not been for her gay, winning smile, her mouth, her glorious shining eyes, and her whole captivating, youthful being."

"Ivan Vasilyevich certainly does lay it on thick!"

"However thick I were to lay it on, I could not make you understand

---

"After the Ball" from *Six Short Story Masterpieces by Tolstoy*, translated by Margaret Wettlin. Reprinted by permission of the publisher, Dell Publishing Co., Inc.

what she was really like. But that is beside the point. The events I shall recount took place in the forties.

"I was then a student at a provincial university. I don't know whether it was a good or a bad thing, but in those days there were none of your study circles, none of your theorizing, at our university; we were just young and lived in the way of young folk—studying and having a good time. I was a very gay and energetic youth, and rich in the bargain. I owned a spirited carriage horse and used to take the girls out for drives (skating had not yet become the fad); I went on drinking parties with my fellow students (in those days we drank nothing but champagne; if we were out of money, we drank nothing, for we never drank vodka as they do now); but most of all I enjoyed parties and balls. I was a good dancer and not exactly ugly."

"Come, don't be modest," put in one of the listeners. "We've all seen your daguerreotype. You were a very handsome youth."

"Perhaps I was, but that isn't what I wanted to tell you. When my love was at its height I attended a ball given on the last day of Shrovetide[1] by the Marshal of Nobility, a good-natured old man, wealthy, and fond of entertaining. His wife, as amiable as he was, stood beside him to receive us. She was wearing a velvet gown and a diamond tiara in her hair, and her aging neck and shoulders, plump and white, were exposed, as in the portraits of Empress Yelizaveta Petrovna. The ball was magnificent. The ballroom was charming, there were famous serf singers and musicians belonging to a certain landowner who was a lover of music, the food was abundant, the champagne flowed in rivers. Much as I loved champagne, I did not drink—I was drunk with love. But I danced till I dropped. I danced quadrilles, and waltzes, and polonaises, and it goes without saying that I danced as many of them as I could with Varenka. She was wearing a white dress with a pink sash, white kid gloves that did not quite reach her thin, pointed elbows, and white satin slippers. A wretched engineer named Anisimov cheated me out of a mazurka with her. I have never forgiven him for that. He invited her the moment she entered the ballroom, while I had been delayed by calling at the hairdresser's for my gloves. And so instead of dancing the mazurka with her, I danced it with a German girl I had once had a crush on. But I am afraid I was very neglectful of her that evening; I did not talk to her or look at her, for I had eyes for no one but a tall, slender girl in a white dress with a pink sash, with radiant, flushed, dimpled cheeks and soft, gentle eyes. I was not the only one; everyone looked at her and

---

[1] *Shrovetide:* the three days immediately preceding Ash Wednesday.

admired her, even the women, though she outshone them all. It was impossible not to admire her.

"Formally I was not her partner for the mazurka, but as a matter of fact I did dance it with her—at least most of it. Without the least embarrassment she danced straight to me down the length of the whole room, and when I leapt up to meet her without waiting for the invitation, she smiled to thank me for guessing what she wanted. When we had been led up to her and she had not guessed my nature, she had given a little shrug of her thin shoulders as she held out her hand to another, turning upon me a little smile of regret and consolation.

"When the figures of the mazurka changed into a waltz, I waltzed with her for a long time, and she smiled breathlessly and murmured *'encore.'*[1] And I waltzed on and on with her, quite unaware of my own body, as if it were made of air."

"Unaware of it? I'm sure you must have been very much aware of it as you put your arm about her waist—aware of not only *your* body, but of hers as well," said one of the guests.

Ivan Vasilyevich suddenly turned crimson and almost shouted:

"That may apply to you, modern youth—all you think of is the body. In our day things were different. The more deeply I loved a girl, the more incorporeal she seemed to me. Today you are aware of legs, ankles, and other things; you disrobe the ladies with whom you are in love, but for me, as Alphonse Karr has said—and a very good writer he was—the object of my love was always clad in bronze raiment. Far from exposing, we tried to hide nakedness, as did the good son of Noah. But you cannot understand this."

"Pay no attention to him. Go on with your story," said another of the listeners.

"Well, I danced mostly with her and did not notice the passage of time. The musicians were so exhausted—you know how it always is at the end of a ball—that they kept playing the mazurka; mamas and papas were rising from the card tables in the drawing room in anticipation of supper; footmen were rushing about. It was going on three o'clock. We had to take advantage of the few minutes left us. I invited her once more, and for the hundredth time we passed down the length of the room.

" 'Will I be your partner for the quadrille after supper?' I asked her as I took her back to her place.

" 'Oh, yes, if they do not take me home,' she said with a smile.

---

[1] *encore:* again.

"'I won't let them,' I said.

"'Give me my fan,' she said.

"'I am sorry to give it back to you,' I said as I handed her her little white fan.

"'Here, then, to keep you from being sorry,' she said, plucking a feather out of the fan and giving it to me.

"I took the feather, unable to express my rapture and gratitude except with a glance. I was not only gay and content — I was happy, I was blissful, I was benevolent, I was no longer myself, but some creature not of this earth, who knew no evil and could do nothing but good.

"I tucked the feather in my glove and stood riveted to the spot, unable to move away from her.

"'Look, they are asking Papa to dance,' she said, indicating a tall, stately man who was her father, a colonel, in silver epaulets, standing in the doorway with the hostess and some other women.

"'Varenka, come here,' called the hostess in the diamond tiara.

"Varenka made for the door and I followed her.

"'Do talk your father into dancing with you, *ma chère*.[1] Please do, Pyotr Vladislavich,' said the hostess to the colonel.

"Varenka's father was a tall, handsome, stately, and well-preserved old man. He had a ruddy face with a white mustache curled *à la* Nicholas I, white side whiskers that met his mustache, hair combed forward over his temples, and the same smile as his daughter's lighting up his eyes and lips. He was very well built, with a broad chest swelling out in military style and with a modest display of decorations on it, with strong shoulders and long, fine legs. He was an officer of the old type with a military bearing of the Nicholas school.

"As we came up to the door the colonel was protesting that he had forgotten how to dance, but nevertheless he smiled, reached for his sword, drew it out of its scabbard, handed it to a young man eager to offer his services, and, drawing a suede glove on to his right hand ('Everything according to rule,' he said with a smile), he took his daughter's hand and struck a pose in a quarter turn, waiting for the proper measure to begin.

"As soon as the mazurka phrase was introduced he stamped one foot energetically and swung out with the other, and then his tall heavy figure sailed round the ballroom. He kept striking one foot against the other, now slowly and gracefully, now quickly and energetically. The willowy form of Varenka floated beside him. Imperceptibly and always

---

[1] *ma chère:* my dear.

just in time, she kept lengthening or shortening the step of the little white satin feet to fit his.

"All the guests stood watching the couple's every movement. The feeling I experienced was less admiration than a sort of deep ecstasy. I was especially touched by the sight of the colonel's boots. They were good calfskin boots, but they were heelless and had blunt toes instead of fashionable pointed ones. Obviously they had been made by the battalion cobbler. 'He wears ordinary boots instead of fashionable ones so that he can dress his beloved daughter and take her into society,' I thought to myself, and that is why I was particularly touched by his blunt-toed boots. Anyone could see he had once danced beautifully, but now he was heavy and his legs were not flexible enough to make all the quick and pretty turns he attempted. But he went twice round the room very well, and everybody applauded when he quickly spread out his feet, then snapped them together again and fell, albeit rather heavily, on one knee. And she smiled as she freed her caught skirt and floated gracefully round him. When he had struggled back to his feet, he touchingly put his hands over his daughter's ears and kissed her on the forehead, then led her over to me, who he thought had been her dancing partner. I told him I was not.

"'It doesn't matter; you dance with her,' he said, smiling warmly as he slipped his sword back into the scabbard.

"Just as the first drop poured out of a bottle brings a whole stream in its wake, so my love for Varenka released all the love in my soul. I embraced the whole world with love. I loved the hostess with her diamond tiara, and her husband, and her guests, and her footmen, and even the wretched Anisimov, who was clearly angry with me. As for her father with his blunt-toed boots and a smile so much like hers—I felt a rapturous affection for him.

"The mazurka came to an end and our hosts invited us to the supper table. But Colonel B. declined, saying that he must be up early in the morning. I was afraid he would take Varenka with him, but she remained behind with her mother.

"After supper I danced the promised quadrille with her. And while it had seemed that my happiness could not be greater, it went on growing and growing. We said nothing of love; I did not ask her, nor even myself, whether she loved me. It was sufficient that I loved her. The only thing I feared was that something might spoil my happiness.

"When I got home, undressed myself and thought of going to bed, I realized that sleep was out of the question. I held in my hand the feather from her fan and one of her gloves, which she had given to me when I put her and her mother into their carriage. As I gazed at these keepsakes I saw her again at the moment when, choosing one of two partners, she had guessed my nature and said in a sweet voice, 'Too proud? Is that it?' then joyfully held out her hand to me; or when, sipping champagne at the supper table, she had gazed at me over her glass with loving eyes. But I saw her best as she danced with her father, floating gracefully beside him, looking at all the admiring spectators with joy and pride for his sake as well as her own. And involuntarily the two of them became merged in my mind and enveloped in one deep and tender feeling.

"At that time my late brother and I lived alone. My brother had no use for society and never went to balls. He was getting ready to take his examinations for a master's degree and was leading the most exemplary of lives. He was asleep. I felt sorry for him as I looked at his head buried in the pillow, half covered by the blanket—sorry because he did not know and did not share the happiness which was mine. Petrusha, our serf valet, met me with a candle and would have helped me undress, but I dismissed him. I was touched by the sight of the man's sleepy face and disheveled hair. Trying to make no noise, I tiptoed to my own room and sat down on the bed. I was too happy, I could not sleep. I found it hot in the room, and so without taking off my uniform I went quietly out into the hall, put on my greatcoat, opened the entrance door, and went out.

"It had been almost five o'clock when I left the ball; about two hours had passed since, so that it was already light when I went out. It was typical Shrovetide weather—misty, with wet snow melting on the roads and water dripping from all the roofs. At that time the B.'s lived on the outskirts of town, at the edge of an open field with a girls' school at one end and a space used for promenading at the other. I went down our quiet little bystreet and came out upon the main street, where I met passers-by and carters with timber loaded on sledges whose runners cut through the snow to the very pavement. And everything—horses bobbing their heads rhythmically under their lacquered yokes, and the carters with bast[1] matting on their shoulders plodding in their enormous boots through the slush beside their sledges, and the houses on either side of the street standing tall in the mist—everything seemed particularly dear and significant.

"When I reached the field where their house stood I saw something big and black at the promenade end of it, and I heard the sounds of a fife and drum. My heart had been singing all this time, and occasionally the strains of the mazurka had come to my mind. But this was different music, harsh and sinister.

" 'What could it be?' I wondered, and made my way in the direction of

[1] *bast:* fiber, often rope.

the sounds, down the slippery wagon road that cut across the field. When I had gone about a hundred paces I began to distinguish in the mist a crowd of people. They were evidently soldiers. 'Drilling,' I thought, and continued on my way in the company of a blacksmith in an oil-stained apron and jacket who was carrying a large bundle. A double row of soldiers in black coats were standing facing each other motionless, their guns at their sides. Behind them stood a fifer and a drummer-boy who kept playing that shrill tune over and over.

" 'What are they doing?' I asked the blacksmith who was standing next to me.

" 'Driving a Tartar down the line for having tried to run away,' replied the blacksmith brusquely, glaring at the far end of the double row.

"I looked in the same direction and saw something horrible coming toward me between the rows. It was a man bare to the waist and tied to a horizontal gun held at either end by a soldier. Beside him walked a tall officer in a greatcoat and forage cap whose figure seemed familiar to me. The prisoner, his whole body twitching, his feet squashing through the melting snow, advanced through the blows raining down on him from either side, now cringing back, at which the soldiers holding the gun would pull him forward, now lunging forward, at which the soldiers would jerk him back to keep him from falling. And next to him, walking firmly, never lagging behind, came the tall officer. It was her father, with his ruddy face and white mustache and side whiskers.

"At every blow the prisoner turned his pain-distorted face to the side from which the blow had come, as if in surprise, and kept repeating something over and over through bared white teeth. I could not make out the words until he came closer to me. He was sobbing rather than speaking them. 'Have mercy, brothers; have mercy, brothers.' But the brothers had no mercy, and when the procession was directly opposite me I saw one of the soldiers step resolutely forward and bring his lash down so hard on the Tartar's back that it whistled through the air. The Tartar fell forward, but the soldiers jerked him up, and then another blow fell from the opposite side, and again from this, and again from that. . . . The colonel marched beside him, now glancing down at his feet, now up at the prisoner, drawing in deep breaths of air, blowing out his cheeks, slowly letting the air out between pursed lips. When the procession passed the spot where I was standing I got a glimpse of the prisoner's back through the row of soldiers. It was something indescribable: striped, wet, crimson, outlandish. I could not believe it was part of a human body.

" 'God in heaven!' murmured the blacksmith standing next to me.

"The procession moved on. The blows kept falling from both sides on the cringing, floundering creature, the drum kept beating, the fife shrilling, and the tall, stately colonel walking firmly beside the prisoner. Suddenly the colonel stopped and went quickly over to one of the soldiers.

" 'Missed? I'll show you!' I heard him say in a wrathful voice. 'Here, take this! And this!' And I saw his strong hand in its suede glove strike the small weak soldier in the face because the man's lash had not come down hard enough on the crimson back of the Tartar.

" 'Bring fresh whips!' shouted the colonel. As he spoke he turned round and caught sight of me. Pretending not to recognize me, he gave a vicious, threatening scowl and turned quickly away. I felt so ashamed that I did not know where to turn my eyes, as if I had been caught doing something disgraceful. With hanging head I hurried home. All the way I kept hearing the rolling of the drum, the shrilling of the fife, the words, 'Have mercy, brothers,' and the wrathful, self-confident voice of the colonel shouting, 'Here, take this! And this!' And the aching of my heart was so intense as to be almost physical, making me feel nauseated, so that I had to stop several times. I felt I must throw up all the horror that this sight had filled me with. I do not remember how I reached home and got into bed, but the moment I began to doze off I saw and heard everything all over again. I jumped up.

" 'There must be something he knows that I do not know,' I said to myself, thinking of the colonel. 'If I knew what he knows, I would understand, and what I saw would not cause me such anguish.' But rack my brains as I might, I could not understand what it was the colonel knew, and I could not fall asleep until evening, and then only after having gone to see a friend and drinking myself into forgetfulness.

"Do you suppose I concluded that what I had seen was bad? Nothing of the sort. 'If what I saw was done with such assurance and was accepted by everyone as being necessary, it means they know something I do not know,' was the conclusion I came to, and I tried to find out what it was. But I never did. And not having found out, I could not enter military service, as it had been my intention to do, and not only military service, but any service at all, and so I turned out to be the good-for-nothing, that you see."

"We know very well what a 'good-for-nothing' you turned out to be," said one of the guests. "It would be more to the point to say how many people would have turned out to be good-for-nothing had it not been for you."

"Now that's a foolish thing to say," said Ivan Vasilyevich with real vexation.

"Well, and what about your love?" we asked.

"My love? From that day on my love languished. Whenever we went out walking and she smiled that pensive smile of hers, I could not help recalling the colonel out in the field, and this made me feel uncomfortable and unhappy, and I gradually stopped going to see her. My love petered out.

"So that is what sometimes happens, and it is incidents like this that change and give direction to a man's whole life. And you talk about environment," he said.

FOR WRITING OR DISCUSSION

1. How does the first paragraph set the problem of the story? How is the problem in this story similar to that posed in "The Raid"?

2. What kind of person is the narrator? Why do you suppose Tolstoy chose to use the first-person point of view? What difference would it have made in the tale if Tolstoy had chosen to tell the story from the daughter's or the colonel's viewpoint?

3. Summarize the events of the story. At what point in the story does the contrast in the two "public" views of the military become apparent?

4. How is the balance between heaviness and lightness developed? What objects and gestures are "heavy" or awkward? Which are light and graceful? How are these contrasts used to reinforce the theme of the story?

5. What seems ironic about the daughter's relationship to the storyteller in regard to her "single" image and his "double" one?

REACTING TO CRITICISM: "THE RAID" AND "AFTER THE BALL"

1. Relate the passages below to what you consider the "realistic" elements of "The Raid":

> Within the limitation of the short-story form, the principal characterizations of the military figures in these Caucasian tales are studies in some depth, and the significant action is nearly always narrated with a realism quite fresh for that time. In this military environment it was almost inevitable that the youthful Tolstoy, with his restless questing mind, should reveal an interest in such abstract questions as "What constitutes bravery? Into what categories should soldiers be classified?" Yet these concerns are never allowed to obtrude on the essential unity of the stories. And the subject that was to dominate so much of his thinking in later years — the rightness or wrongness of war — is also touched upon. In

fact, in "The Raid" ... there is more than a suggestion of his later ruthless analysis of conventional thinking about military glory. But he was not yet blind to the heroism of the simple plain soldier or officer, and his accounts of incidents in this connection in "The Raid" provide the main charm of the tale.[1] [*Ernest Simmons*]

The romantic military life in the Caucasus is not portrayed romantically. The "romantic hero" is played down; the realistic virtues of prudence and patience played up. The soldier's role is summed up by Khlopov's sitting bravely, expertly, wisely on his horse while the young Alanin plunges daringly and foolishly into the forest to return wounded and die. The young officer admits he disobeyed Khlopov, but Khlopov, in his remove, understands more than mere obedience, duty, and adventure, and says simply that it was God's will. Even in such an early story, Tolstoy deeply questioned conventional standards of bravery—witness the opening discussion of bravery between Khlopov and the narrator—and the glorification of war and of heroism. The vanity of the young would-be hero—of Alanin, or better, of the poseur Rosenkranz—is exposed by contrast to the reliable and steadfast honesty of Khlopov, who is in the army because he must be in service, who is in the Caucasus because of double pay, and whose only concern is to do his job well. How can there be glamor about it, he tells the narrator, when you know that on every raid one or more of your comrades will be killed. This same understanding runs through all of Tolstoy's work involving war and led finally to his condemnation of all violence.[2] [*F. D. Reeve*]

2. Both these critics refer to Tolstoy's later, more positive stand against war. How do these two stories—one written very early in Tolstoy's career and one very late—reflect the attitudes stated much more plainly in the following excerpt from an article Tolstoy wrote after he had given up literature as a full-time pursuit?

And in the end, however peaceful Alexander III may be, circumstances will so combine that he will be unable to avoid war, which will be demanded by all who surround him, by the press, and, as always seems in such cases, by the entire public opinion

---

[1]From Introduction by Ernest Simmons to *Leo Tolstoy's Short Stories*, Vol. 1, edited by Ernest Simmons. Reprinted by permission of the publisher, Random House, Inc.
[2]From "Afterword" by F. D. Reeve from *The Cossacks and The Raid* by Leo Tolstoy. Reprinted by permission of The New American Library, Inc., New York.

of the nation. And before we can look round, the usual ominous absurd proclamation will appear in the papers: —

"We, by God's grace, the autocratic great Emperor of all Russia, King of Poland, Grand Duke of Finland, etc., etc. proclaim to all our true subjects, that, for the welfare of these our beloved subjects, bequeathed by God into our care we have found it our duty before God to send them to slaughter. God be with us."

The bells will peal, long-haired men will dress in golden sacks and pray for successful slaughter. And the old story will begin again, the awful customary acts.

The editors of the daily press, happy in the receipt of an increased income, will begin virulently to stir men up to hatred and manslaughter in the name of patriotism. Manufacturers, merchants, contractors for military stores will hurry joyously about their business, in the hope of double receipts.

All sorts of government functionaries will buzz about, foreseeing a possibility of purloining something more than usual. The military authorities will hurry hither and thither, drawing double pay and rations, and with the expectation of receiving for the slaughter of other men various silly little ornaments which they so highly prize, as ribbons, crosses, orders, and stars. Idle ladies and gentlemen will make a great fuss, entering their names in advance for the Red Cross Society, and ready to bind up the wounds of those whom their husbands and brothers will mutilate, and they will imagine that in so doing they are performing a most Christian work.

And, smothering despair within their soul by songs, licentiousness and wine, men will trail along, torn from peaceful labor, from their wives, mothers, and children — hundreds of thousands of simple-minded, good-natured men with murderous weapons in their hands — anywhere they may be driven.

They will march, freeze, hunger, suffer sickness, and die from it, or finally come to some place where they will be slain by thousands, or kill thousands themselves with no reason — men whom they have never seen before, and who neither have done nor could do them any mischief.

And when the number of sick, wounded, and killed becomes so great that there are not hands enough left to pick them up, and when the air is so infected with the putrefying scent of the "food for cannon" that even the authorities find it disagreeable, a truce will be made, the wounded will be picked up anyhow, the sick will be brought in and huddled together in heaps, the killed will be covered with earth and lime, and once more all the crowd of deluded men will be led on and on till those who have devised the project weary of it, or till those who thought to find it profitable receive their spoil.

And so once more men will be made savage, fierce, and brutal, and love will wane in the world, and the Christianizing of mankind, which has already begun, will lapse for scores and hundreds of years. And so once more the men who reaped profit from it all will assert with assurance that since there has been a war there must needs have been one, and that other wars must follow, and they will again prepare future generations for a continuance of slaughter, depraving them from their childhood.[1] [*Leo Tolstoy*]

3. "The Raid" and "After the Ball" reflect Tolstoy's interest in the various ways of viewing military life, both in active combat and in garrisons, as a career, as an adventure, as "glory," often as a means of indulging natural cruelty, and as a waste. Which characters in either story exhibit these attitudes?

Tolstoy's interest in military attitudes, however, goes beyond these specific types of soldiers to the deeper question of the difference between the appearance and the realities of military life. The difference is apparent in the characters of the captain in "The Raid" and the colonel in "After the Ball." Read the following statement about "After the Ball." Then discuss in class the ways in which the "reality" of life as a ball versus the "reality" of the running of the gauntlet compares with the reality of war as a glamorous adventure of young soldiers versus the reality of war as a career officer sees it in "The Raid."

> In another short story, also unfinished, "The Morning After the Ball," written in 1903, when the author was seventy-five years old, Tolstoy, with obvious intention, confronts his old and new visions. The story is in two parts: the first describes, with an art unequaled in Russian literature before or since, a gay, elegant, and amusing ball. It is a really marvelous ball: there are music and dancing, there is champagne, the young people are of the highest class, charming and aristocratic; naturally there is also a charming young lady there and a young man who is in love with

---

[1]From "On Patriotism" from *Tolstoy, on Civil Disobedience and Non-Violence* by Leo Tolstoy, copyright 1967 by Bergman Publishers, New York. Reprinted by permission of the publishers.

her; it is he who tells the story. An hour after the ball,[1] the narrator, still gay, excited, and possessed by his "refined" emotions, is witness of quite another scene in the street[2]; a Tatar deserter is being made to run the gauntlet. And this is being done at the orders of the colonel, the father of the charming young girl, the very man who, to the universal delight, himself had danced the mazurka with his daughter at the end of the ball, displaying such charm and old-world gallantry. I have said that the scene at the ball is described by Tolstoy with inimitable art; the torture of the Tartar is described with no less strength and feeling.... The important point is to compare and contrast the two ways of looking at reality. And considering the whole of Tolstoy's work, one might say, metaphorically of course and with certain reservations, that in his youth Tolstoy described life as a fascinating ball; and later when he was old, it was like the running of the gauntlet.[3]
[*Leo Shestov*]

PEASANTS: *Alyosha*

As both Prince Mirsky and Gorky emphasized, Tolstoy, though leading an adventurous, wordly life in his youth, eventually found his true interest in life on his country estate, Yasnaya Polyana, where he lived, wrote, raised a large family, worked to improve the conditions of the serfs, and gradually became more interested in teaching and advancing his numerous programs for reform than in literature or art for its own sake. In his search for the meaning of life, Tolstoy finally identified the saving graces as simplicity and innocence, two qualities that he associated, rightly or wrongly, with the peasants. He himself, you will recall, emulated the peasants by adopting peasant garb and ways.

The story you are about to read is a masterpiece of simple, straightforward narration, which was written as a tribute to the qualities in the peasant that Tolstoy venerated. As you read, notice the way in which the main character is described. Does he seem like a hero to you? What is his most noticeable personality trait? How is his constant smile related to this trait?

[1]*An ... ball:* actually, two hours later (see text of story).
[2]*in ... street:* actually, in a field (see text of story).
[3]From "The Last Judgment: Tolstoy's Last Works" from *In Job's Balances* by Leo Shestov, translated by Coventry and Macartney. Reprinted by permission of J. M. Dent & Sons Ltd., Publishers.

Alyosha

Alyosha was the younger brother. He had been nicknamed "Pot" because his mother had once sent him to carry a pot of milk to the deacon's wife, and he had stumbled and broken it. His mother had given him a beating and the boys began to tease him about "the pot." "Alyosha the Pot" they called him, and the nickname stuck.

Alyosha was a skinny fellow, with large ears. They stuck out like wings, and he had a big nose. "Alyosha's nose is like a dog on a hillock," the boys would call after him.

There was a school in the village, but Alyosha had no head for learning; besides, he had no time to study. His elder brother was in town working for a merchant, so Alyosha began to help his father at a very early stage. He was only six when he started going out with his little sister to watch the cow and the few sheep in the pasture, and a little later he looked after the horses by day as well as by night, while they grazed in the fields. At twelve he had begun to plow and to drive the cart. He was not strong, but he was able. He was always cheerful. The boys made fun of him; he either said nothing or laughed with them. If his father scolded him, he listened in silence, and as soon as the scolding was over, he would smile and go on with his work.

Alyosha was nineteen when his brother was drafted. So his father had him take his brother's place with the merchant as a porter. He was given his brother's old boots, his father's cap and coat, and was taken to town. Alyosha was delighted with his clothes, but the merchant was not pleased with his appearance.

"I thought you would give me a man in Semyon's place," said the merchant, eyeing Alyosha, "and you've brought me a runt. What good is he to me?"

"He can do everything. He can hitch horses and drive a cart, he's a glutton for work, he only looks spindly, but he's a tough one."

"Well, I'm not sure."

"One thing, he never talks back. And he just eats up work."

"Well, what can I do? Leave him here."

So Alyosha remained with the merchant.

The merchant's family was not a large one: it included his wife, his old

---

"Alyosha" by Leo Tolstoy, translated by Avrahm Yarmolinsky, from *A Treasury of Great Russian Short Stories* edited by Avrahm Yarmolinsky. Published by The Macmillan Company, 1944.

mother, a married son with little education who was in his father's business, a younger son who had finished school and studied at the university, but, having been expelled, was living at home, and a daughter who still went to school.

At first they did not take to Alyosha—he was loutish, was badly dressed, was rough spoken and unmannerly; but they soon got used to him. He did the work even better than his brother had done, and he actually never talked back. Whatever he was ordered to do, he did willingly and quickly, going from one task to another without a pause. And so here, even as at home, all manner of chores were heaped upon his shoulders. And the more he did, the more work everyone found for him to do. The mistress, the master's mother, his daughter, his son, the shop assistant and the cook, all sent him hither and yon, all demanded services from him. You never heard anything but: "Alyosha, run an errand for me," or "Alyosha, do this," or "What, have you forgotten, Alyosha?" and "Mind you, don't forget, Alyosha!" And Alyosha ran, looked after this and that, forgot nothing, managed to do everything, and kept smiling.

He soon wore out his brother's boots, and the master scolded him for going about with his bare toes sticking out of the holes, and ordered other boots bought for him in the market. The boots were new and Alyosha was delighted with them, but his feet were the same, and by the end of the day they ached with so much running about and he was annoyed. And then he was afraid that his father, coming to town to fetch his wages, would be put out to find that the merchant had deducted the cost of the boots.

In winter Alyosha got up before daybreak. He would chop wood, sweep the yard, feed and water the horse and cow. Then he would light the stoves, black the boots, brush the master's clothes, and heat the samovar, which it was his duty to keep bright. Then the shop assistant would summon him to move the goods, or the cook would set him to knead the dough and clean the pots. Then he was sent to town on various errands: to deliver a note, to fetch the daughter from school, to buy oil for the old woman. "Where have you been dawdling, damn you?" one or another would say to him. Or, it would be: "Why should you trouble? Alyosha will go, Alyosha! Hey, Alyosha!" and Alyosha went.

He ate his breakfast on the run, and he hardly ever managed to be around when dinnertime came. The cook scolded him for failing to show up with the others. Nevertheless she was sorry for him and would save something hot for his dinner and supper. Work piled up on him particularly before and during holiday time, but Alyosha liked holidays, especially because he got tips then. Not much money certainly, perhaps some sixty kopeks in all; but it was his very own, that he could spend as he pleased. Alyosha never so much as set eyes on his wages. His father would come, take them from the merchant, and only scold Alyosha for wearing out his boots so fast.

When he had saved up two rubles in tips, he bought himself a red knitted jacket on the cook's advice, and when he put it on, he was so happy that his mouth gaped in a perpetual grin.

Alyosha had little to say, and when he spoke he did so abruptly and briefly. When ordered to do anything or asked if he could do it, he always answered unhesitatingly, "Sure I can," and set to work at once.

He did not know any prayers: he had forgotten those his mother had taught him. But he prayed just the same, morning and evening—he prayed with his hands, crossing himself.

Thus Alyosha lived for a year and a half, and when the second year was drawing to a close a most extraordinary event took place in his life. This event was the amazing discovery that, in addition to the relations existing between human beings because they want to make use of you, there are also relations of a quite different kind: not that they want you to black their boots, or to carry a package or hitch up the horses, but just that they want you around, as you are, so that they may look after you and be tender towards you, and that he, Alyosha, was wanted just that way.

He learned this through Ustinya, the cook. She was an orphan, a young girl, and as hard-working as Alyosha. She began to feel sorry for Alyosha, and for the first time in his life Alyosha felt that he, he himself, not his services, was necessary to another human being. When his mother had been sorry for him, he had not paid any attention to it, he took it for granted, it was just as though he were sorry for himself. But here he suddenly noticed that Ustinya, a perfect stranger, was sorry for him; she would leave some porridge with butter in a pot for him and would sit watching him while he ate it, her chin propped on her bare arm with its sleeve tucked up. And he would look at her, she would laugh, and he too would laugh.

This was so novel and strange that at first it frightened Alyosha. He felt that it would prevent him from performing his services as well as before. But he was glad all the same, and when he looked at the trousers that Ustinya had mended for him, he shook his head and smiled. Often while at work or while running an errand he thought of Ustinya and would say admiringly: "Oh, that Ustinya!" Whenever she could, she helped him, and he helped her. She told him about her life, how she had lost her parents, how an aunt had taken her in, how she had been given a situation in town, how the master's son had tried to lead her astray and how she had sent him about his business. She liked to talk and he liked to listen to her. He had heard it said that peasants who worked in town often got to marry cooks. One day she asked him if he was soon to be married off. He said he didn't know, but he didn't care to have a wife from the village.

"Well, have you found a girl that suits you?"

"I would marry you. Would you be willing?"

"Look at the fellow. They call him 'Pot,' but he has managed to speak up," she said, slapping him on the back with a towel. "Why shouldn't I?"

At Shrovetide Alyosha's father came to town for the lad's wages. The merchant's wife had gotten wind of the fact that Alyosha was thinking of marrying Ustinya, and she did not like it. "She will become pregnant, and what good will she be with a baby?" She spoke to her husband about it.

The merchant handed the old man Alyosha's wages.

"How's the boy getting on?" he asked. "I told you, he wasn't one to talk back."

"You're right about the back talk, but he has gotten a foolish notion into his head. He wants to marry the cook. Now, I won't have married servants. It doesn't suit me."

"Well, who would have thought the fool would get such a notion into his head?" cried the old man. "But don't worry. I'll tell him to drop this nonsense."

He made his way into the kitchen and sat down at the table waiting for his son. Alyosha was out on an errand and came back out of breath.

"I thought you were a decent boy, but now what's this you've taken into your head?" said the old man.

"I? Nothing."

"How—nothing? You're thinking of getting married. I'll marry you off when the time comes, and I'll find the right kind of wife for you, not a town slut."

The father had a great deal to say. Alyosha stood before him and sighed. When the old man had finished, Alyosha smiled.

"Well, I can drop it."

"That's better!"

When his father had gone, and he was left alone with Ustinya, he told her what the old man had said (there was no need for it, though, for she had listened at the door).

"It's all come to nothing. D'you hear? He got angry. He put his foot down."

Ustinya cried quietly into her apron.

Alyosha clicked his tongue.

"Can't disobey. I figure we'll have to give it up."

In the evening when the mistress called him to close the shutters, she said to him:

"Well, are you going to mind your father? Will you give up that nonsense of yours?"

"Looks that way," said Alyosha with a laugh, and then burst into tears.

From that day on Alyosha no longer spoke to Ustinya about marriage, and his life was what it had been earlier.

One day in Lent the shop assistant told Alyosha to clear the snow from the roof. Alyosha climbed onto the roof and cleared all the snow away. Then he started loosening up the ice in the gutters, when his foot slipped and he fell off the roof with his shovel in his hands. As ill luck would have it, he fell not into the snow, but on the sheet of iron covering the cellar door. Ustinya and the master's daughter came running up to him.

"Are you hurt, Alyosha?"

"Hurt indeed! It's nothing."

He tried to raise himself, but could not, and began to smile. He was taken into the lodge. The doctor's assistant came, examined him, and asked him where it hurt him.

"It hurts all over, but that's nothing. I'm only afraid the master will be angry. Word ought to be sent to father."

Alyosha lay in bed for two days, and on the third day they sent for the priest.

"Well, are you going to die?" asked Ustinya.

"What do you think? Can we live forever? Some day we must make an end," Alyosha said briefly in his usual way. "Thank you, Ustinya, for having been kind to me. It's a good thing they didn't let us marry. What would have been the use? Now all's well."

When the priest came, Alyosha prayed only with his hands and his heart, which held this thought: As it is well with a man in this world if he is obedient and does no one any harm, so it will be well with him in the world beyond.

He spoke little. He only kept asking for a drink of water, and there was a puzzled expression in his eyes.

He looked round wonderingly, stretched himself, and died.

FOR WRITING OR DISCUSSION

1. Contrast the peasants in this tale with the peasants portrayed in Turgenev's stories. Which writer seems more objective in his characterization? Explain your answer.

2. How is Alyosha's reaction to death similar to his reactions to life? Do you think Tolstoy considered Alyosha's death pathetic, or do you think he admires the peasant's acceptance of death as a part of life? How is the peasant's attitude contrasted to that of the soldiers in "The Raid"? How is it similar to Khlopov's attitude toward death?

3. Although the story is, of course, a translation from the Russian, which makes talking about vocabulary choice and sentence structure difficult, how would you characterize Tolstoy's style? Are the sentences long or short? Examine the verbs in any narrative passage; compare the numbers of nouns and verbs to the number of modifiers. Why do you suppose Tolstoy relied so heavily on the two basic parts of speech?

4. How is the style in which the story is written related to the theme and the plot?

REACTING TO CRITICISM

"Alyosha" illustrates one facet of Tolstoy's idealized view of the peasant; it also illustrates the demeaning and foolish subjection of a man. Discuss the story as an example of the contrasting views of the peasant as expressed in the following quotations, one by Tolstoy himself and one by the famous British novelist and critic, D. H. Lawrence:

> The range of feelings experienced by the powerful and the rich who have no experience of labor for the support of life is far poorer, more limited, and more insignificant than the range of feelings natural to working people. . . . .
> . . . The life of a laboring man, with its endlessly varied forms of labor and the dangers connected with this labor on sea and underground; his migrations, the intercourse with his employers, overseers, and companions, and with men of other religions and other nationalities; his struggles with nature and with wild beasts, the associations with domestic animals, the work in the forest, on

the steppe, in the field, the garden, the orchard; his intercourse with wife and children, not only as with people near and dear to him but as with co-workers and helpers in labor, replacing him in time of need; his concern in all economic questions, not as matters of display or discussion, but as problems of life for himself and his family; his pride in self-suppression and service to others, his pleasures of refreshment; and with all these interests permeated by a religious attitude toward these occurrences—all this to us who have not these interests and possess no religious perception seems monotonous in comparison with those small enjoyments and insignificant cares of our life—a life not of labor nor of production, but of consumption and destruction of that which others have produced for us.[1] [*Leo Tolstoy*]

What Tolstoy somewhat perversely worshiped in the peasants was poverty itself, and humility, and what Tolstoy perversely hated was instinctive pride or spontaneous passion. Tolstoy has a perverse pleasure in making the later Vronsky[2] abject and pitiable: because Tolstoy so meanly envied the healthy passionate male in the young Vronsky. Tolstoy cut off his own nose to spite his face. He envied the reckless passionate male with a carking envy, because he must have felt himself in some way wanting in comparison. So he exalts the peasant: not because the peasant may be a more natural and spontaneous creature than the city man or the guardsman, but just because the peasant is poverty-stricken and humble. This is malice, the envy of weakness and deformity.

We know now that the peasant is no better than anybody else; no better than a prince or a selfish young army officer or a governor or a merchant. In fact, in the mass, the peasant is worse than any of these. The peasant mass is the ugliest of all human masses, most greedily selfish and brutal of all. Which Tolstoy leaning down from the gold bar of heaven, will have had opportunity to observe. If we have to trust to a mass, then better trust the upper- or middle-class mass, all masses being odious.[3] [*D. H. Lawrence*]

---

[1]From *What Is Art?* by Leo N. Tolstoy, translated by Aylmer Maude, copyright © 1960, by The Liberal Arts Press, Inc. Reprinted by permission of the Liberal Arts Press Division of The Bobbs-Merrill Company, Inc.

[2]*Vronsky:* In Tolstoy's *Anna Karenina*, Aleksei Vronsky is the handsome young officer for whom the heroine abandons her husband and child.

[3]From *Phoenix: The Posthumous Papers of D. H. Lawrence*, edited by Edward D. McDonald. Copyright 1936 by Frieda Lawrence, renewed 1964 by the Estate of the late Frieda Lawrence Ravagli. All rights reserved. Reprinted by permission of The Viking Press, Inc.

PEASANTS: *Elias* and *A Grain as Big as a Hen's Egg*

One of the pursuits to which Tolstoy turned, both when he was completing his great novels and later when he had condemned his imaginative writings, was the teaching of the peasants on his estate. The following passage from a recent biography of Tolstoy describes the school he ran on Yasnaya Polyana:

The school, which he had reopened with a few young teachers selected and paid by himself, was now located in a small, two-story building next to their [the Tolstoy's] own house; two rooms for classes, two for the teachers, and one used as a study. A bell and bell-rope hung under the porch roof. Gymnastic apparatus had been installed in the downstairs vestibule; in the upstairs hall, there was a carpenter's bench. A schedule — purely symbolic, since the motto of the establishment was "Do as you like!" — was posted on the wall.

At eight in the morning a child rang the bell. Half an hour later, "through fog, rain, or the slanting rays of the sun," the black silhouettes of little muzhiks (peasants) appeared by twos and threes, swinging their empty arms. As in the previous years, they brought no books or notebooks with them — nothing at all, save the desire to learn. The classrooms were painted pink and blue.

In one, mineral samples, butterflies, dried plants and physics apparatus lined the shelves. But no books. Why books? The pupils came to the classrooms as though it were home; they sat where they liked, on the floor, on the window-ledge, on a chair or the corner of a table, they listened or did not listen to what the teacher was saying, drew near when he said something that interested them, left the room when work or play called them elsewhere — but were silenced by their fellow pupils at the slightest sound. Self-imposed discipline. The lessons — if these casual chats between an adult and some children could be called that — went on from eight-thirty to noon and from three to six in the afternoon, and covered every conceivable subject from grammar to carpentry, by way of religious history, singing, geography, gymnastics, drawing and composition. Those who lived too far away to go home at night slept in the school. In the summer they sat around their teacher outdoors in the grass. Once a week they all went to study plants in the forest.[1] [*Henri Troyat*]

Although Tolstoy did not use the customary textbooks in his school, he did use collections of his own simple folk tales and parables that illustrated a moral or religious principle. He had been writing these for some time, and many of them were his own versions of Russian legends. The two stories that follow are typical of the kind of story Tolstoy wrote in the last years of his life.

Elias

There once lived, in the Government of Ufa, a Bashkir[2] named Elias. His father, who died a year after he had found his son a wife, did not leave him much property. Elias then had only seven mares, two cows, and about a score of sheep. He was a good manager, however, and soon began to acquire more. He and his wife worked from morn till night; rising earlier than others and going later to bed; and his possessions increased year by year. Living in this way, Elias little by little acquired great wealth. At the end of thirty-five years he had 200 horses, 150 head of cattle, and 1200 sheep. Hired laborers tended his flocks and herds, and hired women milked his mares and cows, and made kumiss,[3] butter, and cheese. Elias had an abundance of everything, and everyone in the district envied him. They said of him:

"Elias is a fortunate man: he has plenty of everything. This world must be a pleasant place for him."

People of position heard of Elias and sought his acquaintance. Visitors came to him from afar; and he welcomed everyone, and gave them food and drink. Whoever might come, there was always kumiss, tea, sherbet, and mutton to set before them. Whenever visitors arrived a sheep would be killed, or sometimes two; and if many guests came he would even slaughter a mare for them.

Elias had three children: two sons and a daughter; and he married them all off. While he was poor, his sons worked with him and looked after the flocks and herds themselves; but when he grew rich they got spoiled, and one of them took to drink. The elder was killed in a brawl; and the younger, who had married a self-willed woman, ceased to obey

---

[1] Excerpt from *Tolstoy* by Henri Troyat, translated by Nancy Amphoux, copyright © 1967 by Doubleday & Company, Inc. Reprinted by permission of the publisher.
[2] *Bashkir:* a person living in Bashkir, in eastern Russia.
[3] *kumiss* (or more properly *kumys*): a fermented drink prepared from mare's milk.

"Elias" from *Leo Tolstoy's Short Stories*, Vol. 2, edited by Ernest Simmons. Translation by Louise and Aylmer Maude; reprinted by permission of Oxford University Press.

his father, and they could not live together any more.

So they parted, and Elias gave his son a house and some of the cattle, and this diminished his wealth. Soon after that, a disease broke out among Elias's sheep, and many died. Then followed a bad harvest, and the hay crop failed; and many cattle died that winter. Then the Kirghiz[1] captured his best herd of horses; and Elias's property dwindled away. It became smaller and smaller, while at the same time his strength grew less; till, by the time he was seventy years old, he had begun to sell his furs, carpets, saddles, and tents. At last he had to part with his remaining cattle, and found himself face to face with want. Before he knew how it had happened, he had lost everything, and in their old age he and his wife had to go into service. Elias had nothing left, except the clothes on his back, a fur cloak, a cup, his indoor shoes and overshoes, and his wife, Sham-Shemagi, who also by this time was old. The son who had parted from him had gone into a far country, and his daughter was dead, so that there was no one to help the old couple.

Their neighbor, Muhammad-Shah, took pity on them. Muhammad-Shah was neither rich nor poor, but lived comfortably, and was a good man. He remembered Elias's hospitality, and, pitying him, said:

"Come and live with me, Elias, you and your old woman. In summer you can work in my melon-garden as much as your strength allows, and in winter feed my cattle; and Sham-Shemagi shall milk my mares and make kumiss. I will feed and clothe you both. When you need anything, tell me, and you shall have it."

Elias thanked his neighbor, and he and his wife took service with Muhammad-Shah as laborers. At first the position seemed hard to them, but they got used to it, and lived on, working as much as their strength allowed.

Muhammad-Shah found it was to his advantage to keep such people, because, having been masters themselves, they knew how to manage and were not lazy, but did all the work they could. Yet it grieved Muhammad-Shah to see people brought so low who had been of such high standing.

It happened once that some of Muhammad-Shah's relatives came from a great distance to visit him, and a Mullah[2] came too. Muhammad-Shah told Elias to catch a sheep and kill it. Elias skinned the sheep and boiled it, and sent it in to the guests. The guests ate the mutton, had some tea, and then began drinking kumiss. As they were sitting with their host on down cushions on a carpet, conversing and sipping kumiss

---

[1]*Kirghiz:* people from Kirghiz, in a part of Russia located in central Asia.
[2]*Mullah:* a Moslem religious leader or teacher.

from their cups, Elias having finished his work, passed by the open door. Muhammad-Shah, seeing him pass, said to one of the guests:

"Did you notice that old man who passed just now?"

"Yes," said the visitor, "what is there remarkable about him?"

"Only this—that he was once the richest man among us," replied the host. "His name is Elias. You may have heard of him."

"Of course I have heard of him," the guest answered, "I never saw him before, but his fame has spread far and wide."

"Yes, and now he has nothing left," said Muhammad-Shah, "and he lives with me as my laborer, and his old woman is here too—she milks the mares."

The guest was astonished: he clicked with his tongue, shook his head, and said:

"Fortune turns like a wheel. One man it lifts, another it sets down! Does not the old man grieve over all he has lost?"

"Who can tell? He lives quietly and peacefully, and works well."

"May I speak to him?" asked the guest. "I should like to ask him about his life."

"Why not?" replied the master, and he called from the kibitka[1] in which they were sitting:

"Babay," (which in the Bashkir tongue means "Grandfather") "come in and have a cup of kumiss with us, and call your wife here also."

Elias entered with his wife; and after exchanging greetings with his master and the guests, he repeated a prayer and seated himself near the door. His wife passed in behind the curtain and sat down with her mistress.

A cup of kumiss was handed to Elias; he wished the guests and his master good health, bowed, drank a little, and put down the cup.

"Well, Daddy," said the guest who had wished to speak to him, "I suppose you feel rather sad at the sight of us. It must remind you of your former prosperity and of your present sorrows."

Elias smiled, and said:

"If I were to tell you what is happiness and what is misfortune, you would not believe me. You had better ask my wife. She is a woman, and what is in her heart is on her tongue. She will tell you the whole truth."

The guest turned toward the curtain.

"Well, Granny," he cried, "tell me how your former happiness compares with your present misfortune."

And Sham-Shemagi answered from behind the curtain:

---

[1] *kibitka:* a movable dwelling, made up of detachable wooden frames and covered over with felt.

"This is what I think about it: My old man and I lived for fifty years seeking happiness and not finding it; and it is only now, these last two years, since we had nothing left and have lived as laborers, that we have found real happiness, and we wish for nothing better than our present lot."

The guests were astonished, and so was the master; he even rose and drew the curtain back, so as to see the old woman's face. There she stood with her arms folded, looking at her old husband, and smiling; and he smiled back at her. The old woman went on:

"I speak the truth and do not jest. For half a century we sought for happiness, and as long as we were rich we never found it. Now that we have nothing left and have taken service as laborers, we have found such happiness that we want nothing better."

"But in what does your happiness consist?" asked the guest.

"Why, in this," she replied, "when we were rich, my husband and I had so many cares that we had no time to talk to one another, or to think of our souls, or to pray to God. Now we had visitors, and had to consider what food to set before them, and what presents to give them, lest they should speak ill of us. When they left we had to look after our laborers, who were always trying to shirk work and get the best food, while we wanted to get all we could out of them. So we sinned. Then we were in fear lest a wolf should kill a foal or a calf, or thieves steal our horses. We lay awake at night worrying lest the ewes should overlie their lambs, and we got up again and again to see that all was well. One thing attended to, another care would spring up: how, for instance, to get enough fodder for the winter. And besides that, my old man and I used to disagree. He would say we must do so and so, and I would differ from him; and then we disputed—sinning again. So we passed from one trouble to another, from one sin to another, and found no happiness."

"Well, and now?"

"Now, when my husband and I wake in the morning we always have a loving word for one another, and we live peacefully having nothing to quarrel about. We have no care but how best to serve our master. We work as much as our strength allows, and do it with a will, that our master may not lose, but profit by us. When we come in, dinner or supper is ready and there is kumiss to drink. We have fuel to burn when it is cold, and we have our fur cloak. And we have time to talk, time to think of our souls, and time to pray. For fifty years we sought happiness, but only now at last have we found it."

The guests laughed.

But Elias said:

"Do not laugh, friends. It is not a matter for jesting—it is the truth of life. We also were foolish at first and wept at the loss of our wealth; but now God has shown us the truth, and we tell it, not for our own consolation, but for your good."

And the Mullah said:

"That is a wise speech. Elias has spoken the exact truth. The same is said in Holy Writ."

And the guests ceased laughing and became thoughtful.

A Grain as Big as a Hen's Egg

One day some children found, in a ravine, a thing shaped like a grain of corn, with a groove down the middle, but as large as a hen's egg. A traveler passing by saw the thing, bought it from the children for a penny, and taking it to town sold it to the King as a curiosity.

The King called together his wise men, and told them to find out what the thing was. The wise men pondered and pondered and could not make head or tail of it, till one day, when the thing was lying on a windowsill, a hen flew in and pecked at it till she made a hole in it, and then every one saw that it was a grain of corn. The wise men went to the King, and said:

"It is a grain of corn."

At that the King was much surprised; and he ordered the learned men to find out when and where such corn had grown. The learned men pondered again and searched in their books, but could find nothing about it. So they returned to the King and said:

"We can give you no answer. There is nothing about it in our books. You will have to ask the peasants; perhaps some of them may have heard from their fathers when and where grain grew to such a size."

So the King gave orders that some very old peasant should be brought before him; and his servants found such a man and brought him to the King. Old and bent, ashy pale and toothless, he just managed with the help of two crutches to totter into the King's presence.

The King showed him the grain, but the old man could hardly see it; he took it, however, and felt it with his hands. The King questioned him, saying:

"Can you tell us, old man, where such grain as this grew? Have you ever bought such corn, or sown such in your fields?"

"A Grain as Big as a Hen's Egg" from *Leo Tolstoy's Short Stories*, Vol. 2, edited by Ernest Simmons. Translation by Louise and Aylmer Maude; reprinted by permission of Oxford University Press.

The old man was so deaf that he could hardly hear what the King said, and only understood with great difficulty.

"No!" he answered at last, "I never sowed nor reaped any like it in my fields, nor did I ever buy any such. When we bought corn, the grains were always as small as they are now. But you might ask my father. He may have heard where such grain grew."

So the King sent for the old man's father, and he was found and brought before the King. He came walking with one crutch. The King showed him the grain, and the old peasant, who was still able to see, took a good look at it. And the King asked him:

"Can you not tell us, old man, where corn like this used to grow? Have you ever bought any like it, or sown any in your fields?"

Though the old man was rather hard of hearing, he still heard better than his son had done.

"No," he said, "I never sowed nor reaped any grain like this in my field. As to buying, I never bought any, for in my time money was not yet in use. Everyone grew his own corn, and when there was any need we shared with one another. I do not know where corn like this grew. Ours was larger and yielded more flour than present-day grain, but I never saw any like this. I have, however, heard my father say that in his time the grain grew larger and yielded more flour than ours. You had better ask him."

So the King sent for this old man's father, and they found him too, and brought him before the King. He entered walking easily and without crutches: his eye was clear, his hearing good, and he spoke distinctly. The King showed him the grain, and the old grandfather looked at it and turned it about in his hand.

"It is long since I saw such a fine grain," said he, and he bit a piece off and tasted it.

"It's the very same kind," he added.

"Tell me, grandfather," said the King, "when and where was such corn grown? Have you ever bought any like it, or sown any in your fields?"

And the old man replied:

"Corn like this used to grow everywhere in my time. I lived on corn like this in my young days, and fed others on it. It was grain like this that we used to sow and reap and thresh."

And the King asked:

"Tell me, grandfather, did you buy it anywhere, or did you grow it all yourself?"

The old man smiled.

"In my time," he answered, "no one ever thought of such a sin as buying or selling bread, and we knew nothing of money. Each man had corn enough of his own."

"Then tell me, grandfather," asked the King, "where was your field, where did you grow corn like this?"

And the grandfather answered:

"My field was God's earth. Wherever I plowed, there was my field. Land was free. It was a thing no man called his own. Labor was the only thing men called their own."

"Answer me two more questions," said the King. "The first is, Why did the earth bear such grain then, and has ceased to do so now? And the second is, Why your grandson walks with two crutches, your son with one, and you yourself with none? Your eyes are bright, your teeth sound, and your speech clear and pleasant to the ear. How have these things come about?"

And the old man answered:

"These things are so, because men have ceased to live by their own labor and have taken to depending on the labor of others. In the old time, men lived according to God's law. They had what was their own and coveted not what others had produced."

FOR WRITING OR DISCUSSION

1. How are these two tales different from the legends and stories that the boys in Turgenev's story "Bezhin Lea" were telling around their campfire? How does the different artistic purpose of each writer explain his choice of folk material?

2. How do these folk tales illustrate Tolstoy's idea about the relative merit of the lives of the wealthy and of the poor as described in the passage from *What Is Art?* (See pages 149–50.)

3. Compare the narrative structure and style of these two stories with the structure and style of "The Raid" and "After the Ball." How are they similar or dissimilar? How is "After the Ball" more like these two simple tales than it is like "The Raid"?

4. Do these stories, well written as they are, explain in any way the distress that many Russian writers of Tolstoy's day felt about his abandoning his former literary career in favor of more didactic writing?

5. Do you think most modern American readers of your generation would enjoy these two folk tales as much as the other Tolstoy stories you have read? Why or why not?

REACTING TO CRITICISM

How do these two folk tales illustrate Tolstoy's social and economic theories as described in the following summary by a contemporary critic?

After a thorough study of the most diverse theories of money, Tolstoy arrives at his famous formula: "Money is a certificate for the work of the poor and disinherited." Therefore it follows that money can be of no help to the poor, whose exploitation cannot be lessened just because these certificates of their sweat and blood change hands. This technically untenable theory of money came to Tolstoy in an especially paradoxical and tragic manner when, on a visit to the Moscow almshouse, he saw that he was in no position to help the miserable inmates with money.

Tolstoy drew the conclusion from his radical rejection of money that the capitalistic economic system was the worst and most unjust that had ever existed. In regard to the sociological bases of the capitalist system, he explored in a most original manner the principle upon which modern society rests, that of the division of labor. The representatives of the professions emerged especially poorly. In *What Shall We Do Then?* his attack on all the professions is characterized by particular severity but also by stylistic splendor. One feels that here not only social theories are being developed but attacks made on the society of which Tolstoy is bitterly conscious of being a member. In this book, this attack is especially effective, because one has the feeling that it is a direct attack upon himself. He could no longer bear to see good, earnest men of the people attend his household, have them fell trees in the forest and chop wood so that he would be warm in the winter. It distressed him to see them draw water for the kitchen so that his food would be cooked; to have them groom the horses for his use; to milk cows for cream in his coffee; to make them brush his clothes and clean his boots — in short, to have them do everything that was necessary for his daily existence. And what did he offer in return? Nothing but his novels that could not possibly be of interest to the people — and even could not be read by most of them, because they were illiterate. Was not such an exchange pure and simple theft? Could such a person who was conscious of this situation continue his parasitic life in good conscience? Tolstoy denied this for himself and for the whole class of landed people and of those who are dominant by dint of wealth.

Tolstoy, always attacking a problem in its entirety, asked himself what could be done to eliminate this inequitable division of labor in society and how it could be substituted with something more just. In answering the fundamental question of his book Tolstoy's famous "four teams" theory arose. As may be anticipated from his criticism of the principle of the division of labor, the basic idea was for every person to do for himself everything that had to be done for the interest of all. According to Tolstoy's scheme, everyone's day should be divided into four sections, or as he calls it, four "teams," which should be divided in natural order by the usual meals. Before breakfast everyone should do heavy manual work and "earn his bread by the sweat of his brow." Between breakfast and the noon meal each person should improve his skill at some craft; and from noon until vespers all should engage in some mental exercise to sharpen their wits and imagination. Evening should be devoted to the cultivation of good relations with one's fellow beings, in friendly association with one's neighbor.[1] [*Fedor Stepun*]

SUMMARY DISCUSSION OF TOLSTOY'S STORIES

Use the following quotations as the basis of a discussion in which you summarize your own reactions to Tolstoy's stories. To support your general statements, cite examples from any of the Tolstoy works you have read.

> The enemy is always the same: experts, professionals, men who claim special authority over other men. . . . Tolstoy was convinced that men have certain basic material and spiritual needs in all places at all times. If these needs are fulfilled they lead harmonious lives, which is the goal of their nature. . . . Moreover, Tolstoy constantly defended the proposition that human beings are more harmonious in childhood than under the corrupting influence of education in later life; and also something that he believed much more deeply and expressed in everything he wrote or said—that simple people, peasants, Cossacks, and the like, have a more "natural" and correct attitude than civilized men toward these

---

[1]From "The Religious Tragedy of Tolstoy" by Fedor Stepun from *The Russian Review*, April 1960. Reprinted by permission of The Russian Review, Inc.

basic values, and they are free and independent in a sense in which civilized men are not.[1] [*Isaiah Berlin*]

The man is much more prominent than the writer. . . . [*George Saintsbury*]

. . . a sense of incompleteness, something still to come [in his stories]. . . .[*George Saintsbury*]

. . . the artistic center of gravity is not in the dialogue between the characters, but in the telling of the story; not in what they say, but in what is said of them; not in what we hear with our ears, but in what we see with our eyes.[2] [*D. S. Merezhkovsky*]

In its essence the language of all the characters in Tolstoy is the same, or all but the same; it is colloquial parlance, as it were, the sound of the voice of Leo himself, whether in gentleman's or peasant's dress. And merely for this reason we overlook the fact that in his works it is not what the characters *say* that matters, *but how they are silent,* or else groan, howl, roar, yell, or grunt: it is not their human words that matter, but their half-animal, inarticulate sounds. . . . The repetition of the same vowels, a–o–u, seems sufficient to express the most complex, terrible, heartrending, mental and bodily emotions.[3] [*D. S. Merezhkovsky*]

[1] From "Tolstoy and Enlightenment" from *Mightier Than the Sword* by Isaiah Berlin, from the P. E. N. Herman Ould Memorial Lectures. Reprinted by permission of Macmillan & Co. Ltd., London.

[2] From *Tolstoy as Man and Artist*, London: Constable & Co., 1902.

[3] *Ibid.*

II. The Reader as Critic

Talking and Writing About Literature: Art as Transmission of Feeling

You will recall that one of the burning issues in the literary world of Turgenev's and Tolstoy's day was the question of the value of art to society. Although Turgenev took the position that art should be considered an end in itself and not just a means to social reform, he nevertheless produced in his sketches and longer works the kind of fiction that was influential in ameliorating the lot of the serfs. Tolstoy presents the interestingly ironic case of a great artist who began his career by writing simply for the pleasure and enjoyment of the tale, and who ended his life by repudiating the very art that had made him famous. As Prince Mirsky says in his account of Tolstoy's life, after his "conversion," Tolstoy regarded literature as the pursuit of dabblers, an unworthy expenditure of time unless it was aimed at teaching great spiritual truths.

In discussing Turgenev's differences with the critics of his time, you took the role of a reader who sided with one or the other literary factions. Now you can take the role of a fellow writer, an admirer of Tolstoy both as a person and an artist, an admirer who is increasingly concerned about Tolstoy's abandonment of his literary career to become a farm manager, teacher, and religious leader. This role was, in fact, the one that Turgenev, among other Russian writers and readers, played. Although Turgenev and Tolstoy had been friends as well as fellow artists, Tolstoy quarreled with Turgenev over a rather trifling personal matter. When Turgenev was dying, he wrote Tolstoy this generous letter:

> Dearest Leo Nikolaevich,
>
> It is long since I wrote to you. I have been in bed, and it is my deathbed. I cannot get well; that is no longer to be thought of. I write to you expressly to assure you how happy I have been to be your contemporary, and to present to you a last, a most urgent request. Dear friend, come back to literary work! This gift came to you whence all gifts come to us. Ah, how happy should I be if I could think that you would listen to my request. My friend, great writer of our land of Russia, grant me this request.[1]

---

[1] From "Turgenev and Tolstoy" from *Avowals* by *George Moore*, copyright by J. C. Medley and R. G. Medley. Reprinted by permission of Field Fisher & Co.

Tolstoy's Theories of Literature

What prompted Turgenev to write a letter like this? What theories had Tolstoy been advancing that seemed contrary to Turgenev's own ideals of art? Turgenev died in 1883, thirteen years before Tolstoy's famous book containing his artistic credo, *What Is Art?,* was published; but the ideas and actions that Tolstoy stated explicitly in this extended essay were the ideas by which he was living and writing since the time of the religious and personal crisis that occurred just a few years before Turgenev's death.

Long before the 1880's, in a speech to the Moscow Society of Lovers of Russian Literature (1859), Tolstoy expressed his regret that so many critics advocated literature that was directed only to social or civic reform. He pleaded for a more universal literature: "There is another literature, reflecting eternal and universal interest, the most precious, sincere consciousness of people, a literature accessible to every people and to all times, a literature without which no single people, gifted with strength and richness, has ever developed." But this statement is not to be construed as support for Turgenev's position that literature is an end in itself. Actually, in *What Is Art?* Tolstoy repudiated both the "art for art's sake" position and the view of the social critics that literature should be a handmaiden of the social sciences.

For a general idea of Tolstoy's theories, read the following excerpts from *What Is Art?* Use the questions that follow as you discuss these theories from the point of view of a fellow writer who considers Tolstoy Russia's greatest living novelist.

Tolstoy's Definition of Art

... beauty, or that which pleases us, can in no sense serve as the basis for the definition of art; nor can a series of objects which afford us pleasure serve as the model of what art should be. To see the aim and purpose of art in the pleasure we get from it is like assuming that the purpose and aim of food is the pleasure derived from consuming it. ...

In order correctly to define art, it is necessary, first of all, to cease to consider it as a means to pleasure and to consider it as one of the conditions of human life. Viewing it in this way we cannot fail to observe that art is one of the means of intercourse between man and man. Every work of art causes the receiver to enter into a certain kind of relationship both with him who produced, or is producing, the art, and with all those who, simultaneously, previously, or subsequently, receive the same artistic impression.

Speech, transmitting the thoughts and experience of men, serves as a means of union among them, and art acts in a similar manner. The peculiarity of this latter means of intercourse, distinguishing it from intercourse by means of words, consists in this, that whereas by words a man transmits his thoughts to another, by means of art he transmits his feelings. The activity of art is based on the fact that a man, receiving through his sense of hearing or sight another man's expression of feeling, is capable of experiencing the emotion which moved the man who expressed it. . . .

To evoke in oneself a feeling one has once experienced, and having evoked it in oneself, then, by means of movements, lines, colors, sounds, or forms expressed in words, so to transmit that feeling that others may experience the same feeling — that is the activity of art. Art is a human activity consisting in this, that one man consciously, by means of certain external signs, hands on to others feelings he has lived through, and that other people are infected by these feelings and also experience them.[1] [Leo Tolstoy]

1. How does Tolstoy differ from Turgenev in his definition of art?
2. Do you think the utilitarian critics of Tolstoy's day would have considered art "one of the conditions of human life" or a means to improve certain conditions of human life? Explain.
3. How, according to Tolstoy, is art related to speech? What is the difference in the sorts of communications we make in ordinary speech and the communications that make art possible?
4. Do you agree that literature — and indeed, all art — communicates feeling to you? Does it also communicate ideas? To provide support for your opinions, refer to any of the stories you have read by Turgenev or Tolstoy.

"Good" Art and "Bad" Art

Modern readers are aware that art transmits feelings, but most of us have accepted the idea that literature and the other arts may deal with any human experience, transmit any human feeling, and still be considered art. Most of us would probably agree that a story, a poem, a play, or a painting can be "about" something unpleasant or be written by a morally weak writer and still be "good" art. But here Tolstoy would disagree violently with us and with his writer-friends:

[1] From *What Is Art?*

If feelings bring men nearer the ideal their religion indicates, if they are in harmony with it and do not contradict it, they are good; if they estrange men from it and oppose it, they are bad.

How are we to decide what is good or bad in the subject matter of art? . . . it is by the standard of this religious perception of the age that the feelings transmitted by art have always been estimated. . . . The religious perception of our time, in its widest and most practical application, is the consciousness that our well-being, both material and spiritual, individual and collective, temporal and eternal, lies in the growth of brotherhood among all men — in their loving harmony with one another. . . . The expression "unite men with God and with one another" . . . indicates that the Christian union of man is that which unites all without exception. Art, all art, has this characteristic, that it unites people . . . the art of our time should be catholic in the original meaning of the word, i.e., universal, and therefore it should unite all men. And only two kinds of feeling do unite all men: first, feelings flowing from the perception of our sonship to God and of the brotherhood of man; and next, the simple feelings of common life, accessible to every one without exception. . . . Only these two kinds of feelings can now supply material for art good in its subject matter.[1] [*Leo Tolstoy*]

1. How does Tolstoy differentiate between "good" and "bad" art?
2. What are the two kinds of feelings that he finally came to believe were the only two human experiences worth transmitting?
3. Which of the stories that you have read seem to illustrate Tolstoy's own ideas of good and bad art? Are they the stories that seem to evoke the greatest intensity of response? Why or why not?

The Universality of Art

Tolstoy was not satisfied with limiting the kinds of subject matter that art could deal with — and the feelings it could transmit — to religious and moral experiences and experiences of the common man. He went even further by insisting that art should be understandable even to the uneducated; otherwise, it was not to be considered "good" or universal art.

Since the upper classes of the Christian nations lost faith in Church Christianity, the art of those upper classes has separated itself from the art of the rest of the people, and there have been two arts — the art of the people and genteel art. . . .

[1] *Ibid.*

I can only conclude that art, becoming ever more and more exclusive, has become more and more incomprehensible to an ever-increasing number of people, and that in this its progress toward greater and greater incomprehensibility, it has reached a point where it is understood by a very small number of the elect, and the number of these chosen people is ever becoming smaller and smaller. . . .

The assertion that art may be good art and at the same time incomprehensible to a great number of people is extremely unjust, and its consequences are ruinous to art itself. . . . Perverted art may not please everyone. . . .

Art is differentiated from activity of the understanding, which demands preparation and a certain sequence of knowledge by the fact that it acts on people independently of their state of development and education, that the charm of a picture, sounds, or of forms, infects any man whatever his plane of development.

The business of art lies just in this—to make that understood and felt which [otherwise] might be incomprehensible and inaccessible. Usually it seems to the recipient of a truly artistic impression that he knew the thing before but had been unable to express it.[1] [*Leo Tolstoy*]

1. Do you agree with Tolstoy that all "good" art should be understandable to all people?

2. At the present moment, what would you say are the two most popular kinds of literature for the "masses"? Are these kinds of literature, in your opinion, "good" art? Why or why not?

3. Have you read anything that you considered good literature, but which you also found difficult to understand at first? What do you think Tolstoy would have said about such a work?

4. How do Tolstoy's theories of art, expressed after his "conversion," help explain his repudiation of his early stories and novels?

Your Own Theories

Fortunately for us, Tolstoy's verdict about his own work has not influenced the opinion of other writers and of countless readers all over the world who consider the very novels and stories he repudiated among the greatest we have. In a sense, Tolstoy presents the ironic spectacle of an artist who was so talented that he produced great art in spite of himself.

[1]*Ibid.*

Read the comments that follow, comments by critics and writers who disagree with Tolstoy's theories but who admire his art. Then select any one of these comments as the basis of a round-table discussion or a short theme, in which you agree or disagree with Tolstoy or with the writer of the comments you have chosen to discuss. To support your opinions, refer to any works of literature you yourself consider "good."

1. ... for though the artist may teach, it must be indirectly: only with beautiful images and ideas may he draw men's minds from baser things. For man is made up of many needs ... and one of these is beauty, but Tolstoy looks upon art as a means whereby we communicate our ideas.[1] [*George Moore*]

2. This is one of Tolstoy's most prominent traits: he sees, and strongly feels, all physical details in nature and man. . . . And he loves this world, and all that he finds in it appeals to his senses and enchants him. No other writer in Russian literature is as fundamentally realistic as this moral preacher, and nobody is so attached to the concreteness, the texture of earthly existence. The overflowing vitality of Tolstoy found its expression in the richness of all his art. When he became convinced of the necessity of renunciation for the sake of his soul, he had to wage a war against the foundations of his nature, against the temptations of the world he cherished with genuine passion. He loved the flesh, the sense, the joys of being, and they are what convey such a feeling of life to his novels.[2] [*Marc Slonim*]

3. He [Tolstoy] had a marvelous sensuous understanding, and very little clarity of mind. So that, in his metaphysic, he had to deny himself, his own being, in order to escape his own disgust of what he had done to himself, and to escape admission of his own failure, which made all the later part of his life a crying falsity and shame. Reading the reminiscences of Tolstoy, one can only feel shame at the way Tolstoy denied all that was great in him, with vehement cowardice. He degraded himself infinitely ... elaborating his own weakness, blaspheming his own strength. It was only as a moralist and a personal being that Tolstoy was perverse. As a true artist, he worshiped every manifestation of pure, spon-

---

[1] From "Turgenev and Tolstoy" from *Avowals* by George Moore, copyright by J. C. Medley and R. G. Medley. Reprinted by permission of Field Fisher & Co.
[2] From *The Epic of Russian Literature: From Its Origins Through Tolstoy* by Marc Slonim, copyright 1950 by Oxford University Press, Inc. Reprinted by permission of the publisher.

taneous, passionate life, life kindled to vividness. As a perverse moralist with a sense of some subtle deficiency in himself, Tolstoy tries to insult and to damp out the vividness of life.[1] [*D. H. Lawrence*]

4. Tolstoy is the greatest depictor of that side of the flesh which approaches the spirit, and that side of the spirit which approaches the flesh, the mysterious border region where the struggle between the animal and the God in man takes place. Therein lies the struggle and the tragedy of his own life. He is a "man of the sense," half-heathen, half-Christian; neither to the full. In proportion as he recedes from this neutral ground in either direction ... toward the region of nature or as he essays the opposite region, human spirituality, almost set free from the body, released from animal nature, the region of pure thought, the power of artistic delineation in Tolstoy decreases, and in the end collapses, so that there are limits which are for him wholly unattainable. But within the limits of the purely natural man he is the supreme artist of the world.[2] [*D. S. Merezhkovsky*]

[1] From *Phoenix: The Posthumous Papers of D. H. Lawrence.*
[2] From *Tolstoy as Man and Artist.*

III. The Reader as Writer
"External" Characterization

Although critics disagree about which elements of Tolstoy's work are superior, most agree that Tolstoy was a great writer of fiction; and the quality many of them single out for praise is Tolstoy's ability to convey a sense of physical reality, a feeling of the immediacy and the tangibility of the concrete that actually makes the reader feel that he is a part of the action, that he would recognize the characters in Tolstoy's stories if he should ever meet them. One of the things we can learn from Tolstoy is a way of describing people that makes them come alive instead of remaining mere characters in a story.

You will recall that Turgenev's advice to young writers and his answers to critics implied his awareness of his own techniques. But Tolstoy, the master of realistic character portrayal, considered technique subordinate to the sincerity of the writer:

> There is one indubitable indication distinguishing real art from its counterfeit; namely, the infectiousness of art. If a man, without exercising effort and without altering his standpoint on reading, hearing, or seeing another man's work, experiences a mental condition which unites him with that man and with other people who also partake of that work of art, then the object evoking that condition is a work of art. . . . most of all is the degree of infectiousness of art increased by the degree of sincerity in the artist. . . . As soon as the spectator, hearer, or reader feels that the artist is infected by his own production, and writes, sings, or plays for himself, and not merely to act on others, this mental condition of the artist infects the receiver. . . .[1] [*Leo Tolstoy*]

The trouble with a statement like this is that no one can decide just what Tolstoy meant by "sincerity." Turgenev put his faith in *talent,* which manifested itself in the form of the work of art; Tolstoy put his in the sincere feelings of the artist—though fortunately, he was himself so talented that his feelings were transmitted regardless of the reader's

[1] From *What Is Art?*

awareness of his "sincerity." At any rate, if you are learning to write, and looking for help in writing, admonitions to be "sincere" are just the beginning. All great artists have tried to arrive at their particular "truth," and Tolstoy said that the hero of all his tales was truth itself. So the first step in portraying character realistically is to study the person you wish to describe carefully, as you observed the character or natural setting you wrote about during your study of Turgenev. But after you have selected a person, what aspects of that person should you observe? Since you cannot possibly tell everything you observe about your character, what principle of selection should you use? Tolstoy did not comment on his own technique to any extent, so let the critics who have studied his work help you.

Tolstoy's Technique: Revealing the Internal Through External Description

The Russian critic D. S. Merezhkovsky discusses Tolstoy's ways of treating descriptions and characterizations of people:

> In all literature there is no writer equal to Tolstoy in depicting the human body.... He is accurate, simple, and as short as possible, selecting only the few, small, unnoticed facial or personal features and producing them, not all at once, but gradually and one by one, distributing them over the whole course of the story, weaving them into the living web of the action.... All these scattered, single features complete and tally with one another, as in beautiful statues the shape of one limb always corresponds to the shape of another. The traits are so harmonized that they naturally and involuntarily unite, in the fancy of the reader, into one living, personal whole....
>
> The secret of his effects consists, among other things, in his noticing what others do not, as too commonplace, and which, when illumined by consciousness, precisely in consequence of this commonplace character, seems unusual. Thus he first made the discovery, apparently so simple and easy, but which for thousands of years had evaded all observers, that the smile is reflected, not only on the face, but in the sound of the voice, that the voice as well as the face can be smiling.... The living web of art consists in such small but striking observations and discoveries....
>
> The language of gesture, if less varied than words, is more direct, expressive, and suggestive. It is easier to lie in words than by gesture or facial expression. One glance, one wrinkle, one

quiver of a muscle in the face, may express the unutterable. Succeeding series of these unconscious, involuntary movements, impressing and stratifying themselves on the face and physique, form the expression of the face and the countenance of the body. Certain feelings impel us to corresponding movement, and, on the other hand, certain habitual movements impel to the corresponding *internal* states. The man who prays, folds his hands and bends his knees, and the man too who folds his hands and bends his knees is near to the praying frame of mind. Thus there exists an uninterrupted current, not only from the internal to the external, but from the external to the internal.

Tolstoy, with inimitable art, uses this convertible connection between the external and the internal. By the same law of mechanical sympathy which makes a stationary tense chord vibrate in answer to a neighboring chord, the sight of another crying or laughing awakes in us the desire to cry or laugh; we experience, when we read, similar descriptions in the nerves and muscles. And so by the motions of muscles or nerves we enter shortly and directly into the internal world of his characters, begin to live with them, and in them.[1] [*D. S. Merezhkovsky*]

To test Merezhkovsky's idea that Tolstoy shows us the internal frames of mind of his characters through description of their outer appearance and gestures, recall the description of Alyosha. How do his name, his physical appearance, his manner of moving, and his gestures indicate what kind of person he is? Does Tolstoy ever *tell* the reader what Alyosha is thinking, how he is feeling? How *does* he indicate Alyosha's patient disposition? At what point in the story, and by what action that Tolstoy mentions, does the reader know that Alyosha, too, feels disappointment and pain?

Tolstoy's Technique: Repetition of Detail

One of the most noticeable ways in which Tolstoy drives home the unity of a character's personality is through repeated mention of a particular gesture, habit, expression, or idea:

> Another variety of repetition, and one which is characteristically Tolstoyan, is the constant reiteration of some external detail designed to characterize an individual: a repetition which has nothing to do with the fact that the novel is long and the reader's memory is short. No one can fail to notice how the essence of a

[1] From *Tolstoy as Man and Artist*.

Tolstoyan character is distilled into a mannerism, a gesture, a physical feature, an outward and visible sign which recurs continually and is the permanent property of that character. Such attributes are not repeated to remind us of something we may have forgotten.... They resemble rather musical *leitmotivs*. They identify the person by something more meaningful than a name, and something less ossified than a stock epithet. The repeated reference to Napoleon's small white hands, Helen's bare white shoulders, Princess Marya's[1] radiant eyes is not a conscious epic device. It is a combination of the assertion of a permanent, individualizing feature with the expression of a moral judgment. As well as suggesting what is most significant about his heroes, Tolstoy tries to evoke in the reader at the same time a positive or negative response to them.... This type of repetition of external detail, involving as it does the frequent recurrence of identical words, is an example of how closely related a novelist's language and character are. Words are repeated because aspects of character have to be repeated, and once the words chosen to convey those aspects are altered, the characterization itself is altered, however slightly....

The crux of Tolstoy's thought is that every human being has features which mark him off from every other human being. While at the same time human beings in the mass exhibit a sameness, a uniformity, a predictability, an inevitability which is conveyed in Tolstoy's language by the repetition of "as is always the case," "as all people do," or "all this must be so."... Tolstoy repeats the same words because he wants to repeat the same ideas.[2] [*R. F. Christian*]

Tolstoy himself felt that sometimes he was too heavy-handed in his piling up of detail:

In comparing himself with Pushkin[3] as an artist, Tolstoy said that the difference between them, among other things, was this, that Pushkin in depicting a characteristic detail does it lightly, not troubling whether it will be noticed or understood by the reader, while he himself, as it were, stood over the reader with this artistic detail, until he had set it forth distinctly. The comparison is acute. He *does* "stand over the reader," not afraid of sickening

---

[1]Napoleon, Helen, and Princess Marya are characters in Tolstoy's most famous novel, *War and Peace*.
[2]From "Language" from *Tolstoy's War and Peace, A Study* by R. F. Christian, published in 1962 by The Clarendon Press, Oxford. Reprinted by permission of the publisher.
[3]*Pushkin:* Alexander Pushkin (1799–1837), Russian poet.

him, and flogs in the trait, repeats, lays on colors, layer after layer, thickening them more and more, where Pushkin, barely touching, slides his brush over in light and careless, but invariably sure and faithful strokes. It seems as if Pushkin, especially in prose harsh, and even niggardly, gave little, that we might want more. But Tolstoy gives so much that there is nothing more for us to want; we are sated, if not glutted.[1] [*D. S. Merezhkovsky*]

How many times in "Alyosha" does Tolstoy mention Alyosha's smile or laugh? How do the many references to Alyosha's smiles heighten the effect of the one moment of pain that the reader knows Alyosha feels?

Next observe the times that Tolstoy refers to Varenka's smile and to her father's smile in "After the Ball." Do the smiles of Alyosha, Varenka, and the officer indicate the same feelings? What *are* the personality traits that these three very different smiles connote? How does Tolstoy make the reader aware of the differences in kinds of people through the kinds of smiles and the situations in which they occur?

In "After the Ball," Tolstoy refers on several occasions to the colonel's boots. What are these occasions? What traits of the colonel do these references to his boots betray? How does Tolstoy use a similar repeated detail about the young daughter to point up a contrast between the colonel and his child?

Look through "The Raid" and notice what gestures, ideas, and mannerisms characterize the young lieutenant. What recurrent question does the narrator pose to himself and others? How is the question related to the theme of the entire story as well as to the characterization of the young man? How is this deviation from Tolstoy's usual habit—of not letting the reader into the character's mind except through a description of external details—a result of the point of view from which this story is told? How is Tolstoy's use of Khlopov's pipe similar to that of the colonel's boots? How does the pipe represent a different kind of person from the wearer of the boots?

Writing a Characterization from an "External" Point of View

To try your hand at learning from Tolstoy, as you learned from Turgenev earlier, select a person you know quite well whom you have seen at a time of stress or good fortune. Try to feel your way into the person's emotions as if you yourself had experienced the sorrow, dismay, fear, joy, or whatever emotion your character indicated through observable gestures, words, facial characteristics, or other external manifestations

[1] From *Tolstoy as Man and Artist*.

of inner states of mind. Next, list the external details that seem most clearly to demonstrate the emotion you wish to convey. These should be the gestures, expression, and physical mannerisms and traits you know to be most typical and characteristic of the character's personality. Write a short description of the person at the moment of his great emotional tension. By describing external evidence only, convey the personality of the character about whom you are writing as well as the typical way in which he or she is reacting to a particular feeling at a particular time.

A final word of advice: Use the present tense and put yourself in the position of a first-person narrator, like the young observer in "The Raid."

PART FOUR

Theodore Dostoevsky

THEODORE DOSTOEVSKY

If Turgenev's search was for beauty and Tolstoy's for truth, then the quest of the third great Russian writer of fiction—Theodore Dostoevsky—was for the freedom of the inner man in each of us. Where Turgenev observes and imposes on his observations his own reaction to people and places, and Tolstoy records human experience in generous detail or strips life to a few moral and religious precepts, Dostoevsky conducts his search in the laboratory of the human subconscious. Turgenev and Tolstoy were aristocrats who wrote about the lives of their own class and of the peasants their families owned and later cared for; Dostoevsky was the representative of the physically, mentally, and emotionally impoverished and rejected. As you read the following account of Dostoevsky's life, contrast his background and the kind of problems he faced with those of his two great contemporaries.

Dostoevsky

MARC SLONIM

One May evening in 1845 Dmitri Grigorovich, a young nobleman, brought a manuscript, written by a friend of his and entitled *Poor Folk*, to Nekrasov,[1] who was about to publish a literary anthology. They read the manuscript aloud. The pathetic story of a humble clerk and his self-sacrificing love made Nekrasov so enthusiastic that he wanted to rush out and make the author's acquaintance forthwith. Grigorovich objected that the author must be asleep at that late hour. "Who cares?" retorted Nekrasov. "We'll wake him up. This is more important than sleep."

And so, at four o'clock in the morning, they were congratulating and embracing a baffled young man named Fedor[2] Dostoevsky. The impression made on the latter by this surprising visit was everlasting. "This was the most delightful moment of all my life," he wrote later. Glory it-

---

[1]*Nekrasov:* Nikolai Alekseyevich Nekrasov (1821–1877), Russian poet, editor, and publisher.
[2]*Fedor:* a variant spelling of the Anglicized "Theodore," just as "Lev" is a variant of "Leo."

"Dostoevsky" from *The Epic of Russian Literature: From Its Origins Through Tolstoy* by Marc Slonim, copyright 1950 by Oxford University Press, Inc. Reprinted by permission of the publisher.

self descended upon him and illuminated his poor lodgings amid the tremulous pallor of a St. Petersburg dawn.

Dostoevsky, like Turgenev, was a man of the forties, brought up in an atmosphere of idealistic philosophy and romantic longings. His background, however, was completely different from that of the wealthy patrician. He came from an impoverished family of obscure gentry. His paternal grandfather was a priest; his father, a former army surgeon, who was on the staff of a Moscow Hospital for the poor, had married a merchant's daughter, a kindhearted and meek woman who bore him eight children. Fedor Mikhailovich Dostoevsky, born in 1821, spent a rather gloomy childhood in the hospital yards and in the low-ceiling rooms of the doctor's cottage, filled with religious pictures and icons. His father, an irritable and morose man, ruled his large family with an iron hand: his sons had to ask permission to sit in his presence. The strict discipline, the unyielding paternal authority, the religious devotion, and the whole traditional way of life in the Dostoevsky household were more typical of the merchant class than of the petty nobility, which explains certain features of Fedor's character and what he himself later called his "lack of form," of *savoir faire*.

At the age of seventeen he was sent to the Academy of Military Engineering in St. Petersburg, where he found a regime of rigid formality, severe punishments, and strict drilling. He suffered atrociously because of his poverty, his ill health, and the mockery of his companions, who laughed at the clumsiness and shyness of this silent, nervous, odd-looking youth. His only joy was reading: he was passionately fond of Sir Walter Scott and E. T. A. Hoffmann, knew Schiller by heart, read the French novelists avidly, adored Pushkin, and later, Gogol. He wrote himself—historical tales, dramas, poems in a high-flown style—and was making bold plans for other literary undertakings. A commissioned officer by 1842 and a draftsman at the engineering section of the War Department by 1843, he nevertheless had very little liking for his position and finally resigned with the intention of devoting himself entirely to literature. The following years he lived in utter destitution, earning a few rubles by translating Balzac, his favorite writer, and the works of several French Romantics, paying frequent visits to the pawnshops, and forced, on cold winter nights, to seek shelter in disreputable dives. On those rare occasions when he came into some money, as when he received his inheritance from his father, he spent it on theater tickets, gay suppers, and gambling. His life was as irregular and unpredictable as his mind: he could pass, with amazing rapidity, from elation to despondency and from wonderful hopes to grim despair. The success of *Poor Folk,* published in

1846 and acclaimed as an example of "Realistic Humanism," had not improved his financial status but it did open to him the doors of literary salons, where he lost his heart to the attractive Panaeva and met a number of prominent writers, Turgenev among them. However, his next novel, *The Double,* as well as some of his short stories, did not please the critics — and apparently not the readers either.

In 1846–47 Dostoevsky went through a period of discouragement and inner crisis. His vanity had been hurt by hostile criticism, he was burdened with debts, exhausted by work, exasperated by the bondage of his literary commitments — mostly translations, the main source of his meager income. His health, undermined by bad food, cold and damp lodgings, an irregular, occasionally dissipated life, was also impaired by hypochondria and what he called "fits of mystical horror." His irritability, his outbreaks of lust or his passion for gambling, alternating with repentance and abasement, his pathological sensitivity and the contradictions of his character worried his few friends. But he also enchanted them by imparting to them his fantasies and wonderful dreams.

In 1848 most of these were fervent visions of a regenerated mankind and an ideal future. Under the influence of Belinsky[1] he became interested in social problems and read Saint-Simon, Cabet, Fourier, Owen, and other Utopian-Socialists. He joined the circle of Petrashevsky,[2] moved everybody to tears by his comments on the Christian-Socialist Lamennais, and made inspired speeches — without ever suspecting that all his words were being recorded by an agent of the secret police.

In April 1849, all the members of the circle were arrested and imprisoned in the Fortress of Saints Peter and Paul. The imprisonment worsened Dostoevsky's physical condition, and it is almost certain he had his first fit of epilepsy while under solitary confinement. Eight months later, on December 22, the prisoners were taken to Semenovsky Place and lined up before a scaffold surrounded by stakes. Despite the fierce frost they were stripped to their shirts and, shivering, were compelled to listen to sentence of death for all of them. The first group of three, sentenced to be shot, wearing white shrouds and blindfolded, were tied to stakes. Dostoevsky waited for his turn in a second group. The firing squad pointed its rifles at the victims.

Then, suddenly, the commanding officer waved a white handkerchief: the execution was stopped at the last moment, and a commutation of the

---

[1]*Belinsky:* V. G. Belinsky (1811–1848), important Russian literary critic who started out as a member of a group of young "idealist" authors and ultimately became spokesman for a new realistic and didactic literature. See also pages 5–7.

[2]*Petrashevsky:* Mikhail V. Petrashevsky (1821–1866), leader of a progressive political circle of the 1840's.

sentence, at the "Czar's merciful behest," was proclaimed. The bonds of the three men were loosed. The hair of one of the three had turned white; another had gone mad. Dostoevsky, under the new sentence, was condemned to four years of hard labor and four years of military service as a private in Siberia. On Christmas Eve, wearing chains weighing ten pounds each, his body covered with sores, he was put into an open sleigh which, through blizzards and storms, was to take him all the way to Siberia.

The journey lasted two months. In the prison at Omsk he found himself in the company of murderers whose nostrils had been torn out by the public executioner, of criminals branded on their foreheads, of grimacing and blaspheming humanity jangling its chains. For four years he had to endure the heavy toil, the dirt and darkness of prison barracks, the inhuman regulations: the prisoners were flogged if they did not sleep on their right side or moaned too loudly at night. The only book Dostoevsky was allowed to read was the New Testament, and all his religous feelings, dormant during his association with Belinsky and Petrashevsky, emerged with redoubled force.

In the letter to his brother ten days after his term was over (February 1854), Dostoevsky wrote:

> My stomach was ruined. I was repeatedly ill. As a result of my bad nerves I became epileptic. And I have rheumatism in my legs. I shall not tell you—it would take too long—what happened to my soul, my beliefs, my mind and heart, during these years. But the constant concentration on my inner self, to which I escaped from bitter reality, bore its fruit.

By comparison with the penal servitude the life of a private in the garrison at Semipalatinsk, on the border of Siberia and Central Asia, seemed to Dostoevsky a great relief: he could at last correspond with his brothers and friends and could read and write.

In 1855, he started to write the first drafts of works that were to appear later (*The Village of Stepanchikovo, Notes from the House of the Dead, The Humiliated and the Wronged*). He felt attracted, at this period, by Maria Isaeva, an intelligent and sensitive woman of twenty-eight, who sympathized with the former convict and showed an almost maternal affection toward him. After the death of Maria's husband, Dostoevsky proposed to her, but he had to go through many sufferings and difficulties before their marriage in 1857. The jealous Dostoevsky reproached his wife with not responding adequately to his frantic passion, and the marriage proved a failure. By 1859 Dostoevsky's love seemed extinct, while Maria's health (she had tuberculosis) deteriorated rapidly. In the following years he took care of her as he would have of an unhappy and lonely friend.

By 1858 Dostoevsky was at last permitted to return to Russia proper and to publish his writings. Now he was free and, after a break of nine years, could resume the lifework he had begun as a young enthusiast. In his late thirties his past was already extraordinarily oppressive; he looked old and tired, this silent and grim man with a short and stocky body, a big head set on broad shoulders, a nervous tic on his thin, bloodless lips, and with a sunken, yellowish and tormented face.

When, in 1859, Dostoevsky moved to St. Petersburg, the intelligentsia and particularly the youth, stirred by expectations of reforms, warmly greeted the writer who had been a political martyr. They learned soon enough that he was not their man. His devotion to the Church, his Slavophile sympathies, his sharp anti-Nihilist and antirevolutionary attitude all disappointed the radicals. His popularity as a writer, however, grew steadily. After "Uncle's Dream," a short story, and the satirical short novel, *The Village of Stepanchikovo* (1860), his novel *The Humiliated and the Wronged* (1861) was called by Dobrolybuv the best book of the year. It was followed by *Notes from the House of the Dead*, which was widely read and highly appreciated by liberal Westernizers as a realistic exposé of prison life and by the Slavophiles for its faith in the Russian people.

By this time Dostoevsky was strongly attracted to journalism. In 1861 he founded, with his brother Mikhail, the review *Time,* wherein he preached "the reunion of educated society with the people" and prophesied that Russia would save the West.

Unlike Leo Tolstoy and Turgenev, for whom literature never was a profession, Dostoevesky was a professional writer: writing was his daily routine, the very essence of his life, and his only way of earning a living. Like most people of his time, he was convinced that the artist's supreme duty was to assume political and moral leadership, that one should write about life and respond to the calls of contemporary events. He fervently defended these ideas in numerous articles, and they made him popular with the Radicals and Nihilists.

All the ordeals he had gone through could not break his vitality and his tempestuous temperament. As his friend and biographer Strakhov remarked, Dostoevsky *felt* his ideas and expressed them with the same inspired enthusiasm he had displayed years before, at the meetings of the Petrashevsky circle. But now an emotional climax would often be followed by an epileptic seizure: he would stop suddenly in the middle of a sentence, a wild scream would escape from his distorted lips, and he would fall down in convulsions. Each fit made him ill for two or three days, and sometimes these seizures occurred weekly, or even at intervals of a few days. They were preceded by moments of elation and creative energy, during which he wrote his best pages or kept his friends spellbound with his talk. Vladimir Solovyov, the philosopher, said that after two hours of conversation with Dostoevsky one felt as if drugged or in a state of voluptuous torment, of feverish inebriation.

His disease was aggravated by his restless existence, his worries and ceaseless work. *Time* was suspended by the government; publishers who had advanced him money were pressing him hard for copy; he had endless financial and moral troubles; his wife, staying in a provincial town, was dying—and, at the same time, he was desperately in love with Appollinaria Suslova, a beautiful, self-willed, and capricious young woman in her twenties. The story of this love reads like one of Dostoevsky's own novels: the proud Suslova served as a model for the figures of Paulina in *The Gambler*, of Nastasya Philippovna in *The Idiot*, of Lizaveta in *The Possessed,* among others. . . .

Dostoevsky [was] supplanted in Suslova's heart by less interesting . . . lovers, and she did not hide this from her former friend. . . . The agony of a dying love was made more painful for him by the humiliating consequences of his gambling madness. An inveterate gambler since early youth, he lost everything in the casinos of Germany and had to beg his distant friends for help. After the death of his wife in 1865 he went abroad again, officially to attend to his health but actually to meet Suslova, who had definitely settled in Paris. The few months of flaring passion, quarrels, ruptures, renewed attraction, short reconciliations coupled with the most humiliating concessions, ended in a final break and a fever of gambling that left him penniless. He returned to St. Petersburg completely exhausted, physically and mentally.

His new venture, the review *Epoch,* had to fold up, and its bankruptcy left Dostoevsky with heavy financial obligations. His brother Mikhail died, and he had to provide for his family as well as to help Maria's boy, his stepson. In this dreadful situation, harassed by creditors and publishers, Dostoevsky published his *Notes from the Underground* (1864), *Crime and Punishment* (1866), proclaimed his masterpiece by stunned critics and deeply impressed readers, and *The Gambler.*

The last, a highly revealing autobiographical work, he had dictated to his young and pretty stenographer, Anna Snitkina, who impressed him by her kindness and simplicity. A month later he proposed to her and they were married in 1867. Anna became a good angel to the man she loved and admired with rare devotion. She gave him the feeling of security he so badly needed and made his life altogether easier and more normal. He fully appreciated her affection and returned it with all the tenderness and love he had.

After the marriage they went abroad to escape the creditors and to work in peace. The first year away was not too bright: they had to live in poverty, almost in destitution; Dostoevsky was as addicted to roulette as ever; and their first child died. But nothing could stop the creative urge: he kept writing *The Idiot* (published in 1868) and made numerous plans for new novels. In 1871-72 *The Possessed*, that violent attack against the revolutionaries and Nihilists, provoked endless polemics and contained what was little more than a caricature of Turgenev—under the name of Karmazinov—a vain and hypocritical literary lion.

The years between 1871 and his death a decade later were the most quiet and normal period of Dostoevsky's life. He led a more or less regular existence under the watchful eye of his wife, who bore him three children. Although the wolf frequently returned to his door, his financial situation improved greatly as the sales of his books kept mounting. In the seventies he was celebrated throughout the country as Russia's outstanding writer. He continued to work in his usual, intensive way. In 1876 he began the monthly publication of *A Writer's Diary*—a miscellany, written entirely by himself and consisting of philosophical or literary essays and articles on current events, occasionally interspersed with some short story, such as "The Boy at Christ's Christmas Tree" or "The Muzhik Marey." Despite its special character the *Diary* had fourteen thousand subscribers. Although its political articles alienated the liberals, Dostoevsky's nationalism was of so individual and peculiar a kind that they seemed ready to discuss his ideas without any prejudice. Also in 1876, he published *A Raw Youth* and, by 1879, had finished his most important book, *The Brothers Karamazov*—the result of many years of work.

In 1880 his popularity reached its zenith. His speech at the unveiling of the monument to Pushkin in Moscow, when Dostoevsky expressed his faith in Russia's great destiny and its universal role in the reunion of all nations, won rapturous acclaim. Russian society suddenly realized that Dostoevsky, like Pushkin, was a truly national writer, an artist of titanic stature and, above all political dissensions, the exponent of the unexpressed hopes of many generations. But this success was the last Dostoevsky was to enjoy.

In January 1881, he fell ill and had a pulmonary hemorrhage, followed by frequent losses of consciousness. In a moment of lucidity he asked his wife to open at random the New Testament he had brought back from his Siberian exile. She read aloud: "Suffer it to be so now: for thus it becometh us to fulfil all righteousness:" "You see," said Dostoevsky, "suffer it to be now—which means I am to die."

And he closed his eyes in resignation. He passed away on the evening of the same day.

FOR WRITING OR DISCUSSION

1. Describe Dostoevsky's social and educational background. How did it differ from that of Turgenev and Tolstoy? What professional experience, including his writing, did Dostoevsky have? How did he make his living?

2. When, and on what occasions, was Dostoevsky in close contact with the very poor, the criminal, and the other "disinherited" people of Russia? What effect did these contacts have on the subject matter of his stories and on his own personality?

3. Describe Dostoevsky's arrest and imprisonment. How did his political and religious views change as a result of these experiences?

4. What were the physical and personal obstacles to Dostoevsky's happiness? How did his second wife help him overcome them?

5. How did his professional aspirations conflict with his personal habits?

6. What was the public reaction to Dostoevsky's work by the time of his death?

I. Reading Literature

TERROR

What sets Dostoevsky apart from all other novelists of his day is a fearful experience: his arrest, condemnation to death, reprieve on the scaffold; then eight years of prison labor and military service in Siberia.[1] [*Henry Gifford*]

As you learned in Marc Slonim's biographical sketch, Dostoevsky was at one point a member of the Petrashevsky Circle, a group of liberals who met to exchange ideas and make plans for the particular form of a socialist Utopia in which they believed. The Petrashevsky followers were evidently quite ineffectual, and scarcely the type of wild-eyed revolutionaries we usually think of as prototypes of radicals. But they were made to suffer nonetheless. The terrible experience of the mock execution turned the hair of one of the prisoners white, caused insanity in another, and ultimately resulted in Dostoevsky's turning from the liberals to support the czar and the Orthodox Church.

One of Russia's most highly regarded poets of the present day, Yevgeny Yevtushenko, has memorialized the event of the execution in the following poem. As you read it, try to imagine the feeling experienced by Dostoevsky and his fellow prisoners as they witnessed the following scene.

Followers of Petrashevsky[2]

YEVGENY YEVTUSHENKO

Drums,
      drums ...
Petrashevsky's followers are being taken to the scaffold!
Hoods for hanging,

---

[1]From Henry Gifford, *The Novel in Russia*. London: Hutchinson & Co., 1964.
[2]*Petrashevsky:* Mikhail V. Petrashevsky (1821–1866) was a leader of liberal movements in the nineteenth century and of a progressive political circle in the 1840's.
"Followers of Petrashevsky" from *Bratsk Station and Other New Poems* by Yevgeny Yevtushenko, copyright 1966 by Sun Books Pty. Ltd. Reprinted by permission of Doubleday & Company, Inc.

                        hoods for hanging,
    like shrouds
                to their heels.
    The army line
                cold, infernal,
    and They —
                standing shoulder to shoulder.
    There is an evil smell of the Senate square,
    on the Semenorvsky parade ground.
    The same snow —
                lying in blinding sheets,
    and blizzards with the very same whine.
    In each real Russian there is
    somewhere hidden a Decembrist.[1]
    Drums,
            drums . . .
    left-right,
            left-right . . .
    There will still be barricades,
    but for the time being —
                only the scaffold.
    But for the time being —
                alarmingly,
    the light of Russia is being executed by darkness,
    the hoods,
            the hoods
    are being pulled over their eyes.
    But one,
            wrapped up in the blizzard,
    silent and aloof,
    secretly sees all of Russia
    through the futile hood.
    Across Russia goes Rogozhin;[2] tattered, face distorted,
    among visions and lights,
                crying, blustering.
    Myshkin dashes across her,
    and among her banks and granaries,
    among her prisons and orphans,

[1] *Decembrist:* one who conspired against Czar Nicholas I of Russia on his accession to the throne in December 1825.
[2] *Rogozhin:* a character in Dostoevsky's *The Idiot*, of which Prince Myshkin is the hero.

Alyosha Karamazov[1]
roams like a peaceful monk.
Hangmen, undoubtedly
fear doesn't let you understand
that you —
             not those under sentence of death —
have hoods over your eyes.
You don't see anything of Russia
her nakedness,
              her bareness,
her pains,
        her strength,
her freedom,
         her beauty . . .

Horses are foaming!
                      Horses are foaming!
At the gallop comes the Czar's decree!
Sentence of death has been changed
for sentence of life . . .

But only one man
              pitifully —
in a fit of humiliation
tearing wildly at his coat,
cried out praise to the Czar.
Clumsily he made haste,
tearing hooks and loops,
but the coat would not come off,
grown to his body, forever.

Drums,
        drums . . .
Those whose will is not strong enough
are fated to be slaves, to be slaves,
fated to be slaves forever!
Drums,
        drums
and men of high rank.
Oh, in old Russia,
              what jolly puppet shows!

[1]*Alyosha Karamazov:* one of the brothers in *The Brothers Karamazov.*

FOR WRITING OR DISCUSSION

1. Reread the section in Slonim's biography that describes the event that is central in this poem. How was the execution to be accomplished? What time of year was it? How does Yevtushenko indicate the time of year? What images in the poem contribute to the reader's impression of the weather? of the participants in the drama?
2. What in the poem do the hangmen represent?
3. What is ironic about the last line of the poem? Do you think Yevtushenko might be criticizing some of the tendencies in modern Soviet Russia, even though he is a loyal citizen of the Soviet Union?
4. What in your previous reading might lead you to believe that Dostoevsky was the man who "cried out praise to the Czar"? What reason does the poet imply for the failure to remove that "coat" forever?

Dostoevsky's Account of Prison: A Letter to His Brother

Dostoevsky was not permitted to write to his family during his imprisonment in Siberia, but in a letter to his brother written later, during his military service at Semipalatinsk, he described his prison experiences with heartrending vividness.

February 22, 1854

At last I can talk with you somewhat more explicitly, and, I believe, in a more reasonable manner. But before I write another line I *must* ask you: tell me, for God's sake, why you have never written me a single syllable till now? Could I have expected this from you? Believe me, in my lonely and isolated state, I sometimes fell into utter despair, for I believed that you were no longer alive; through whole nights I would brood upon what was to become of your children, and I cursed my fate because I could not help them. . . .

How can I impart to you what is now in my mind—the things I thought, the things I did, the convictions I acquired, the conclusions I came to? I cannot even attempt the task. It is absolutely impossible. I don't like to leave a piece of work half done; to say only a part is to say nothing. At any rate, you now have my detailed report in your hands: read it, and get from it what you will. It is my duty to tell you all, and so I will begin with my recollections. Do you remember how we parted

From "Dostoevsky in His Correspondence" from *Dostoevsky* by André Gide. All Rights Reserved. Copyright © 1961 by New Directions Publishing Corporation. Reprinted by permission of the publisher.

from each other, dear beloved fellow? You had scarcely left me when we three, Dourov, Yastryembsky, and I, were led out to have the irons put on. Precisely at midnight on that Christmas Eve (1849) did chains touch me for the first time. They weigh about ten pounds, and make walking extraordinarily difficult. Then we were sent into open sledges, each with a gendarme; and so, in four sledges, the orderly opening the procession, we left Petersburg. I was heavy-hearted, and the many different impressions filled me with confused and uncertain sensations. My heart beat with a peculiar flutter, and that numbed its pain. Still, the fresh air was reviving in its effect, and, since it is usual before all new experiences to be aware of a curious vivacity and eagerness, so I was at the bottom quite tranquil. I looked attentively at all the festively lit houses of Petersburg and said good-by to each. They drove us past your abode, and at Krayevsky's the windows were brilliantly lit. You had told me he was giving a Christmas party and tree, and that your children were going to it, with Emilie Fyodorovna; I did feel dreadfully sad as we passed that house. I took leave, as it were, of the little ones. I felt so lonely for them, and even years afterwards I often thought of them with tears in my eyes. We were driven beyond Yaroslavl; after three or four stations we stopped, in the first gray of morning, at Schlüsselburg, and went into an inn. There we drank tea with as much avidity as if we had not touched anything for a week. After the eight months' captivity, sixty versts[1] in a sledge gave us appetites of which, even today, I think with pleasure.

I was in a good temper. Dourov chattered incessantly, and Yastryembsky expressed unwonted apprehensions for the future. We all laid ourselves out to become better acquainted with our orderly. He was a good old man, very friendly toward us: a man who had seen a lot of life; he had traveled all over Europe with dispatches. On the way he showed us many kindnesses. His name was Kusma Prokofyevitch Prokofyev. Among other things he let us have a covered sledge, which was very welcome, for the frost was fearful.

The second day was a holiday; the drivers, who were changed at the various stations, wore cloaks of gray German cloth and bright red belts; in the village streets there was not a soul to be seen. It was a splendid winter day. They drove us through the remote parts of the Petersburg, Novgorod, and Yaroslavl Governments. There were quite insignificant little towns, at great distances from one another. But as we were passing through on a holiday, there was always plenty to eat and drink; we drove —drove terribly. We were warmly dressed, it is true, but we had to sit

[1] *verst:* a Russian measure of distance—about two thirds of a mile.

for ten hours at a time in the sledges, halting at only five or six stations; it was almost unendurable. I froze to the marrow, and could scarcely thaw myself in the warm rooms at the stations. Strange to say, the journey completely restored me to health. Near Perm, we had a frost of 40 degrees[1] during some of the nights. I don't recommend that to you. It was highly disagreeable.

Mournful was the moment when we crossed the Urals. The horses and sledges sank deep in the snow; a snowstorm was raging. We got out of the sledge—it was night—and waited, standing, till they were extricated. All about us whirled the snowstorm. We were standing on the confines of Europe and Asia; before us lay Siberia and the mysterious future—behind us, our whole past; it was very melancholy. Tears came to my eyes. On the way, the peasants would stream out of all the villages to see us; and although we were fettered, prices were trebled to us at all the stations. Kusma Prokofyevitch took half our expenses on himself, though we tried hard to prevent him; in this way each of us, during the whole journey, spent only fifteen rubles.

On January 12, 1850, we came to Tobolsk. After we had been paraded before the authorities, and searched, in which proceeding all our money was taken from us, myself, Dourov and Yastryembsky were taken into one cell; the others, Spejechynov, etc., who had arrived before us, were in another section, and during the whole time we hardly once saw each other. I should like to tell you more of our six days' stay in Tobolsk, and of the impression it made upon me. But I haven't room here. I will only tell you that the great compassion and sympathy which was shown to us there, made up to us, like a big piece of happiness, for all that had gone before. The prisoners of former days[2] (and still more their wives) cared for us as if they had been our kith and kin. Those noble souls, tested by five-and-twenty years of suffering and self-sacrifice! We saw them but seldom, for we were very rigidly guarded; still they sent us clothes and provisions, they comforted and encouraged us. I had brought far too few clothes, and had bitterly repented it; but they sent me clothes. Finally we left Tobolsk, and reached Omsk in three days.

While I was in Tobolsk, I gathered information about my future superiors. They told me that the Commandant was a very decent fellow, but that the Major, Krivzov, was an uncommon brute, a petty tyrant, a drunkard, a trickster—in short, the greatest horror that can be imagined. From the very beginning, he called both Dourov and me blockhead, and

[1] *frost of 40 degrees:* that is, forty degrees below zero.
[2] *prisoners . . . days:* that is, the Decembrists, who conspired against Czar Nicholas I.

vowed to chastise us bodily at the first transgression. He had already held his position for two years, and done the most hideous and unsanctioned things; two years later he was court-martialed for them. So God protected me from him! He used to come to us mad drunk (I never once saw him sober), and would seek out some inoffensive person and flog him on the pretext that he—the prisoner—was drunk.

Often he came at night and punished at random—say, because such and such a one was sleeping on his left side instead of his right, or because he talked or moaned in his sleep—in fact, anything that occurred to his drunken mind. I should have had to break out in the long run against such a man as that, and it was he who wrote the monthly reports of us to Petersburg.

I spent the whole four years behind dungeon walls, and only left the prison when I was taken on "hard labor." The work was hard, though not always; sometimes in bad weather, in rain, or in winter during the unendurable frosts, my strength would forsake me. Once I had to spend four hours at a piece of extra work, and in such frost that the quicksilver froze; it was perhaps 40 degrees below zero. One of my feet was frostbitten. We all lived together in one barrack room. Imagine an old, crazy, wooden building, that should long ago have been broken up as useless. In the summer it is unbearably hot, in the winter unbearably cold. All the boards are rotten; on the ground filth lies an inch thick; every instant one is in danger of slipping and coming down. The small windows are so frozen over that even by day one can hardly read. The ice on the panes is three inches thick. The ceilings drip, there are drafts everywhere. We are packed like herrings in a barrel. The stove is heated with six logs of wood, but the room is so cold that the ice never thaws; the atmosphere is unbearable—and so through all the winter long.

In the same room, the prisoners wash their linen, and thus make the place so wet that one scarcely dares to move. From twilight till morning we are forbidden to leave the barrack room; the doors are barricaded; in the anteroom a great wooden trough for the calls of nature is placed; this makes one almost unable to breathe. All the prisoners stink like pigs; they say that they can't help it, for they must live, and are but men. We sleep upon bare boards; each man was allowed one pillow only. We covered ourselves with short sheepskins, and our feet were outside the covering all the time. It was thus that we froze night after night. Fleas, lice, and other vermin by the bushel. In the winter we got thin sheepskins to wear, which didn't keep us warm at all, and boots with short legs; thus equipped, we had to go out into the frost.

To eat we got bread and cabbage soup; the soup should, by the regulations, have contained a quarter pound of meat per head; but they put in sausage meat, and so I never came across a piece of genuine flesh. On feast days we got porridge, but with scarcely any butter. On fast days, cabbage and nothing else. My stomach went utterly to pieces, and I suffered tortures from indigestion.

From all this you can see yourself that one couldn't live there at all without money; if I had had none, I should most assuredly have perished; no one could endure such a life. But every convict does some sort of work and sells it, thus earning, every single one of them, a few pence. I often drank tea and bought myself a piece of meat; it was my salvation. It was quite impossible to do without smoking, for otherwise the stench would have choked one. All these things were done behind the backs of the officials.

I was often in the hospital. My nerves were so shattered that I had some epileptic fits—however, that was not often. I have rheumatism in my legs now, too. But except for that, I feel right well. Add to all these discomforts the fact that it was almost impossible to get one's self a book, and that when I did get one, I had to read it on the sly; that all around me was incessant malignity, turbulence, and quarreling; then perpetual espionage, and the impossibility *of ever being alone,* even for an instant—and so without variation for four long years. You'll believe me when I tell you I was not happy! And imagine, in addition, the ever-present dread of drawing down some punishment on myself, the irons, and the utter oppression of spirits—and you have the picture of my life.

I won't even try to tell you what transformations were undergone by my soul, my faith, my mind, and my heart, in those four years. It would be a long story. Still, the eternal concentration, the escape into myself from bitter reality, did bear its fruit. I now have many new needs and hopes of which I never thought in other days. But all this will be pure enigma for you, so I'll pass to other things. I will say only one word: do not forget me, and do help me! I need books and money. Send them me, for heaven's sake.

Omsk is a hateful hole. There is hardly a tree there. In summer, heat and winds that bring sandstorms; in winter, snowstorms. I have scarcely seen anything of the country around. The place is dirty, almost exclusively inhabited by military, and dissolute to the last degree. I mean the common people. If I hadn't discovered some human beings here, I should have gone utterly to the dogs.

Constantine Ivanovitch Ivanov is like a brother to me. He has done everything that he in any way could for me. I owe him money. If he ever goes to Petersburg, show him some recognition. I owe him twenty-five rubles. But how can I repay his kindness, his constant willingness to carry out all my requests, his attention and care for me, just like a brother's? And he is not the only one I have to thank in that way. *Brother, there are very many noble natures in the world.*

I have already said that your silence often tortures me. I thank you for the money you sent. In your next letter (even if it's "*official,*" for I don't know yet whether it is possible for me to correspond with you)—in your next, write as fully as you can of all your affairs, of Emilie Fyodorovna, the children, all relations and acquaintances; also of those in Moscow— who is alive and who is dead; and of your business; tell me what capital you started with, whether it is lucrative, whether you are in funds, finally, whether you will help me financially, and how much you will send me a year. But send no money with the official letter—particularly if I don't find a covering address. For the present, give Michael Petrovitch as the consignor of all packets (you understand, don't you?). For the time, I have some money, but I have no books. If you can, send me the magazines for this year, or at any rate the *O.Z. (Annals of the Homeland).*

But what I urgently need are the following: I need (very necessary!) ancient historians (in French translation), modern historians: Guizot, Thierry, Thiers, Ranke, and so forth; national studies, and the Fathers of the Church. Choose the cheapest and most compact editions. Send them by return.

People try to console me: "They're quite simple sort of fellows there." But I dread simple men more than complex ones. For that matter, men everywhere are just—men. Even among the robber-murderers in the prison, I came to know some men in those four years. Believe me, there were among them deep, strong, beautiful natures, and it often gave me great joy to find gold under a rough exterior. And not in a single case, or even two, but in several cases. Some inspired respect, others were downright fine. I taught the Russian language to a young Circassian—he had been transported to Siberia for robbery with murder. How grateful he was to me! Another convict wept when I said good-by to him. Certainly I had often given him money, but it was so little, and his gratitude so boundless! My character, though, was deteriorating; in my relations with others I was ill-tempered and impatient. They accounted for it by my mental condition, and bore all without grumbling. A propos, what a number of national types and characters I became familiar with in prison! I lived *into* their lives, and so I believe I know them really well. Many tramps' and thieves' careers were laid bare to me and, above all, the whole wretched existence of the common people. Decidedly I have not spent my time there in vain. I have learned to know the Russian people as only a few know them. I am a little vain of it. I hope that such vanity is pardonable. . . .

Send me the Koran, and Kant's *Critique of Pure Reason,* and if you have the chance of sending me anything not officially, then be sure to send Hegel, but particularly Hegel's *History of Philosophy.* Upon that depends my whole future. For God's sake, exert yourself to get me transferred to the Caucasus; try to find out from well-informed sources whether I shall be permitted to print my works, and in what way I should seek this sanction. I intend to try for permission in two or three years. I beg you to sustain me so long. Without money I shall be destroyed by military life. So please! . . .

Now I mean to write novels and plays. But I must still read a great deal. Don't forget me.

Once again farewell.

F. D.

FOR WRITING OR DISCUSSION

1. Describe Dostoevsky's life in prison and on hard labor. According to Slonim's account, what permanent physical and emotional effects did these experiences have on Dostoevsky?

2. What did Dostoevsky learn about the nature of criminals as compared to that of ordinary men? In what sense are we all "doubles"?

3. How does this letter help you to understand Dostoevsky's lifelong alternation between happiness and despair, his extremes of behavior and thought, his struggle to understand the problems of evil and suffering?

4. This letter is extraordinary not only because of its content but also because of its style. Point out passages that convey the experiences of pathos and suffering by means of objective realism rather than by overstatement or sentimentality.

5. Do you think that Tolstoy would have considered this letter "good" art according to his standard of the author's "sincerity"? Why or why not?

The Peasant Marey

Years after his experience in Siberia, when Dostoevsky was publishing a periodical called *A Writer's Diary,* he included in one of the issues a story based on an episode that took place while he was a prisoner. The story, called "The Peasant Marey," reiterates the idea of the duality of human nature and makes one wonder if the terror within Dostoevsky dates back to his childhood life with a father who was brutal enough to be killed by his own serfs.

The Peasant Marey

It was Easter Monday. The air was warm, the sky blue, the sun high, warm and bright, but I was plunged in gloom. I wandered aimlessly behind the barracks in the prison yard, looked at the palings of the strong prison fence, counting them mechanically, though I did not particularly want to count them, but doing it more out of habit than anything else. It was the second day of "holidays" in prison. The convicts were not taken out to work; lots of them were drunk; cursing and quarreling broke out every minute in different corners of the prison. Disgusting, coarse songs; groups of convicts playing cards under the bunks; several convicts who had run amok and had been dealt with summarily by their own comrades, were lying half dead on the bunks, covered with sheepskins, until they should recover consciousness; the knives that had already been drawn several times—all this had so harrowing an effect on me during the two days of holidays that it made me ill. I could never bear without disgust the wild orgies of the common people, and here in this place this was specially true. On such days even the officials never looked into the prison, carried out no searches, did not look for drinks, realizing that once a year even these outcasts had to be given a chance of enjoying themselves and that otherwise things would be much worse. At last blind fury blazed up in my heart. I met the Pole, M———ski,[1] one of the political prisoners. He gave me a black look, with flashing eyes and trembling lips. "*Je hais ces brigands!*"[2] he hissed at me in an undertone and walked past me. I went back to the barracks, although I had rushed out of them like a madman only a quarter of an hour before, when six strong peasants had hurled themselves on the drunken Tartar Gazin in an attempt to quiet him and had begun beating him. They beat him senselessly—a camel might have been killed by such blows. But they knew that it was not easy to kill this Hercules, and they beat him therefore without any qualms. Now, on my return, I noticed Gazin lying unconscious and without any sign of life on a bunk in a corner at the other

---

[1]*M———ski:* O. Miretski, who was serving a prison sentence with Dostoevsky.
[2]"*Je ... brigands!*": "I hate these bandits."

"The Peasant Marey" from *The Best Short Stories of Dostoevsky,* translated by David Magarshack. Reprinted by permission of Random House, Inc. All rights reserved.

end of the barracks; he lay covered with a sheepskin, and they all passed by him in silence, knowing very well that if the man was unlucky he might die from a beating like that. I made my way to my place opposite the window with the iron bars and lay on my back with my eyes closed and my hands behind my head. I liked to lie like that: no one would bother a sleeping man, and meanwhile one could dream and think. But I found it difficult to dream: my heart was beating uneasily and M——ski's words were still echoing in my ears: "*Je hais ces brigands!*" However, why dwell on these scenes; I sometimes even now dream of those times at night, and none of my dreams is more agonizing. Perhaps it will be noticed that to this day I have hardly ever spoken in print of my life in prison; *The House of the Dead* I wrote fifteen years ago in the person of a fictitious character who was supposed to have killed his wife. I may add, incidentally, just as an interesting detail, that many people have thought and have been maintaining ever since the publication of that book of mine, that I was sent to Siberia for the murder of my wife.

By and by I did forget my surroundings and became imperceptibly lost in memories. During the four years of my imprisonment I was continually recalling my past and seemed in my memories to live my former life all over again. These memories cropped up by themselves; I seldom evoked them consciously. It would begin from some point, some imperceptible feature, which then grew little by little into a complete picture, into some clear-cut and vivid impression. I used to analyze those impressions, adding new touches to an event that had happened long ago, and, above all, correcting it, correcting it incessantly, and that constituted my chief amusement. This time I for some reason suddenly remembered one fleeting instant in my early childhood when I was only nine years old—an instant that I seemed to have completely forgotten; but at that time I was particularly fond of memories of my early childhood. I remembered an August day in our village; a dry, bright day, though rather cold and windy; summer was drawing to a close, and we should soon have to leave for Moscow and again have to spend all winter over the boring French lessons, and I was so sorry to leave the country. I walked past the threshing floors and, going down a ravine, climbed up into the dense thicket of bushes which stretched from the other side of the ravine to the wood. I got among the bushes, and I could hear not very far away, about thirty yards perhaps, a peasant plowing by himself on a clearing. I knew he was plowing up the steep slope of a hill. The horse must have found it very hard going, for from time to time I heard the peasant's call from a distance: "Gee up! Gee up!" I knew almost all our peasants, but I did not know which of them was plowing now, nor did it really matter to me who it was because I was occupied with my own affairs—I too was busy, breaking off a switch from a hazel tree to strike frogs with; hazel twigs are very lovely, but they are also very brittle, much more brittle than birch twigs. I was also interested in beetles and other insects, and I was collecting them; some of them were very beautiful. I also liked the small quick red and yellow lizards with black spots, but I was afraid of snakes. However, there were many fewer snakes than lizards. There were not many mushrooms there; to get mushrooms one had to go to the birch wood, and I was about to go there. And there was nothing in the world I loved so much as the wood with its mushrooms and wild berries, its beetles and its birds, its hedgehogs and squirrels, and its damp smell of rotten leaves. And even as I write this I can smell the fragrance of our birch wood: these impressions remain with you for your whole life. Suddenly amid the dead silence I heard clearly and distinctly the shout, "Wolf! Wolf!" I uttered a shriek and, panic-stricken, screamed at the top of my voice and rushed out to the clearing straight to the plowing peasant.

It was our peasant Marey. I do not know if there is such a name, but everybody called him Marey. He was a peasant of about fifty, thickset and over medium height, with a large, grizzled, dark-brown beard. I knew him, but till that day I had scarcely ever spoken to him. When he heard my cry, he even stopped his old mare, and when, unable to stop myself I clutched at his wooden plow with one hand and at his sleeve with the other, he saw how terrified I was.

"There's a wolf there!" I cried, breathless.

He threw up his head and looked round involuntarily, for a moment almost believing me.

"Where's the wolf?"

"Someone shouted—shouted just now 'Wolf! Wolf!'" I stammered.

"There, there! There are no wolves hereabouts," he murmured, trying to calm me. "You've been dreaming, sonny. Who ever heard of wolves in these parts?"

But I was trembling all over and I was still clutching at his smock, and I suppose I must have been very pale. He looked at me with a worried smile, evidently anxious and troubled about me.

"Dear, dear, how frightened you are," he said, shaking his head. "Don't be frightened, sonny. Oh, you poor thing, you! There, there."

He stretched out his hand and suddenly stroked my cheek.

"There now! Christ be with you, cross yourself, there's a good lad!"

But I did not cross myself; the corners of my mouth were still twitching, and that seemed to strike him particularly. He quietly stretched out his thick finger with its black nail, smeared with earth, and gently touched my trembling lips.

"Dear, oh dear," he smiled at me with a slow motherly sort of smile, "Lord, how frightened he is, the poor lad!"

I realized at last that there was no wolf and that I had imagined the shout, "Wolf! Wolf!" The shout, though, was very clear and distinct, but such shouts (and not only about wolves) I had imagined once or twice before, and I knew it. (I grew out of these hallucinations a few years later.)

"Well, I'll go now," I said, looking up at him, questioningly and shyly.

"Run along, run along, son, I'll be awatching you," he said, adding, "Don't you worry, I shan't let the wolf get you!" and he smiled at me with the same motherly smile. "Well, Christ be with you. Run along, run along, sonny," and he made the sign of the cross over me, and then crossed himself too.

I walked away, looking back anxiously every few yards. While I was walking away, Marey stood still with his mare and looked after me, nodding his head at me every time I looked round. As a matter of fact, I was a little ashamed of myself for having let him see how frightened I was, but I was still very much afraid of the wolf as I was walking away till I climbed up the steep side of the ravine and came to the first threshing barn. There my terror left me completely, and our watchdog Volchok suddenly appeared out of nowhere and rushed at me. With Volchok at my side I completely recovered my spirits and turned round to Marey for the last time. I could no longer see his face clearly, but I felt that he was still nodding and smiling tenderly at me. I waved to him and he waved back to me and started his mare.

"Gee-up!" I heard his call in the distance again, and the mare pulled at the wooden plow once more.

All this came back to me all at once, I don't know why, but with an amazing accuracy of detail. I suddenly came to and sat up on my bunk and, I remember, I could still feel the gentle smile of memory on my lips. For another minute I went on recalling that incident from my childhood.

When I returned home from Marey that day I did not tell anybody about my "adventure." It was not much of an adventure, anyway. And, besides, I soon forgot all about Marey. Whenever I happened to come across him now and then, I never spoke to him either about the wolf or anything else, and now twenty years later in Siberia I suddenly remembered this meeting so distinctly that not a single detail of it was lost, which means of course that it must have been hidden in my mind without my knowing it, of itself and without any effort on my part, and came back to me suddenly when it was wanted. I remembered the tender, motherly smile of that serf, the way he made the sign of the cross over me and crossed himself, the way he nodded at me. "Lord, how frightened he is, the poor lad!" And particularly that thick finger of his, smeared with earth, with which he touched my twitching lips so gently and with such shy tenderness. No doubt, anyone would have done his best to calm a child, but something quite different seemed to have happened during that solitary meeting; and if I had been his own son, he could not have looked at me with eyes shining with brighter love. And who compelled him to look like that? He was one of our serfs, a peasant who was our property, and after all I was the son of his master. No one would have known that he had been so good to me, and no one would have rewarded him for it. Did he really love little children as much as that? There are such people, no doubt. Our meeting took place in a secluded spot, in a deserted field, and only God perhaps saw from above with what profound and enlightened human feeling, and with what delicate, almost womanly, tenderness the heart of a coarse, savagely ignorant Russian serf was filled, a serf who at the time neither expected nor dreamed of his emancipation.

Tell me, was not this what Konstantin Akaskov[1] perhaps meant when he spoke of the high degree of culture of our people?

And so when I got off the bunk and looked round, I suddenly felt, I remember, that I could look at these unhappy creatures with quite different eyes, and that suddenly by some miracle all hatred and anger had vanished from my heart. I walked round the prison peering into the faces I came across. That rascal of a peasant with his shaven head and branded face, yelling his hoarse drunken song at the top of his voice—why, he, too, may be the same sort of peasant as Marey: I cannot possibly look into his heart, can I? That evening I again met M——ski. Poor man! He could have no memories about Marey or peasants like him and he could have no other opinion of these people except, *"Je hais ces brigands!"* Yes, it was much harder for those Poles than for us!

FOR WRITING OR DISCUSSION

1. What contrasts are made in this story between brutality and kindness, terror and security, ignorance and understanding?

2. How is Marey like Tolstoy's peasant Alyosha? In what sense could he represent Tolstoy's ideal peasant?

3. What is meant toward the end of the story by "the high degree of culture of our people"?

[1] *Konstantin Akaskov:* a leading member of the Slavophiles.

THE PEASANT MAREY   199

4. What, according to the narrator, is the cure for terror and hatred?

5. What did the narrator mean by saying that the Polish prisoners had more to bear than he?

6. Would you say that this story or Dostoevsky's letter to his brother reveals more about the actual emotions and feelings of men in prison? Explain.

REACTING TO CRITICISM

Both Turgenev and Tolstoy based much of their work on autobiographical material; Tolstoy especially, you may recall, wrote "direct from life." But Dostoevsky relied as heavily on his own experience as material for his fiction as any other writer in the world. The difference between Dostoevsky and Tolstoy in this respect is that Dostoevsky's life was an inner-directed, psychological drama. The terrors he wrote about, though often physically real, were terrors of the mind, and in writing about himself, he managed to write about us all. That is the secret of his universality. As you read the commentaries that follow, relate Dostoevsky's letter to his brother and "The Peasant Marey" to what is said here.

> Dostoevsky belonged to that race of writers to whom it is given to express themselves in their work; he gave voice to all the doubts and contradictions of his own mind, and perhaps it is because he hid nothing of what was going on in himself that he was able to find out such astonishing things about mankind in general. The destiny of his characters is his own, their doubts and dualities are his, their iniquities are the sins hidden in his own soul. The story of Dostoevsky's life is therefore much less interesting than his writings; his letters tell us less than his novels; in his fiction he strips himself bare, and thanks to his confession he is much less of a puzzle than other writers. . . . The nature of Dostoevsky's genius was such that in the exploration and analysis of his own life he showed at the same time the universal destiny of man. He hides from us nothing of his contrary ideals, from the Evil and Sodom to our Lady and the Good: man torn between the two was one of his great themes. Even his epilepsy was something more to him than just an accidental malady.[1] [*Nicholas Berdyaev*]

Unjustifiably, Dostoevsky's acquiescence in hardship has been held against him. He has been thought cowardly and even hypocritical for having proclaimed that his imprisonment had been a

---

[1]From *Dostoevsky* by Nicholas Berdyaev, translated by Donald Attwater, published by Sheed & Ward, Inc., New York. Reprinted by permission of the publisher.

salutary experience. But however unusual his change of views—after his return from Siberia, to which he had been sent for his revolutionary sympathies, he became a friend of the notoriously reactionary Pobedonostsev—this apparent reversal was logical and certainly not opportunist. Nothing worse can be imagined than the circumstances under which he had been obliged to live....
It is characteristic of Dostoevsky that what should have hurt him most in the hardships he catalogues here [that is, in his letter to his brother] was not physical discomfort but estrangement from people. The reason for this alienation was not only the herd proximity he describes, but the fact that he was looked on suspiciously by his fellow convicts because of his education and social position. He managed to break down the barrier and, as a result, was able to write a remarkable book about them when he returned to European Russia. This book, *Memoirs from the House of the Dead,* shows clearly why Dostoevsky considered his period of exile a time of growth, not a break in his development.

Before Siberia his concern for the underdog had expressed his knowledge of himself. He invented symbols for what he knew most intimately—the duality of his humiliated ego. In Siberia he found his own experience objectified and corroborated a hundred times over. There were among the convicts the meek whose meekness harbored depths of violence, and monsters of cruelty who could not tolerate the sickness of a pet dog; mildest, humblest individuals who were guilty of atrocious crimes, and willful bullies who were in essence weaklings and cowards. For many years, Dostoevsky found, a man would live quietly, submitting to a harsh lot; then, all of a sudden, something would go wrong and he would stab a neighbor. That, he observed, happened with the quietest, the least noticed of them. And they would give way to crime not in moments of blind passion, but knowing perfectly well that they would be severely punished in consequence. There was an irresistible thrill in perpetrating such deeds, like that of a man on a high tower who feels he must jump off; he knows he will be killed, but not to jump would be more disastrous. This is a feeling that comes as the climax of long suppression and accumulated hurt; it is the ego crying out for recognition, ready to extinguish itself for the sake of a moment's self-assertion. Barring certain criminal monsters to whom the rule did not apply, a man would commit a crime just to prove himself a human being in his own right. Even in jail the murderer demanded a certain amount of respect. Without ever forgetting that he was an offender, and knowing perfectly well that he was at the mercy of the jailers, he always demanded to be treated as a human being. . . . A man's sense of his own dignity was even more important, Dostoevsky decided, than he hitherto realized. And, he discovered, this dignity could be destroyed not only by the absence but by an overabundance of power, as was true of the jailers who were always tyrants, often sadists. . . . Furthermore, a sense of power was tempting and contagious. It was destructive not only to individuals but to states, and a society that looked on it indifferently was already contaminated in essence. The executioner was to be found in embryo in every modern man.[1] [*Helen Muchnic*]

1. How do Yevtushenko's poem, Dostoevsky's letter to his brother, and the story about the peasant Marey illustrate Berdyaev's statement that Dostoevsky "hides from us nothing of his contrary ideals, from the Evil . . . to . . . the Good: man torn between the two was one of his great themes."

2. Helen Muchnic speaks of an "overabundance of power." How are the hangmen in Yevtushenko's poem an example of the dangers of the overabundance of power in Dostoevsky's jailers?

THE RUSSIANS

The Crocodile

Although Dostoevsky's major contributions to literature have been in the realm of psychological explorations of the inner man confronted by his own peculiar "terror," he considered himself a social and religious commentator on the Russian scene. After his return to St. Petersburg, he founded the review called *Time*, in which, as Marc Slonim has explained, he predicted that Russia would eventually absorb the West into its cultural circle and thereby save it. When this review was suspended by the government, Dostoevsky established another one, called *Epoch*. It was in *Epoch* that, in 1865, the story you are about to read was first published. Having begun life as a liberal, Dostoevsky became an arch-conservative. As you read this story, notice how humor is used

[1]From the book *An Introduction to Russian Literature* by Helen Muchnic, copyright, 1947, ©, 1964, by Helen Muchnic. Reprinted by permission of E. P. Dutton & Co., Inc.

to poke fun at Westernized Russians, social reformers, and political progressives. As you meet each new character ask yourself what the character represents to Dostoevsky in terms of a trend in Russian life that he deplores.

The Crocodile

AN EXTRAORDINARY INCIDENT

A true story of how a gentleman of a certain age and of respectable appearance was swallowed alive by the crocodile in the Arcade, and of the consequences that followed.

> Ohé Lambert! Où est Lambert?
> As tu vu Lambert?[1]

1

On the thirteenth of January of this present year, 1865, at half past twelve in the day, Elena Ivanovna, the wife of my cultured friend Ivan Matveitch, who is a colleague in the same department, and may be said to be a distant relation of mine, too, expressed the desire to see the crocodile now on view at a fixed charge in the Arcade. As Ivan Matveitch had already in his pocket his ticket for a tour abroad (not so much for the sake of his health as for the improvement of his mind), and was consequently free from his official duties and had nothing whatever to do that morning, he offered no objection to his wife's irresistible fancy, but was positively aflame with curiosity himself.

"A capital idea!" he said, with the utmost satisfaction. "We'll have a look at the crocodile! On the eve of visiting Europe it is as well to acquaint ourselves on the spot with its indigenous inhabitants." And with these words, taking his wife's arm, he set off with her at once for the Arcade. I joined them, as I usually do, being an intimate friend of the family. I have never seen Ivan Matveitch in a more agreeable frame of mind than he was on that memorable morning—how true it is that we know beforehand the fate that awaits us! On entering the Arcade he was at once full of admiration for the splendors of the building, and when we reached the shop in which the monster lately arrived in Petersburg was being exhibited, he volunteered to pay the quarter-ruble for me to the

---

[1] *Ohé . . . Lambert?:* Oh Lambert! Where is Lambert? Have you seen Lambert?
"The Crocodile" from *An Honest Thief and Other Stories* by Dostoevsky, translated by Constance Garnett. Published in England by William Heinemann Ltd. and reprinted with their permission.

crocodile owner—a thing which had never happened before. Walking into a little room, we observed that besides the crocodile there were in it parrots of the species known as cockatoo, and also a group of monkeys in a special case in a recess. Near the entrance, along the left wall stood a big tin tank that looked like a bath covered with a thin iron grating, filled with water to the depth of two inches. In this shallow pool was kept a huge crocodile, which lay like a log absolutely motionless and apparently deprived of all its faculties by our damp climate, so inhospitable to foreign visitors. This monster at first aroused no special interest in any one of us.

"So this is the crocodile!" said Elena Ivanovna, with a pathetic cadence of regret. "Why, I thought it was . . . something different."

Most probably she thought it was made of diamonds. The owner of the crocodile, a German, came out and looked at us with an air of extraordinary pride.

"He has a right to be proud," Ivan Matveitch whispered to me, "he knows he is the only man in Russia exhibiting a crocodile."

This quite nonsensical observation I ascribe also to the extremely good-humored mood which had overtaken Ivan Matveitch, who was on other occasions of rather envious disposition.

"I fancy your crocodile is not alive," said Elena Ivanovna, piqued by the irresponsive stolidity of the proprietor, and addressing him with a charming smile in order to soften his churlishness—a maneuver so typically feminine.

"Oh, no, madam," the latter replied in broken Russian; and instantly moving the grating half off the tank, he poked the monster's head with a stick.

Then the treacherous monster, to show that it was alive, faintly stirred its paws and tail, raised its snout and emitted something like a prolonged snuffle.

"Come, don't be cross, Karlchen," said the German caressingly, gratified in his vanity.

"How horrid that crocodile is! I am really frightened," Elena Ivanovna twittered, still more coquettishly. "I know I shall dream of him now."

"But he won't bite you if you do dream of him," the German retorted gallantly, and was the first to laugh at his own jest, but none of us responded.

"Come, Semyon Semyonitch," said Elena Ivanovna, addressing me exclusively, "let us go and look at the monkeys. I am awfully fond of monkeys; they are such darlings . . . and the crocodile is horrid."

"Oh, don't be afraid, my dear!" Ivan Matveitch called after us, gallantly displaying his manly courage to his wife. "This drowsy denison of the realms of the Pharaohs will do us no harm." And he remained by the tank. What is more, he took his glove and began tickling the crocodile's nose with it, wishing, as he said afterwards, to induce him to snort. The proprietor showed his politeness to a lady by following Elena Ivanovna to the case of monkeys.

So everything was going well, and nothing could have been foreseen. Elena Ivanovna was quite skittish in her raptures over the monkeys, and seemed completely taken up with them. With shrieks of delight she was continually turning to me, as though determined not to notice the proprietor, and kept gushing with laughter at the resemblance she detected between these monkeys and her intimate friends and acquaintances. I, too, was amused, for the resemblance was unmistakable. The German did not know whether to laugh or not, and so at last was reduced to frowning. And it was at that moment that a terrible, I may say unnatural, scream set the room vibrating. Not knowing what to think, for the first moment I stood still, numb with horror, but noticing that Elena Ivanovna was screaming too, I quickly turned round — and what did I behold! I saw — oh, heavens! — I saw the luckless Ivan Matveitch in the terrible jaws of the crocodile, held by them round the waist, lifted horizontally in the air and desperately kicking. Then — one moment, and no trace remained of him. But I must describe it in detail, for I stood all the while motionless, and had time to watch the whole process taking place before me with an attention and interest such as I never remember to have felt before. "What," I thought at that critical moment, "what if all that had happened to me instead of to Ivan Matveitch — how unpleasant it would have been for me!"

But to return to my story. The crocodile began by turning the unhappy Ivan Matveitch in his terrible jaws so that he could swallow his legs first; then bringing up Ivan Matveitch, who kept trying to jump out and clutching at the sides of the tank, sucked him down again as far as his waist. Then bringing him up again, gulped him down, and so again and again. In this way Ivan Matveitch was visibly disappearing before our eyes. At last, with a final gulp, the crocodile swallowed my cultured friend entirely, this time leaving no trace of him. From the outside of the crocodile we could see the protuberances of Ivan Matveitch's figure as he passed down the inside of the monster. I was on the point of screaming again when destiny played another treacherous trick upon us. The crocodile made a tremendous effort, probably oppressed by the magnitude of the object he had swallowed, once more opened his terrible jaws, and with a final hiccup he suddenly let the head of Ivan Matveitch pop out for a second, with an expression of despair on his face. In that brief instant the spectacles dropped off his nose to the bottom of the tank. It seemed as though that despairing countenance had only popped out to cast one last look on the objects around it, to take its last farewell of all earthly pleasures. But it had not time to carry out its intention; the crocodile made another effort, gave a gulp and instantly it vanished again — this time forever. This appearance and disappearance of a still living human head was so horrible, but at the same — either from its rapidity and unexpectedness or from the dropping of the spectacles — there was something so comic about it that I suddenly quite unexpectedly exploded with laughter. But pulling myself together and realizing that to laugh at such a moment was not the thing for an old family friend, I turned at once to Elena Ivanovna and said with a sympathetic air:

"Now it's all over with our friend Ivan Matveitch!"

I cannot even attempt to describe how violent was the agitation of Elena Ivanovna during the whole process. After the first scream she seemed rooted to the spot, and stared at the catastrophe with apparent indifference, though her eyes looked as though they were starting out of her head; then she suddenly went off into a heart-rending wail, but I seized her hands. At this instant the proprietor, too, who had at first been also petrified by horror, suddenly clasped his hands and cried, gazing upwards:

"Oh, my crocodile! *Oh mein allerliebster Karlchen! Mutter, Mutter, Mutter!*"[1]

A door at the rear of the room opened at this cry, and the *Mutter,* a rosy-cheeked, elderly but disheveled woman in a cap, made her appearance, and rushed with a shriek to her German.

A perfect bedlam followed. Elena Ivanovna kept shrieking out the same phrase, as though in a frenzy, "Flay him! flay him!" apparently entreating them — probably in a moment of oblivion — to flay somebody for something. The proprietor and *Mutter* took no notice whatever of either of us; they were both bellowing like calves over the crocodile.

"He did for himself! He will burst himself at once, for he did swallow a *ganz*[2] official!" cried the proprietor.

"*Unser Karlchen, unser allerliebster Karlchen wird sterben,*"[3] howled his wife.

"We are bereaved and without bread!" chimed in the proprietor.

[1]*"Oh . . . Mutter!":* "Oh my dearest Karl! Mother, Mother, Mother!"
[2]*ganz:* whole.
[3]*Unser . . . sterben":* "Our Karl, our dearest Karl will die."

"Flay him! flay him!" clamored Elena Ivanovna, clutching at the German's coat.

"He did tease the crocodile. For what did your man tease the crocodile?" cried the German, pulling away from her. "You will if *Karlchen wird*[1] burst, therefore pay, *das war mein Sohn, das war mein einziger Sohn.*"[2]

I must own I was intensely indignant at the sight of such egoism in the German and the coldheartedness of his disheveled *Mutter;* at the same time Elena Ivanovna's reiterated shriek of "Flay him! flay him!" troubled me even more and absorbed at last my whole attention, positively alarming me. I may as well say straight off that I entirely misunderstood this strange exclamation: it seemed to me that Elena Ivanovna had for the moment taken leave of her senses but, nevertheless wishing to avenge the loss of her beloved Ivan Matveitch, was demanding by way of compensation that the crocodile should be severely thrashed, while she was meaning something quite different. Looking round at the door, not without embarrassment, I began to entreat Elena Ivanovna to calm herself, and above all not to use the shocking word "flay." For such a reactionary desire here, in the midst of the Arcade and of the most cultured society, not two paces from the hall where at this very minute Mr. Lavrov was perhaps delivering a public lecture, was not only impossible but unthinkable, and might at any moment bring upon us the hisses of culture and the caricatures of Mr. Stepanov. To my horror I was immediately proved to be correct in my alarmed suspicions: the curtain that divided the crocodile room from the little entry where the quarter-rubles were taken suddenly parted, and in the opening there appeared a figure with mustaches and beard, carrying a cap, with the upper part of its body bent a long way forward, though the feet were scrupulously held beyond the threshold of the crocodile room in order to avoid the necessity of paying the entrance money.

"Such a reactionary desire, madam," said the stranger, trying to avoid falling over in our direction and to remain standing outside the room, "does no credit to your development, and is conditioned by lack of phosphorus in your brain. You will be promptly held up to shame in the *Chronicle of Progress* and in our satirical prints. . . ."

But he could not complete his remarks; the proprietor coming to himself, and seeing with horror that a man was talking in the crocodile room without having paid entrance money, rushed furiously at the progressive stranger and turned him out with a punch from each fist. For a moment

---

[1] *Karlchen wird:* Karl will.
[2] *das . . . Sohn:* that was my son, that was my only son.

both vanished from our sight behind a curtain, and only then I grasped that the whole uproar was about nothing. Elena Ivanovna turned out quite innocent; she had, as I have mentioned already, no idea whatever of subjecting the crocodile to a degrading corporal punishment, and had simply expressed the desire that he should be opened and her husband released from his interior.

"What! You wish that my crocodile be perished!" the proprietor yelled, running in again. "No! let your husband be perished first, before my crocodile! . . . *Mein Vater* showed crocodile, *mein Grossvater* showed crocodile, *mein Sohn*[1] will show crocodile, and I will show crocodile! All will show crocodile! I am known to *ganz Europa,*[2] and you are not known to *ganz Europa,* and you must pay me a *strafe!*"[3]

"*Ja, ja,*" put in the vindictive German woman, "we shall not let you go. *Strafe,* since Karlchen is burst!"

"And, indeed, it's useless to flay the creature," I added calmly, anxious to get Elena Ivanovna away home as quickly as possible, "as our dear Ivan Matveitch is by now probably soaring somewhere in the empyrean."

"My dear"—we suddenly heard, to our intense amazement, the voice of Ivan Matveitch—"my dear, my advice is to apply direct to the superintendent's office, as without the assistance of the police the German will never be made to see reason."

These words, uttered with firmness and aplomb, and expressing an exceptional presence of mind, for the first minute so astounded us that we could not believe our ears. But, of course, we ran at once to the crocodile's tank, and with equal reverence and incredulity listened to the unhappy captive. His voice was muffled, thin and even squeaky, as though it came from a considerable distance. It reminded one of a jocose person who, covering his mouth with a pillow, shouts from an adjoining room, trying to mimic the sound of two peasants calling to one another in a deserted plain or across a wide ravine—a performance to which I once had the pleasure of listening in a friend's house at Christmas.

"Ivan Matveitch, my dear, and so you are alive!" faltered Elena Ivanovna.

"Alive and well," answered Ivan Matveitch, "and, thanks to the Almighty, swallowed without any damage whatever. I am only uneasy as to the view my superiors may take of the incident; for after getting a

---

[1]*Mein Vater . . . Sohn:* My father . . . my grandfather . . . my son.
[2]*ganz Europa:* the whole of Europe.
[3]*strafe:* fine, penalty.

permit to go abroad I've got into a crocodile, which seems anything but clever."

"But, my dear, don't trouble your head about being clever; first of all we must somehow excavate you from where you are," Elena Ivanovna interrupted.

"Excavate!" cried the proprietor. "I will not let my crocodile be excavated. Now the *publicum*[1] will come many more, and I will *fünfzig*[2] kopecks ask and Karlchen will cease to burst."

"*Gott sei dank!*"[3] put in his wife.

"They are right," Ivan Matveitch observed tranquilly; "the principles of economics before everything."

"My dear! I will fly at once to the authorities and lodge a complaint, for I feel that we cannot settle this mess by ourselves."

"I think so too," observed Ivan Matveitch; "but in our age of industrial crisis it is not easy to rip open the belly of a crocodile without economic compensation, and meanwhile the inevitable question presents itself: What will the German take for his crocodile? And with it another: How will it be paid? For, as you know, I have no means. . . ."

"Perhaps out of your salary. . . ." I observed timidly, but the proprietor interrupted me at once.

"I will not the crocodile sell; I will not for three thousand the crocodile sell! I will not for four thousand the crocodile sell! Now the *publicum* will come very many. I will not for five thousand the crocodile sell!"

In fact he gave himself insufferable airs. Covetousness and a revolting greed gleamed joyfully in his eyes.

"I am going!" I cried indignantly.

"And I! I too! I shall go to Andrey Osipitch himself. I will soften him with my tears," whined Elena Ivanovna.

"Don't do that, my dear," Ivan Matveitch hastened to interpose. He had long been jealous of Andrey Osipitch on his wife's account, and he knew she would enjoy going to weep before a gentleman of refinement, for tears suited her. And I don't advise you to do so either, my friend," he added, addressing me. "It's no good plunging headlong in that slapdash way; there's no knowing what it may lead to. You had much better go today to Timofey Semyonitch as though to pay an ordinary visit; he is an old-fashioned and by no means brilliant man, but he is trustworthy, and what matters most of all, he is straightforward. Give him my greetings

[1] *publicum:* public.
[2] *fünfzig:* fifty.
[3] *"Gott . . . dank!":* "Thank God!"

and describe the circumstances of the case. And since I owe him seven rubles over our last game of cards, take the opportunity to pay him the money; that will soften the stern old man. In any case his advice may serve as a guide for us. And meanwhile take Elena Ivanovna home. . . . Calm yourself, my dear," he continued, addressing her. "I am weary of these outcries and feminine squabblings, and should like a nap. It's soft and warm in here, though I have hardly had time to look round in this unexpected haven."

"Look round! Why, is it light in there?" cried Elena Ivanovna in a tone of relief.

"I am surrounded by impenetrable night," answered the poor captive, "but I can feel and, so to speak, have a look round with my hands. . . . Good-by; set your mind at rest and don't deny yourself recreation and diversion. Till tomorrow! And you, Semyon Semyonitch, come to me in the evening, and as you are absent-minded and may forget it, tie a knot in your handkerchief."

I confess I was glad to get away, for I was overtired and somewhat bored. Hastening to offer my arm to the disconsolate Elena Ivanovna, whose charms were only enhanced by her agitation, I hurriedly led her out of the crocodile room.

"The charge will be another quarter-ruble in the evening," the proprietor called after us.

"Oh, dear, how greedy they are!" said Elena Ivanovna, looking at herself in every mirror on the walls of the Arcade, and evidently aware that she was looking prettier than usual.

"The principles of economics," I answered with some emotion, proud that passers-by should see the lady on my arm.

"The principles of economics," she drawled in a touching little voice. "I did not in the least understand what Ivan Matveitch said about those horrid economics just now."

"I will explain to you," I answered, and began at once telling her of the beneficial effects of the introduction of foreign capital into our country, upon which I had read an article in the *Petersburg News* and the *Voice* that morning.

"How strange it is," she interrupted, after listening for some time. "But do leave off, you horrid man. What nonsense you are talking. . . . Tell me, do I look purple?"

"You look perfect, and not purple!" I observed, seizing the opportunity to pay her a compliment.

"Naughty man!" she said complacently. "Poor Ivan Matveitch," she added a minute later, putting her little head on one side coquettishly. "I am really sorry for him. Oh, dear!" she cried suddenly, "how is he going to have his dinner ... and ... and ... what will he do ... if he wants anything?"

"An unforeseen question," I answered, perplexed in my turn. To tell the truth, it had not entered my head, so much more practical are women than we men in the solution of the problems of daily life!

"Poor dear! how could he have got into such a mess ... nothing to amuse him, and in the dark. ... How vexing it is that I have no photograph of him. ... And so now I am a sort of widow," she added, with a seductive smile, evidently interested in her new position. "Hm! ... I am sorry for him, though."

It was, in short, the expression of the very natural and intelligible grief of a young and interesting wife for the loss of her husband. I took her home at last, soothed her, and after dining with her and drinking a cup of aromatic coffee, set off at six o'clock to Timofey Semyonitch, calculating that at that hour all married people of settled habits would be sitting or lying down at home.

Having written this first chapter in a style appropriate to the incident recorded, I intend to proceed in a language more natural though less elevated, and I beg to forewarn the reader of the fact.

2

The venerable Timofey Semyonitch met me rather nervously, as though somewhat embarrassed. He led me to his tiny study and shut the door carefully, "that the children may not hinder us," he added with evident uneasiness. There he made me sit down on a chair by the writing-table, sat down himself in an easy chair, wrapped round him the skirts of his old wadded dressing gown, and assumed an official and even severe air, in readiness for anything, though he was not my chief nor Ivan Matveitch's, and had hitherto been reckoned as a colleague and even a friend.

"First of all," he said, "take note that I am not a person in authority, but just such a subordinate official as you and Ivan Matveitch. ... I have nothing to do with it, and do not intend to mix myself up in the affair."

I was surprised to find that he apparently knew all about it already. In spite of that I told him the whole story over in detail. I spoke with positive excitement, for I was at that moment fulfilling the obligations of a true friend. He listened without special surprise, but with evident signs of suspicion.

"Only fancy," he said, "I always believed that this would be sure to happen to him."

"Why, Timofey Semyonitch? It is a very unusual incident in itself...."

"I admit it. But Ivan Matveitch's whole career in the service was leading up to this end. He was flighty—conceited indeed. It was always 'progress' and ideas of all sorts, and this is what progress brings people to!"

"But this is a most unusual incident and cannot possibly serve as a general rule for all progressives."

"Yes, indeed it can. You see, it's the effect of overeducation, I assure you. For overeducation leads people to poke their noses into all sorts of places, especially where they are not invited. Though perhaps you know best," he added, as though offended. "I am an old man and not of much education. I began as a soldier's son, and this year has been the jubilee of my service."

"Oh, no, Timofey Semyonitch, not at all. On the contrary, Ivan Matveitch is eager for your advice; he is eager for your guidance. He implores it, so to say, with tears."

"So to say, with tears! Hm! Those are crocodile's tears and one cannot quite believe in them. Tell me, what possessed him to want to go abroad? And how could he afford to go? Why, he has no private means!"

"He had saved the money from his last bonus," I answered plaintively. "He only wanted to go for three months—to Switzerland ... to the land of William Tell."

"William Tell? Hm!"

"He wanted to meet the spring at Naples, to see the museums, the customs, the animals...."

"Hm! The animals! I think it was simply from pride. What animals? Animals, indeed! Haven't we animals enough? We have museums, menageries, camels. There are bears quite close to Petersburg! And here he's got inside a crocodile himself...."

"Oh, come, Timofey Semyonitch! The man is in trouble, the man appeals to you as to a friend, as to an older relation, craves for advice— and you reproach him. Have pity at least on the unfortunate Elena Ivanovna!"

"You are speaking of his wife? A charming little lady," said Timofey Semyonitch, visibly softening and taking a pinch of snuff with relish. "Particularly prepossessing. And so plump, and always putting her pretty little head on one side.... Very agreeable. Andrey Osipitch was speaking of her only the other day."

"Speaking of her?"

"Yes, and in very flattering terms. Such a figure, he said, such eyes, such hair.... A sugarplum, he said, not a lady—and then he laughed. He is still a young man, of course," Timofey Semyonitch blew his nose with a loud noise. "And yet, young though he is, what a career he is making for himself."

"That's quite a different thing, Timofey Semyonitch."

"Of course, of course."

"Well, what do you say then, Timofey Semyonitch?"

"Why, what can I do?"

"Give advice, guidance, as a man of experience, a relative! What are we to do? What steps are we to take? Go to the authorities and...."

"To the authorities? Cetainly not," Timofey Semyonitch replied hurriedly. "If you ask my advice, you had better, above all, hush the matter up and act, so to speak, as a private person. It is a suspicious incident, quite unheard of. Unheard of, above all; there is no precedent for it, and it is far from creditable.... And so discretion above all.... Let him lie there a bit. We must wait and see...."

"But how can we wait and see, Timofey Semyonitch? What if he is stifled there?"

"Why should he be? I think you told me that he made himself fairly comfortable there?"

I told him the whole story over again. Timofey Semyonitch pondered.

"Hm!" he said, twisting his snuffbox in his hands. "To my mind it's really a good thing he should lie there a bit, instead of going abroad. Let him reflect at his leisure. Of course he mustn't be stifled, and so he must take measures to preserve his health, avoiding a cough, for instance, and so on.... And as for the German, it's my personal opinion he is within his rights, and even more so than the other side, because it was the other party who got into *his* crocodile without asking permission, and not *he* who got into Ivan Matveitch's crocodile without asking permission, though, so far as I recollect, the latter has no crocodile. And a crocodile is private property, and so it is impossible to slit him open without compensation."

"For the saving of human life, Timofey Semyonitch."

"Oh, well, that's a matter for the police. You must go to them."

"But Ivan Matveitch may be needed in the department. He may be asked for."

"Ivan Matveitch needed? Ha-ha! Besides, he is on leave, so that we may ignore him—let him inspect the countries of Europe! It will be a different matter if he doesn't turn up when his leave is over. Then we shall ask for him and make inquiries."

"Three months! Timofey Semyonitch, for pity's sake!"

"It's his own fault. Nobody thrust him there. At this rate we should have to get a nurse to look after him at government expense, and that is not allowed for in the regulations. But the chief point is that the crocodile is private property, so that the principles of economics apply in this question. And the principles of economics are paramount. Only the other evening, at Luka Andreitch's, Ignaty Prokofyitch was saying so. Do you know Ignaty Prokofyitch? A capitalist, in a big way of business, and he speaks so fluently. 'We need industrial development,' he said; 'there is very little development among us. We must create it. We must create capital, so we must create a middle class, the so-called bourgeoisie. And as we haven't capital we must attract it from abroad. We must, in the first place, give facilities to foreign companies to buy up lands in Russia as is done now abroad. The communal holding of land is poison, is ruin.' And, you know, he spoke with such heat; well, that's all right for him — a wealthy man, and not in the service. 'With the communal system,' he said, 'there will be no improvement in industrial development or agriculture. Foreign companies,' he said, 'must as far as possible buy up the whole of our land in big lots, and then split it up, split it up, split it up, in the smallest parts possible' — and do you know he pronounced the words 'split it up' with such determination — 'and then sell it as private property. Or rather, not sell it, but simply let it. When,' he said, 'all the land is in the hands of foreign companies they can fix any rent they like. And so the peasant will work three times as much for his daily bread and he can be turned out at pleasure. So that he will feel it, will be submissive and industrious, and will work three times as much for the same wages. But as it is, with the commune, what does he care? He knows he won't die of hunger, so he is lazy and drunken. And meanwhile money will be attracted into Russia, capital will be created and the bourgeoisie will spring up. The English political and literary paper, *The Times,* in an article the other day on our finances stated that the reason our financial position was so unsatisfactory was that we had no middle class, no big fortunes, no accommodating proletariat.' Ignaty Prokofyitch speaks well. He is an orator. He wants to lay a report on the subject before the authorities, and then to get it published in the *News*. That's something very different from verses like Ivan Matveitch's...."

"But how about Ivan Matveitch?" I put in, after letting the old man babble on.

Timofey Semyonitch was sometimes fond of talking and showing that he was not behind the times, but knew all about things.

"How about Ivan Matveitch? Why, I am coming to that. Here we are, anxious to bring foreign capital into the country—and only consider: as soon as the capital of a foreigner, who has been attracted to Petersburg, has been doubled through Ivan Matveitch instead of protecting the foreign capitalist, we are proposing to rip open the belly of his original capital—the crocodile. Is it consistent? To my mind, Ivan Matveitch, as the true son of his fatherland, ought to rejoice and to be proud that through him the value of a foreign crocodile has been doubled and possibly trebled. That's just what is wanted to attract capital. If one man succeeds, mind you, another will come with a crocodile, and a third will bring two or three of them at once, and capital will grow up about them—there you have a bourgeoisie. It must be encouraged."

"Upon my word, Timofey Semyonitch!" I cried, "you are demanding almost supernatural self-sacrifice from poor Ivan Matveitch."

"I demand nothing, and I beg you, before everything—as I have said already—to remember that I am not a person in authority and so cannot demand anything of anyone. I am speaking as a son of the fatherland, that is, not as the *Son of the Fatherland*, but as a son of the fatherland. Again, what possessed him to get into the crocodile? A respectable man, a man of good grade in the service, lawfully married—and then to behave like that! Is it consistent?"

"But it was an accident."

"Who knows? And where is the money to compensate the owner to come from?"

"Perhaps out of his salary, Timofey Semyonitch?"

"Would that be enough?"

"No, it wouldn't, Timofey Semyonitch," I answered sadly. "The proprietor was at first alarmed that the crocodile would burst, but as soon as he was sure that it was all right, he began to bluster and was delighted to think that he could double the charge for entry."

"Treble and quadruple perhaps! The public will simply stampede the place now, and crocodile owners are smart people. Besides, it's not Lent yet, and people are keen on diversions, and so I say again, the great thing is that Ivan Matveitch should preserve his incognito, don't let him be in a hurry. Let everybody know, perhaps, that he is in the crocodile, but don't let them be officially informed of it. Ivan Matveitch is in particularly favorable circumstances for that, for he is reckoned to be abroad. It will be said he is in the crocodile, and we will refuse to believe it. That is how it can be managed. The great thing is that he should wait; and why should he be in a hurry?"

"Well, but if . . ."

"Don't worry, he has a good constitution. . . ."

"Well, and afterward, when he has waited?"

"Well, I won't conceal from you that the case is exceptional in the highest degree. One doesn't know what to think of it, and the worst of it is there is no precedent. If we had a precedent we might have something to go by. But as it is, what is one to say? It will certainly take time to settle it."

A happy thought flashed upon my mind.

"Cannot we arrange," I said, "that if he is destined to remain in the entrails of the monster and it is the will of Providence that he should remain alive, that he should send in a petition to be reckoned as still serving?"

"Hm! . . . Possibly as on leave and without salary. . . ."

"But couldn't it be with salary?"

"On what grounds?"

"As sent on a special commission."

"What commission and where?"

"Why, into the entrails, the entrails of the crocodile. . . . So to speak, for exploration, for investigation of the facts on the spot. It would, of course, be a novelty, but that is progressive and would at the same time show zeal for enlightenment."

Timofey Semyonitch thought a little.

"To send a special official," he said at last, "to the inside of a crocodile to conduct a special inquiry is, in my personal opinion, an absurdity. It is not in the regulations. And what sort of special inquiry could there be there?"

"The scientific study of nature on the spot, in the living subject. The natural sciences are all the fashion nowadays, botany. . . . He could live there and report his observations. . . . For instance, concerning digestion or simply habits. For the sake of accumulating facts."

"You mean as statistics. Well, I am no great authority on that subject, indeed I am no philosopher at all. You say 'facts'—we are overwhelmed with facts as it is, and don't know what to do with them. Besides, statistics are a danger."

"In what way?"

"They are a danger. Moreover, you will admit he will report facts, so to speak, lying like a log. And, can one do one's official duties lying like a log? That would be another novelty and a dangerous one; and again, there is no precedent for it. If we had any sort of precedent for it, then, to my thinking, he might have been given the job."

"But no live crocodiles have been brought over hitherto, Timofey Semyonitch."

"Hm ... yes," he reflected again. "Your objection is a just one, if you like, and might indeed serve as a ground for carrying the matter further; but consider again, that if with the arrival of living crocodiles government clerks begin to disappear, and then on the ground that they are warm and comfortable there, expect to receive the official sanction for their position, and then take their ease there ... you must admit it would be a bad example. We should have everyone trying to go the same way to get a salary for nothing."

"Do your best for him, Timofey Semyonitch. By the way, Ivan Matveitch asked me to give you seven rubles he had lost to you at cards."

"Ah, he lost that the other day at Nikifor Nikiforitch's. I remember. And how gay and amusing he was — and now!"

The old man was genuinely touched.

"Intercede for him, Timofey Semyonitch!"

"I will do my best. I will speak in my own name, as a private person, as though I were asking for information. And meanwhile, you find out indirectly, unofficially, how much would the proprietor consent to take for his crocodile?"

Timofey Semyonitch was visibly more friendly.

"Certainly," I answered. "And I will come back to you at once to report."

"And his wife ... is she alone now? Is she depressed?"

"You should call on her, Timofey Semyonitch."

"I will. I thought of doing so before; it's a good opportunity. ... And what on earth possessed him to go and look at the crocodile? Though, indeed, I should like to see it myself."

"Go and see the poor fellow, Timofey Semyonitch."

"I will. Of course, I don't want to raise his hopes by doing so. I shall go as a private person. ... Well, good-by, I am going to Nikifor Nikiforitch's again; shall you be there?"

"No, I am going to see the poor prisoner."

"Yes, now he is a prisoner! ... Ah, that's what comes of thoughtlessness!"

I said good-by to the old man. Ideas of all kinds were straying through my mind. A good-natured and most honest man, Timofey Semyonitch, yet, as I left him, I felt pleased at the thought that he had celebrated his fiftieth year of service, and that Timofey Semyonitches are now a rarity among us. I flew at once, of course, to the Arcade to tell poor Ivan Matveitch all the news. And, indeed, I was moved by curiosity to know how he was getting on in the crocodile and how it was possible to live in a crocodile. And, indeed, was it possible to live in a crocodile at all? At times it really seemed to me as though it were all an outlandish, monstrous dream, especially as an outlandish monster was the chief figure in it.

3

And yet it was not a dream, but actual, indubitable fact. Should I be telling the story if it were not? But to continue.

It was late, about nine o'clock, before I reached the Arcade, and I had to go into the crocodile room by the back entrance, for the German had closed the shop earlier than usual that evening. Now in the seclusion of domesticity he was walking about in a greasy old frock coat, but he seemed three times as pleased as he had been in the morning. It was evidently that he had no apprehensions now, and that the public had been coming "many more." The *Mutter* come out later, evidently to keep an eye on me. The German and the *Mutter* frequently whispered together. Although the shop was closed he charged me a quarter-ruble. What unnecessary exactitude!

"You will every time pay; the public will one ruble, and you one quarter pay; for you are the good friend of your good friend; and I a friend respect..."

"Are you alive, are you alive, my cultured friend?" I cried, as I approached the crocodile, expecting my words to reach Ivan Matveitch from a distance and to flatter his vanity.

"Alive and well," he answered, as though from a long way off or from under the bed, though I was standing close beside him. "Alive and well; but of that later.... How are things going?"

As though purposely not hearing the question, I was just beginning with sympathetic haste to question him how he was, what it was like in the crocodile, and what, in fact, there was inside a crocodile. Both friendship and common civility demanded this. But with capricious annoyance he interrupted me.

"How are things going?" he shouted, in a shrill and on this occasion particularly revolting voice, addressing me peremptorily as usual.

I described to him my whole conversation with Timofey Semyonitch down to the smallest detail. As I told my story I tried to show my resentment in my voice.

"The old man is right," Ivan Matveitch pronounced as abruptly as usual in his conversation with me. "I like practical people, and can't endure sentimental milksops. I am ready to admit, however, that your idea about a special commission is not altogether absurd. I certainly have a great deal to report, both from a scientific and from an ethical point of view. But now all this has taken a new and unexpected aspect, and it is not worth while to trouble about mere salary. Listen attentively. Are you sitting down?"

"No, I am standing up."

"Sit down on the floor if there is nothing else, and listen attentively."

Resentfully I took a chair and put it down on the floor with a bang, in my anger.

"Listen," he began dictatorially. "The public came today in masses. There was no room left in the evening, and the police came in to keep order. At eight o'clock, that is, earlier than usual, the proprietor thought it necessary to close the shop and end the exhibition to count the money he had taken and prepare for tomorrow more conveniently. So I know there will be a regular fair tomorrow. So we may assume that all the most cultivated people in the capital, the ladies of the best society, the foreign ambassadors, the leading lawyers and so on, will all be present. What's more, people will be flowing here from the remotest provinces of our vast and interesting empire. The upshot of it is that I am the cynosure of all eyes, and though hidden to sight, I am eminent. I shall teach the idle crowd. Taught by experience, I shall be an example of greatness and resignation to fate! I shall be, so to say, a pulpit from which to instruct mankind. The mere biological details I can furnish about the monster I am inhabiting are of priceless value. And so, far from repining at what has happened, I confidently hope for the most brilliant of careers."

"You won't find it wearisome?" I asked sarcastically.

What irritated me more than anything was the extreme pomposity of his language. Nevertheless, it all rather disconcerted me. "What on earth, what, can this frivolous blockhead find to be so cocky about?" I muttered to myself. "He ought to be crying instead of being cocky."

"No!" he answered my observation sharply, "for I am full of great ideas, only now can I at leisure ponder over the amelioration of the lot of humanity. Truth and light will come forth now from the crocodile. I shall certainly develop a new economic theory of my own and I shall be proud of it—which I have hitherto been prevented from doing by my official duties and by trivial distractions. I shall refute everything and be a new Fourier.[1] By the way, did you give Timofey Semyonitch the seven rubles?"

"Yes, out of my own pocket," I answered, trying to emphasize that fact in my voice.

---

[1] *Fourier:* François Fourier (1772–1837), a French socialist.

"We will settle it," he answered superciliously. "I confidently expect my salary to be raised, for who should get a raise if not I? I am of the utmost service now. But to business. My wife?"

"You are, I suppose, inquiring after Elena Ivanovna?"

"My wife?" he shouted, this time in a positive squeal.

There was no help for it! Meekly, though gnashing my teeth, I told him how I had left Elena Ivanovna. He did not even hear me out.

"I have special plans in regard to her," he began impatiently. "If I am celebrated *here,* I wish her to be celebrated *there.* Savants, poets, philosophers, foreign mineralogists, statesmen, after conversing in the morning with me, will visit her *salon* in the evening. From next week onward she must have an 'At Home' every evening. With my salary doubled, we shall have the means for entertaining, and as the entertainment must not go beyond tea and hired footmen—that's settled. Both here and there they will talk of me. I have long thirsted for an opportunity for being talked about, but could not attain it, fettered by my humble position and low grade in the service. And now all this has been attained by a simple gulp on the part of the crocodile. Every word of mine will be listened to, every utterance will be thought over, repeated, printed. And I'll teach them what I am worth! They shall understand at last what abilities they have allowed to vanish in the entrails of a monster. 'This man might have been Foreign Minister or might have ruled a kingdom,' some will say. 'And that man did not rule a kingdom,' others will say. In what way am I inferior to a Garnier-Pagesishky[1] or whatever they are called? My wife must be a worthy second—I have brains, she has beauty and charm. 'She is beautiful, and that is why she is his wife,' some will say. 'She is beautiful *because* she is his wife,' others will amend. To be ready for anything let Elena Ivanovna buy tomorrow the Encyclopedia edited by Andrey Kraevsky, that she may be able to converse on any topic. Above all, let her be sure to read the political leader in the *Petersburg News,* comparing it every day with the *Voice.* I imagine that the proprietor will consent to take me sometimes with the crocodile to my wife's brilliant *salon.* I will be in a tank in the middle of the magnificent drawing room, and I will scintillate with witticisms which I will prepare in the morning. To the statesman I will impart my projects; to the poet I will speak in rhyme; with the ladies I can be amusing and charming without impropriety, since I shall be no danger to their husbands' peace of mind. To all the rest I shall serve as a pattern of resignation to fate and the will of Providence. I shall make my wife a brilliant literary lady; I shall bring

---

[1] *Garnier-Pagès:* Étienne Garnier-Pagès (1801–1841), one of the leaders of the French republican party during the 1830's.

her forward and explain her to the public; as my wife she must be full of the most striking virtues; and if they are right in calling Andrey Alexandrovitch our Russian Alfred de Musset, they will be still more right in calling her our Russian Yevgenia Tour."

I must confess that although this wild nonsense was rather in Ivan Matveitch's habitual style, it did occur to me that he was in a fever and delirious. It was the same everyday Ivan Matveitch, but magnified twenty times.

"My friend," I asked him, "are you hoping for a long life? Tell me, in fact, are you well? How do you eat, how do you sleep, how do you breathe? I am your friend, and you must admit that the incident is most unnatural, and consequently my curiosity is most natural."

"Idle curiosity and nothing else," he pronounced sententiously, "but you shall be satisfied. You ask how I am managing in the entrails of the monster? To begin with, the crocodile, to my amusement, turns out to be perfectly empty. His inside consists of a sort of huge empty sack made of gutta-percha, like the elastic goods sold in the Gorohovy Street, in the Morskaya, and, if I am not mistaken, in the Voznesensky Prospect. Otherwise, if you think of it, how could I find room?"

"Is it possible?" I cried, in a surprise that may well be understood. "Can the crocodile be perfectly empty?"

"Perfectly," Ivan Matveitch maintained sternly and impressively. "And in all probability, it is so constructed by the laws of Nature. The crocodile possesses nothing but jaws furnished with sharp teeth, and besides the jaws, a tail of considerable length—that is all, properly speaking. The middle part between these two extremities is an empty space enclosed by something of the nature of gutta-percha, probably really gutta-percha."

"But the ribs, the stomach, the intestines, the liver, the heart?" I interrupted quite angrily.

"There is nothing, absolutely nothing of all that, and probably there never has been. All that is the idle fancy of frivolous travelers. As one inflates an air cushion, I am now with my person inflating the crocodile. He is incredibly elastic. Indeed, you might, as the friend of the family, get in with me if you were generous and self-sacrificing enough—and even with you here there would be room to spare. I even think that in the last resort I might send for Elena Ivanovna. However, this void, hollow formation of the crocodile is quite in keeping with the teachings of natural science. If, for instance, one had to construct a new crocodile, the question would naturally present itself. What is the fundamental characteristic of the crocodile? The answer is clear: to swallow human beings. How is one, in constructing the crocodile, to secure that he should swallow people? The answer is clearer still: construct him hollow. It was settled by physics long ago that Nature abhors a vacuum. Hence the inside of the crocodile must be hollow so that it may abhor the vacuum, and consequently swallow and so fill itself with anything it can come across. And that is the sole rational cause why every crocodile swallows men. It is not the same in the constitution of man: the emptier a man's head is, for instance, the less he feels the thirst to fill it, and that is the one exception to the general rule. It is all as clear as day to me now. I have deduced it by my own observation and experience, being so to say, in the very bowels of Nature, in its retort, listening to the throbbing of its pulse. Even etymology supports me, for the very word "crocodile" means voracity. Crocodile—*crocodillo*—is evidently an Italian word, dating perhaps from the Egyptian Pharaohs, and evidently derived from the French verb *croquer,* which means to eat, to devour, in general to absorb nourishment. All these remarks I intend to deliver as my first lecture in Elena Ivanovna's *salon* when they take me there in the tank."

"My friend, oughtn't you at least to take some purgative?" I cried involuntarily.

"He is in a fever, a fever, he is feverish!" I repeated to myself in alarm.

"Nonsense!" he answered contemptuously. "Besides, in my present position it would be most inconvenient. I knew, though, you would be sure to talk of taking medicine."

"But, my friend, how . . . how do you take food now? Have you dined today?"

"No, I am not hungry, and most likely I shall never take food again. And that, too, is quite natural; filling the whole interior of the crocodile I make him feel always full. Now he need not be fed for some years. On the other hand, nourished by me, he will naturally impart to me all the vital juices of his body; it is the same as with some accomplished coquettes who embed themselves and their whole persons for the night in raw steak, and then, after their morning bath, are fresh, supple, buxom and fascinating. In that way nourishing the crocodile, I myself obtain nourishment from him, consequently we mutually nourish one another. But as it is difficult even for a crocodile to digest a man like me, he must, no doubt, be conscious of a certain weight in his stomach—an organ which he does not, however, possess—and that is why, to avoid causing the creature suffering, I do not often turn over, and although I could turn over I do not do so from humanitarian motives. This is the one drawback of my present position, and in an allegorical sense Timofey Semyonitch was right in saying I was lying like a log. But I will prove that even lying like a log—nay, that only lying like a log—one can revolutionize the lot of mankind. All the great ideas and movements of our newspapers and magazines have evidently been the work of men who were lying like logs; that is why they call them divorced from the realities of life—but what does it matter, their saying that! I am constructing now a complete system of my own, and you wouldn't believe how easy it is! You have only to creep into a secluded corner or into a crocodile, to shut your eyes, and you immediately devise a perfect millennium for mankind. When you went away this afternoon I set to work at once and have already invented three systems, now I am preparing the fourth. It is true that at first one must refute everything that has gone before, but from the crocodile it is so easy to refute it; besides, it all becomes clearer, seen from the inside of the crocodile.... There are some drawbacks, though small ones, in my position, however; it is somewhat damp here and covered with a sort of slime; moreover, there is rather a smell of India rubber exactly like the smell of my old galoshes. That is all, there are no other drawbacks."

"Ivan Matveitch," I interrupted, "all this is a miracle in which I can scarcely believe. And can you, can you intend never to dine again?"

"What trivial nonsense you are troubling about, you thoughtless, frivolous creature! I talk to you about great ideas, and you ... Understand that I am sufficiently nourished by the great ideas which light up the darkness in which I am enveloped. The good-natured proprietor has, however, after consulting the kindly *Mutter,* decided with her that they will every morning insert into the monster's jaws a bent metal tube, something like a whistle pipe, by means of which I can absorb coffee or broth with bread soaked in it. The pipe has already been bespoken in the neighborhood, but I think this is superfluous luxury. I hope to live at least a thousand years, if it is true that crocodiles live so long, which, by the way—good thing I thought of it—you had better look up in some natural history tomorrow and tell me, for I may have been mistaken and have mixed it up with some excavated monster. There is only one reflection that rather troubles me: as I am dressed in cloth and have boots on, the crocodile can obviously not digest me. Besides, I am alive, and so am opposing the process of digestion with my whole will power; for you can understand that I do not wish to be turned into what all nourishment turns into, for that would be too humiliating for me. But there is one thing I am afraid of: in a thousand years the cloth of my coat, unfortunately of Russian make, may decay, and then, left without clothing, I might perhaps, in spite of my indignation, begin to be digested; and though by day nothing would induce me to allow it, at night, in my sleep, when a man's will deserts him, I may be overtaken by the humiliating destiny of a potato, a pancake, or veal. Such an idea reduces me to fury. This alone is an argument for the revision of the tariff and the encouragement of the importation of English cloth, which is stronger and so will withstand Nature longer when one is swallowed by a crocodile. At the first opportunity I will impart this idea to some statesman and at the same time to the political writers on our Petersburg dailies. Let them publish it abroad. I trust this will not be the only idea they will borrow from me. I foresee that every morning a regular crowd of them, provided with quarter-rubles from the editorial office, will be flocking round me to seize my ideas on the telegrams of the previous day. In brief, the future presents itself to me in the rosiest light."

"Fever, fever!" I whispered to myself.

"My friend, and freedom?" I asked, wishing to learn his views thoroughly. "You are, so to speak, in prison, while every man has a right to the enjoyment of freedom."

"You are a fool," he answered. "Savages love independence, wise men love order; and if there is no order . . ."

"Ivan Matveitch, spare me, please!"

"Hold your tongue and listen!" he squealed, vexed at my interrupting him. "Never has my spirit soared as now. In my narrow refuge there is only one thing that I dread—the literary criticisms of the monthlies and the hiss of our satirical papers. I am afraid that thoughtless visitors, stupid and envious people and nihilists in general, may turn me into ridicule. But I will take measures. I am impatiently awaiting the response of the public tomorrow, and especially the opinion of the newspapers. You must tell me about the papers tomorrow."

"Very good; tomorrow I will bring a perfect pile of papers with me."

"Tomorrow it is too soon to expect reports in the newspapers, for it will take four days for it to be advertised. But from today come to me every evening by the back way through the yard. I am intending to employ you as my secretary. You shall read the newspapers and magazines to me, and I will dictate to you my ideas and give you commissions. Be particularly careful not to forget the foreign telegrams. Let all the European telegrams be here every day. But enough; most likely you are sleepy by now. Go home, and do not think of what I said just now about criticisms: I am not afraid of it, for the critics themselves are in a critical position. One has only to be wise and virtuous and one will certainly get on to a pedestal. If not Socrates, then Diogenes, or perhaps both of them together—that is my future role among mankind."

So frivolously and boastfully did Ivan Matveitch hasten to express himself before me, like feverish weak-willed women who, as we are told by the proverb, cannot keep a secret. All that he told me about the crocodile struck me as suspicious. How was it possible that the crocodile was absolutely hollow? I don't mind betting that he was bragging from vanity and partly to humiliate me. It is true that he was an invalid and one must make allowances for invalids; but I must frankly confess, I never could endure Ivan Matveitch. I have been trying all my life, from a child up, to escape from his tutelage and have not been able to! A thousand times over I have been tempted to break with him altogether, and every time I have been drawn to him again, as though I were still hoping to prove something to him or to revenge myself on him. A strange thing, this friendship! I can positively assert that nine tenths of my friendship for him was made up of malice. On this occasion, however, we parted with genuine feeling.

"Your friend a very clever man!" the German said to me in an undertone as he moved to see me out; he had been listening all the time attentively to our conversation.

"*À propos,*" I said, "while I think of it: how much would you ask for your crocodile in case any one wanted to buy it?"

Ivan Matveitch, who heard the question, was waiting with curiosity for the answer; it was evident that he did not want the German to ask too little; anyway, he cleared his throat in a peculiar way on hearing my question.

At first the German would not listen—was positively angry.

"No one will dare my own crocodile to buy!" he cried furiously, and turned as red as a boiled lobster. "Me not want to sell the crocodile! I would not for the crocodile a million thalers[1] take. I took a hundred and thirty thalers from the public today, and I shall tomorrow ten thousand take, and then a hundred thousand every day I shall take. I will not him sell."

Ivan Matveitch positively chuckled with satisfaction. Controlling myself—for I felt it was a duty to my friend—I hinted coolly and reasonably to the crazy German that his calculations were not quite correct, that if he made a hundred thousand every day, all Petersburg will have visited him in four days, and then there will be no one left to bring him rubles, that life and death are in God's hands, that the crocodile may burst or Ivan Matveitch may fall ill and die, and so on and so on.

The German grew pensive.

---

[1] *thaler:* a German silver coin no longer in use.

"I will him drops from the chemist's get," he said, after pondering, "and will save your friend that he die not."

"Drops are all very well," I answered, "but consider, too, that the thing may get into the law courts. Ivan Matveitch's wife may demand the restitution of her lawful spouse. You are intending to get rich, but do you intend to give Elena Ivanovna a pension?"

"No, me not intend," said the German in stern decision.

"No, we not intend," said the *Mutter,* with positive malignancy.

"And so would it not be better for you to accept something now, at once, a secure and solid though moderate sum, than to leave things to chance? I ought to tell you that I am inquiring simply from curiosity."

The German drew the *Mutter* aside to consult with her in a corner where there stood a case with the largest and ugliest monkey of his collection.

"Well, you will see!" said Ivan Matveitch.

As for me, I was at that moment burning with the desire, first, to give the German a thrashing, next, to give the *Mutter* an even sounder one, and, thirdly, to give Ivan Matveitch the soundest thrashing of all for his boundless vanity. But all this paled beside the answer of the rapacious German.

After consultation with the *Mutter* he demanded for his crocodile fifty thousand rubles in bonds of the last Russian loan with lottery voucher attached, a brick house in Gorohovy Street with a chemist's shop attached, and in addition the rank of Russian colonel.

"You see!" Ivan Matveitch cried triumphantly. "I told you so! Apart from this last senseless desire for the rank of a colonel, he is perfectly right, for he fully understands the present value of the monster he is exhibiting. The economic principle before everything!"

"Upon my word!" I cried furiously to the German. "But what should you be made a colonel for? What exploit have you performed? What service have you done? In what way have you gained military glory? You are really crazy!"

"Crazy!" cried the German offended. "No, a person very sensible, but you very stupid! I have a colonel deserved for that I have a crocodile shown and in him a live *hofrath*[1] sitting! And a Russian can a crocodile not show and a live *hofrath* in him sitting! Me extremely clever man and much wish colonel to be!"

"Well, good-by, then, Ivan Matveitch!" I cried, shaking with fury, and I went out of the crocodile room almost at a run.

I felt that in another minute I could not have answered for myself.

---

[1] *hofrath:* privy counselor.

The unnatural expectations of these two blockheads were insupportable. The cold air refreshed me and somewhat moderated my indignation. At last, after spitting vigorously fifteen times on each side, I took a cab, got home, undressed and flung myself into bed. What vexed me more than anything was my having become his secretary. Now I was to die of boredom there every evening, doing the duty of a true friend! I was ready to beat myself for it, and I did, in fact, after putting out the candle and pulling up the bedclothes, punch myself several times on the head and various parts of my body. That somewhat relieved me, and at last I fell asleep fairly soundly, in fact, for I was very tired. All night long I could dream of nothing but monkeys, but toward morning I dreamed of Elena Ivanovna.

4

The monkeys I dreamed about, I surmise, because they were shut up in the case at the German's; but Elena Ivanovna was a different story.

I may as well say at once, I loved the lady, but I make haste—posthaste—to make a qualification. I loved her as a father, neither more nor less. I judge that because I often felt an irresistible desire to kiss her little head or her rosy cheek. And though I never carried out this inclination, I would not have refused even to kiss her lips. And not merely her lips, but her teeth, which always gleamed so charmingly like two rows of pretty, well-matched pearls when she laughed. She laughed extraordinarily often. Ivan Matveitch in demonstrative moments used to call her his "darling absurdity"—a name extremely happy and appropriate. She was a perfect sugarplum, and that was all one could say of her. Therefore I am utterly at a loss to understand what possessed Ivan Matveitch to imagine his wife as a Russian Yevgenia Tour? Anyway, my dream, with the exception of the monkeys, left a most pleasant impression upon me, and going over all the incidents of the previous day as I drank my morning cup of tea, I resolved to go and see Elena Ivanovna at once on my way to the office—which, indeed, I was bound to do as the friend of the family.

In a tiny little room out of the bedroom—the so-called little drawing room, though their big drawing room was little too—Elena Ivanovna was sitting, in some half-transparent morning wrapper, on a smart little sofa before a little teatable, drinking coffee out of a little cup in which she was dipping a minute biscuit. She was ravishingly pretty, but struck me as being at the same time rather pensive.

"Ah, that's you, naughty man!" she said, greeting me with an absent-minded smile. "Sit down, feather-head, have some coffee. Well, what were you doing yesterday? Were you at the masquerade?"

"Why, were you? I don't go, you know. Besides, yesterday I was visiting our captive...." I sighed and assumed a pious expression as I took the coffee.

"Whom? ... What captive? ... Oh, yes! Poor fellow! Well, how is he — bored? Do you know ... I wanted to ask you ... I suppose I can ask for a divorce now?"

"A divorce!" I cried in indignation and almost spilled the coffee. "It's that swarthy fellow," I thought to myself bitterly.

There was a certain swarthy gentleman with little mustaches who was something in the architectural line, and who came far too often to see them, and was extremely skillful in amusing Elena Ivanovna. I must confess I hated him and there was no doubt that he had succeeded in seeing Elena Ivanovna yesterday either at the masquerade or even here, and putting all sorts of nonsense into her head.

"Why," Elena Ivanovna rattled off hurriedly, as though it were a lesson she had learned, "if he is going to stay on in the crocodile, perhaps not come back all his life, while I sit waiting for him here! A husband ought to live at home, and not in a crocodile...."

"But this was an unforeseen occurrence," I was beginning, in very comprehensible agitation.

"Oh, no, don't talk to me, I won't listen, I won't listen," she cried, suddenly getting quite cross. "You are always against me, you wretch! There's no doing anything with you, you will never give me any advice! Other people tell me that I can get a divorce because Ivan Matveitch will not get his salary now."

"Elena Ivanovna! is it you I hear!" I exclaimed pathetically. "What villain could have put such an idea into your head? And divorce on such a trivial ground as a salary is quite impossible. And poor Ivan Matveitch, poor Ivan Matveitch is, so to speak, burning with love for you even in the bowels of the monster. What's more, he is melting away with love like a lump of sugar. Yesterday while you were enjoying yourself at the masquerade, he was saying that he might in the last resort send for you as his lawful spouse to join him in the entrails of the monster, especially as it appears the crocodile is exceedingly roomy, not only able to accommodate two but even three persons...."

And then I told her all that interesting part of my conversation the night before with Ivan Matveitch.

"What, what!" she cried, in surprise. "You want me to get into the monster too, to be with Ivan Matveitch? What an idea!" And how am I to get in there, in my hat and crinoline? Heavens, what foolishness! And what should I look like while I was getting into it, and very likely there would be someone there to see me! It's absurd! And what should I have to eat there? And . . . and . . . and what should I do there when . . . Oh, my goodness, what will they think of next? . . . And what should I have to amuse me there? . . . You say there's a smell of gutta-percha? And what should I do if we quarreled—should we have to go on staying there side by side? Foo, how horrid!"

"I agree, I agree with all those arguments, my sweet Elena Ivanovna," I interrupted, striving to express myself with that natural enthusiasm which always overtakes a man when he feels the truth is on his side. "But one thing you have not appreciated in all this, you have not realized that he cannot live without you if he is inviting you there; that is a proof of love, passionate, faithful, ardent love. . . . You have thought too little of his love, dear Elena Ivanovna!"

"I won't, I won't, I won't hear anything about it!" waving me off with her pretty little hand with glistening pink nails that had just been washed and polished. "Horrid man! You will reduce me to tears! Get into it yourself, if you like the prospect. You are his friend, get in and keep him company, and spend your life discussing some tedious science. . . ."

"You are wrong to laugh at this suggestion"—I checked the frivolous woman with dignity—"Ivan Matveitch has invited me as it is. You, of course, are summoned there by duty; for me, it would be an act of generosity. But when Ivan Matveitch described to me last night the elasticity of the crocodile, he hinted very plainly that there would be room not only for you two, but for me also as a friend of the family, especially if I wished to join you, and therefore . . ."

"How so, the three of us?" cried Elena Ivanovna, looking at me in surprise. "Why, how should we . . . are we going to be all three there together? Ha-ha-ha! How silly you both are! Ha-ha-ha! I shall certainly pinch you all the time, you wretch! Ha-ha-ha! Ha-ha-ha!"

And falling back on the sofa, she laughed till she cried. All this—the tears and the laughter—were so fascinating that I could not resist rushing eagerly to kiss her hand, which she did not oppose, though she did pinch my ears lightly as a sign of reconciliation.

Then we both grew very cheerful, and I described to her in detail all Ivan Matveitch's plans. The thought of her evening receptions and her salon pleased her very much.

"Only I should need a great many new dresses," she observed, "and so Ivan Matveitch must send me as much of his salary as possible and as soon as possible. Only . . . only I don't know about that," she added thoughtfully. "How can he be brought here in the tank? That's very absurd. I don't want my husband to be carried about in a tank. I should feel quite ashamed for my visitors to see it. . . . I don't want that, no, I don't."

"By the way, while I think of it, was Timofey Semyonitch here yesterday?"

"Oh, yes, he was; he came to comfort me, and do you know, we played cards all the time. He played for sweetmeats, and if I lost he was to kiss my hands. What a wretch he is! And only fancy, he almost came to the masquerade with me, really!"

"He was carried away by his feelings!" I observed. "And who would not be with you, you charmer?"

"Oh, get along with your compliments! Stay, I'll give you a pinch as a parting present. I've learned to pinch awfully well lately. Well, what do you say to that? By the way, you say Ivan Matveitch spoke several times of me yesterday?"

"N-no, not exactly. . . . I must say he is thinking more now of the fate of humanity, and wants . . ."

"Oh, let him! You needn't go on! I am sure it's fearfully boring. I'll go and see him some time. I shall certainly go tomorrow. Only not today; I've got a headache, and besides, there will be such a lot of people there today. . . . They'll say, 'That's his wife,' and I shall feel ashamed. . . . Good-by. You will be . . . there this evening, won't you?"

"To see him, yes. He asked me to go and take him the papers."

"That's capital. Go and read to him. But don't come and see me today. I am not well, and perhaps I may go and see someone. Good-by, you naughty man."

"It's that swarthy fellow who is going to see her this evening," I thought.

At the office, of course, I gave no sign of being consumed by these cares and anxieties. But soon I noticed some of the most progressive papers seemed to be passing particularly rapidly from hand to hand among my colleagues, and were being read with an extremely serious expression of face. The first one that reached me was the *Newsheet,* a paper of no particular party but humanitarian in general, for which it was regarded with contempt among us, though it was read. Not without surprise I read in it the following paragraph:

"Yesterday strange rumors were circulating among the spacious ways and sumptuous buildings of our vast metropolis. A certain well-known *bon vivant* of the highest society, probably weary of the cuisine at Borel's and at the X. Club, went into the Arcade, into the place where an immense crocodile recently brought to the metropolis is being exhibited, and insisted on its being prepared for his dinner. After bargaining with the proprietor he at once set to work to devour him (that is, not the proprietor, a very meek and punctilious German, but his crocodile), cutting juicy morsels with his penknife from the living animal, and swallowing them with extraordinary rapidity. By degrees the whole crocodile disappeared into the vast recesses of his stomach, so that he was even on the point of attacking an ichneumon,[1] a constant companion of the crocodile, probably imagining that the latter would be as savory. We are by no means opposed to that new article of diet with which foreign gourmands have long been familiar. We have, indeed, predicted that it would come. English lords and travelers make up regular parties for catching crocodiles in Egypt, and consume the back of the monster cooked like beefsteak, with mustard, onions and potatoes. The French who followed in the train of Lesseps prefer the paws baked in hot ashes, which they do, however, in opposition to the English, who laugh at them. Probably both ways would be appreciated among us. For our part, we are delighted at a new branch of industry, of which our great and varied fatherland stands preeminently in need. Probably before a year is out crocodiles will be brought in hundreds to replace this first one, lost in the stomach of a Petersburg gourmand. And why should not the crocodile be acclimatized among us in Russia? If the water of the Neva is too cold for these interesting strangers, there are ponds in the capital and rivers and lakes outside it. Why not breed crocodiles at Pargolovo, for instance, or at Pavlovsk, in the Presnensky Ponds and in Samoteka in Moscow? While providing agreeable, wholesome nourishment for our fastidious gourmands, they might at the same time entertain the ladies who walk about these ponds and instruct the children in natural history. The crocodile skin might be used for making jewel-cases, boxes, cigar-cases, pocketbooks, and possibly more than one thousand saved up in the greasy notes that are peculiarly beloved of merchants might be laid by in crocodile skin. We hope to return more than once to this interesting topic."

Though I had foreseen something of the sort, yet the reckless inaccuracy of the paragraph overwhelmed me. Finding no one with whom to share my impression, I turned to Prohor Savvitch who was sitting opposite to me, and noticed that the latter had been watching me for some time, while in his hand he held the *Voice* as though he were on the point of passing it to me. Without a word he took the *Newsheet* from me, and as he handed me the *Voice* he drew a line with his nail against an article to which he probably wished to call my attention. This Prohor Savvitch was a very queer man: a taciturn old bachelor, he was not on intimate

[1] *ichneumon:* a large fly.

terms with any of us, scarcely spoke to anyone in the office, always had an opinion of his own about everything, but could not bear to impart it to anyone. He lived alone. Hardly anyone among us had ever been in his lodging.

This was what I read in the *Voice*.

"Everyone knows that we are progressive and humanitarian and want to be on a level with Europe in this respect. But in spite of all our exertions and the efforts of our paper we are still far from maturity, as may be judged from the shocking incident which took place yesterday in the Arcade and which we predicted long ago. A foreigner arrives in the capital bringing with him a crocodile which he begins exhibiting in the Arcade. We immediately hasten to welcome a new branch of useful industry such as our powerful and varied fatherland stands in great need of. Suddenly yesterday at four o'clock in the afternoon a gentleman of exceptional stoutness enters the foreigner's shop in an intoxicated condition, pays his entrance money, and immediately without any warning leaps into the jaws of the crocodile, who was forced, of course, to swallow him, if only from a instinct of self-preservation, to avoid being crushed. Tumbling into the inside of the crocodile, the stranger at once dropped asleep. Neither the shouts of the foreign proprietor, nor the lamentations of his terrified family, nor threats to send for the police made the slightest impression. Within the crocodile was heard nothing but laughter and a promise to flay him (*sic*), though the poor mammal, compelled to swallow such a mass, was vainly shedding tears. An uninvited guest is worse than a Tartar. But in spite of the proverb, the insolent visitor would not leave. We do not know how to explain such barbarous incidents which prove our lack of culture and disgrace us in the eyes of foreigners. The recklessness of the Russian temperament has found a fresh outlet. It may be asked what was the object of the uninvited visitor? A warm and comfortable abode? But there are many excellent houses in the capital with very cheap and comfortable lodgings, with the Neva water laid on, and a staircase lighted by gas, frequently with a hall-porter maintained by the proprietor. We would call our readers' attention to the barbarous treatment of domestic animals: it is difficult, of course, for the crocodile to digest such a mass all at once, and now he lies swollen out to the size of a mountain, awaiting death in insufferable agonies. In Europe persons guilty of inhumanity towards domestic animals have long been punished by law. But in spite of our European enlightenment, in spite of our European pavements, in spite of the European architecture of our houses, we are still far from shaking off our time-honored traditions.

'Though the houses are new, the conventions are old.'

"And, indeed, the houses are not new, at least the staircases in them are not. We have more than once in our paper alluded to the fact that in the Petersburg Side in the house of the merchant Lukyanov the steps of the wooden staircase have decayed, fallen away, and have long been a danger for Afimya Skapidarov, a soldier's wife who works in the house and is often obliged to go up the stairs with water or armfuls of wood. At last our predictions have come true: yesterday evening at half past eight Afimya Skapidarov fell down with a basin of soup and broke her leg. We do not know whether Lukyanov will mend his staircase now, Russians are often wise after the event, but the victim of Russian carelessness has by now been taken to the hospital. In the same way we shall never cease to maintain that the house-porters who clear away the mud from the wooden pavement in the Viborgsky Side ought not to spatter the legs of passers-by, but should throw the mud up into heaps as is done in Europe," and so on, and so on.

"What's this?" I asked in some perplexity, looking at Prohor Savvitch. "What's the meaning of it?"

"How do you mean?"

"Why, upon my word! Instead of pitying Ivan Matveitch, they pity the crocodile!"

"What of it? They have pity even for a beast, a mammal. We must be up to Europe, mustn't we? They have a very warm feeling for crocodiles there too. He-he-he!"

Saying this, queer old Prohor Savvitch dived into his papers and would not utter another word.

I stuffed the *Voice* and the *Newssheet* into my pocket and collected as many old copies of the newspapers as I could find for Ivan Matveitch's diversion in the evening, and though the evening was far off, yet on this occasion I slipped away from the office early to go to the Arcade and look, if only from a distance, at what was going on there, and to listen to the various remarks and currents of opinion. I foresaw that there would be a regular crush there, and turned up the collar of my coat to meet it. I somehow felt rather shy—so unaccustomed are we to publicity. But I feel that I have no right to report my own prosaic feelings when faced with this remarkable and original incident.

FOR WRITING OR DISCUSSION

1. How does the humor in this story exemplify Dostoevsky's intensity and his portrayal of "extremes"?

2. What types of humor does Dostoevsky use, and for what pur-

pose? Find examples of burlesque, caricature, parody, hyperbole, and satire. Would you say that ridicule is a more or less effective way to call attention to social trends than deadpan serious invective or reportage? Explain your answer.

3. The reader usually identifies with the narrator of a story. How far into the story were you before you began to look on the narrator as a character in the story rather than as an observer with whom you could identify?

4. Cite examples from the story where the rational and irrational are juxtaposed or mixed. How is the rational mixed with the irrational? How is the irrational or fantastic made to appear acceptable to the characters in the story? Where, if ever, does the reader cross the borderline of irrationality to a point where he believes in the central event of the story? What *is* believable to the reader?

5. What inferences can you draw from "The Crocodile" about the ideas of Westernized Russians as regards the natural sciences, economics, manufactured goods, travel? What do you think Dostoevsky himself believed about these subjects?

6. What inferences can you draw about Dostoevsky's opinion of the social life of the "intelligentsia"? of government officials, petty bureaucrats and their wives? Do you think Turgenev would have agreed with Dostoevsky's views entirely or in part? Explain.

7. Where does Dostoevsky seem to stand on corporal punishment? How do you account for this point of view in a man who had witnessed such brutal beatings during his prison life? Do you think Dostoevsky approved of cruelty, or did he simply consider it an ineradicable part of any social order? How do you think Tolstoy would have felt about this matter?

8. What does Dostoevsky think of foreigners? How do you know?

9. What aspects of Russian thought does each of these characters represent: Ivan Matveitch; Elena Ivanovna; the narrator; Timofey Semyonitch?

10. Probably the single most noticeable quality of "The Crocodile" is its absurdity. The situation is absurd, the characters are absurd, and their remarks are most absurd of all. Modern playgoers and readers should find this type of absurdity quite up-to-date, although much modern use of the absurd is philosophical in thrust rather than specifically social or political. Comment on the nature of the absurdity in each of the following passages of dialogue in the story. What specific aspects of Russian life or thought are being satirized in each?

a. Ivan: "We'll have a look at the crocodile! On the eve of visiting Europe it is as well to acquaint ourselves on the spot with its indigenous inhabitants."

b. Narrator: "... I began to entreat Elena Ivanovna to calm herself, and above all not to use the shocking word 'flay.' For such a reactionary desire here, in the midst of the Arcade and of the most cultured society, not two paces from the hall where at this very minute Mr. Lavrov was perhaps delivering a public lecture, was not only impossible but unthinkable, and might at any moment bring upon us the hisses of culture and the caricatures of Mr. Stepanov."

c. Ivan: "Never has my spirit soared as now. In my narrow refuge there is only one thing that I dread—the literary criticisms of the monthlies and the hiss of our satirical papers. I am afraid that thoughtless visitors, stupid and envious people and nihilists in general, may turn me into ridicule. But I will take measures. I am impatiently awaiting the response of the public tomorrow, and especially the opinion of the newspapers."

d. Elena: "Oh, dear! ... how is he going to have his dinner ... and what will he do ... if he wants anything?" Narrator: "An unforeseen question. ... To tell the truth, it had not entered my head, so much more practical are women than men in the solution of the problems of daily life!"

e. Timofey Semyonitch: "To my mind, it's really a good thing he should lie there a bit, instead of going abroad.... And a crocodile is private property, and so it is impossible to slit him open without compensation." Narrator: "For the saving of human life, Timofey Semyonitch." Timofey Semyonitch: "Oh, well, that's a matter for the police.... But the chief point is that the crocodile is private property, so that the principles of economics apply in this question. And the principles of economics are paramount. ... To my mind, Ivan Matveitch, as the true son of his fatherland, ought to rejoice and to be proud that through him the value of a foreign crocodile has been doubled and possibly even trebled."

f. Ivan: "What is the fundamental characteristic of the crocodile? The answer is clear: to swallow human beings. How is one, in constructing the crocodile, to secure that he should swallow people? The answer is clearer still: construct him hollow. It was settled by physics long ago that Nature abhors a vacuum. Hence the inside of the crocodile must be hollow so that it may abhor the vacuum, and consequently swallow and so fill itself with anything it can come across.

And that is the sole rational cause why every crocodile swallows men. It is not the same in the constitution of man: the emptier a man's head is, for instance, the less he feels the thirst to fill it, and that is the one exception to the general rule."

Find other examples of absurdities of the same sort. Discuss with the class the way in which Dostoevsky has contrived to make the "rational" absurd and the "irrational," or unexplainable, sensible.

REACTING TO COMMENTARY ABOUT "THE CROCODILE"

Many Russian readers took "The Crocodile" as an insulting satire of N. G. Chernyshevsky's liberal views. You will recall Chernyshevsky as a commentator on Turgenev's work and as a critic who advocated the use of literature for social reform. In 1862 Chernyshevsky was arrested for his radical views and in 1864 was exiled to Siberia. Before his exile, however, he wrote a work, *What Is to Be Done?,* in which he set forth his ideas of the rational ways in which men could achieve social and political harmony.

Dostoevsky answered the charges of personal insult to Chernyshevsky in an issue of *A Writer's Diary,* that appeared eleven years after the publication of "The Crocodile."

> About eighteen months ago it occurred to me to write a fantastic tale—something along the lines of Gogol's story "The Nose." Never before did I attempt to write in a fantastic vein. This was a purely literary prank, solely for the sake of humor. In fact, I had come across several comical situations which I sought to unfold....
>
> ... it is not finished. Some day, by all means, I will finish it, even though I have forgotten it and have to read it over to recall it.
>
> And yet, here is what people managed to make out of this bagatelle. No sooner had the story appeared in the magazine *Epoch* (in 1865), than the *Voice,* unexpectedly, printed a strange notice. I do not literally recall its contents and, besides, it would take too much trouble to check it, but its meaning was somewhat along these lines: "In vain, it would seem, does the author of "The Crocodile" choose this path; it will bring him neither honor nor anticipated advantage," etc., etc., followed by a few most nebulous and inimical stings. I read it in passing, understood nothing, but perceived much venom without comprehending why. This vague feuilletonistic[1] comment, in itself, of course, could cause

---

[1]*feuilletonistic:* journalistic.

me no damage: all the same no one among the readers could have understood it—even as myself. Yet, a week later, N. N. S. said to me: "Do you know what they are thinking there?—There they are convinced that your 'Crocodile' is an allegory, the story of Chernyshevsky's exile, and that it was your intention to portray and ridicule him." Although surprised, I wasn't much worried—what kind of conjectures can't be set forth? This opinion seemed to me too isolated and farfetched to produce any effect, and I deemed it altogether unnecessary to protest. This I will never forgive myself, since the opinion took root and did spread. *Calomniez, il en restera toujours quelque chose.*[1]

However, even now I am certain that here there was no calumny at all—and what would be the purpose?—In literary circles I had quarreled with almost no one—at least, seriously....

Wherein is the allegory?—Why, certainly—the crocodile signifies Siberia; the self-conceited and light-minded bureaucrat is Chernyshevsky. He got into the crocodile, but still hopes to teach the whole world. The pusillanimous friend of his typifies all the local friends of Chernyshevsky. The good-looking but stupid little wife of the bureaucrat, enjoying her status "as that of a widow"—this is... But this is dirty to such an extent that I decline to soil myself and to continue the explanation of the allegory. (And yet it did take root; and it did so, perhaps, precisely because of this last insinuation. I have irrefutable proof thereof.)

So that the presumption was made that I, myself a former exile and a convict, rejoiced in the exile of another "unfortunate"; even more—I wrote on this occasion a diatribe. Yet, where is the proof of that? In the allegory? But give me whatever you please: *The Memoirs of a Lunatic,* the ode *God, Uri Miloslavsky,* the verses of Fet[2]—anything—and I undertake to prove to you by the very first ten lines, designated by you, that therein is precisely an allegory on the Franco-Prussian War or a pasquinade on the actor Gorbunov—in a word, on anyone you please, on anyone you may insist upon.

Please recall how, in olden days, at the end of the forties, for instance, censors used to examine manuscripts: there wasn't a line, there wasn't a dot in which something, some allegory, wouldn't have been suspected. Let them produce anything at all

---

[1]*Calomniez . . . chose:* Even if you are innocent, once you have been slandered, you will always be open to suspicion.
[2]*Fet:* Afanasi Afanasievich Fet, Russian poet. (See page 85.)

from the record of my whole life in support of the fact that I resemble a malicious, heartless lampooner and that one may expect from me allegories of this kind.

On the contrary, the very haste and promptitude of such inferences prove a certain vileness of spirit in the accusers, the coarseness and inhumanity of their views. Here, the simplemindedness of the conjecture itself is no excuse. Why not?—One can be simplemindedly vile—and that's all.

Perhaps, I had a personal hatred of Chernyshevsky?—To forestall this accusation I gave above an account of our brief and cordial acquaintance. It may be said: this is not enough, for I may have nourished a concealed hate. Then, let them set forth pretexts for such animosity, if they have anything to produce. But there were no such pretexts. On the other hand, I am certain that Chernyshevsky himself would corroborate the veracity of my account of our meeting, if some day he should read it. And I pray God that he be given an opportunity to do so. I am longing for this as warmly, as ardently as I sincerely regretted, and do regret, his misfortune.[1] [*Theodore Dostoevsky*]

Does Dostoevsky's explanation of the critic's interpretation of his story seem sincere? How would you explain the allegory of "The Crocodile" in a more generalized way?

The allegory of "The Crocodile" is perhaps an allegory based on what has become known as the "Russian Idea." You have already learned something of the Slavophiles and Westernized Russians from the Introduction (pages 3-13) of this book and from the Muchnic passage which accompanies Turgenev's "The Reformer and the Russian German" (pages 61-62). Dostoevsky is usually considered a Slavophile. Actually, as Janko Lavrin so well explains, Dostoevsky began as a liberal, became a conservative after his Siberian experience, and ended by adopting and, in a sense, formulating the "Russian Idea," which aimed at the combining of West and East under the messianic drive of pan-Russianism.

A careful study of his novels and correspondence only confirms the difficulty he had in fighting his own "crucible of doubts," his latent nihilism. Even the Russian Idea, as formulated by him in the end, was above all a projection of his desire to integrate some of those contrasts and conflicts within himself which threatened to

[1] From *The Diary of a Writer, F. M. Dostoevsky*, translated by Boris Brasol; copyright 1949 Charles Scribner's Sons. Reprinted by permission of Charles Scribner's Sons.

undermine his personality. Identifying his own needs and wishes with the prospective mission of his country, he could not help but see her as a universal peacemaker, reconciling all the contrasts — Russian and European — in a higher synthesis to come.

Such an attitude demanded, however, that tolerant view of the European West which he finally adopted. In spite of his loathing of Western philistinism, he could hardly dismiss the cultural achievements of the European past. In fact, he admired them, even if they seemed to him more like a "beautiful cemetery" — a view expressed clearly enough through Versilov and Ivan Karamazov. But if so, the mission of Russia as he saw or wished to see it, assumed an all-the-greater significance. Her destiny was, in short, to reveal to Europe a new scale of values, and the ideal of a true integrated unity of mankind, as distinct from a compulsory external unification. Outside and apart from such a unity Dostoevsky saw no creative future either for Russia or mankind as a whole, but only a rapidly growing Tower of Babel, whose very productivity was doomed to hasten its ruin.

It was for this reason that he wrote: "The future Russian Idea is not yet born, but the entire earth awaits it in pain and suffering." And again (in his *Journal of an Author*): "I make no attempt to compare Russia with the Western nations in the matter of economic and scientific renown. I only say that the Russian people are perhaps among all nations the most capable of upholding the ideal of universal union of mankind, of brotherly love, of the calm conception which forgives contrasts. This is not an economic, but a moral trait." In his Pushkin speech he went even further, when saying that "to a true Russian Europe and the destiny of all the mighty Aryan [sic] family are as dear as Russia herself; because our destiny is universality won not by the sword, but by the strength of brotherhood and our fraternal aspirations, to reunite mankind. And, in course of time, I believe that we shall, without exception, understand that to be a Russian does indeed mean to aspire finally to reconcile the contradictions of Europe, to show the end of our European yearning in our Russian soul, omnihuman and all-uniting, to include within our soul by brotherly love all our brethren, and at last it may be, to pronounce the final word of the great general harmony, of the general brotherly communion of all nations in accordance with the law and the gospel of Christ."

Passages such as this may seem—especially in the light of our present-day history—mere rhetoric. Yet to a Russian they still can mean something that might some time become real. . . .[1]
[*Janko Lavrin*]

From what you know of modern Russia, is there anything prophetic about the last lines of this passage?

THE MEEK ONES

An Honest Thief

Dostoevsky's interest in duality—his dramatization of the inner struggle in man between good and evil, pride and humility, reason and will—was objectified in two kinds of characters, the "proud" and the "meek." The following story presents an example of the latter. As you read, notice how the submissive, spineless, and dishonest beggar gradually becomes the "hero" of the tale.

An Honest Thief

One morning, just as I was about to set off to my office, Agrafena, my cook, washerwoman and housekeeper, came in to me and, to my surprise, entered into conversation.

She had always been such a silent, simple creature that, except for her daily inquiry about dinner, she had not uttered a word for the last six years. I, at least, had heard nothing else from her.

"Here I have come in to have a word with you, sir," she began abruptly, "you really ought to let the little room."

"Which little room?"

"Why, the one next the kitchen, to be sure."

"What for?"

"What for? Why because folks do take in lodgers, to be sure."

"But who would take it?"

"Who would take it? Why, a lodger would take it, to be sure."

---

[1] From *Dostoevsky: A Study* by Janko Lavrin (1943); New York: Russell & Russell, 1968. Reprinted by permission of Janko Lavrin and Russell & Russell.

"An Honest Thief" from *An Honest Thief and Other Stories* by Dostoevsky, translated by Constance Garnett. Published in England by William Heinemann Ltd. and reprinted with their permission.

"But, my good woman, one could not put a bedstead in it; there wouldn't be room to move! Who could live in it?"

"Who wants to live there! As long as he has a place to sleep in. Why, he would live in the window."

"In what window?"

"In what window! As though you didn't know! The one in the passage, to be sure. He would sit there, sewing or doing anything else. Maybe he would sit on a chair, too. He's got a chair; and he has a table, too; he's got everything."

"Who is 'he' then?"

"Oh, a good man, a man of experience. I will cook for him. And I'll ask him three rubles a month for his board and lodging."

After prolonged efforts I succeeded at last in learning from Agrafena that an elderly man had somehow managed to persuade her to admit him into the kitchen as a lodger and boarder. Any notion Agrafena took into her head had to be carried out; if not, I knew she would give me no peace. When anything was not to her liking, she at once began to brood, and sank into a deep dejection that would last for a fortnight or three weeks. During that period my dinners were spoiled, my linen was mislaid, my floors went unscrubbed; in short, I had a great deal to put up with. I had observed long ago that this inarticulate woman was incapable of conceiving a project, of originating an idea of her own. But if anything like a notion or a project was by some means put into her feeble brain, to prevent its being carried out meant, for a time, her moral assassination. And so, as I cared more for my peace of mind than for anything else, I consented forthwith.

"Has he a passport anyway, or something of the sort?"

"To be sure, he has. He is a good man, a man of experience; three rubles he's promised to pay."

The very next day the new lodger made his appearance in my modest bachelor quarters; but I was not put out by this, indeed I was inwardly pleased. I lead as a rule a very lonely hermit's existence. I have scarcely any friends; I hardly ever go anywhere. As I had spent ten years never coming out of my shell, I had, of course, grown used to solitude. But another ten or fifteen years or more of the same solitary existence, with the same Agrafena, in the same bachelor quarters, was in truth a somewhat cheerless prospect. And therefore a new inmate, if well behaved, was a heaven-sent blessing.

Agrafena had spoken truly: my lodger was certainly a man of experience. From his passport it appeared that he was an old soldier, a fact which I should have known indeed from his face. An old soldier is easily recognized. Astafy Ivanovitch was a favorable specimen of his class. We got on very well together. What was best of all, Astafy Ivanovitch would sometimes tell a story, describing some incident in his own life. In the perpetual boredom of my existence such a storyteller was a veritable treasure. One day he told me one of these stories. It made an impression on me. The following event was what led to it.

I was left alone in the flat; both Astafy and Agrafena were out on business of their own. All of a sudden I heard from the inner room somebody—I fancied a stranger—come in; I went out; there actually was a stranger in the passage, a short fellow wearing no overcoat in spite of the cold autumn weather.

"What do you want?"

"Does a clerk called Alexandrov live here?"

"Nobody of that name here, brother. Good-by."

"Why, the dvornik[1] told me it was here," said my visitor, cautiously retiring towards the door.

"Be off, be off, brother, get along."

Next day after dinner, while Astafy Ivanovitch was fitting on a coat which he was altering for me, again someone came into the passage. I haif opened the door.

Before my very eyes my yesterday's visitor, with perfect composure, took my wadded greatcoat from the peg and, stuffing it under his arm, darted out of the flat. Agrafena stood all the time staring at him, agape with astonishment and doing nothing for the protection of my property. Astafy Ivanovitch flew in pursuit of the thief and ten minutes later came back out of breath and empty-handed. He had vanished completely.

"Well, there's a piece of luck, Astafy Ivanovitch!"

"It's a good job your cloak is left! Or he would have put you in a plight, the thief!"

But the whole incident had so impressed Astafy Ivanovitch that I forgot the theft as I looked at him. He could not get over it. Every minute or two he would drop the work upon which he was engaged, and would describe over again how it had all happened, how he had been standing, how the greatcoat had been taken down before his very eyes, not a yard away, and how it had come to pass that he could not catch the thief. Then he would sit down to his work again, then leave it once more, and at last I saw him go down to the dvornik to tell him all about it, and to upbraid him for letting such a thing happen in his domain. Then he came back and began scolding Agrafena. Then he sat down to his work again, and long afterward he was still muttering to himself how it had all hap-

---

[1]*dvornik:* porter or doorman.

pened, how he stood there and I was here, how before our eyes, not a yard away, the thief took the coat off the peg, and so on. In short, though Astafy Ivanovitch understood his business, he was a terrible slowpoke and busybody.

"He's made fools of us, Astafy Ivanovitch," I said to him in the evening, as I gave him a glass of tea. I wanted to while away the time by recalling the story of the lost greatcoat, the frequent repetition of which, together with the great earnestness of the speaker, was beginning to become very amusing.

"Fools, indeed, sir! Even though it is no business of mine, I am put out. It makes me angry though it is not my coat that was lost. To my thinking there is no vermin in the world worse than a thief. Another takes what you can spare, but a thief steals the work of your hands, the sweat of your brow, your time.... Ugh, it's nasty! One can't speak of it! it's too vexing. How is it you don't feel the loss of your property, sir?"

"Yes, you are right, Astafy Ivanovitch, better if the thing had been burned; it's annoying to let the thief have it, it's disagreeable."

"Disagreeable! I should think so! Yet, to be sure, there are thieves and thieves. And I have happened, sir, to come across an honest thief."

"An honest thief? But how can a thief be honest, Astafy Ivanovitch?"

"There you are right indeed, sir. How can a thief be honest? There are none such. I only meant to say that he was an honest man, sure enough, and yet he stole. I was simply sorry for him."

"Why, how was that, Astafy Ivanovitch?"

"It was about two years ago, sir. I had been nearly a year out of a place, and just before I lost my place I made the acquaintance of a poor lost creature. We got acquainted in a public house.[1] He was a drunkard, a vagrant, a beggar, he had been in a situation of some sort, but from his drinking habits he had lost his work. Such a ne'er-do-well! God only knows what he had on! Often you wouldn't be sure if he'd a shirt under his coat; everything he could lay his hands upon he would drink away. But he was not one to quarrel; he was a quiet fellow. A soft, good-natured chap. And he'd never ask, he was ashamed; but you could see for yourself the poor fellow wanted a drink, and you would stand it him. And so we got friendly, that's to say, he stuck to me.... It was all one to me. And what a man he was, to be sure! Like a little dog he would follow me; wherever I went there he would be; and all that after our first meeting, and he as thin as a thread paper! At first it was 'let me stay the night'; well, I let him stay.

"I looked at his passport, too; the man was all right.

[1] *public house:* tavern, saloon.

"Well, the next day it was the same story, and then the third day he came again and sat all day in the window and stayed the night. 'Well,' thinks I, 'he is sticking to me; give him food and drink and shelter at night, too—here am I, a poor man, and a hanger-on to keep as well!' And before he came to me, he used to go in the same way to a government clerk's; he attached himself to him; they were always drinking together; but he, through trouble of some sort, drank himself into the grave. My man was called Emelyan Ilyitch. I pondered and pondered what I was to do with him. To drive him away I was ashamed. I was sorry for him; such a pitiful, God-forsaken creature I never did set eyes on. And not a word said either; he does not ask, but just sits there and looks into your eyes like a dog. To think what drinking will bring a man down to!

"I keep asking myself how am I to say to him: 'You must be moving, Emelyanoushka, there's nothing for you here, you've come to the wrong place; I shall soon not have a bite for myself, how am I to keep you too?'

"I sat and wondered what he'd do when I said that to him. And I seemed to see how he'd stare at me, if he were to hear me say that, how long he would sit and not understand a word of it. And when it did get home to him at last, how he would get up from the window, would take up his bundle—I can see it now, the red-check handkerchief full of holes, with God knows what wrapped up in it, which he had always with him, and then how he would set his shabby old coat to rights, so that it would look decent and keep him warm, so that no holes would be seen—he was a man of delicate feelings! And how he'd open the door and go out with tears in his eyes. Well, there's no letting a man go to ruin like that. . . . One's sorry for him.

"'And then again,' I think, 'how am I off myself? Wait a bit, Emelyanoushka,' says I to myself, 'you've not long to feast with me: I shall soon be going away and then you will not find me.'

"Well, sir, our family made a move; and Alexandr Filimonovitch, my master (now deceased, God rest his soul), said, 'I am thoroughly satisfied with you, Astafy Ivanovitch; when we come back from the country we will take you on again.' I had been butler with them; a nice gentleman he was, but he died that same year. Well, after seeing him off, I took my belongings, what little money I had, and I thought I'd have a rest for a time, so I went to an old woman I knew, and took a corner in her room. There was only one corner free in it. She had been a nurse, so now she had a pension and a room of her own. Well, now good-by, Emelyanoushka, thinks I, you won't find me now, my boy.

"And what do you think, sir? I had gone out to see a man I knew, and when I came back in the evening, the first thing I saw was Emelyanoushka! There he was, sitting on my box and his check bundle beside him; he was sitting in his ragged old coat, waiting for me. And to while away the time he had borrowed a church book fom the old lady, and was holding it wrong side upwards. He'd scented me out! My heart sank. 'Well,' thinks I, 'there's no help for it — why didn't I turn him out at first?' So I asked him straight off: 'Have you brought your passport, Emelyanoushka?'

"I sat down on the spot, sir, and began to ponder: will a vagabond like that be very much trouble to me? And on thinking it over it seemed he would not be much trouble. 'He must be fed,' I thought. 'Well, a bit of bread in the morning, and to make it go down better I'll buy him an onion. At midday I should have to give him another bit of bread and an onion; and in the evening, onion again with kvass,[1] with some more bread if he wanted it.' And if some cabbage soup were to come our way, then we should both have had our fill. I am no great eater myself, and a drinking man, as we all know, never eats; all he wants is herb-brandy or green vodka. 'He'll ruin me with his drinking,' I thought, but then another idea came into my head, sir, and took great hold on me. So much so that if Emelyanoushka had gone away I should have felt that I had nothing to live for, I do believe. . . . I determined on the spot to be a father and guardian to him. 'I'll keep him from ruin,' I thought, 'I'll wean him from the glass! You wait a bit,' thought I; 'very well, Emelyanoushka, you may stay, only you must behave yourself; you must obey orders.'

" 'Well,' thinks I to myself, 'I'll begin by training him to work of some sort, but not all at once; let him enjoy himself a little first, and I'll look round and find something you are fit for, Emelyanoushka.' For every sort of work a man needs a special ability, you know, sir. And I began to watch him on the quiet; I soon saw Emelyanoushka was a desperate character. I began, sir, with a word of advice: I said this and that to him. 'Emelyanoushka,' said I, 'you ought to take a thought and mend your ways. Have done with drinking! Just look what rags you go about in: that old coat of yours, if I may make bold to say so, is fit for nothing but a sieve. A pretty state of things! It's time to draw the line, sure enough.' Emelyanoushka sat and listened to me with his head hanging down. Would you believe it, sir? It had come to such a pass with him, he'd lost his tongue through drink and could not speak a word of sense. Talk to him of cucumbers and he'd answer back about beans! He would listen and listen to me and then heave such a sigh. 'What are you sighing for, Emelyan Ilyitch?' I asked him.

---

[1] *kvass:* a fermented drink resembling sour beer.

"'Oh, nothing; don't you mind me, Astafy Ivanovitch. Do you know there were two women fighting in the street today, Astafy Ivanovitch? One upset the other woman's basket of cranberries by accident.'

"'Well, what of that?'

"'And the second one upset the other's cranberries on purpose and trampled them under foot, too.'

"'Well, and what of it, Emelyan Ilyitch?'

"'Why, nothing, Astafy Ivanovitch, I just mentioned it.'

"'Nothing, I just mentioned it!' 'Emelyanoushka, my boy,' I thought, 'you've squandered and drunk away your brains!'

"'And do you know, a gentleman dropped a money note on the pavement in Gorohovy Street, no, it was Sadovy Street. And a peasant saw it and said, "That's my luck"; and at the same time another man saw it and said, "No, it's my bit of luck. I saw it before you did."'

"'Well, Emelyan Ilyitch?'

"'And the fellows had a fight over it, Astafy Ivanovitch. But a policeman came up, took away the note, gave it back to the gentleman and threatened to take up both the men.'

"'Well, but what of that? What is there edifying about it, Emelyanoushka?'

"'Why, nothing, to be sure. Folks laughed, Astafy Ivanovitch.'

"'Ach, Emelyanoushka! What do the folks matter? You've sold your soul for a brass farthing! But do you know what I have to tell you, Emelyan Ilyitch?'

"'What, Astafy Ivanovitch?'

"'Take a job of some sort, that's what you must do. For the hundredth time I say to you, set to work, have some mercy on yourself!'

"'What could I set to, Astafy Ivanovitch? I don't know what job I could set to, and there is no one who will take me on, Astafy Ivanovitch.'

"'That's how you came to be turned off, Emelyanoushka, you drinking man!'

"'And do you know Vlass, the waiter, was sent for to the office today, Astafy Ivanovitch?'

"'Why did they send for him, Emelyanoushka?' I asked.

"'I could not say why, Astafy Ivanovitch. I suppose they wanted him there, and that's why they sent for him.'

"'A-ach,' thought I, 'we are in a bad way, poor Emelyanoushka! The Lord is chastising us for our sins.' Well, sir, what is one to do with such a man?

"But a cunning fellow he was, and no mistake. He'd listen and listen to me, but at last I suppose he got sick of it. As soon as he sees I am beginning to get angry, he'd pick up his old coat and out he'd slip and leave no trace. He'd wander about all day and come back at night drunk. Where he got the money from, the Lord only knows; I had no hand in that.

" 'No,' said I, 'Emelyan Ilyitch, you'll come to a bad end. Give over drinking, mind what I say now, give it up! Next time you come home in liquor, you can spend the night on the stairs. I won't let you in!'

"After hearing that threat, Emelyanoushka sat at home that day and the next; but on the third he slipped off again. I waited and waited; he didn't come back. Well, at last I don't mind owning, I was in a fright, and I felt for the man too. 'What have I done to him?' I thought. 'I've scared him away. Where's the poor fellow gone to now? He'll get lost maybe. Lord have mercy upon us!'

"Night came on, he did not come. In the morning I went out into the porch; I looked, and if he hadn't gone to sleep in the porch! There he was with his head on the step, and chilled to the marrow of his bones.

" 'What next, Emelyanoushka, God have mercy on you! Where will you get to next!'

" 'Why, you were—sort of—angry with me, Astafy Ivanovitch, the other day, you were vexed and promised to put me to sleep in the porch, so I didn't—sort of—venture to come in, Astafy Ivanovitch, and so I lay down here....'

"I did feel angry and sorry too.

" 'Surely you might undertake some other duty, Emelyanoushka, instead of lying here guarding the steps,' I said.

" 'Why, what other duty, Astafy Ivanovitch?'

" 'You lost soul'—I was in such a rage, I called him that—'if you could but learn tailoring work! Look at your old rag of a coat! It's not enough to have it in tatters, here you are sweeping the steps with it! You might take a needle and boggle up your rags, as decency demands. Ah, you drunken man!'

"What do you think, sir? He actually did take a needle. Of course I said it in jest, but he was so scared he set to work. He took off his coat and began threading the needle. I watched him; as you may well guess, his eyes were all red and bleary, and his hands were all of a shake. He kept shoving and shoving the thread and could not get it through the eye of the needle; he kept screwing his eyes up and wetting the thread and twisting it in his fingers—it was no good! He gave it up and looked at me.

" 'Well,' said I, 'this is a nice way to treat me! If there had been folks by to see, I don't know what I should have done! Why, you simple fellow, I said it to you in joke, as a reproach. Give over your nonsense, God bless you! Sit quiet and don't put me to shame, don't sleep on my stairs and make a laughingstock of me.'

" 'Why, what am I to do, Astafy Ivanovitch? I know very well I am a drunkard and good for nothing! I can do nothing but vex you, my bene—bene—factor. . . .'

"And at that his blue lips began all of a sudden to quiver, and a tear ran down his white cheek and trembled on his stubbly chin, and then poor Emelyanoushka burst into a regular flood of tears. Mercy on us! I felt as though a knife were thrust into my heart! The sensitive creature! I'd never have expected it. Who could have guessed it? 'No, Emelyanoushka,' thought I, 'I shall give you up altogether. You can go your way like the rubbish you are.'

"Well, sir, why make a long story of it? And the whole affair is so trifling; it's not worth wasting words upon. Why, you, for instance, sir, would not have given a thought to it, but I would have given a great deal —if I had a great deal to give—that it never should have happened at all.

"I had a pair of riding breeches by me, sir, deuce take them, fine, first-rate riding breeches they were too, blue with a check on it. They'd been ordered by a gentleman from the country, but he would not have them after all; said they were not full enough, so they were left on my hands. It struck me they were worth something. At the secondhand dealer's I ought to get five silver rubles for them, or if not I could turn them into two pairs of trousers for Petersburg gentlemen and have a piece over for a waistcoat for myself. Of course for poor people like us everything comes in. And it happened just then that Emelyanoushka was having a sad time of it. There he sat day after day: he did not drink, not a drop passed his lips, but he sat and moped like an owl. It was sad to see him —he just sat and brooded. 'Well,' thought I, 'either you've not got a copper to spend, my lad, or else you're turning over a new leaf yourself, you've given it up, you've listened to reason.' Well, sir, that's how it was with us; and just then came a holiday. I went to vespers; when I came home I found Emelyanoushka sitting in the window, drunk and rocking to and fro.

"Ah! so that's what you've been up to, my lad! And I went to get something out of my chest. And when I looked in, the breeches were not there. . . . I rummaged here and there; they'd vanished. When I'd ransacked everywhere and saw they were not there, something seemed to stab me to the heart. I ran first to the old dame and began accusing her; of Emelyanoushka I'd not the faintest suspicion, though there was cause for it in his sitting there drunk.

" 'No,' said the old body, 'God be with you, my fine gentleman, what good are riding breeches to me? Am I going to wear such things? Why, a skirt I had I lost the other day through a fellow of your sort ... I know nothing; I can tell you nothing about it,' she said.

" 'Who has been here, who has been in?' I asked.

" 'Why, nobody has been, my good sir,' says she; 'I've been here all the while; Emelyan Ilyitch went out and came back again; there he sits, ask him.'

" 'Emelyanoushka,' said I, 'have you taken those new riding breeches for anything; you remember the pair I made for that gentleman from the country?'

" 'No, Astafy Ivanovitch,' said he; 'I've not—sort of—touched them.'

"I was in a state! I hunted high and low for them—they were nowhere to be found. And Emelyanoushka sits there rocking himself to and fro. I was squatting on my heels facing him and bending over the chest, and all at once I stole a glance at him.... 'Alack,' I thought; my heart suddenly grew hot within me and I felt myself flushing up too. And suddenly Emelyanoushka looked at me.

" 'No, Astafy Ivanovitch,' said he, 'those riding breeches of yours, maybe, you are thinking, maybe, I took them, but I never touched them.'

" 'But what can have become of them, Emelyan Ilyitch?'

" 'No, Astafy Ivanovitch,' said he, 'I've never seen them.'

" 'Why, Emelyan Ilyitch, I suppose they've run off of themselves, eh?'

" 'Maybe they have, Astafy Ivanovitch.'

"When I heard him say that, I got up at once, went up to him, lighted the lamp and sat down to work to my sewing. I was altering a waistcoat for a clerk who lived below us. And wasn't there a burning pain and ache in my breast! I shouldn't have minded so much if I had put all the clothes I had in the fire. Emelyanoushka seemed to have an inkling of what a rage I was in. When a man is guilty, you know, sir, he scents trouble far off, like the birds of the air before a storm.

" 'Do you know what, Astafy Ivanovitch,' Emelyanoushka began, and his poor old voice was shaking as he said the words, 'Antip Prohoritch, the apothecary, married the coachman's wife this morning, who died the other day——'

"I did give him a look sir, a nasty look it was; Emelyanoushka understood it too. I saw him get up, go to the bed, and begin to rummage there for something. I waited—he was busy there a long time and kept muttering all the while, 'No, not there, where can the blessed things have got to!' I waited to see what he'd do; I saw him creep under the bed on all fours. I couldn't bear it any longer. 'What are you crawling about under the bed for, Emelyan Ilyitch?' said I.

" 'Looking for the breeches, Astafy Ivanovitch. Maybe they've dropped down there somewhere.'

" 'Why should you try to help a poor simple man like me,' said I, 'crawling on your knees for nothing, sir?' — I called him that in my vexation.

" 'Oh, never mind, Astafy Ivanovitch, I'll just look. They'll turn up, maybe, somewhere.'

" 'H'm,' said I, 'look here, Emelyan Ilyitch!'

" 'What is it, Astafy Ivanovitch?' said he.

" 'Haven't you simply stolen them from me like a thief and a robber, in return for the bread and salt you've eaten here?' said I.

"I felt so angry, sir, at seeing him fooling about on his knees before me.

" 'No, Astafy Ivanovitch.'

"And he stayed lying as he was on his face under the bed. A long time he lay there and then at last crept out. I looked at him and the man was white as a sheet. He stood up, and sat down near me in the window and sat so for some ten minutes.

" 'No, Astafy Ivanovitch,' he said, and all at once he stood up and came towards me, and I can see him now; he looked dreadful. 'No, Astafy Ivanovitch,' said he, 'I never — sort of — touched your breeches.'

"He was all of a shake, poking himself in the chest with a trembling finger, and his poor old voice shook so that I was frightened, sir, and sat as though I was rooted to the window seat.

" 'Well, Emelyan Ilyitch,' said I, 'as you will, forgive me if I, in my foolishness, have accused you unjustly. As for the breeches, let them go hang; we can live without them. We've still our hands, thank God; we need not go thieving or begging from some other poor man; we'll earn our bread.'

"Emelyanoushka heard me out and went on standing there before me. I looked up, and he had sat down. And there he sat all the evening without stirring. At last I lay down to sleep. Emelyanoushka went on sitting in the same place. When I looked out in the morning, he was lying curled up in his old coat on the bare floor; he felt too crushed even to come to bed. Well, sir, I felt no more liking for the fellow from that day, in fact for the first few days I hated him. I felt, as one may say, as though my own son had robbed me, and done me a deadly hurt. 'Ach,' thought I,

'Emelyanoushka, Emelyanoushka!' And Emelyanoushka, sir, went on drinking for a whole fortnight without stopping. He was drunk all the time, and regularly besotted. He went out in the morning and came back late at night, and for a whole fortnight I didn't get a word out of him. It was as though grief was gnawing at his heart, or as though he wanted to do for himself completely. At last he stopped; he must have come to the end of all he'd got, and then he sat in the window again. I remember he sat there without speaking for three days and three nights; all of a sudden I saw that he was crying. He was just sitting there, sir, and crying like anything: a perfect stream, as though he didn't know how his tears were flowing. And it's a sad thing, sir, to see a grown-up man and an old man, too, crying from woe and grief.

" 'What's the matter, Emelyanoushka?' said I.

"He began to tremble so that he shook all over. I spoke to him for the first time since that evening.

" 'Nothing, Astafy Ivanovitch.'

" 'God be with you, Emelyanoushka, what's lost is lost. Why are you moping about like this?' I felt sorry for him.

" 'Oh, nothing, Astafy Ivanovitch, it's no matter. I want to find some work to do, Astafy Ivanovitch.'

" 'And what sort of work, pray, Emelyanoushka?'

" 'Why, any sort; perhaps I could find a situation such as I used to have. I've been already to ask Fedosay Ivanitch. I don't like to be a burden on you, Astafy Ivanovitch. If I can find a situation, Astafy Ivanovitch, then I'll pay it you all back, and make you a return for all your hospitality.'

" 'Enough, Emelyanoushka, enough; let bygones be bygones — and no more to be said about it. Let us go on as we used to do before.'

" 'No, Astafy Ivanovitch, you, maybe, think — but I never touched your riding breeches.'

" 'Well, have it your own way; God be with you, Emelyanoushka.'

" 'No, Astafy Ivanovitch, I can't go on living with you, that's clear. You must excuse me, Astafy Ivanovitch.'

" 'Why, God bless you, Emelyan Ilyitch, who's offending you and driving you out of the place — am I doing it?'

" 'No, it's not the proper thing for me to live with you like this, Astafy Ivanovitch. I'd better be going.'

"He was so hurt, it seemed, he stuck to his point. I looked at him, and sure enough, up he got and pulled his old coat over his shoulders.

" 'But where are you going, Emelyan Ilyitch? Listen to reason: what are you about? Where are you off to?'

" 'No, good-by, Astafy Ivanovitch, don't keep me now' — and he was blubbering again — 'I'd better be going. You're not the same now.'

" 'Not the same as what? I am the same. But you'll be lost by yourself like a poor helpless babe, Emelyan Ilyitch.'

" 'No, Astafy Ivanovitch, when you go out now, you lock up your chest and it makes me cry to see it, Astafy Ivanovitch. You'd better let me go, Astafy Ivanovitch, and forgive me all the trouble I've given you while I've been living with you.'

"Well, sir, the man went away. I waited for a day; I expected he'd be back in the evening — no. Next day no sign of him, nor the third day either. I began to get frightened; I was so worried, I couldn't drink, I couldn't eat, I couldn't sleep. The fellow had quite disarmed me. On the fourth day I went out to look for him, I peeped into all the taverns, to inquire for him — but no, Emelyanoushka was lost. 'Have you managed to keep yourself alive, Emelyanoushka?' I wondered. 'Perhaps he is lying dead under some hedge, poor drunkard, like a sodden log.' I went home more dead than alive. Next day I went out to look for him again. And I kept cursing myself that I'd been such a fool as to let the man go off by himself. On the fifth day it was a holiday — in the early morning I heard the door creak. I looked up and there was my Emelyanoushka coming in. His face was blue and his hair was covered with dirt as though he'd been sleeping in the street; he was as thin as a match. He took off his old coat, sat down on the chest and looked at me. I delighted to see him, but I felt more upset about him than ever. For you see, sir, if I'd been overtaken in some sin, as true as I am here, sir, I'd have died like a dog before I'd have come back. But Emelyanoushka did come back. And a sad thing it was, sure enough, to see a man sunk so low. I began to look after him, to talk kindly to him, to comfort him.

" 'Well, Emelyanoushka,' said I, 'I am glad you've come back. Had you been away much longer I should have gone to look for you in the taverns again today. Are you hungry?'

" 'No, Astafy Ivanovitch.'

" 'Come, now, aren't you really? Here, brother, is some cabbage soup left over from yesterday; there was meat in it; it is good stuff. And here is some bread and onion. Come, eat it, it'll do you no harm.'

"I made him eat it, and I saw at once that the man had not tasted food for maybe three days — he was as hungry as a wolf. So it was hunger that had driven him to me. My heart was melted looking at the poor dear. 'Let me run to the tavern,' thought I, 'I'll get something to ease his heart, and then we'll make an end of it. I've no more anger in my heart against you, Emelyanoushka!' I brought him some vodka. 'Here, Eme-

Iyan Ilyitch, let us have a drink for the holiday. Like a drink? And it will do you good.' He held out his hand, held it out greedily; he was just taking it, and then he stopped himself. But a minute after, I saw him take it, and lift it to his mouth, spilling it on his sleeve. But though he got it to his lips he set it down on the table again.

" 'What is it, Emelyanoushka?'

" 'Nothing, Astafy Ivanovitch, I—sort of——'

" 'Won't you drink it?'

" 'Well, Astafy Ivanovitch, I'm not—sort of—going to drink any more, Astafy Ivanovitch.'

" 'Do you mean you've given it up altogether, Emelyanoushka, or are you only not going to drink today?'

"He did not answer. A minute later I saw him rest his head on his hand.

" 'What's the matter, Emelyanoushka, are you ill?'

" 'Why, yes, Astafy Ivanovitch, I don't feel well.'

"I took him and laid him down on the bed. I saw that he really was ill: his head was burning hot and he was shivering with fever. I sat by him all day; toward night he was worse. I mixed him some oil and onion and kvass and bread broken up.

" 'Come, eat some of this,' said I, 'and perhaps you'll be better.' He shook his head. 'No,' said he, 'I won't have any dinner today, Astafy Ivanovitch.'

"I made some tea for him, I quite flustered our old woman—he was no better. 'Well,' thinks I, 'it's a bad outlook!' The third morning I went for a medical gentleman. There was one I knew living close by, Kostopravov by name. I'd made his acquaintance when I was in service with Bosomyagins; he'd attended me. The doctor came and looked at him. 'He's in a bad way,' said he, 'it was no use sending for me. But if you like I can give him a powder.' Well, I didn't give him a powder, I thought that's just the doctor's little game; and then the fifth day came.

"He lay, sir, dying before my eyes. I sat in the window with my work in my hands. The old woman was heating the stove. We were all silent. My heart was simply breaking over him, the good-for-nothing fellow; I felt as if it were a son of my own I was losing. I knew that Emelyanoushka was looking at me. I'd seen the man all the day long making up his mind to say something and not daring to.

"At last I looked up at him; I saw such misery in the poor fellow's eyes. He had kept them fixed on me, but when he saw that I was looking at him, he looked down at once.

" 'Astafy Ivanovitch.'

"'What is it, Emelyanoushka?'

"'If you were to take my old coat to a secondhand dealer's, how much do you think they'd give you for it, Astafy Ivanovitch?'

"'There's no knowing how much they'd give. Maybe they would give me a ruble for it, Emelyan Ilyitch.'

"But if I had taken it they wouldn't have given a farthing for it, but would have laughed in my face for bringing such a trumpery thing. I simply said that to comfort the poor fellow, knowing the simpleton he was.

"But I was thinking, Astafy Ivanovitch, they might give you three rubles for it; it's made of cloth, Astafy Ivanovitch. How could they only give one ruble for a cloth coat?'

"'I don't know, Emelyan Ilyitch,' said I, 'if you are thinking of taking it you should certainly ask three rubles to begin with.'

"Emelyanoushka was silent for a time, and then he addressed me again —

"'Astafy Ivanovitch.'

"'What is it, Emelyanoushka?' I asked.

"'Sell my coat when I die, and don't bury me in it. I can lie as well without it; and it's a thing of some value — it might come in useful.'

"I can't tell you how it made my heart ache to hear him. I saw that the death agony was coming on him. We were silent again for a bit. So an hour passed by. I looked at him again: he was still staring at me, and when he met my eyes he looked down again.

"'Do you want some water to drink, Emelyan Ilyitch?' I asked.

"'Give me some, God bless you, Astafy Ivanovitch.'

"I gave him a drink.

"'Thank you, Astafy Ivanovitch,' said he.

"'Is there anything else you would like, Emelyanoushka?'

"'No, Astafy Ivanovitch, there's nothing I want, but I — sort of ——'

"'What?'

"'I only ——'

"'What is it, Emelyanoushka?'

"'Those riding breeches — it was — sort of — I who took them — Astafy Ivanovitch.'

"'Well, God forgive you, Emelyanoushka,' said I, 'you poor, sorrowful creature. Depart in peace.'

"And I was choking myself, sir, and the tears were in my eyes. I turned aside for a moment.

"'Astafy Ivanovitch ——'

"I saw Emelyanoushka wanted to tell me something; he was trying to sit up, trying to speak, and mumbling something. He flushed red all over suddenly, looked at me ... then I saw him turn white again, whiter and whiter, and he seemed to sink away all in a minute. His head fell back, he drew one breath and gave up his soul to God."

FOR WRITING OR DISCUSSION

1. Where does the actual plot of "An Honest Thief" begin? Who tells the story?

2. What purpose do you think Dostoevsky had in mind by creating a "story within a story" instead of having Astafy as the only narrator?

3. How much of the story is told in dialogue? Why is this method more effective in a story where characterization is of greater importance than plot?

4. How does Astafy reveal as much of himself to the reader as he does of his parasitic dependent? What do Astafy and Emlyan Ilyitch have in common? What binds them together?

5. In what sense is this story both humorous and pathetic? How is the humor in this story different from that in "The Crocodile"?

6. The critic Ernest Simmons has called Emelyan a "special type of the meek character." What aspects of meekness does Emelyan exhibit? How does he use his meekness to gain his point almost as effectively, or perhaps more effectively, than Dostoevsky's overassertive and ruthless "proud" characters? How is Emelyan's meekness an example of an "extreme" point of view?

7. Why did Emelyan finally confess his theft? Do you think Astafy really wanted him to confess? Why or why not?

8. How do Astafy's reactions to Emelyan represent the duality of feeling so usual in Dostoevsky? Do we all have these mixed feelings? What does this tell you about Dostoevsky as a psychologist?

9. Dostoevsky has been called the writer of the city. What details of the life of the city poor are given in the story?

REACTING TO CRITICISM

There are at least two ways of looking at Dostoevsky's obsessive interest in "meek" characters. One views his preoccupation with the extremes of submissiveness and humility in a Freudian way—that is, as the obsessions of a masochistic personality, which actually enjoys suffering. The other views his treatment of submissiveness as an example of his ideal of Christ's humility, in its religious sense of "turning the other cheek." A modification of this latter view holds that by demonstrating in his meek characters the capriciousness of fate in the life of the poor and humble, Dostoevsky was pointing out the irrational nature of justice in the world.

The passages that follow imply one of these points of view more than the others. After you read each one, discuss with the class the relationship of each passage to "An Honest Thief."

> His heroes are drifters, pariahs, from the lowest strata of society, yet from the moral point of view they are the salt of the earth. The condemnation of the society that rejects or mistreats them is therefore made on ethical grounds. Makar[1] is good and pure; yet he suffers and rots in his misery. This offends our sense of justice; there is a gap between man's condition and the moral order as expressed in Christianity. This is the precise significance of Dostoevsky's first novel *Poor Folk,* and it heralds the main theme of all his work. It also reveals the author's almost morbid interest in human suffering, his mastery in portraying pathetic figures and evoking those poignant scenes of destitution and doom that are in all his novels. His contemporaries say it is evidence of his realistic humanity; in the twentieth century this tendency was attributed to Dostoevsky's sense of Christian compassion—or to his sadistic or masochistic impulses.[2] [*Marc Slonim*]

> The favorite themes of Dostoevsky are the men who have been brought so low by the circumstances of their lives that they have not even a conception of there being a possibility of rising above these conditions. You feel moreover that Dostoevsky finds a real pleasure in describing the sufferings, moral and physical, of the downtrodden—that he revels in representing that misery of mind, that absolute hopelessness of redress, and that completely broken-down condition of human nature which is characteristic of neuropathological cases. By the side of such sufferers you find a few others who are so deeply human that all your sympathies go with them; but the favorite heroes of Dostoevsky are the man and the woman who consider themselves as not having either the force to compel respect, or even the right of being treated as human beings. They once have made some timid attempt at defending their personalities, but they have succumbed, and never will try it again. They will sink deeper and deeper in their

---

[1] *Makar:* hero of Dostoevsky's first novel, *Poor Folk.*
[2] From *The Epic of Russian Literature: From Its Origins Through Tolstoy* by Marc Slonim, copyright 1950 by Oxford University Press, Inc. Reprinted by permission of the publisher.

wretchedness, and die, either from consumption or from exposure, or they will become the victims of some mental affliction—a sort of half-lucid lunacy, during which men occasionally rise to the highest conceptions of human philosophy—while some will conceive an embitterment which will bring them to commit some crime, followed by repentance the very next instant after it has been done.[1] *[Prince Kropotkin]*

The reason that Dostoevsky could understand pain so deeply was that, from the first, his own experience of it was all but overwhelming. From earliest days he had known cruelty of various kinds. His father was an ill-balanced, suspicious man who tyrannized his family and was eventually murdered by one of his own peasants; his mother, to whom he was devoted, died when he was sixteen; the engineering school to which he was sent was a torment to him; the years after his graduation were years of poverty and bitter hurt, when he was coldly dropped by the literary circles that had first taken him up and then decided they had exaggerated his importance; then came imprisonment for the crime of discussing socialist doctrines with a group of friends; the famous mock condemnation, brutally contrived to "teach a lesson," when the prisoners were led out to the place of execution and suffered to hear the death penalty read before their last-minute, melodramatic reprieve; exile in Siberia; an unfortunate marriage; a tormenting love affair; bankruptcy—and with all this, a nervous ailment that early in life developed into epilepsy. It was only the devotion of his second wife and the growing development of artistic power that brought a measure of stability and happiness into this tragic life. His mind was able to make a triumph of this suffering. Poetic, philosophic, independent, it shaped its own patterns, set its own standards, and reached conclusions that were far ahead of its generation.[2] *[Helen Muchnic]*

The most striking of Dostoevsky's discoveries in the psychology of self-assertion are, however, the ones referring to the "insulted and injured"; to persons suffering from irreparable injustice on the one hand, and from an acute feeling of their own inferiority on the other. Again and again he took up the weakling who has been insulted without being able to retaliate, and therefore

---

[1]From *Ideals and Realities in Russian Literature* by Prince Kropotkin. Reprinted by permission of the publisher, Alfred A. Knopf, Inc.
[2]From *Introduction to Russian Literature.*

turns all his rancor against himself, humiliating himself even more, as if reveling in his own degradation. "Strange to say," reasons Arkady in *A Raw Youth,* "I always had, perhaps from my earliest childhood, one characteristic: if I were ill treated, absolutely wronged and insulted to the last degree, I always showed at once an irresistible desire to submit passively to the insult, and even to accept more than my assailant wanted to inflict on me, as though I would say: 'All right, you have humiliated me, so I will humiliate myself even more; look, and enjoy it.' " Such voluntary self-degradation can in fact give one the illusion of what might be called self-will from the other end: one is utterly humiliated at least through one's *own* (and not other people's) volition.

An aggressive counterpart of it is the sadistic self-assertion of a weakling who wants to bully and tyrannize over everyone he can get hold of. It is a known fact that erotic sadists often suffer from sexual inferiority or even impotence. Similarly, mental and moral cruelty is to be found above all in people who are not sure either of their own value or of their own convictions. The Holy Inquisition was not a child of faith, but of incipient doubt. And the cruelest inquisitors were probably those who feared their own latent unbelief. According to Dostoevsky (*Crime and Punishment*), even murder can arise from the urge to prove and to assert one's "will to power" over another human being in an absolute way, i.e. by taking his life.

Exaggerated moral cruelty finds, however, its masochist contrast in that exaggerated pity which was another favorite motive of Dostoevsky the psychologist. But through certain kinds of pity one can affirm oneself against the person one pities nearly as much as one does through cruelty. Pity is often but cruelty turned inside out, and—in contrast to love—is equally devoid of respect. The dividing line between the two is much narrower than is generally thought. Did not Dostoevsky often invent the greatest torments for his characters that he might shed tears of pity over them? And as for certain motives of charity, he made this remark (in his drafts for *The Life of a Great Sinner*) about one of his heroes: "Out of pride and infinite haughtiness toward people he becomes meek and charitable to all, because he is already higher than all." Such meekness is perhaps the subtlest form of *indirect* self-assertion.[1] [*Janko Lavrin*]

---

[1] From *Dostoevsky: A Study.*

II. The Reader as Critic

Art as the "Higher Realism"

Ernest Simmons, one of the most scholarly and well-known American biographers and critics of Russian literature, contrasts Dostoevsky's views about the purpose and place of literature with Turgenev's and Tolstoy's in this way:

> Compared with his landed gentry rivals, Dostoevsky regarded himself as an intellectual proletarian with an entirely different outlook on life. They were novelists of the countryside; he was a poet of the city. In their works they chronicled the biographies of members of their own class, whereas he wrote about off-center city dwellers living in an off-center world of their own. He thought that their realism, at its best, dealt with the typical and surface features of existence, at its worst, with the irrelevant; whereas he was completely immersed in the realities of the spiritual life of men. That is, he preferred to shift the action from the external world to that of the mind and heart of his characters. For him art was a medium of conveying the wisdom of life, the emotions of the soul.[1] [*Ernest Simmons*]

Most people have assumed that writing was a sort of psychological therapy for Dostoevsky, a way of writing out his neuroses, and that his art is entirely autobiographical in that sense. But Simmons warns against taking this view too exclusively. He makes the point that the extensive scholarship on Dostoevsky's life and art has made it possible

> ... to establish the extent to which his fiction is autobiographical, the prototypes of some of his principal characters and the influence of foreign models on the form, plots, and incidents of his novels. Then the publication of the rich material in the notebooks bearing on the composition of all his major novels takes us into the writing laboratory of Dostoevsky and allows us to study, in unexampled detail, the whole process involved in the creation of these masterpieces. This process, as well as the abundant information about the conception and plans of his works which Dostoevsky

[1] From *Introduction to Russian Realism* by Ernest Simmons. Reprinted by permission of the publisher, Indiana University Press.

often provides in his letters, may in turn be most fruitfully checked for fulfillment of artistic intentions against the finished novels. Finally, the vexed question of the correspondences of Dostoevsky's thought and ideas and those of his characters may be substantially resolved by correlating his views, fully expressed in the pages of his two magazines, *Time* and *Epoch*, in *The Diary of a Writer,* and in his letters, with those of the characters in the novels.

None of this is meant to suggest that one can explain the deep mystery of genius in the creation of enduring art, but simply to warn critics of the futility of attempting to do just that. Conscious that he was an innovator in fiction, Dostoevsky was not disposed to keep his future commentators in the dark about it. He did not consider himself a writer of any definite social group. Rather he regarded his work as of universal significance, an effort, he said, "with complete realism to find man in man." He defined his innovation as a attempt to represent in fiction spiritual phenomena above and beyond social practices, to resolve the psychological contradictions of man in terms of true and external "humanness." "They call me a psychologist," he wrote in his notebook. "It is not true. I am only a realist in the higher sense; that is, I portray all the depths of the human soul."[1] [*Ernest Simmons*]

What did Dostoevsky mean by "higher" realism? Both Turgenev and Tolstoy were realists of a kind—Turgenev with his objective attitude and technique, and Tolstoy because of his ability to present the totality of human experience with absolute accuracy to life and with an honesty that has scarcely ever been equaled in literature. It is surprising that the fables and legends he wrote to convey the "truth" that he was convinced of seem less "realistic" to us than the novels and stories he himself repudiated.

But we must remember that neither Turgenev nor Tolstoy defined art as "realism" of one kind or another. Tolstoy, in fact, said that

> to value a work of art by the degree of its realism, by the accuracy of the details reproduced, is as strange as to judge of the nutritive quality of food by its external appearance. When we appraise a work according to its realism, we only show that we are talking, not of a work of art, but of its counterfeit.[2] [*Leo Tolstoy*]

[1] *Ibid.*
[2] From *What Is Art?* by Leo N. Tolstoy, translated by Aylmer Maude, copyright © 1960, by The Liberal Arts Press, Inc. Reprinted by permission of the Liberal Arts Press Division of The Bobbs-Merrill Company, Inc.

Tolstoy was referring, of course, to the kind of realistic writer who tried to duplicate the events and characters in life exactly as they were.

But Dostoevsky—the writer whose characters seem sometimes to have come from nightmares and whose situations seem to come from fantastic dreams (think of "The Crocodile"!)—how can this writer claim that art, his own writing, represents a "higher" reality? One's definition of "realism" and "reality" determines, in part, the answer to that question.

Varieties of Realism and Reality

Janko Lavrin discusses this very question at some length in his long critical work, *Dostoevsky: A Study*. In the introduction to the chapter "Dostoevsky as Artist," he says:

> If we consider works of art and literature from the angle of their genesis, we notice several, often contradictory impulses of creation. One of them is the author's need to find a refuge from the burden of actual life either in an imaginary world or in wishful thinking. Another is the secret craving to take revenge upon life for one's frustrations, especially for one's disappointed idealism. In this case satirical mockery and sneering realism are likely to come into their own. At the opposite end is the impulse to play with reality in the benevolently humorous mood, known only to a man whose sense of proportion is strong enough to prevent him from taking too seriously either himself or the world—a disposition which makes him smile where a wounded idealist would grin or gnash his teeth. Then there is the urge to enlarge one's perception of reality through exploring its wider aspects, its secrets, beauties, and also its horrors. Insofar as this urge is expressed through the medium of literature, we obtain various grades of realism.
>
> An artist who is on the lookout for an escape is usually drawn towards "romance." He indulges in imaginary substitutes for an intense life and clings to them all the more tenaciously the more he is repelled by the actual world. Exotic romanticism and hothouse aestheticism are often but shelters, prompted by one's inability to accept life, or to grapple with its difficulties. A true realist, on the other hand, enjoys above all the manifold variety of existence. In contrast to a romantic, he feels at home in this world even when he rebels against its negative aspects. His art gives us an intensified picture of life as seen through his creative eye. Yet

this picture is never entirely "detached." It is bound to be more or less subjective for the very reason that the world it presents is sifted through his personal vision and temperament.

Such impulses need not function singly. Some of them pass into each other, intertwining in a startling manner. Thus a romantic "escapist" whose imagination is too weak to provide an adequate shelter, often goes back to real life, but with an aggressive and rancorous attitude. What he wants is to take revenge upon life. He watches it, preys upon it, all the time anxious to show up its squalor and meanness. In this process he uses realistic methods, but the impulse behind it all is romantic. What he is after is the refutation of life as it is. . . .

A more complicated realist is the man who for some reason or other accepts life as an artist, even if his moral or social sense takes up a highly negative attitude. An example of a full-blooded biological acceptance of life in the teeth of one's protesting moral sense is Tolstoy. Tolstoy's work as a whole shows a tragic contest between the two attitudes—a contest which eventually turned that great artist into a moral preacher. . . .

A very intensive kind of realism can be obtained however by concentrating on man's inner world. It results in the psychological novel pure and simple, or else in that type of novel in which a religious-philosophic quest merges with "psychology" to such an extent as to become one with it. A quest of this kind frequently represents the author's own inner travail—exteriorized and projected into human characters whose "philosophy" is not a matter of intellect only, but of what might be called one's total inner experience. . . .

We may perhaps find a clue to [an author's] realism by drawing a line between reality and actuality. The two are often regarded as identical. Yet reality is more than actuality. It includes all the hidden forces and agents of life, whereas actuality is confined to its external or else "topical" aspects. The proportion between these two planes varies and is reflected in the two different although complementary directions in art, especially in the novel: the horizontal and the vertical.

The "horizontal" novel is concerned with manners, with life as expressed in terms of external contacts and relationships of the persons described. But it must not stop here. Unless it has a fringe, suggestive of something more important and universal than what it shows, it will remain only a picture or document of a certain period

—nearer to journalism than to art. The "vertical" novel, however, concentrates above all upon human destinies as they work in and through the characters presented. Hence it is predominantly psychological. It is more intensive than extensive; for which purpose it reduces the number of characters, as well as the area of the background, to a minimum.[1] [*Janko Lavrin*]

1. How does Lavrin explain "romantic" attitudes?
2. What two types of romantics does he identify? Which type turns toward a "surface" realism? Why?
3. Where does Lavrin place Tolstoy in his scale of realisms?
4. What distinctions does the critic draw between reality and actuality?
5. What is the difference between a "horizontal" and a "vertical" story? Which type did Dostoevsky write?

Dostoevsky's "Realism"

Lavrin, then, feels that Dostoevsky was justified in calling himself a realist and in defining his art as the essence of "truth":

> "Spiritual realism" is the label applied to Dostoevsky's art by Melchior de Vogüé, in his pioneering work on the Russian novel. And Dostoevsky himself is quite explicit about it when he says in one of his letters: "I have a totally different conception of truth and realism from that of our 'realists' and critics. My God! If one could tell but categorically all that we Russians have gone through during the last ten years in the way of spiritual development, all the realists would shriek that it was pure fantasy! And yet it would be pure realism! It is the one true, deep realism. Theirs is altogether too superficial." And again, "I have my own ideas about art, and it is this: what most people regard as fantastic and lacking in universality, I hold to be the inmost essence of truth. Arid observations of everyday trivialities I have long ceased to regard as realism...."
>
> If a label were necessary at all, we could perhaps call his art *visionary* realism, as distinct from mere visual realism. He strains the actual and the average to its utmost limits mainly in order to reach that reality which lies beyond it. His wildest and cruelest situations are often but experiments upon the human soul with the object of extracting its "inmost essence." Hence there is some-

[1] From *Dostoevsky: A Study*.

thing paradoxical about Dostoevsky's exaggerated characters: they are most real when they seem least realistic from the standpoint of the mere visual realism.[1] [*Janko Lavrin*]

1. How is "spiritual" realism different from what we ordinarily conceive of as realism in literature?
2. How does Dostoevsky reverse the usual connotations of fantasy and reality?
3. Do you agree that one can arrive at an inner reality by intensifying the "experiments upon the human soul" to a degree that seldom is experienced in actual life?

Another very famous Russian critic, D. S. Merezhkovsky, agrees that Dostoevsky's intense explorations of the human heart and soul are realistic portrayals of man's inner life.

> We are accustomed to think that the more abstract thought is, the more cold and dispassionate it is. It is not so; or at least, it is not so with us. From the heroes of Dostoevsky we may see how abstract thought may be passionate, how metaphysical theories and deductions are rooted, not only in cold reason, but in the heart, emotions and will.
>
> There are thoughts which pour oil on the fire of the passions and inflame man's flesh and blood more powerfully than the most unrestrained license. There is a logic of the passions, but there are also passions in logic. And these are essentially *our* new passions, peculiar to us and alien to the men of former civilizations.
>
> The great poets of the past ages, in depicting the passions of the heart, left out of consideration the passions of the mind, as if they thought them a subject out of the reach of the painter's delineation. If Faust and Hamlet are nearest to us of all heroes, because they think more than any, yet they feel less, they act less, precisely because they think more. The tragedy of both men lies in the contradiction which they cannot solve, between the *passionate heart and passionless thought*. But is not a tragedy of *thinking* passion or passionate *thought* possible? The future belongs to this tragedy and no other. And Dostoevsky was one of the first to make an approach to it.
>
> He has overcome the superstitious timidity, common to modern artists, of feeling in presence of the mind. He has recognized and

[1] *Ibid.*

showed us the connection there is between the tragedy of our hearts and that of our reason, our philosophical and religious consciousness. . . .

As in our bodily impressionability something is altered after reading Tolstoy, so after reading Dostoevsky something is changed in our spiritual impressionability. It is impossible to forget, to either reject or accept him with impunity. His reasonings penetrate not only into the mind, but into the heart and will. They are momentous events which must have consequences. We remember them some time or other, and perhaps precisely at the most decisive impassioned crises of our lives. "Once touch the heart," he says himself, "and the wound remains." Or, as the Apostle Paul puts it, he "is quick and powerful, sharper than any two-edged sword, piercing even to the dividing asunder of soul and spirit, of joints and marrow."

There are simple-minded readers, with the effeminate, sickly sentimentality of our day, to whom Dostoevsky will always seem "cruel," merely "a cruel genius." In what intolerable, what incredible situations he places his heroes!

And is all this suffering natural, possible, real? Does it occur? Where has it been seen? And even if it occurs, what have we sane-thinking people to do with these rare among the rare, exceptional among the exceptional cases, these moral and mental monstrosities, deformities, and abortions, fancies of fever and delirium?

Here is the main objection to Dostoevsky, one that all can understand, unnaturalness, unusualness, apparent artificiality, the absence of what is called "healthy realism.". . .

But he is a searcher into human nature; also at times "a realist in the highest sense of the word" [sic] — the realist of a new kind of experimental realism. In making scientific researches he surrounds in his machines and contrivances the phenomena of nature with artificial and exceptional conditions. He observes how, under the influence of those conditions, the phenomenon undergoes changes. We might say that the essence of all scientific research consists precisely in deliberately "artificializing" the surrounding conditions. Thus the chemist, increasing the pressure of atmospheres to a degree impossible in the conditions of nature as known to us, gradually densifies the air and changes it from gaseous to liquid. May we not call unreal, unnatural, supernatural, nay miraculous, that transparent liquid, dark blue as the clearest sky, evaporating, boiling and yet cold, inconceivably colder than ice?[1] [*D. S. Merezhkovsky*]

Another Point of View: Art as Symbol

Nicholas Berdyaev, a Russian critic and writer who left Russia to live in Paris (see also page 200), believes that the kinds of truths Dostoevsky was interested in transmitting do not lend themselves to the ordinary realistic treatment:

> Was Dostoevsky a realist? Before this question can be answered it must be decided in what measure great art can be realistic. It is true that Dostoevsky liked to call himself so, and regarded his realism as being the very realism of life itself. But he certainly did not use the word in the sense given to it by official critics when they affirm the existence of a "realistic school.". . . The truth is that all essential art is symbolical: it is a bridge built between two worlds, a sign that expresses a deep, authentic reality; the end of art surpasses experimental reality and is to express hidden reality, not in a direct way but by means of projected shadows. Now nobody was less preoccupied with the empirical world than Dostoevsky; his art is completely immersed in the profound realities of the spiritual universe. . . . For Dostoevsky, the ultimate realities are not the external forms of life, flesh, and blood men, but their inner depths, the destiny of the human spirit . . . though it is absolutely wrong to call Dostoevsky a "realist," we may say that he is a "mystical realist."[2] [*Nicholas Berdyaev*]

To conclude your study of Dostoevsky's artistic intention, discuss with the class, or with small groups of other students, any or all of the following questions, or, if you prefer, read "The Dream of a Ridiculous Man" (page 350) before drawing your conclusions about Dostoevsky's realism.

1. How were Dostoevsky's ideas of literature and art different from both Turgenev's and Tolstoy's?

2. In what sense are all three writers "realists"?

3. Do you think that Dostoevsky's attempt to transmit man's inner experience, even through fantastic means, is a "higher" realism than Turgenev's or Tolstoy's? Explain your answer.

[1]From *Tolstoy as Man and Artist*. London: Constable & Co., 1902.
[2]From *Dostoevsky*.

III. The Reader as Writer

Writing "Dramatic" Dialogue

Some critics would scarcely advise young writers to use Dostoevsky as a model of good writing; they attribute his immense popularity less to his skill as a technician than to his psychological insights, fantastic imagination, intricate plots, and intense emotions:

> Today, when Dostoevsky is recognized as one of the greatest masters in world literature, we can imagine how the uncouth qualities of his novels must have shocked Victorian tastes. He wrote hastily and often under the duress of harsh circumstances: always in debt, always taking advances for works he had no time to begin, publishing most of his writings in reviews, in monthly installments. . . . The language is unseemly and loose, lapsing into journalese or the dryness of a report; it is devoid of poetic smoothness, with unnerving changes of pace and rhythm. The exposition is often lengthy and repetitious, although some of the repetitions have a distinct functional value. . . . Dostoevsky seems to be always in a hurry to unload all he has on his mind—hence all the many digressions and stories-within-the-story.[1] [*Marc Slonim*]

Slonim's opinion is not a recent one. Prince Kropotkin, writing fifty years earlier, expressed some of the same ideas, but goes on to insist that even with its faults, Dostoevsky's writing accomplishes its purpose:

> If Dostoevsky's work had been judged from the purely aesthetic point of view, the verdict of critics concerning its literary value would have been anything but flattering. Dostoevsky wrote with such rapidity and he so little cared about the working out of his novels, that the literary form is in many places almost below criticism. His heroes speak in a slipshod way, continually repeating themselves, and whatever hero appears in the novel, you feel it is the author who speaks. Besides, to these serious defects one must add the extremely romantic and obsolete forms of the plots of his novels, the disorder of their construction, and the unnatural suc-

---

[1] From *The Epic of Russian Literature*.

cession of their events—to say nothing of the atmosphere of the lunatic asylum with which the later ones are permeated. And yet, with all this, the works of Dostoevsky are penetrated with such a deep feeling of reality, and by the side of the most unreal characters one finds characters so well known to every one of us, and so real, that all these defects are redeemed. Even when you think that Dostoevsky's record of the conversations of his heroes is not correct, you feel that the men whom he describes—at least some of them—were exactly such as he wanted to describe them.[1]
[*Prince Kropotkin*]

Even though these critics were speaking of Dostoevsky's longer novels, the stylistic qualities they mention are evident, to a degree, in his stories.

1. What examples from "The Crocodile" and "An Honest Thief" can you provide to support these criticisms by Slonim and Kropotkin:
   a. "lengthy and repetitious" exposition
   b. "many digressions and stories-within-the-story"
   c. "heroes ... continually repeating themselves"
   d. "the atmosphere of the lunatic asylum"

2. Do you agree with Kropotkin that Dostoevsky's characters, even the most fantastic, seem real? Explain.

Dostoevsky's Method of Working

Scholarly examination of Dostoevsky's notebooks and letters has revealed that "slipshod" is an overstated way of referring to Dostoevsky's admittedly rapid writing habits. Sipping cold tea from a nearby samovar, he usually worked from midnight until dawn every night, after others had retired. He slept during the morning and rose in the early afternoon to join his family and guests. When an idea had intense hold on him, he wrote at fever heat until he was exhausted, sometimes to the point of precipitating an epileptic attack. And he had, as André Gide tells us, an immense pride in his work and a desire always to improve what he had written:

"I want each of my works to be good in itself"[2] ... we can, without cavilling, admit that he did not break his vow.

But he cherished throughout his life the belief that with more time and freedom he could have given better expression to his

---
[1] From *Ideals and Realities in Russian Literature*.
[2] From a letter to his brother Michael, March 24, 1845.

thought. "There is one consideration that troubles one greatly: if I spent a year writing the novel beforehand, and then two or three months in copying and revising it, I guarantee the result would be very different." Self-delusion, maybe? Who can tell? With greater leisure, to what could he have attained? After what was he still striving? Greater simplicity, no doubt, and a more complete subordination of detail. As they are, his best works rise, almost throughout, to a degree of precision and clarity that it is not easy to imagine excelled.

And to reach this, what expenditure of effort! It is only now and again that sudden inspiration is vouchsafed; everything else means painful toil. To his brother, who doubtless had reproached him with not writing "simply" enough, meaning to say "quickly" enough, and with not "surrendering himself to inspiration," he replied, young as he was: "It is clear that you are confusing, as often happens, inspiration, that is, first momentary creation of the picture, or the stirring of the soul, with work. Thus, for instance, I make note at once of a scene just as it appeared to me, and I am delighted: then, for months, for a year even, I work at it . . . and believe me, the finished article is much superior. Provided, of course, that the inspiration is vouchsafed! Naturally without inspiration nothing can be accomplished. . . ." Must I crave pardon for this prodigality of quotation, or will you not rather be grateful to me for allowing Dostoevsky to be his own spokesman as much as possible? "At the beginning, that is at the end of last year, I thought the novel (he refers to *The Possessed*) very *made* and artificial and rather scorned it. But later I was overtaken by real enthusiasm. I fell in love with my work of a sudden, and made a big effort to get all that I had written into good trim. . . ."[1] "The whole year," he goes on to say (1870), "I have done nothing but destroy. . . . I have altered my plan at least ten times, and I've rewritten the first part entirely. Two or three months ago I was in despair. Now everything has fallen into place together and cannot be changed." And again the everpresent obsession: "If I had had time to write without hurrying myself, without a time limit in view, it is possible that something good might have developed out of it."[2]

This anguish and this dissatisfaction with himself were gone through for every work that he wrote. "It is a long novel, in six parts *(Crime and Punishment)*. At the end of November a large

[1] From a letter to N. N. Strakhov, Dresden, October 9, 1870.
[2] From a letter to N. N. Strakhov, Dresden, December 2, 1870.

part of it was written and ready; I burned the lot! Now I can frankly admit that it did not please me. A new form, a new plan hurried me along. I have made a fresh start. I am working night and day; still, progress is slow." — "I am working hard and little comes of it," he says elsewhere: "I am constantly tearing my work up. I am terribly discouraged." And again: "I have done so much work that I've become stupid, and my head is dazed." — "I am working here (Staraia Roussa) like a convict in spite of the fine weather to be taken advantage of; I am tied night and day to my task."

Sometimes a mere article gives him as much trouble as a book, because his conscientiousness is as rigid in little things as in great.

"I have let it drag on till now" (i.e., a memoir on Belinsky, which has not been traced), "and at last I've finished it, gnashing my teeth the while. Ten pages of a novel are more easily written than these two sheets. Consequently I've written, all in all, this confounded article five times at least, and even then I've scored everything out and changed what I'd written. Finally I've completed the article after a fashion, but it is so bad that I am full of disgust." For while he clings to the profound belief in his worth, in the worth of his ideas at least, he is always exacting while the work is in progress, and never pleased when it is completed.

And the year of his death,[1] writing to Melle N____, he says: "I am conscious that, as a writer, I have many defects, because I am the first to be dissatisfied with my own efforts. You can just picture the times when I cross-examine myself to find that I have literally not expressed the twentieth part of what was in my mind, and could, perhaps, have been expressed! My salvation lies in the sure hope that one day God may grant me such strength and inspiration that I shall find perfect self-expression and be able to make plain all that I carry in my heart and imagination."[2] [*André Gide*]

Is it possible that a talented writer could try as hard as Dostoevsky evidently did to improve his work and simply not have the time or the strength to keep on revising? Would you agree perhaps that Dostoevsky's style is suitable to the kind of subject matter he dealt with, that one's inner worlds *are* disordered, repetitious, and often irrational or confused?

---

[1] Actually, this letter was written in the spring of 1880; Dostoevsky died in 1881.
[2] From *Dostoevsky* by André Gide. All Rights Reserved. Copyright © 1961 New Directions Publishing Corporation. Reprinted by permission of the publisher.

Dostoevsky's Narrative Method

When you compare the initial part of a Dostoevsky story with the beginning of a story like "Bezhin Lea" or "After the Ball," you realize that Dostoevsky's stories either begin abruptly, right in the midst of the main event, or else they seem to begin a tale that turns out not to be the main thread of plot interest, as in "An Honest Thief." You will observe, too, that the action shifts from place to place or speech to speech in a series of "scenes," usually conversations or confrontations between two characters in conflict or sometimes within one character who is carrying on something like an inner conversation with himself. This method of telling a story is called dramatic. When this term is applied to Dostoevsky's narrative method, it usually refers both to the intensely melodramatic quality of some of his actions (plot) and to the use of dialogue or monologue as the principle way of telling a story or revealing character.

Dostoevsky's dialogue has been praised by a number of critics:

> The story is not quite a text, but, as it were, small writing in brackets, notes on the drama, explaining the time and place of the action, the events that have gone before, the surroundings and exterior of the characters; it is the setting up of the scenery, the indispensable theatrical paraphernalia — when the characters come on and begin to speak, then at length the piece begins. In Dostoevsky's dialogue is concentrated all the artistic power of his delineation: it is in the dialogue that all is revealed and unrevealed. There is not in all contemporary literature a writer equal to him for mastery of dialogue....
>
> In Dostoevsky it is impossible not to recognize the personage speaking, at once, at the first words uttered.... In this way Dostoevsky has no need to describe the appearance of his characters, for by their peculiar form of language and tones of voices they themselves depict, not only their thoughts and feelings, but their faces and bodies.[1] [*D. S. Merezhkovsky*]

The narrative or rather dramatic interest of his novels never flags. His most potent method in achieving this constant tension of interest is his mastery in dialogue. Dostoevsky's novels contain more dialogue than anything else; in fact, all the rest is no more important than stage directions in a play. It has been found very easy to turn his novels into plays without adding a single word. The dialogue is marvelously individualized. In the Russian origi-

---

[1] From *Tolstoy as Man and Artist*.

nal you recognize every character by the peculiar intonations and rhythm of his speech as easily as you recognize the voice of a friend. It is difficult to lay one's hand on the processes by which the novelist arrives at the effect. The dialogue is kept up at a high pitch of emotional tension which communicates itself to the reader, making it impossible for him to lay down the book before he has finished it. . . . The contrast is strong between the dialogue and the narrative part: his narrative prose, like his journalism, is slovenly, unkempt journalese. His dialogue is a marvel of effectiveness.[1] [*D. S. Mirsky*]

You can see that Mirsky and Merezhkovsky disagree with Prince Kropotkin's view that whatever hero is speaking, it seems to be Dostoevsky himself who is talking. To test your own awareness of the relation of dialogue to characterization in the stories you have read, identify the speakers of the following remarks:

1. "I demand nothing, and I beg you, before everything—as I have said already—to remember that I am not a person in authority and so cannot demand anything of anyone. I am speaking as a son of the fatherland, that is, not as the *Son of the Fatherland,* but as a son of the fatherland."

2. "Why, you have had a fright, *aie, aie!*"

3. "I am intending to employ you as my secretary. You shall read the newspapers and magazines to me, and I will dictate to you my ideas and give you commissions. Be particularly careful not to forget the foreign telegrams."

4. "I will him drops from the chemist's get and will save your friend that he die not."

5. "'And then again,' I think 'how am I off myself? Wait a bit,' says I to myself, 'you've not long to feast with me: I shall soon be going away and then you will not find me.'"

6. "There, there, you have had a fright, little one!"

7. "Now I was to die of boredom there every evening, doing the duty of a true friend!"

8. "Horrid man! You will reduce me to tears!"

9. "'I don't like to be a burden on you. . . . If I can find a situation . . . then I'll pay it you all back, and make a return for all your hospitality.'"

10. "I like practical people, and can't endure sentimental milksops."

How revealing do *you* think Dostoevsky's dialogue is?

[1] From *Modern Russian Literature* by Prince D. S. Mirsky, published in 1925 by The Clarendon Press, Oxford. Reprinted by permission of the publisher.

Writing a Dramatic Dialogue or Monologue

Your writing assignment for Tolstoy was to develop a characterization of a person under emotional stress of some sort, in which you indicated both the person's habitual gestures and mannerisms and also the nature of the stressful situation. Using the same character or person you chose for that assignment, develop a monologue or a dialogue in which you are the person to whom your character is revealing himself—after the moment of tension has passed. If you participate in the dialogue, your main role will be to ask questions, or to interrupt the character's speaking so as to create some suspense for the reader as to the outcome of the dialogue. If you choose to write a monologue, remember to account for the action or event that caused the emotional stress as well as to explain the speaker's interpretation of the effect of the event.

A CONCLUDING PORTRAIT

Although you may have read a number of stories or a longer work in addition to the selections by Dostoevsky that you have discussed in class, you are still in a position to form no more than tentative opinions about his works. Perhaps, however, by reading the short concluding chapter from the biography of Dostoevsky by a distinguished scholar and critic, Ernest Simmons, quoted extensivly earlier, you will gain an idea of Dostoevsky's stature in world as well as in Russian literature. Perhaps Simmons's evaluation also may extend your interest in reading other novels and stories by this strange but immensely talented writer.

Dostoevsky: The Making of a Novelist

ERNEST SIMMONS

In a letter that accompanied the manuscript of the Epilogue to *The Brothers Karamazov,* Dostoevsky hopefully remarked to his publisher that he intended to live another twenty years and to go on writing. Less than three months later (January 28, 1881), he was dead. The continuation of his masterpiece and the writing of several projected works, the titles of which he jotted down in his notebook—a Russian *Candide,* a

---

"Conclusion" from *Dostoevsky, The Making of a Novelist* by Ernest Simmons, published by Alfred A. Knopf, Inc. Reprinted by permission of the author.

book about Christ, an epic on *The Commemoration of the Dead,* and his reminiscences—were literary hopes that were buried with him. His toil, however, had not been without great honor, even before he died. In June 1880, on the occasion of the dedication of the Pushkin statue in Moscow, he had delivered a speech that had electrified a distinguished audience and aroused the people to a recognition of him as a national literary hero. Taking the famous poet and his works as a prophetic symbol of Russia's destiny, he pronounced a ringing message on the world-mission of his country that inspired his enraptured listeners to shout "genius!" "saint!" "prophet!" Both Westerners and Slavophiles, and even the young generation of radicals in the audience, found something in his speech which they could accept with enthusiasm. In reality, he had simply repeated, in a more effective manner, the deeply felt convictions that he had uttered in his novels and journalism for many years. His praise of European culture and Russia's indebtedness to it satisfied the Westerners; the Slavophiles were pleased with his glorification of native genius; and the young radicals saw a hint of the coming revolution in his insistence that for the Russian sufferer universal happiness is necessary if he is to find peace. Throughout the whole performance, however, ran his own special message of meekness and faith in Christ, whose precepts of suffering and love will enable the Russian people to bring about the brotherhood of man.

The fact that adherents of opposing schools of thought could take comfort in Dostoevsky's speech must be regarded as a final reflection of his dualism. In truth, the evidence of the present study seems to justify the conclusion that the dual impulses of his nature were the most significant factor in the development of his creative art and profoundly influenced his opinions on religious, social, and political questions. Herein lies a certain consistency which explains his creative process and defines his thinking.

It is necessary, however, to resist the tyranny of labels and refuse to designate Dostoevsky by any of the commonly accepted names which we apply to the literary artist and thinker. His divided soul rendered him incapable of unbroken allegiance to any credo of art or philosophy. Tolstoy said of him that his whole life was a struggle between good and evil, which is as true for the great characters of his novels as for their creator. Out of this struggle came his lifelong search for freedom—moral and spiritual freedom. He accepted the most autocratic government in the world, because he believed that it did not interfere with the equality that is to be found only in the spiritual dignity of man. Authority became repulsive to him when it attempted to organize man's existence on a purely rational basis and thus deprive him of the free choice between good and evil, so essential to his self-perfection. It was not disillusionment with the hopes of socialism to remedy abuses in Russia that turned him to a mystical and religious panacea—a reaction painfully common today among intellectuals who have lost their faith, perhaps prematurely, in the efficacy of man's rational schemes for political and social betterment. From the very beginning of his creative life, Dostoevsky had profoundly distrusted the capacity of the intellect to establish those principles by which men may live in universal peace and happiness. He felt that hate, not love, was the medium through which the socialists would attempt to achieve the unification of man. They did not understand that love, like God, was apprehended by the heart, not by the reason. This conviction led him to God, and to his religion, for he perceived that without religion, morality was impossible. In the sense that he was intensely dissatisfied with the world in which he lived, Dostoevsky was perhaps more radical than the revolutionists of his day. Like Christ, however, his vision of a purer and finer world was founded on the love and innate goodness that dwell in the hearts of men. Equality did not mean for him an equal distribution of property and work, or an equal share in power and subjugation. Rather equality existed in a union of people through love and meekness, and in a lofty expression of moral feeling through service to each other.

Often the famous works of an artist seem infinitely nobler than their creator; in the same sense, the novels of Dostoevsky are more noble than the man himself and will outlive his religious and social thinking. Intellectuality can never be the sole measure of a great novelist; he achieves immortality, as it were, in spite of it. It is no mere accident or paradox that Dostoevsky, a powerful if sometimes inconsistent thinker, should have been so deeply skeptical of reason as a key to the understanding of the individual and of life itself. His personal dualism continually led him into an impasse between the head and the heart. If God seemed to be the ultimate irrationality of man's mind, an unreasoning faith in him appeared to be absolutely essential to assure the harmony of man's relation to the world in which he lived. Although Dostoevsky's finest characters, the Doubles, reflect the mental struggle of his own split personality, his heart went out to his Meek creations, whose spirituality and goodness are expressed not through ratiocination, but through an outpouring of moral feeling.

Feeling, however, is not confined to the Meek characters, for the whole intellectual climate of Dostoevsky's fiction is pervaded by it in the sense that he *felt* his thoughts. All the ordinary surface features of the consummate novelist he possessed to an extraordinary degree, but this quality of *feeling* suffuses them and gives to his best productions a high seriousness and a sense of vital experience. Unlike the rationalist, Ivan Karamazov, Dostoevsky was more concerned with life than with the meaning of life. If he regarded life as a mystery, he did not seek to explain by reason what reason is powerless to explain. Life never became an abstraction, void of sense and value. Although he is commonly accepted as one of the most eminent precursors of the so-called psychological novelists, unlike many modern writers, he did not allow psychological analysis to become an end in itself. He emphatically believed that the novelist's business was not simply to explain life, but to see that life was lived in his books. Despite his almost excessive emphasis upon dialogue, his conversation is not pervaded by a desiccated intellect, which provides us with infinite talk about life, characters, emotions, sex, and about political, economic, and social theories. In his own life, he was never afraid of expressing his genuine feelings, sentiments, and emotions, nor did he ever deny these profoundly human attributes to the creatures of his imagination. If he is ever happy, he tells us, it is during the long nights when he sits with these men and women of his fancy as he would with real individuals. He loves them, rejoices and grows sad with them, and at times he even weeps sincere tears over their misfortunes. This is what is meant by *feeling*. He imaginatively and emotionally identifies himself with his characters, with all their experiences and actions. Even their political, religious, and social theories he apprehends passionately and sensitively so that they never seem like cold, artificial products of the mind. This quality of *feeling,* which we never fail to identify with life itself, contributes perhaps more than anything else to the deep and abiding experience we enjoy in reading his great novels.

FOR WRITING OR DISCUSSION

1. Why was Dostoevsky considered a "national" literary hero? What accounts for Dostoevsky's appeal to Westerners and Slavophiles, Europeans and Russians alike?

2. What, according to Simmons, were the most significant aspects of Dostoevsky's personality and writing? How are these traits related to his "lifelong search for freedom"?

3. Which kinds of freedom—political, moral, spiritual—did Dostoevsky consider most important? How does this priority account for Dostoevsky's political stance?

4. One critic, you recall, said that Tolstoy was a greater man than he was a writer. How does Simmons feel about Dostoevsky in this respect?

5. In what ways is Dostoevsky the supreme writer about feelings? Give examples from your reading (in or outside class) of his ability to convey psychological and emotional insights.

6. Recall Marc Slonim's short biographical sketch of Dostoevsky (page 177) and other critical materials you have read. How might Dostoevsky's own relationships with his father and mother have resulted in his polarizing the meek and the proud, or cruel, types?

PART FIVE

Variations on a Theme

THE "NEGATIVE HERO" IN RUSSIAN LITERATURE

VARIATIONS ON A THEME: THE "NEGATIVE HERO" IN RUSSIAN LITERATURE

Although Turgenev, Tolstoy, and Dostoevsky came from different kinds of backgrounds and took various roads to literary artistry and eventual fame, they all shared one theme and one character in common, a theme and a character typically Russian at the time. The theme is that of the ineffective or "negative" response to life. The characters who dramatize this response are the "negative heroes" that now seem so modern to contemporary Americans and Europeans because they are similar to the "antiheroes" of existentialist literature and of "absurd" dramas. The Russian negative heroes were men who, faced with the need to make a decision or choice, reacted mentally instead of physically, who talked instead of acting, whose will to *do* or to *be* was paralyzed by their circuitous rationalizations. The negative heroes reflected, in the case of Turgenev and Tolstoy, the aristocratic liberal of the 1840's who, because he was not raised to work or to accept responsibility, or because he was ineffectual against the czarist military and police power, recognized the social or personal problems intellectually but failed to respond with appropriate actions. Dostoevsky's negative heroes are not undecided or inactive because of failure of nerve or overintellectuality; their will to act is polarized between two opposite forces. These "heroes" dramatize Dostoevsky's own duality and *actively* alternate between the extreme possibilities presented to them by the nature of their particular conflicts. And, as is to be anticipated in Dostoevsky, the conflicts of his heroes are largely "inner," or spiritual, conflicts.

Historically, the "negative hero" had a positive counterpart in Russian life and literature. The "positive" hero was the man of action who was, unfortunately, more active than rational, more sensitive than sensible. Turgenev characterized these two types as the "Hamlet" (negative) and "Don Quixote" (positive) types. The three stories you are about to read are variations on the theme of the negative hero. The predecessor and prototype of the heroes in these stories is a man named Oblomov, the principal character in a novel of the same name by the novelist I. A. Goncharov, a contemporary of the three great writers you have been studying. Goncharov is remembered chiefly for his creation of this character. It was a Russian critic, however, N. A. Dobrolyubov, who coined the term describing the disease of inertia and ineffectuality from which people like this character suffer—the disease of "Oblomovitis."

Oblomov: The Prototype of the "Negative Hero"

In a famous review of *Oblomov,* N. A. Dobrolyubov, a renowned Russian critic who, you may remember, reviewed Turgenev's and Dostoevsky's novels, drew from the characterization of the protagonist a composite portrait of the ineffectual, inert, negative hero. As you read excerpts from Dobrolyubov's review, "What Is Oblomovitis?," make note of Oblomov's characteristics for later comparisons with those of Turgenev's, Tolstoy's, and Dostoevsky's negative heroes.

> In the first part Oblomov lies on the couch; in the second part he goes to visit the Ilyinskys and falls in love with Olga, and she falls in love with him; in the third part she realizes that she had been mistaken in Oblomov, and they part; in the fourth part she marries Oblomov's friend Stolz, and Oblomov marries the landlady of the house in which he rents his lodgings. And that is all....
>
> ... The story of how good-natured and indolent Oblomov lies and sleeps, and of how neither friendship nor love can awaken and make him get up, is, after all, not such an important one. But it reflects Russian life; in it there appears before us the living contemporary Russian type presented with relentless severity and truth; it reflects the new word of our social development, pronounced clearly and firmly, without despair and without puerile hopes, but in full consciousness of the truth. This word is—*Oblomovitis;* it is the key to the riddle of many of the phenomena of Russian life, and it lends Goncharov's novel far greater social significance than all our exposure novels possess. In the Oblomov type and in all this *Oblomovitis* we see something more than a successful production by the hand of a strong talent; we see a product of Russian life, a sign of the times.
>
> ... What are the main features of the Oblomov character? Utter inertness resulting from apathy toward everything that goes on in the world. The cause of this apathy lies partly in Oblomov's external position and partly in the manner of his mental and moral development. The external position is that he is a gentleman.... He became accustomed to lolling about at a very early age because he had people to fetch and carry for him, to do things for him.... Perhaps the little gentleman dresses himself, but he

knows that for him it is a pleasant exercise, a whim, that he is by no means obliged to dress himself. In fact there is no need for him to do anything. Why should he trouble? Has he not people to fetch things for him and do everything he needs?...

From their earliest years they [Oblomov characters] see life turned inside out, as it were, and until the end of their days they are unable to understand what their relation to the world and to people should reasonably be.... As a result, chaos reigns in their heads: sometimes a man makes up his mind to do something, but he does not know how to begin, where to turn.... This is not surprising: a normal man always wants to do only what he can do; that is why he immediately does all that he wants to do.... But Oblomov is not accustomed to doing anything; consequently, he cannot really determine what he can do and what he cannot do— and consequently, he cannot seriously *actively,* want anything.... His wishes always assume the form "How good it would be if this were done," but how this can be done he does not know. That is why he is so fond of dreaming, and dreads the moment when his dreams may come in contact with reality.... "Sometimes he liked to picture himself an invincible general, compared with whom not only Napoleon, but even Yeruslan Lazarevich "as a nonentity; he would picture a war and its cause: for example, Africans would come pouring into Europe, or he would organize new crusades and would fight, decide the fate of nations, sack towns, show mercy, execute, perform acts of kindness and generosity." Sometimes he would picture himself as a great thinker or artist who is followed by admiring crowds....

The main trouble was that he could see no meaning in life in general. In the Oblomov world nobody asked himself: Why life, what is life, what is its meaning and purpose? The Oblomovs had a very simple conception of life: "They conceived it as an ideal of repose and inaction, disturbed at times by various unpleasant accidents such as sickness, losses, quarrels, and, incidentally, work. They tolerated work as a punishment imposed on our ancestors, but they could not love it, and they always shirked it whenever possible, deeming this permissible and right."...

Failing to put such questions to himself, failing to clear up his own relation to the world and to society, Oblomov, of course, could not grasp the meaning of his own life, and, therefore, found everything he had to do irksome and tedious.... It was observed long ago that all the heroes in the first Russian stories and novels suffer from their failure to see any purpose in life and their inability to find a decent occupation for themselves. As a consequence they find all occupations tedious and repugnant, and in this they reveal an astonishing resemblance to Oblomov....

... The attitude of all the Oblomovs toward other people, and toward women in particular, also has certain common features. They hold all people in contempt because of the petty labors they engage in, because of their narrow concepts and shortsighted strivings.... They are totally incapable of loving and they have no more idea about what to seek in love than they have about what to seek in life in general.... All the Oblomovs like to humiliate themselves, but they do so in order to have the satisfaction of being contradicted, of hearing praise from those to whom they are speaking deprecatingly about themselves. They delight in this self-abasement....

But what about friendship? What do they all do with their friends? Onegin killed Lensky; Pechorin is always quarreling with Werner; Rudin succeeded in repelling Lezhnev and failed to take advantage of Pokorsky's friendship.... It is needless to speak of love. Every one of the Oblomovs met a woman superior to himself, and every one of them ignominiously fled from her love, or did his best to make her dismiss him....

They merely talk about lofty strivings, consciousness of moral duty and common interests; when put to the test, it all turns out to be words, mere words.... No, all these Oblomovs have never converted into flesh and blood the principles with which they were imbued; they have never carried them to their logical conclusion, have never reached the borderline where words are transformed into deeds, where principle merges with the inherent requirement of the soul, disappears in it and becomes the sole spring to a man's conduct. That is why these people are always telling lies; that is why they are so bankrupt when it comes to definite action. That is why abstract views are more precious to them than living facts, why general principles are more important to them than the simple truths of life.

Now, when I hear a country squire talking about the rights of man and urging the necessity of developing personality, I know from the first words he utters that he is an Oblomov. When I hear a government official complaining that the system of administration is too complicated and cumbersome, I know that he is an Oblomov.... When, in the magazines, I read liberal denunciations of abuses and expressions of joy over the fact that at last something has been done that we have been waiting and hoping for for so long, I think to myself that all this has been written from Oblomovka. When I am in the company of educated people who ardently sympathize with the needs of mankind and who for many years have been relating with undiminished heat the same (and sometimes new) anecdotes about bribery, acts of tyranny, and lawlessness of every kind, in spite of myself I feel that I have been transported to old Oblomovka....[1] [*N. A. Dobrolyubov*]

FOR WRITING OR DISCUSSION

1. List all the habits and personality traits that establish Oblomov as a "negative" character.
2. What are Oblomov's positive qualities? How are these related to and, in some cases, even responsible for his passivity?
3. How do Oblomov's upbringing and background help account for his indecisive behavior?
4. What is the usual connotation of the word "hero"? How could a person like Oblomov be considered a "hero"? Is the "hero" in this sense simply the main character in a story?
5. What is Dobrolyubov's attitude toward "Oblomovitis"? Do you think it fair to judge a character in a story as if the author intended him to be a portrait of actual people? Explain. What could be dangerous about this sort of criticism?
6. In a class discussion, develop a definition of "Oblomovitis" in contemporary terms.

THE DIARY OF A SUPERFLUOUS MAN

IVAN TURGENEV

In "The Diary of a Superfluous Man" (1850), Turgenev portrays one of the typically Russian characters known later as negative heroes or Oblomovs. As you might anticipate, Turgenev's protagonist is a member of the landed gentry who, not forced to work for a livelihood and sickly by nature, grows bored and restless and eventually makes abortive attempts

---

[1]From the book *Belinsky, Chernyshevsky and Dobrolyubov: Selected Criticism*, translated and edited by Ralph E. Matlaw, copyright, ©, 1962, by E. P. Dutton & Co., Inc. Reprinted by permission of the publisher.

to act. Unfortunately, however, his actions are as erratic and misunderstood by others as are his ideas. The title of Turgenev's story indicates the nature of his hero. Where Oblomov is overcome by inertia, Chulkaturin is a victim of his awareness that he is a completely "superfluous," or unnecessary, person. As you read this novella, one of Turgenev's earliest long works of fiction, keep in mind the lists of traits you compiled for Oblomov. In what respect is Chulkaturin a victim of the disease that Dobrolyubov called Oblomovitis?

The Diary of a Superfluous Man

Lambswater Hamlet, March 20, 18——

The doctor has just left me. At last I have gained my point! With all his cunning, he had to tell me in the end. Yes, I shall die soon, very soon. The rivers will be freed of ice again, and I, with the last snows probably, will float away—whither? God knows! Also down to the sea. Well, what of it! If death has to come, then let it be in the spring. Yet isn't it absurd to begin a diary perhaps two weeks before one's death? But what of it? And in what respect are fourteen days less than fourteen years, or fourteen centuries? In face of eternity, they say, everything is a mere nothing; and that is true; but then, eternity itself is a mere nothing. I appear to be embarking on speculation; that is a bad sign—I'm not already funking it, surely? It would be better if I started to write about something more concrete. It is raw and windy outside, I am forbidden to go out. So what can I write about? A decent man doesn't talk about his ailments, and surely to write a story is not my line; deliberations on exalted subjects are beyond my powers; a description of the life surrounding me cannot interest even me. And yet to do nothing is boring; to read is being lazy. I know! I'll tell myself all my own life. An excellent idea! On the eve of my death that is only right, and it cannot offend anyone. I begin.

I was born, some thirty years ago, to quite wealthy landowners. My father was a passionate gambler; my mother was a lady of character—a very virtuous lady. Only I have never known any woman whose virtue caused me less satisfaction. She staggered beneath the burden of her qualities and tortured everybody, beginning with herself. During all the fifty years of her life she never rested once, never folded her arms; she was everlastingly bustling and fussing like an ant—and without any benefit, which cannot be said of an ant. An indefatigable worm gnawed

"The Diary of a Superfluous Man" from *The Vintage Turgenev*, Vol. 2, translated by Harry Stevens, copyright 1950 by Alfred A. Knopf, Inc. Reprinted by permission of the publisher.

at her day and night. Only once did I see her completely at rest, and that was the first day after her death, in her coffin. As I looked at her I, to tell the truth, had the feeling that her face expressed a quiet astonishment; the half-open lips, the sunken cheeks and benignly motionless eyes, seemed to be uttering the words: "How good it is not to stir!" Yes, it is good, it is good to be severed at last from the exhausting consciousness of life, from the importunate and restless feeling of existence! But that is away from the point.

I was brought up badly and not at all cheerfully. My father and mother both loved me; but that did not make things any the easier for me. As a man openly devoted to a shameful and ruinous failing, my father had no authority whatever in his own house and carried no weight at all; he was conscious of his downfall and, not having the strength to renounce his beloved passion, tried at least, by his affectionate and modest demeanor, by his evasive meekness, to deserve the indulgence of his exemplary wife. My mother did, indeed, bear his misfortune with that magnificent and sumptuous long-suffering of the virtuous, in which there is so much selfish pride. She never reproached my father in any respect, silently handed him her last money, and paid his debts. He exalted her to her face and behind her back, but he did not like staying at home and caressed me by stealth, as though he himself were afraid of infecting me by his very presence. But when he was with me his distorted features looked so kindly, the feverish sneer on his lips was replaced by such a touching smile, his hazel eyes, with their meshes of fine furrows, beamed with such love, that I involuntarily pressed my cheek against his cheek, which was damp and warm with tears. With my handkerchief I wiped away those tears; and they flowed again, without effort, like water from an overfilled glass. I too began to cry, and he comforted me, stroked me on the back with his hand, kissed me all over my face with his trembling lips. And even now, more than twenty years after his death, when I recall my poor father, a mute sobbing rises in my throat, and my heart beats, beats so hotly and bitterly, is fretted with such yearning pity, as though he still had a long time to struggle and there were still something to pity!

My mother, on the other hand, was always consistent in the way she treated me, kindly, but coldly. One often finds such mothers, moralizing and just, in children's books. She loved me, but I did not love her. Yes, I shunned my virtuous mother and passionately loved my sinful father.

But that will be enough for today. The beginning is made; and as for the end, no matter what it may be, I have no need to worry. That is for my disease to attend to.

March 21

Today the weather is remarkably fine. Warm and clear; the sun is playing merrily on the thawing snow; everything is glittering, steaming, melting; the sparrows are chattering like mad around the dark sweating fences; the humid air is sweetly and fearfully tickling my chest. Spring, spring is coming! I am sitting by the window and gazing across the little stream into the open field. O nature, nature! I love you so much, and from your womb I have emerged not even viable. Look, a male sparrow is hopping about with outspread wings; it calls—and every sound of its voice, every bristling little feather on its tiny body, is quivering with health and strength. . . .

What deduction follows from that? None whatever. It is healthy and has the right to call and to bristle its feathers; but I am ill and must die— that is all. It is not worth saying any more about it. And in nature lachrymose[1] harangues are exhaustingly funny. Let us return to our story.

I was brought up, as I have already said, very badly and not at all cheerfully. I had no brothers and sisters. I was educated at home. And besides, what would my mother have had to occupy herself with if she had put me into a boarding school or a government educational institution? That is what children are for: to save their parents from being bored. We lived mostly in the country, but from time to time we went to Moscow. I had teachers and tutors, as is proper; I particularly remember one cachectical[2] and lachrymose German named Rikman, an unusually mournful, woebegone creature, vainly consumed with an exhausting fretting for his distant native land. My unshaven old male nurse, Vasily, nicknamed "the Goose," used to sit by the stove in the terrible stuffiness of the crowded anteroom, which was heavy with the sour smell of stale kvass.[3] He would sit in his everlasting cossack-style coat of blue sacking, playing cards with the coachman Potap, who wore a new foamy-white sheepskin greatcoat and everlasting greased boots, while Rikman sang on the other side of the partition:

> *"Herz, mein Herz, warum so traurig?*
> *Was bekümmerts dich so sehr?*
> *S'ist ja schön im fremden Lande—*
> *Herz, mein Herz, was willst du mehr?"*[4]

[1] *lachrymose:* tearful.
[2] *cachectical:* thin, emaciated.
[3] *kvass:* a mildly fermented beer.
[4] *"Herz . . . mehr?":* "Heart, my heart, why are you so sad?/What troubles you so?/ It is beautiful in this foreign land—/ Heart, my heart, what more do you want?"

After my father's death we went to Moscow to live. I was now twelve years old. My father died in the night from a stroke. I shall never forget that night. I was sleeping soundly, as all children commonly sleep; but I remember that even in my sleep I thought I heard a heavy and measured snoring. Suddenly I felt someone take me by the shoulder and shake me. I opened my eyes: I saw Vasily. "What's the matter?" "Get up, get up, Alexei Mikhailich is dying!" I jumped like a madman out of my bed and ran into their room. I looked and saw my father lying with his head flung back, his face all crimson, and snoring stertorously.[1] Servants with terrified faces were crowded at the door; in the anteroom someone asked in a hoarse voice: "Have they sent for the doctor?" In the yard a horse was brought out from the stables, the gate creaked. A tallow candle was burning on the floor in the room; my mother was there lamenting, but without losing either her decorum or the consciousness of her own worth. I flung myself on my father's breast, embraced him, stammered: "Daddy, Daddy! . . ." He lay motionless and with his eyes queerly screwed up. I glanced into his face—an unbearable horror caught my breath. I began to howl with fear; like a bird seized with rough hands, I was dragged off and led away. Only the evening before, he had caressed me so ardently and despondently, as though he had a presentiment of his imminent death.

A rough and sleepy doctor, smelling strongly of herb vodka, arrived. My father died under his lancet, and the very next day, completely numb with grief, I stood with a candle in my hand before the table on which the body was lying, and listened senselessly to the deacon's guttural drone, occasionally interrupted by the priest's feeble voice. The tears streamed again and again down my cheeks, over my lips, my collar, my shirt-front; I cried my eyes out. I stared fixedly, I attentively stared at my father's immobile face, as though I expected him to do something. But meanwhile my mother slowly bowed herself again and again to the ground, slowly rose, and, crossing herself, pressed her fingers firmly to her forehead, her shoulders, and her belly. I had no thoughts whatever in my head; I was completely leaden: but I felt that something terrible was being done to me. . . . That day death looked me in the face and noted me.

We moved to Moscow after my father's death for a very simple reason: all our estate was sold under the hammer to pay the debts—absolutely everything except one little hamlet, the very one in which I am now living out my magnificent existence. I confess that though I was young then, I was saddened by the sale of our nest; or rather, in reality I

[1] *stertorously:* breathing hoarsely, as in apoplexy.

was sad only about our garden. Almost my only happy memories are connected with that garden. There one gentle spring evening I buried my best friend, an old dog with docked tail and crooked paws, named Trixy. There I used to hide in the long grass to eat stolen apples, the red, sweet, Novgorod kind. And there, finally, between bushes of ripe raspberries I first saw the maid Klavdia, who, despite her snub nose and habit of laughing into her handkerchief, aroused such a tender passion in me that in her presence I barely breathed, my heart stopped beating, and I was speechless. But one Easter Sunday, when it was her turn to kiss my hand as her young master, I all but flung myself down to kiss her patched kidskin shoes. My God! Was all that really twenty years ago? It does not seem all that time since I rode my little shaggy chestnut horse along by the old wattle fence[1] of our garden and, rising in the stirrups, picked the two-colored leaves of the poplars. So long as man is living he is not conscious of his own life: like sound, it becomes perceptible to him only when a little has passed.

O my garden, O you overgrown paths beside the shallow pond! O sandy little spot beneath the crumbling dam, where I caught gudgeon and loaches![2] And you, lofty birches, with long, hanging branches, beyond which, along the byroad, rose a peasant's dreary song, unevenly broken by the jolts of his cart — I send you my last farewell.... As I part with life, to you alone do I stretch out my hands. I should like once more to breathe in the bitter freshness of the wormwood, the sweet smell of the reaped buckwheat in the fields of my native parts. I should like once more to hear in the distance the modest tinkle of the cracked bell in our parish church; to lie once more in the cool shade beneath an oaken bush on the slope of the well-known ravine, once more to follow with my gaze the mobile tracks of the wind, running in a darker stream over the golden grass of our meadow....

Ah, to what purpose is all this? But I cannot write any more today. Till tomorrow.

March 22

Today it is cold and overcast again. Such weather is far more suitable. It is in accord with my task. Yesterday quite ineptly aroused in me a multitude of unwanted feelings and memories. That will not happen again. Sentimental outpourings are just like liquorice: when you first begin to suck it, it doesn't seem at all bad, but then it tastes quite unpleasant. I shall simply and calmly tell my life story.

[1] *wattle fence:* a fence made of twigs.
[2] *gudgeon ... loaches:* small, freshwater fish, related to carp.

And so we went to live in Moscow. . . .

But now the thought occurs to me—is it really worth while telling my life story?

No, it simply is not worth it. . . . My life has been in no way different from that of many other people. The parental home, the university, service in minor positions, retirement, a small circle of acquaintances, honest poverty, modest pleasures, humble occupations, moderate desires—for goodness' sake, who doesn't know all that? And so I shall not bother to tell my life story, especially as I am writing for my own satisfaction. And as my past does not suggest anything either excessively cheerful or even excessively sad to me, it cannot contain anything worthy of consideration. I would do better to analyze my character for my own benefit.

What sort of man am I? . . . Someone may remark that no one inquires into that either. Agreed. But then I am dying; don't you see, I am dying; and before one's death surely the desire to know what sort of bird I have been would seem excusable?

Having given some little thought to this important question and, for that matter, having no need whatever to be excessively bitter in regard to myself, as is the manner of people who are strongly convinced of their own virtues, I must confess one thing: in this world I have been a completely superfluous man, or better, a completely superfluous bird. And I intend to demonstrate this tomorrow, because today I am coughing like an old sheep, and my nurse, Terentievna, will not give me any peace. "Lie down," she says, "my master, and have a drink of tea. . . ." I know why she is so persistent: she wants some tea herself. Well, all right! Why not let the poor old woman extract every possible benefit from her master?—while it is not too late.

March 23

Winter again. Snow is falling in great clumps.

Superfluous, superfluous . . . I have thought of an excellent word. The farther I penetrate into myself, the more closely I examine all my past life, the more am I convinced of the stern truth of that expression. Superfluous—precisely. To other people that word is not applicable. People are bad, good, intelligent, stupid, pleasant, and unpleasant; but superfluous . . . no. Yet understand me: even without these people the universe could manage quite well—of course; but uselessness is not their main quality, not their distinctive characteristic, and when you speak of them the word "superfluous" is not the first to come to the tongue. But I —about me it is not possible to say anything else: I am superfluous, and that is all there is to it. A supernumerary man, and nothing more. Evidently nature did not reckon on my turning up, and so she treated me as an unexpected and uninvited guest. Not without reason did one wit, a great lover of the game of preference, say of me that my mother had forfeited a trick. I am writing of myself calmly, without any spleen. . . .

The question is settled. All my life I continually found my place occupied, perhaps because I sought that place where I should not have sought it. I was mistrustful, shy, peevish, like all ailing people; and, moreover, probably owing to excessive self-esteem or in consequence of some unsatisfactory allocation of my being between my feelings and thoughts — and the expression of those feelings and thoughts — I came up against a senseless, incomprehensible, and invincible obstacle. And when I decided to conquer that obstacle by force, to break down that barrier, my movements, the expression of my face, all my being acquired a look of agonizing strain. I not only seemed to be, I actually became unnatural and tense. I myself felt that and hastened to return to my normal state. At such moments a terrible fear arose within me. I analyzed myself down to the last tiny thread, compared myself with others, recalled the least glances, smiles, and words of the people before whom I desired to display myself, interpreted everything in a bad sense, laughed venomously at my own pretensions to "be like everybody else"; and suddenly, in the middle of the laugh, sadly let myself go quite flat, fell into an absurd despondency. And then I returned myself to my previous state. In a word, I spun around like a squirrel in a wheel. Whole days were passed in this agonizing, fruitless activity. Well, now, please tell me, tell me yourself, who and what has any need of such a man? Why this happened to me, what was the cause of this painstaking fussing with my own self — who knows? Who can say?

I remember, one day I left Moscow in the diligence.[1] The going was good, yet to the four-in-hand the driver harnessed yet a fifth horse. This unfortunate, this fifth, this quite useless horse, fastened untidily to the singletree[2] by a thick, short rope, which mercilessly chafes its flank, rubs its tail, forces it to run in a very unnatural manner, and makes all its body look like a comma, always arouses my profound sympathy. I remarked to the driver that surely on this occasion it would have been possible to do without the fifth horse. . . . He was silent for a moment, wagged his head, lashed the animal a dozen times in succession across its meager back and under its swollen belly — and said, not without a sneer: "Why, but there it is; it's been tied on! And what the devil for?"

[1] *diligence:* public stagecoach.
[2] *singletree:* a swinging bar to which a horse is harnessed.

I too have simply been tied on!... But, thank goodness, the post house is not far away now.

Superfluous... I promised to demonstrate the justice of my opinion, and I shall keep my promise. I do not consider it necessary to recall a thousand details, everyday incidents and events, which, for that matter, in the eyes of any thinking man would serve as irrefutable proofs in my favor—I mean in favor of my view. It would be better for me to begin directly with one quite important event, after which I think no doubt whatever will remain of the exactitude of the word "superfluous." I repeat: I have no intention of going into details, but I cannot pass over in silence one quite curious and remarkable circumstance: namely, my friends' (even I had friends) strange behavior toward me whenever I happened to meet them or even when I called on them. They seemed to be made to feel awkward. When they advanced to welcome me they smiled not quite naturally, looked not into my eyes, nor at my feet, as some do, but more often at my cheeks, hurriedly pronounced: "Ah! Good morning, Chulkaturin!" (Fate has favored me with such a name) or "Ah! and here's Chulkaturin," and at once stepped away or even remained motionless for a time, as though trying to recall something.

I noticed all this because I am not lacking in penetration and the gift of observation; I am not at all stupid; quite amusing, and not quite ordinary thoughts sometimes enter my head. But as I am a superfluous man and have imposed an internal constraint on myself, it is fearful for me to express my thoughts, especially as I know in advance that I shall express them very badly. I sometimes wonder how people can talk, and so simply, so easily.... What audacity, you know! I mean, I have to confess it, even I, despite my constraint, quite often had an itching tongue. But really I gave vent to speech only in my youth, and in my more mature years I almost always succeeded in checking myself. I would say in an undertone: "Well now, we would do better to be silent for a moment," and I would calm down. We are all clever at silence; our women especially have been greatly taken by it. Some exalted Russian maiden will be so potently silent that even in a man prepared for such a spectacle it is capable of producing a slight shiver and a cold sweat. But this is not my subject, and it is not for me to criticize others. I set about the story I promised.

Some years ago, owing to a combination of quite insignificant, but for me highly important circumstances, I had to spend about six months in the county town of O——. This town is built entirely on a slope, and is built very inconveniently. It has about eight hundred inhabitants, of more than usual poverty, and the little houses are like nothing on earth.

Along the main street, as a pretext for a roadway, here and there menacing slabs of unhewn limestone show whitely, with the result that even the peasants' carts drive round them. In the very center of the astonishingly untidy square is a tiny, yellow erection with dark holes, and in the holes people wearing large peaked caps sit and pretend to be trading. Right outside it is an extraordinarily tall multicolored pole, and by this pole, for order's sake, on the instructions of the authorities, a cart of yellow hay stands and one official chicken struts about. In a word, in the town of O—— life is excellent. During the first few days of my stay in this town I all but went out of my mind with boredom. I must say of myself that although, of course, I am a superfluous man, it is not by my own choice. I am sickly myself, but I cannot stand anything sickly.... I would not be at all averse to happiness, I have even tried to approach it from one side and another.... And so it is not surprising that I too can be bored, like any other mortal. I was in the town of O—— on official business....

Terentievna is absolutely determined to wear me out. Here is a specimen of our conversation:

Terentievna: "Oh, sir! what are you always writing for? It isn't good for you to write."

I: "But I'm bored, Terentievna."

She: "You have a drink of tea and lie down. If God wills, you'll have a little sweat and get a little sleep."

I: "But I don't want to sleep."

She: "Ah, master, what are you saying? For the Lord's sake! Lie down now, lie down; it's better that way."

I: "I shall die in any case, Terentievna!"

She: "God preserve and forgive!... Well, will you order some tea?"

I: "I shan't live through the week, Terentievna!"

She: "Oh, master, what are you saying?... Then I'll go and get the samovar going."

O decrepit, yellow, toothless creature! So am I not a human being even to you?

March 24. A cracking frost.

On the very day of my arrival in the town of O—— my above-mentioned official business made it necessary for me to call on a certain Kirila Matveevich Ozhogin, one of the chief officials in the country. But I made his acquaintance, or, as we say, made friends with him, only two weeks later. His house was on the main street and was distinguished from all the others by its size, its painted roof, and two lions at the gates, of the species that look uncommonly like the unfortunate dogs whose habitat is Moscow. These lions in themselves showed that Ozhogin was a man of affluence. And in fact he owned four hundred peasant souls. He received all the best people of the town of O—— and had the reputation of being hospitable. He was also called on by the town governor, an unusually bulky man who looked as though cut from long-lying material, who drove in a two-horse ginger-colored droshky.[1] And he was called on by other officials: by the lawyer, a jaundiced and malevolent creature; by the surveyor, a wit, of German extraction, with a Tartar face; by the officer of communications, a tender soul, a singer, but a gossip; and by the former marshal of the county, a gentleman with dyed hair, a swelling shirt-front, tight-fitting pantaloons, and that most noble expression which is peculiar to people who have been submitted to trials. He was also called on by two landowners, friends inseparable, both of them no longer young and even showing signs of wear. The younger of these landowners constantly annihilated the elder, and always closed his friend's mouth with the same protest: "Do stop it, Sergei Sergeich, where are you getting to? Why, you write the word 'cork' with a 'k.' ... Yes, gentlemen," he would go on with all the fire of conviction, turning to the others present, "Sergei Sergeich writes not 'cork,' but 'kork.'" And everybody present laughed, although in all probability not one of them was distinguished by any particular gift for spelling. But the unfortunate Sergei Sergeich lapsed into silence and bowed his head with a fading smile. But I forgot that my days are numbered, I am describing things too minutely. And so, without further circumstantial details, Ozhogin was married, he had a daughter, Yelizaveta Kirillovna, and with this daughter I fell in love.

Ozhogin himself was a commonplace sort of man, neither bad nor good, and his wife was like a perennial chickling; but their daughter did not take after her parents. She was very good-looking, vivacious, and of a gentle character. Her gray, gleaming eyes beamed good-naturedly and frankly below her childishly raised eyebrows; she smiled almost continually, and laughed too, quite often. Her fresh voice sounded very pleasant; she moved easily, swiftly, and blushed merrily. She did not dress with any excess of elegance; only simple dresses suited her. In general I was not quick at making acquaintances, and if I found myself at ease with anyone from the beginning—a thing that, I may mention, hardly every happened—I confess that this was greatly in favor of the new acquaintance. Toward women I did not know how to behave at all, and in

---

[1] *droshky:* a low, open Russian carriage.

their presence I either scowled and adopted an infuriated look, or bared my teeth in the most stupid manner and grew tongue-tied in my embarrassment. With Yelizaveta Kirillovna, on the other hand, I felt completely at home from our very first meeting. This is how it came about.

I went one day to see Ozhogin before dinner, asked if he was at home, and was told: "He's at home, dressing; please come into the hall." I went into the hall and saw a girl in a white dress standing at the window with her back toward me, holding a cage in her hand. As usual, I felt a little awkward; none the less I did nothing, only coughed for the sake of decorum. The girl turned round swiftly—so swiftly that her curls struck her in the face. She saw me, bowed, and with a smile showed me a little box half-filled with seed. "May I go on?" I, of course, as is correct in such circumstances, first bent my head and simultaneously swiftly bent and straightened my knee (just as though someone had struck me from behind in the hock, a movement that, as is known, is a sign of excellent breeding and affable ease of manners). Then I smiled, raised my hand, and passed it cautiously and gently through the air a couple of times. The girl at once turned away, pulled a little board out of the cage, began to scrape it vigorously with a knife, and suddenly, without changing her position, said the following words:

"This is Papa's bullfinch.... Do you like bullfinches?"

"I prefer siskins,"[1] I replied, not without effort.

"And I like siskins too; but look at him, what a nice little bird he is! Look, he's not afraid." (What amazed me was that I was not afraid.) "Come closer. His name is Popka."

I went up to her and bent to look at the bird. "He is a dear, isn't he?" She turned her face to me; but we were standing so close to each other that she had to throw her head back a little in order to look at me with her gleaming eyes. I looked at her: all her youthful, rosy face was smiling with such friendliness that I too smiled and all but laughed with pleasure.

The door opened; Mr. Ozhogin entered. I at once went to him and began to talk to him very easily. I myself don't know how it came about that I remained to dinner, sat on all the evening, and the next day Ozhogin's footman, a lanky and purblind[2] fellow, even smiled at me as a friend of the family while he relieved me of my greatcoat.

To find a shelter, to build oneself at least a temporary nest, to know the comfort of everyday relations and habits—this happiness I, a superfluous man, without family memories, had not experienced hitherto. If

[1] *siskins:* small birds similar to the goldfinch.
[2] *purblind:* lacking in understanding; obtuse.

anything about me had the least reminiscence of a flower, and if that comparison were not so trite, I would have dared to say that from that day I blossomed in my soul. Everything in me and around me changed in an instant. All my life was irradiated with love—absolutely all my life, down to the smallest details, like a dark, neglected room into which a candle has been carried. I lay down to sleep and rose again, I dressed, I breakfasted, I smoked a pipe, all differently from before. I even danced a little as I walked, really I did, as though wings had suddenly sprouted from my shoulders. I, I remember, was not for a single moment unaware of the feeling that Yelizaveta Kirillovna inspired in me; and from the first day I loved her passionately, and from the very first day I knew that I was in love. During the following three weeks I saw her every day. Those three weeks were the happiest time in my life; but the memory of them is oppressive. I cannot think of them in isolation: I involuntarily recall what followed them, and a venomous sorrow slowly takes possession of the heart that a moment before was moved with tenderness.

When a man is very happy his brain, as is well known, functions very little. A calm and joyous feeling, a feeling of satisfaction, penetrates into all his being; he is engulfed by it; his consciousness of personality vanishes—he felicitates, as badly educated poets say. But when, at last, this "enchantment" passes, a man sometimes feels annoyed and regretful that amid his happiness he studied himself so little, that by way of meditation and memory he did not double, did not continue his enjoyment— as though a "felicitating" man has any time, and even finds it worth while, to meditate on his feelings. A happy man is like a fly in the sunlight. And so I too, when I recall those three weeks, find it almost impossible to retain an exact, definite impression, especially as during all this time nothing of any note occurred between us. . . . Those twenty days are to me something warm, young, and scented, a lighter streak in my dim and gray little life. My memory suddenly grows inexorably faithful and clear only from the moment when, to use the words of those same badly educated authors, the blows of fate fell upon me.

Yes; those three weeks. . . . For that matter, they were not entirely without lasting impress on my mind. Sometimes, when I happen to think for long about that time, other memories suddenly float up from the gloom of the past—just as stars unexpectedly emerge in the evening sky to meet the attentive gaze. One walk especially, in a wood outside the town has remained in my memory. There were four of us: old Mrs. Ozhogina, Liza, myself, and a certain Bizmionkov, a petty official of the town, a flaxen-haired, kind, and quiet little man. I shall have more to say about him later. Mr. Ozhogin himself had remained at home: he had a headache through oversleeping. The day was marvelous, warm and still. It has to be observed that pleasure gardens and social walks are not to the mind of the Russian. In the so-called public gardens of the provincial towns you will never meet a living soul at any season of the year, except perhaps some old woman, who sits down with a groan on a sun-baked green bench close to a large tree, and even then only if there is no greasy seat under a nearby gateway. But if there happens to be a scraggy little birch wood in the proximity of the town, on Sundays and holidays the merchants and sometimes the officials readily drive out to it with samovars, pastries, and watermelons; they set out all this profusion of good things on the dusty grass right by the road, sit down in a circle, and eat and drink tea in the sweat of their faces until the very evening. It was exactly this type of wood that existed just over a mile from the town of O——.

We drove there after dinner, drank our fill of tea, as is usual, and then set out, all four of us, to stroll through the wood. Bizmionkov took old Mrs. Ozhogina by the arm, I took Liza. The day was now declining toward evening. At that time I was in the very zenith of my first love (not more than two weeks had passed since the day of our first acquaintance), in that state of passionate and attentive adoration when all your soul innocently and involuntarily follows every movement of the beloved being; when you can never be satiated with her presence, or listen too much to her voice; when you smile and look like a child restored to health, and the least experienced of men can see at one glance a hundred paces away what is happening to you. Until that day I had never had the chance to hold Liza by the arm. I walked beside her, quietly strolling over the green grass. A light breeze literally fluttered around us, between the white trunks of the birches, occasionally flinging her hat ribbon into my face. I persistently watched her gaze until, at last, she gaily turned to me, and we smiled at each other. The birds twittered approvingly above us, the blue sky shone graciously through the delicate foliage. My head was swimming with an excess of delight. I hasten to remark that Liza was not in the least in love with me. She liked me; she never shunned anybody; but not I was destined to disturb her childlike tranquillity. At this period she was seventeen.... And meanwhile, in my very presence, this very same evening that gentle internal ferment began within her which portends the child's transformation into a woman.... I witnessed the transformation of all her being, that innocent bewilderment, that anxious meditation; I was the first to observe that sudden gentleness of gaze, that ringing uncertainty of voice, and—O fool, O superfluous man!

—for a whole week after I was not ashamed to assume that I, I was the cause of the change!

This is how it happened.

We walked for quite a long time, until evening had set in, and we talked little. I was silent, like all inexperienced lovers, and in all probability she had nothing to say to me. But she seemed to be meditating on something and shook her head in a peculiar way, thoughtfully biting a leaf she had plucked. From time to time she started off in front, with such resolution . . . and then she suddenly halted, waited for me, and looked about her with raised eyebrows and an abstracted smile. The evening before, she and I had read *The Caucasian Prisoner*[1] together. With what avidity she had listened to me, resting her little face in both hands and leaning her breast against the table! I began to talk about that reading; she reddened, asked me whether I had given the finch some hempseed before our departure, began to sing some song aloud, and suddenly fell silent. On one side the wood ended in quite a steep and lofty cliff; at the bottom flowed a winding little river, and beyond it endless meadows, here and there intersected with gulleys, and now slightly rising, like waves, then broadly spreading like a tablecloth, stretched into the boundless distance. Liza and I were the first to reach the edge of the wood; Bizmionkov was left behind with the mother. We came out at the edge, halted, and both involuntarily screwed up our eyes: directly in front of us, amid an incandescent haze, the livid, enormous sun was setting. Half the sky was burning and reddening; crimson rays struck across the meadows, casting a lurid reflection even on the shady sides of the gulleys, lying like molten lead on the river wherever it was not concealed beneath overhanging bushes, and seeming to be pressing into the heart of the cliff and the wood. We stood flooded with the burning refulgence.[2] I am not capable of communicating all the passionate exultation of that picture. They say that a blind man once imagined the color of red as a trumpet sound. I don't know how far this comparison is just, but certainly there was something challenging in that flaming gold of the evening air, in the purple gleam of the sky and the earth. I cried out with rapture and turned at once to Liza. She was gazing straight at the sun. I remember that conflagration of the sunset was reflected as tiny points of fire in her eyes. She was overwhelmed, was profoundly moved. She made no response to my exclamation; for long she did not stir; she stood with head hanging. . . . I stretched out my hand to her; she turned away

[1] *The Caucasian Prisoner:* a narrative poem by Alexander Pushkin (1799–1837).
[2] *refulgence:* splendor, radiance.

from me and suddenly burst into tears. I looked at her with a secret, almost joyous amazement. . . .

Bizmionkov's voice sounded a couple of paces away. Liza swiftly wiped away her tears and looked at me with an irresolute smile. Her mother, resting on her fair-haired escort's arm, came out of the wood; they too admired the spectacle. Liza's mother asked her something, and I, I remember, involuntarily trembled when she answered in a broken voice, like a cracked glass. Meanwhile the sun set, the glow began to fade. We walked back. I again took Liza by the arm. It was still light in the wood, and I could distinguish her features clearly. She was embarrassed and did not raise her eyes. The blush that had suffused all her face did not vanish: it was as though she were still standing in the radiance of the setting sun. . . . Her hand gently touched mine. For long I could not say anything, so violently was my heart beating within me. In the distance the carriage appeared through the trees; the coachman was driving to meet us at a walking pace along the crumbling sandy road.

"Lizaveta Kirillovna," I said at last, "why did you weep?"

"I don't know," she replied after a brief silence, and looked at me with her mild, still moist eyes—I thought their look seemed changed—and she was silent again.

"I see you love nature. . . ." I continued. That was not what I had wanted to say at all, and even that phrase I could hardly stammer out. She shook her head. I could not say another word . . . I was waiting for something . . . not an avowal—how could I! I was waiting for a trustful glance, a question. . . . But Liza gazed at the ground and was silent. I repeated yet again in an undertone: "Why?" and did not get an answer. I could see that she was feeling awkward, almost ashamed.

Fifteen minutes later we were sitting in the carriage and approaching the town. The horses moved at a fast trot; we sped swiftly through the darkening, humid air. I suddenly began to talk a great deal, incessantly addressing myself first to Bizmionkov, then to Mrs. Ozhogina, and did not look at Liza. But I was able to observe that her gaze rested on me from time to time as she sat in the corner of the carriage. On arriving home she roused herself; she did not want to read with me, however, and soon retired to bed. The change, that change of which I have spoken, had been accomplished in her. She had ceased to be a girl, she too had begun to wait—like me—for something. She did not wait long.

But that night I returned to my apartments completely enchanted. The vague—was it presentiment or suspicion?—that had stirred within me had vanished. The sudden constraint in Liza's behavior toward me I ascribed to maidenly bashfulness, timidity.... Had I not read a thousand times in innumerable works that the first arrival of love always agitates and frightens a maiden? I felt extremely happy, and was already mentally making various plans....

If anyone had said into my ear: "You're lying, my friend! Something quite different awaits you, brother. You are to die in loneliness, in a wretched little house, to the unbearable grumbling of an old woman who can hardly wait for your death in order to sell your boots for a trifling sum...."

Yes, involuntarily one says with a certain Russian philosopher: "How to know what you don't know?" Till tomorrow.

March 25. A white winter's day.

I have reread what I wrote yesterday, and all but tore up the whole book. It seems to me that I am telling my story too expansively and too fondly. For that matter, as all my other memories of this time are without joy, except that peculiar kind of joy which Lermontov[1] had in mind when he said that it is pleasurable and painful to disturb the sores of old wounds, why shouldn't I indulge myself? But one should have respect for one's honor too. And so I continue without any display of fondness.

For a whole week after that walk outside the town my position did not show any essential improvement, though the transformation in Liza grew more obvious with every day. I, as I have said, interpreted this change in the manner most favorable to myself.... The misfortune of lonely and shy people—shy from self-esteem—consists just in the circumstance that, although they have eyes and even stare those eyes out, they see nothing, or see everything in a false light, as if through tinted spectacles. Their own thoughts and observations hinder them at every step. At the beginning of our acquaintance Liza turned to me trustfully and easily, like a child; perhaps in her attitude to me there was even something still more simple, something of childish attachment.... But when that strange, almost abrupt transformation was accomplished within her, she, after a brief bewilderment, felt constrained in my presence, she involuntarily turned away from me, and at the same time grew sad and thoughtful.... She waited—for what? She herself did not know, but I... as I have said, I rejoiced in this transformation. By God, I all but swooned, as they say, with rapture. For that matter, I am prepared to agree that in my place any other man might have been deluded.... Who is without self-esteem? I need not say that all this became

---

[1] *Lermontov:* Mikhail Yurievich Lermontov (1814–1841), Russian poet and novelist.

clear to me only when I had to fold my broken wings, which were weak enough already.

The misunderstanding that arose between me and Liza continued a whole week—and there is nothing surprising in that: I have had to be witness of misunderstandings that lasted for year after year. And, indeed, who was it who said that the truth is the only reality? A lie is just as viable as truth, if not more so. Certainly, I remember that even during that week a worm occasionally stirred within me.... But a man like me, a solitary individual, I will say again, is just as incapable of understanding what is going on inside him as of that which is being accomplished before his eyes. And besides, is love a natural feeling? Is it inherent in man to love? Love is a sickness; and no law has been laid down for sickness. Granted that at times my heart constricted unpleasantly; but then, everything within me was turned upside down. In such a case how can you demand that a man should recognize what is satisfactory and what not, or the cause, the meaning of every separate sensation?

But in any case all these misunderstandings, presentiments, and hopes were resolved in the following manner.

One day, it was in the morning, about twelve o'clock, as I entered Mr. Ozhogin's vestibule I heard an unknown, ringing voice in the hall. Then the door was thrown open and, accompanied by the master, a tall and well-built man of about twenty-five appeared, swiftly flung round his shoulders his military greatcoat, which had been lying on a bench, took an affectionate leave of Kirila Matveich, carelessly touched his peaked cap as he passed me, and disappeared with a jingle of spurs.

"Who is that?" I asked Ozhogin.

"Prince N.," he answered with a preoccupied air. "He's been sent from Petersburg to take over the recruits. But where have all the servants vanished to?" he continued crossly. "No one handed him his coat."

We entered the hall.

"Has he been here long?" I asked.

"They say he arrived yesterday evening. I offered him a room with us, but he refused. But he seems to be a very charming fellow."

"Has he been with you long?"

"About an hour. He asked me to introduce him to Olimpiada Nikitinichna."

"And did you?"

"Of course."

"And to Lizaveta Kirillovna—?"

"He made her acquaintance too, of course."

I was silent.

"Is he going to stay here long, do you know?"

"Yes; I think he will have to remain here a couple of weeks and more."

And Kirila Matveich hurried off to dress.

I walked up and down the hall several times. I don't remember that Prince N.'s arrival made any special impression on me at the time, apart from that unpleasant feeling that customarily takes possession of us when a new face appears in our domestic circle. Possibly with this feeling went a touch of the jealousy felt by a shy and obscure Moscow man for a brilliant Petersburg officer. "The Prince," I thought, "is a man from the capital; he will look down on us...." I had not seen him for more than a minute, but I had been able to note that he was good-looking, adroit, and free and easy. After walking about the hall for some time I finally halted before a mirror, took a comb out of my pocket, gave my hair a look of picturesque negligence, and, as sometimes happens, was suddenly sunk in contemplation of my own features. I remember my attention was anxiously concentrated on my nose; its rather soft and indefinite outline did not give me any special satisfaction—when suddenly, in the dark depths of the sloping glass, which reflected almost all the room, a door was opened and Liza's graceful figure appeared.

I don't know why, but I did not stir and did not change the expression on my face. Liza craned her neck, stared at me attentively, and, raising her eyebrows, biting her lips, and holding her breath, like someone who is glad he has not been noticed, cautiously fell back and quietly drew the door open behind her. The door creaked a little. She started and froze still.... I did not move.... She reached for the handle again and vanished. There could be no possibility of doubt: the expression on her face at the sight of me, an expression that indicated nothing but a desire to retire unnoticed, to avoid an unpleasant meeting, the sudden flash of satisfaction that I managed to catch in her eyes when she thought she had succeeded in slipping away unobserved—all these things said only too clearly: this girl does not love me. For long, long I could not remove my gaze from the dumb, immobile door, which again appeared as a white patch in the depths of the mirror. I felt like smiling at my own strained figure. I drooped my head, returned home, and flung myself on the sofa. I felt unusually disheartened, so disheartened that I could not weep.... And what was there to weep over?... "Surely not?" I affirmed incessantly as I lay like a corpse on my back, with my hands folded on my chest. "Surely not?" How do you like that "Surely not?"

March 26. A thaw.

When next day, after much vacillation and with sinking heart, I entered the Ozhogins' familiar reception hall, I was no longer the man they had known for the past three weeks. All my former habits, which under the influence of a new feeling I had begun to live down, reappeared and took possession of me, like masters returning to their homes. People like me are guided in general not so much by positive facts as by their own impressions. I, who no longer ago than yesterday had been dreaming of "the raptures of mutual love," now had no doubt whatever of my own "unhappiness," and was in utter despair, though even I could not find any sensible pretext for my despair. I could hardly be jealous of Prince N., and no matter what qualities he abounded with, his arrival was not in itself sufficient to put an end to Liza's predilection for me all at once.... But then, had any such predilection ever existed? I recalled the past. "But what of the walk in the wood?" I asked myself. "But what of her expression in the mirror?" "But," I continued, "the walk in the wood, I think . . ." "Pah, my God, what an insignificant creature I am!" I exclaimed aloud at last. This was the kind of half-expressed, half-formulated thought that, returning a thousand times, circled in my head like a monotonous whirlwind. I repeat, when I called on Ozhogin next day, I was the same mistrustful, suspicious, strange person I had been since childhood....

I found all the family in the reception hall; Bizmionkov also was sitting there, in a corner. They all seemed in good spirits; Ozhogin especially beamed, and with his very first words he informed me that Prince N. had spent all the previous evening with them. Liza greeted me calmly. "Well," I said to myself, "now I understand why you are in good spirits." I confess that this second visit of the Prince rather puzzled me. I hadn't expected it. In general, people like me expect everything in the world except that which should happen in the natural order of things. I sulked and adopted the air of an injured but magnanimous man; I wanted to punish Liza with my disfavor, from which, by the way, it should follow that nonetheless I had not completely given up hope. They say that in certain cases, when you are really loved, it is quite helpful to torment the adored being. But in my position that would have been inexpressibly stupid: in her utter innocence Liza did not pay any attention to me. Only Mrs. Ozhogina noticed my solemn taciturnity and anxiously inquired after my health. Of course I replied with a bitter smile that, thank God, I was quite well. Ozhogin continued to expatiate on his guest. But, noticing that I replied reluctantly, he addressed himself more to Bizmionkov, who was listening to him with greater attention. While he was talking, a manservant entered and announced Prince N.'s arrival. Ozhogin jumped up and ran to meet him; Liza, on whom I at once fixed an eagle gaze, reddened with delight and fidgeted on her chair. The Prince entered, perfumed, gay, gracious. . . .

As I am not composing a novel for a benevolent reader, but am writing simply for my own satisfaction, there is no reason why I should resort to the usual stratagems of the littérateurs. I shall say at once, without further procrastination, that from the first day she met him Liza fell passionately in love with the Prince; and the Prince took a fancy to her, partly because he had nothing to do, partly through a habit he had of turning women's heads, but also partly because Liza was in fact a very pleasant creature. There was nothing surprising in the circumstance that they fell in love with each other. In all probability he had not expected to find such a pearl in such a filthy shell (I am referring to the God-forsaken town of O———), and even in her dreams she had never seen anything in the least resembling this brilliant, intelligent, captivating aristocrat.

After the first greetings Ozhogin introduced me to the Prince, who was very courteous to me. Indeed, he was always courteous to everybody and, despite the immeasurable chasm between him and our obscure county circle, he had the gift not only of setting people at ease, but even of appearing as though he were our equal and only happened to live in St. Petersburg.

The first evening . . . Oh, that first evening! In the happy days of our childhood our teachers taught us to admire and imitate the valiant endurance of that young Lacedaemonian who, having stolen a fox and concealed it beneath his garment, allowed it to devour all his entrails without once crying out, so preferring death itself to dishonor. . . . I cannot find any better comparison to convey my inexpressible sufferings during all that evening, when I first saw the Prince at Liza's side. My constantly strained smile, my agonizing keenness of observation, my stupid silence, my yearning and futile desire to leave, all these were probably very remarkable in their kind. More than one fox devoured my entrails: jealousy, envy, and sense of my own insignificance, and helpless anger, all gnawed at me. I could not but admit that the Prince was indeed a very charming young man. . . . I watched him with consuming eyes; in truth, I think I forgot to blink as I gazed at him. He did not talk only to Liza, but of course he talked only for her. I must have greatly bored him. . . . In all probability he quickly guessed that he had to do with an eliminated lover; but, out of pity for me, and profoundly conscious of my complete impotence, he treated me with unusual mildness. You can imagine how that affronted me!

During the evening, I remember, I attempted to make amends; I (do not laugh at me, whoever you may be whose eyes chance to fall on these lines, especially as this was my last dream) — I, believe me, in the midst of my many and varied torments, suddenly imagined that Liza was trying to punish me for my haughty coldness at the beginning of my visit, that she was angry with me and was flirting with the Prince only out of pique. I seized a suitable moment and, going up to her with a humble but gracious smile, muttered: "Enough, forgive me. . . . Besides, I'm not behaving like this because I'm afraid." And then, without waiting for her reply, I abruptly adopted an extremely animated and jaunty expression, smiled wryly, stretched my arm above my head in the direction of the ceiling (I remember I wanted to adjust my neckerchief), and even prepared to spin round on one leg, as though wishing to say: "It's all over, I'm in good spirits, let's all be in good spirits." However, I didn't spin round on one leg, for I was afraid of falling, owing to some unnatural petrifaction of my knees. . . . Liza did not understand me at all, stared into my face in amazement, hurriedly smiled as though wanting to get away from me as quickly as possible, and went back to the Prince. With all my blindness and stupidity, I could not but confess to myself that she had not been angry at all and had not been vexed with me at the moment: she simply hadn't even been thinking of me. The blow was decisive; my last hopes collapsed with a crash, just as a sheet of ice caught in the spring sunlight suddenly disintegrates into little pieces. I was completely overwhelmed at the very first pressure, and, like the Prussians at Jena, lost everything at once, in one day. No, she had not been angry with me. . . .

Alas, quite the reverse! She herself — I could see that — was being washed around as by a wave. Like a young tree already half cut off from the bank, she avidly leaned over the torrent, ready to yield to it forever not only the first blossoms of her spring, but all her life. Anyone who has happened to be the witness of such an infatuation has known some bitter moments, if he loved and was not loved in return. I shall always remember that consuming attention, that tender gaiety, that innocent self-oblivion, that gaze, still childlike and already womanly, that happy, blossoming smile, which never left the parted lips and the crimsoned cheeks. . . . Everything of which Liza had had a vague presentiment during our walk in the wood had now come to pass. And she, yielding herself entirely to love, at the same time grew completely still, and shone like young wine that has ceased to ferment because its time has come. . . .

I had the patience to sit through that first evening and all the following evenings—right to their end! I could have no hope in anything. With every day Liza and the Prince grew more and more attached to each other. But I had absolutely lost all sense of my own dignity and could not tear myself away from the spectacle of my own unhappiness. I remember one day I attempted to refrain from going; in the morning I gave myself my word of honor to remain at home. And at eight o'clock in the evening (usually I went out at seven) I jumped up like a madman, put on my hat, and, panting, ran to Kirila Matveich's reception room. My position was extremely awkward: I was stubbornly silent; sometimes I did not utter a sound for days at a time. As I have already said, I was never distinguished by eloquence; but now all the sense I had in me seemed to fly out in the Prince's presence, and I was left as bare as a falcon. And with it all, when alone I forced my unfortunate brain to work so hard, pondering over all that I had observed or noticed during the previous day, that when I returned to the Ozhogins', I hardly had the strength to continue my observations. As a sick man I was shown mercy; I saw that. Every morning I made a new, final decision, usually agonizingly hatched out during the past sleepless night; at one time I prepared to have an explanation with Liza, to give her friendly advice. . . . But when I chanced to find myself alone with her, my tongue suddenly ceased to function, as though it had gone stiff, and both of us anxiously looked for the arrival of a third person. Then I wanted to flee, forever, of course, leaving a letter behind for the object of my devotion, a letter filled with reproaches; and one day I even began that letter. But my sense of justice had not completely faded; I realized that I had no right to reproach anybody with anything, and I threw my missive into the fire.

At one moment I magnanimously offered all myself in sacrifice, blessed Liza in her happy love, and from my corner smiled at the Prince mildly and amiably. But the hard-hearted lovers not only did not thank me for my sacrifice; they did not even notice it and evidently had no need of either my blessings or my smiles. . . . Then, in my chagrin, I abruptly passed to the exactly contrary state of mind. I promised myself that, wrapping myself in my cloak like a Spaniard, I would strike down the fortunate rival from around a corner, and took a bestial delight in imagining Liza's despair. . . . But, to begin with, there were very few such corners in the town of O——, and, secondly, a plank fence, a lantern, a policeman in the distance . . . no, at that sort of corner it was somehow more decent to trade in doughnuts than shed human blood. I must confess that among other means for effecting my salvation, as I very indefinitely expressed my thoughts when I talked with myself, I did even think of speaking to Ozhogin—in order to draw this nobleman's attention to his daughter's dangerous situation, to the mournful consequences of her frivolity. . . . One day I even began to talk to him about a certain ticklish subject, but I spoke so cunningly and obscurely that he listened and listened to me and suddenly, as though just waking up, rubbed his hand vigorously and swiftly all over his face, not sparing his nose, then snorted and walked away. I need not say that, having taken this decision, I assured myself that I was acting from the most disinterested of motives; I desired the general good, I was performing the duty of a friend of the family. . . . But I venture to think that even if Kirila Matveich had not cut short my outpourings I would not have had the courage to finish my harangue. Sometimes, with the gravity of an ancient merchant, I took to weighing up the Prince's qualities; sometimes I comforted myself with the hope that it was only temporary, that Liza would come to herself, that her love was not real love. . . . Oh, no! In a word, I cannot think of a single thought that I did not play with at that time. Only one resource, I confess openly, never entered my head: namely, not once did I think of taking my own life. Why I didn't think of that I don't know. . . . Perhaps even then I had a presentiment that in any case I was not to live long.

It is understandable that in such unpropitious circumstances my conduct, my treatment of other people, was more than ever distinguished by unnaturalness and strain. Even old Mrs. Ozhogina—that innately stupid creature—began to shun me and at times did not know how to approach me. Bizmionkov, who had always been polite and ready to do services, avoided me. Even then I had the impression that in him I had a fellow sufferer, that he too was in love with Liza. But he never responded to my hints, and in general talked with me only reluctantly. The Prince treated him very amiably; the Prince, one may say, respected him. Neither Bizmionkov nor I hindered the Prince and Liza; but he did not grow antagonistic to them as I did, did not look like a wolf or a sacrifice, and readily joined them when they desired him to. True, in such cases he was not distinguished by any jocularity, but his cheerfulness had always been of a quiet kind.

Thus about two weeks passed. The Prince was not only good-looking and intelligent; he played the piano, sang, could draw quite well, and could tell a story. His stories, drawn from the higher circles of life in the capital, always made a strong impression on the listeners, all the stronger because he did not appear to attach any special significance to them. . . .

The consequence of this simple artifice of his, if you like to call it so, was that during his brief residence in the town of O—— he absolutely enchanted all the local society. It is always very easy for a man from a higher circle to enchant our steppe nobility. The Prince's frequent visits to the Ozhogins (he spent whole evenings with them) of course aroused the jealousy of the other noblemen and officials. But the Prince, who was a man of the world and intelligent, did not overlook a single one of them, visited them all, said at least one kindly word to all the ladies and young ladies, allowed them to feed him on monstrously heavy dishes and to give him wretched wines with high-sounding names to drink—in a word, he behaved excellently, prudently, and adroitly. Prince N. was in general a man of gay disposition, convivial, amiable by nature, and also, be it added, by calculation; so how could he fail to be a complete success, and in every respect?

From the moment of his arrival everybody in the house found that time flew past with extraordinary speed; everything went well; old Ozhogin, though he pretended that he noticed nothing, in all probability rubbed his hands in secret at the thought of having such a son-in-law. The Prince himself was managing the whole affair very quietly and decorously. When suddenly, one unexpected occurrence . . .

Till tomorrow. I am tired now. These memories irritate me even on the edge of the grave. Terentievna decided today that the tip of my nose is already peaked; and that, they say, is a bad sign.

March 27. The thaw continues.

Affairs had reached the position above described, the Prince and Liza were in love with each other, the old Ozhogins were waiting for something to happen, Bizmionkov was present at all this—more could not be said of him—I was struggling like a fish against the ice, and watching so far as was in my power. I remember I now set myself the task of at least not allowing Liza to perish in the toils of a seducer and so had begun to pay special attention to the maids and the fateful "back door." Though, on the other hand, sometimes I dreamed all night of how in due course I would stretch out my hand with touching magnanimity to the deluded victim and say to her: "The crafty fellow has betrayed you; but I am your faithful friend . . . we will forget the past and will be happy!" When suddenly all through the town spread the joyous news: in honor of the distinguished visitor the county marshal was intending to give a grand ball, to be held at his personal estate of Gornostayovka, also known as

Gubnyakovo. All the officials and authorities of the town of O—— received invitations, from the town governor down to the druggist, who was an unusually carbuncular[1] German with stern pretensions to the ability to talk pure Russian, as the result of which he constantly and by no means aptly used strong expressions, such as "I, may the devil take me to himself, am an absolute lad today...."

As usual, fearful preparations were undertaken. One shopkeeper who stocked cosmetics sold sixteen dark-blue boxes of pomade with the inscription *"A la jesmin"*[2] and with a specifically Slavonic letter after the "n." The young ladies made themselves tight-fitting dresses with agonizing waists, and promontories jutting out at the front. On their own heads the mothers erected menacing embellishments in lieu of mobcaps. The bustling fathers were run off their hind legs, as the saying is. . . .

The longed-for day arrived at last. I was among those invited. It was reckoned to be six miles from the town to Gornostayovka. Kirila Matveich offered me a place in his carriage, but I refused. . . . In like manner punished children refuse their favorite food at table, in order to have a good revenge on their parents. Moreover, I felt that my presence would be irksome to Liza. Bizmionkov took my place. The Prince drove in his own calash, and I in a wretched droshky that I hired at great expense for the solemn occasion.

I shall not stop to describe that ball. Everything was as it should be: the musicians playing in chorus, with trumpets more than usually out of tune, the stupefied landowners with their inveterate families, the lilac ice, the slimy orgeat,[3] the servants in patched boots and knitted cotton gloves, the provincial lions with convulsively grimacing faces, etc., etc. And all this little world revolved around its sun, around the Prince. Lost in the crowd, not noticed even by the forty-eight-year-old maidens with red pimples on their foreheads and blue flowers on their crowns, I constantly watched first the Prince, then Liza. She was very nicely dressed and looked very beautiful that evening. They only danced twice with each other (true, he had the mazurka with her!),[4] but at least to *me* it seemed that some secret, unbroken communication existed between them. Not even looking at her, not talking to her, he seemed continually to be turning to her, to her alone; he was kind, and brilliant, and affable to others—for her alone. She obviously regarded herself as the queen of the ball—and of the beloved; her face simultaneously beamed with child-

---

[1] *carbuncular:* having many skin infections similar to boils.
[2] *"A ... jesmin":* "jasmine."
[3] *orgeat:* a syrup made from barley water and sugar and flavored with almonds.
[4] The mazurka would last an hour or more.

ish joy and innocent pride, and then was abruptly lit up with another, more profound feeling. She radiated happiness. I noticed all this. . . . It was not the first time I had had the opportunity to observe them. . . . At first it greatly afflicted me, then it seemed to move me, and finally it infuriated me. I suddenly felt extremely angry and, I remember, was extremely delighted at this new sensation and even conceived a certain respect for myself. "We'll show them that we've not perished yet," I said to myself.

When the first challenging sounds of the mazurka thundered out I looked about me calmly, coldly and jauntily went up to one long-faced young lady with a red and shining nose, a mouth opened awkwardly as though left unbuttoned, and a scraggy neck, like the neck of a doublebass — went up to her and, dryly clicking my heels, invited her to be my partner. She was wearing a rose-colored dress that looked as though it had only recently, and still not completely, faded; over her head quivered a discolored, despondent fly on an excessively broad copper spring, and altogether this maiden was, if one may put it so, saturated with a kind of sour boredom and inveterate failure. All the evening she had not stirred from her place: no one had thought of asking her to dance. In the absence of any other lady, one sixteen-year-old fair-haired youngster was about to turn to this maiden, and did take a step toward her, but he thought better of it, looked about for a moment, and briskly vanished into the crowd. You can imagine the joyous astonishment with which she accepted my invitation! I triumphantly led her right through the hall, found two chairs, and sat down with her in the ring of the mazurka, as the tenth couple, almost opposite the Prince, who, of course, had been assigned the first place. The Prince, as I have said, had Liza for his partner. Neither I nor my lady was troubled with invitations to dance, so we had ample time for conversation. To tell the truth, my partner was not distinguished by any capacity for uttering words in coherent speech; she used her mouth more for executing a peculiar smile downward, which I had not previously observed, in the course of which she turned her eyes upward, as though some invisible force were elongating her face. But I had no need of her eloquence. Fortunately, I felt angry, and my partner did not inspire me with any feeling of timidity. I began to criticize everybody and everything in the world, especially attacking the youth of the metropolis and the Petersburg *mirliflores*,[1] and finally let myself go so much that my partner gradually ceased to smile and, instead of turning her eyes up, began suddenly — out of astonishment, I suppose — to squint, and so queerly too, as though she had only just no-

[1] *mirliflores:* fops, dandies.

ticed that she had a nose on her face. The gentleman next to me, one of those lions I have already mentioned, threw glances at me more than once, and even turned to me with the expression of an actor who is supposed to awaken in an unknown country and has to convey: "You here too?"

For that matter, even while I sang away like a nightingale, as the saying is, I went on watching the Prince and Liza. They were continually being asked for a turn in the dance; but I suffered less when they were both dancing. And even when they were sitting side by side and talking to each other, smiling that gentle smile which never wishes to leave the faces of happy lovers, even then I was not troubled so much. But when Liza fluttered through the hall with some dashing fop, and the Prince, with her azure gauze scarf on his knees, thoughtfully followed her with his eyes as though enjoying his conquest—then, oh, then I felt unendurable torments and in my fury gave vent to such malicious remarks that both my partner's pupils were fixed on her nose! Meanwhile, the mazurka was drawing to an end. The dancers began to perform the figure known as *la confidante*. In this figure a lady sits in the middle of the ring, chooses another lady as a confidante, and whispers into her ear the name of the gentleman with whom she wishes to dance. A gentleman leads other gentlemen up to her one after another; but the confidante rejects them all until, at last, the previously chosen lucky man arrives. Liza sat in the middle of the ring and selected the host's daughter, a maiden to be reckoned among those of whom one says: "God help them!" The Prince began to seek the chosen one. Having vainly presented at least ten young men (the host's daughter rejected them all with the pleasantest of smiles), he at last turned to me. Something extraordinary occurred within me at that moment; I literally blinked with all my body and wanted to refuse, but I got up and went. The Prince led me to Liza. . . . She did not even look at me. The host's daughter shook her head; the Prince turned to me and, presumably stimulated by the gooselike expression on my face, made me a deep bow. This derisive bow, this rejection, conveyed to me by a triumphant rival, his negligent smile, Liza's unconcerned inattention—all these things carried me away. . . . I drew closer to the Prince and whispered furiously: "You appear to be taking the liberty of laughing at me?"

He looked at me with contemptuous astonishment, took me by the arm again, and, acting as though he were escorting me to my seat, coldly replied: "What?"

"Yes, you, you!" I continued in a whisper, submitting to him nonetheless—in other words, going with him to my seat. "You; but I have no intention of allowing any vacuous Petersburg upstart . . ."

The Prince smiled coldly, almost condescendingly, squeezed my arm, and whispered: "I understand you; but this is not the place; we'll talk about it later." He turned away, went up to Bizmionkov, and led him to Liza. The pale-faced petty official proved to be the chosen one. Liza rose to meet him.

Sitting beside my lady with the despondent fly on her head, I felt myself almost a hero. My heart was beating violently, my breast was heaving nobly beneath my starched shirt-front, I breathed deeply and rapidly. And suddenly I looked so grandly at the adjacent lion that he involuntarily twitched one little foot that he had turned toward me. Having dealt with this person, I ran my eyes round the circle of dancers. . . . I had the impression that two or three gentlemen were looking at me in some astonishment; but, generally speaking, my talk with the Prince had not been observed. . . . My rival was already sitting on his chair, perfectly calm and with his former smile on his face. Bizmionkov led Liza to her seat. She bowed to him amiably and at once turned to the Prince, with some anxiety, it seemed to me. But he smiled to her in reply, graciously waved his hand, and evidently said something very pleasant to her, for she crimsoned deeply with pleasure, dropped her eyes, and then fixed them on him again with affectionate reproach.

The heroic mood that had suddenly developed in me did not vanish until the mazurka was ended; but I no longer uttered sarcasms and did not criticize. I only looked from time to time moodily and sternly at my lady, who was evidently beginning to be afraid of me and was reduced to stuttering and blinking incessantly when I returned her to the natural fortress of her mother, a very fat woman with a red toque on her head. Entrusting the terrified maiden to her rightful ownership, I walked away to the window, folded my arms, and began to wait for what would happen next. I waited quite a long time. The Prince was continually surrounded by the host—literally surrounded, just as Britain is surrounded by the sea—not to speak of the other members of the county marshal's family and other guests. And besides, he could not go up and begin to talk to such an insignificant person as I without arousing general astonishment. I remember that this insignificance of mine even gave me cause for joy. "Have a good time!" I thought, watching as he courteously turned first to one, then to another worthy person who had achieved the honor of being noticed by him if only for the "twinkling of an eye," as the poets say. "Have a good time, my boy—you'll come up to me at last, for, after all, I have insulted you." Finally the Prince, neatly escaping from the crowd of his adorers, passed by me, glanced perhaps at the window, or at my hair, turned back, and suddenly halted, as though he had remembered something.

"Ah, yes! he said, turning to me with a smile. "That reminds me, I have a little business with you."

Two landowners, among the most importunate, who had persistently followed the Prince, must have thought that the "little business" was of an official nature, for they respectfully fell back. The Prince took me by the arm and led me aside. My heart knocked in my chest.

"I think you," he began, drawling the word "you" and gazing at my chin with a contemptuous expression, which, strangely enough, could not have accorded better with his fresh and handsome face, "you made some impertinent remark to me."

"I said what I thought," I retorted, raising my voice.

"Sssh! Quieter!" he remarked. "Gentlemen don't shout. Perhaps you would like to fight a duel with me?"

"That is your business," I replied, drawing myself up.

"I shall be compelled to challenge you," he said carelessly, "if you do not withdraw your expression."

"I have no intention of withdrawing anything," I retorted proudly.

"Really?" he observed, not without a sarcastic smile. "In that case," he continued after a moment's silence, "I shall have the honor to send my second to you tomorrow."

"Very good!" I said in a voice as unconcerned as possible.

He bowed slightly.

"I cannot forbid your regarding me as vacuous," he added, arrogantly narrowing his eyes, "but the Princes N. cannot be upstarts. Good-by, Mr. — Mr. Stuccoturin."

He swiftly turned his back on me and went back to the host, who was beginning to get agitated.

Mr. Stuccoturin! . . . My name is Chulkaturin. . . . I could not think of anything to say to him in reply to that last affront and only stared after him furiously. "Till tomorrow!" I whispered, clenching my teeth, and at once sought out an officer of my acquaintance, an Uhlan captain named Koloberdayev, a desperate reveler and a splendid fellow. I briefly told him about my quarrel with the Prince and asked him to be my second. Of course he agreed at once, and I went home.

I could not sleep all night — out of agitation, not cowardice. I am not a coward. In fact, I thought very little about the possibility that I might be deprived of life, of that highest good on earth, as the Germans call it. I thought only of Liza, of my shattered hopes, of what I ought to do. "Should I attempt to kill the Prince?" I asked myself; and of course I wanted to kill him, not for the sake of vengeance, but in my desire for Liza's good. "But she will not survive that blow," I continued. "No, better that he should kill me!" I confess I also found it pleasant to think that I, an obscure local individual, should have compelled such an important person to fight with me.

Morning came upon me during these meditations; and the morning was immediately followed by Koloberdayev.

"Well," he asked me as he clattered into my bedroom, "and where is the Prince's second?"

"Give him a chance," I replied crossly; "it is only eight o'clock. I expect the Prince is still asleep."

"In that case," the indefatigable captain retorted, "order some tea for me. I've got a headache from yesterday. . . . I haven't even undressed. For that matter," he added with a yawn, "I very rarely do undress."

Tea was brought for him. He drank six glasses with rum, smoked four pipes, told me that the previous day he had bought a horse for almost nothing after the coachmen had rejected it, and that he planned to break it in, tying up one foreleg. And he fell asleep, without undressing, on the sofa, with a pipe in his mouth. I got up and put my papers in order. One note of invitation from Liza, the only note I had ever received from her, I was about to put in my breast; but I thought better of the idea and threw it into my box. Koloberdayev snored quietly, his head hanging half-off the leather upholstery. . . . I remember I spent a long time examining his crumpled, audacious, carefree, goodnatured face. At ten o'clock my servant announced the arrival of Bizmionkov. The Prince had chosen him as his second.

Together we aroused the captain, who was dead asleep. He rose, stared at us with glassy eyes, asked in a hoarse voice for vodka, pulled himself together, and, bowing to Bizmionkov, went with him into the next room for a conference. The seconds' conference did not last long. Fifteen minutes later they both came to me in the bedroom. Koloberdayev informed me: "We shall fight this very day, at three o'clock, with pistols." I silently nodded my agreement. Bizmionkov at once took his leave and departed. He was rather pale and inwardly agitated, like a man unaccustomed to such activities; but he was very courteous and cold. I felt rather conscience-stricken in his presence, I did not dare to look him in the eyes. Koloberdayev again began to tell me about his horse. This conversation was very much to my mind. I was afraid he might make some mention of Liza. But my good captain was not a gossip, and moreover he was contemptuous of all women, calling them salads, God knows why. At two o'clock we had something to eat, and at three were already on the scene of action—in that same birch wood where I had once walked with Liza, two paces from that cliff.

We were the first to arrive. But the Prince and Bizmionkov did not keep us waiting long. Without exaggeration, the Prince was as fresh as a rose; his hazel eyes gleamed with extraordinary affability beneath the peak of his cap. He was smoking a cigar, and when he saw Koloberdayev he shook his hand warmly. Even to me he bowed very amiably. I, on the contrary, felt that I was pale, and my hands, to my great chagrin, were trembling a little . . . my throat was dry . . . I had never fought a duel before. "Oh, God!" I thought, "so long as this derisive gentleman doesn't take my agitation for nervousness!" I mentally consigned my nerves to all the devils; but glancing, at last, straight in the Prince's face and catching an amost imperceptible sneer on his lips, I suddenly grew angry again and at once recovered my equanimity. Meanwhile our seconds were arranging the details, measuring off the paces, loading the pistols. Koloberdayev was the more active; Bizmionkov mostly watched him. The day was excellent—no worse than that of the unforgettable walk. As then, the deep azure of the sky was peering through the gilded green of the leaves. Their murmur seemed to irritate me. The prince continued to smoke his cigar, leaning his back against the trunk of a lime tree. . . .

"Please take up your positions, gentlemen; all is ready," Koloberdayev said at last, handing us the pistols.

The Prince walked away a few paces, halted, and, turning his head round, asked me across his shoulder: "So you don't take back your words?" I wanted to reply, but my voice betrayed me, and I contented myself with a contemptuous gesture. The Prince again smiled sarcastically and took up his position. We began to approach each other. I raised my pistol, intending to aim at my enemy's breast—at that moment he was indeed my enemy—but suddenly I elevated the barrel, as though someone had jogged my elbow, and fired. The Prince staggered and put his left hand to his left temple; a little stream of blood flowed down his cheek from beneath his white chamois glove. Bizmionkov rushed to him.

"It's nothing," he said, taking off his cap, which had been holed by the bullet. "As it didn't enter the head it must be a scratch."

He calmly took a batiste handkerchief out of his pocket and pressed it against his blood-soaked curls. I stared at him as though petrified and did not stir.

"Please go to the line!" Koloberdayev said to me severely.

I obeyed.

"Is the duel to continue?" he added, turning to Bizmionkov.

Bizmionkov made no answer. But the Prince, without removing his handkerchief from the wound and not even giving himself the pleasure of torturing me as I stood, retorted with a smile: "The duel is ended," and fired into the air. I all but burst into tears with chagrin and fury. With all his magnanimity this man had finally trodden me into the mud, had disposed of me. I wanted to object, wanted to demand that he should fire at me. But he came up to me and held out his hand.

"Now everything is forgotten between us, isn't it?" he said in a kindly tone.

I glanced at his white face, at that bloodstained handkerchief, and, completely unmanned, ashamed, and annihilated, I squeezed his hand....

"Gentlemen," he added, turning to the seconds, "I hope that everything will be kept secret?"

"Of course!" Koloberdayev exclaimed. "But, Prince, allow me...."

And he himself tied up the Prince's head.

As the Prince departed he bowed to me once more; but Bizmionkov did not even glance at me. Shattered—morally shattered—I returned home with Koloberdayev.

"Why, what's the matter with you?" the captain asked me. "Don't be alarmed; the wound isn't dangerous. He'll be able to dance even tomorrow, if that's what you want. Or are you sorry you didn't kill him? In that case you're wrong; he's a fine fellow."

"Why did he spare me?" I muttered at last.

"Well, there's a fine thing!" the captain calmly replied. "Oh, these authors!"

I have no idea why it occurred to him to call me an author.

I flatly refuse to describe my sufferings during the evening that followed this unfortunate duel. My self-esteem suffered beyond all my powers of explanation. It was not that I was tormented by conscience; it was the realization of my stupidity that devastated me. "I have myself administered the last, the final blow to my hopes!" I declared as I walked about my room with great strides. "The Prince, wounded by me and forgiving me.... Yes, Liza is his now. Now nothing can save her, can hold her back on the edge of the precipice." I knew quite well that our duel could not remain a secret, despite the Prince's words; in any case, it could not remain a secret to Liza. "The Prince isn't so stupid," I whispered in my rage, "as not to exploit it...." But meanwhile I was mistaken. All the town learned about the duel and its real cause, and the very next day, of course; but it was not the Prince who talked too much; on the contrary. When, with bandaged head and with an explanation already formulated, he presented himself to Liza, she knew everything before he spoke. . . . I cannot say whether it was Bizmionkov who betrayed me or whether the news reached her through other channels. But in any case is it possible to keep anything a secret in a small town?

You can imagine how Liza received him, how all the Ozhogin family received him! As for me, I immediately became the object of general indignation, of abomination. I was a monster, a crazy, jealous fool, and a cannibal. My few acquaintances turned from me as from the plague. The town authorities immediately approached the Prince with the proposal to punish me exemplarily and severely; only the Prince's own insistent and urgent requests averted the disaster that hung over my head. That man was fated to annihilate me in every respect. With his magnanimity he slammed me down as if with a coffin lid. I need not say that the Ozhogin house was at once closed to me. Kirila Matveich even returned an ordinary pencil that I had forgotten to bring away with me. In reality, he in particular had no good reason to be angry with me. My "crazy" jealousy, as it was called in the town, defined, elucidated, so to speak, the Prince's relations with Liza. The old Ozhogins themselves, and all the other citizens began to regard him almost as a fiancé. In fact this could not have been altogether pleasant for him. But he liked Liza very much; moreover, he had not yet gained his end. . . . With all the adroitness of an intelligent man of the world he adapted himself to his new situation and at once entered into the spirit, as one says, of his new role. . . .

But I! . . . Now I turned my back on my hopes, on all the hopes of my future. When one's sufferings reach the point of causing all one's entrails to crack and groan like an overloaded cart, it would be desirable for those sufferings to cease being laughable. . . . But no! Laughter not only accompanies tears to the end, to the point of exhaustion, the impossibility of shedding any more—no, it goes on ringing and echoing even when the tongue is petrified and lamentation itself dies away. . . . And so, firstly because I have no intention of seeming ludicrous even to myself, and secondly as I am terribly tired, I postpone the continuation and, if God wills, the end of my story until tomorrow. . . .

March 29. A light frost. Yesterday it thawed.

Yesterday I did not have the strength to continue my diary; like Poprishchin, I spent most of the day lying in bed and talking to Terentievna. Now there's a woman! She lost her first husband with the plague sixty years ago, she has survived all her children, she is herself unforgivably old, she drinks as much tea as you like, she is well fed, warmly clothed; but what do you think she talked to me about all day yesterday? I had given orders that the half-moth-eaten collar of some outworn livery was to be given to another completely plucked old woman for a waistcoat (she wears breastplates in the form of a waistcoat). . . . And what do you think?—Terentievna wanted to know why she couldn't have it. "I am your nurse, I believe. . . . Oh, my dear master, it's a sin on your part. . . . And what did I look after you so tenderly for, I'd like to know? . . ." and so on. The merciless old woman completely wore me out with her reproaches. . . . But to return to the story.

And so I suffered like a dog that has had its hind parts run over. Only then, only after my final banishment from the Ozhogins' house, did I fully realize how much satisfaction a man may draw from contemplation of his own unhappiness! O humankind, truly thou art a wretched generation! But all the same, away with philosophic reflections! . . . I spent the days in utter loneliness and only by the most roundabout and sneaking ways discovered what was happening in the Ozhogin family and what the Prince was doing: my servant had made the acquaintance of his coachman's first cousin once removed. This acquaintance afforded me some relief, and, as the result of my hints and little presents, my servant quickly guessed what he should talk about when he was dragging off his master's boots each evening. Sometimes I happened to meet one of the Ozhogin family, or Bizmionkov, or the Prince, in the street. . . . I bowed to the Prince and Bizmionkov, but did not enter into conversation with them. I saw Liza only three times altogether: once with her mother in a fashionable shop; once in an open carriage, with her father, mother, and the Prince; and once in church. I need not say that I did not have the temerity to go up to her, and I gazed at her only from afar. In the shop she was very preoccupied, but gay. She was ordering something for herself and was fussily measuring out ribbons. Her mother stood watching her, her arms folded over her belly, her nose tilted up, and smiling with that stupid and devoted smile which is permissible only to loving mothers. In the carriage with the Prince, Liza was—I shall never forget that meeting! The old Ozhogins were sitting on the back seat of the carriage, the Prince and Liza in front. She was paler than usual; the two rosy patches were hardly visible on her cheeks. She was half-turned to him; resting on her outstretched right hand (she was holding an umbrella in the left) and languidly bending her little head, she was gazing straight into his face with her expressive eyes. At that moment she was entirely his, she trusted him irrevocably. I did not have a good chance of observing his face — the carriage dashed by too quickly — but it seemed to me that he too was deeply moved.

The third time I saw her in church. Not more than ten days had passed since I had met her in the carriage with the Prince, not more than three weeks since the day of my duel. The business on which the Prince had come to O—— was now completed, but he continued to procrastinate with his departure; he reported to Petersburg that he was unwell. The town was every day expecting him to make a formal proposal to Kirila Matveich. I myself was only waiting for this last blow in order to go away forever. I had taken a violent dislike to the town of O——. I could not remain indoors, and I wandered about its neighborhood from morning till evening. One gray unpleasant day, returning from a walk interrupted by rain, I went into the church. Evening service had only just begun, there were very few people present. I looked about me, and suddenly, close to a window, noticed a familiar figure. I did not recognize her at first; that pale face, that faded glance, those sunken cheeks — surely that was not the same Liza whom I had seen two weeks before? Wrapped in a cloak, hatless, half-illuminated by the cold light falling from a broad clear window, she gazed fixedly at the altar screen and seemed to be trying to pray, trying to shake off a despondent torpor. Behind her a red-faced, fat little page with yellow cartridge pockets across his chest was standing with his hands folded behind his back and gazing at his mistress with sleepy bewilderment. I trembled all over and was about to go up to her, but I stopped. An agonizing presentiment crushed my heart. Liza stood without moving in the least till the end of the service. Everybody else had left, the verger began to sweep the church, and still she did not stir from the spot. The page went up to her, said something to her, touched her dress. She looked round, passed her hand over her face, and went out. I followed her home, keeping some little distance behind, then returned to my house.

"She is lost!" I exclaimed as I entered my room.

To this day I, as a man, do not know what my sensations were at that moment; I remember that, folding my arms, I flung myself on the sofa and fixed my gaze on the floor; yet I don't know, but in the midst of my misery I seemed to have a feeling of satisfaction. . . . I would not have admitted this feeling for anything if I had not been writing this only for my own pleasure. . . . Truly, I was racked by terrible, agonizing presentiments . . . and, who knows, perhaps I would have been greatly embarrassed if they had not been fulfilled. "Such is the human heart!" some middle-aged Russian moralizer would exclaim in an expressive voice at this point, raising his fat forefinger adorned with a carnelian ring. But what do we care for the opinion of a Russian moralizer with an expressive voice, and a carnelian ring on his finger?

Rightly or wrongly, my presentiments were justified. Suddenly the news spread through the town that the Prince had gone, apparently as the result of an order received from Petersburg; that he had gone without making any proposal either to Kirila Matveich or to his wife, and that Liza was left to weep over his infidelity to the end of her days. The Prince's departure was quite unexpected, because only the previous evening his coachman, so my servant assured me, had had no suspicions whatever of his master's intentions. This news put me in a fever; I dressed at once and was about to hurry to the Ozhogins'. But after thinking it over, I deemed it decorous to wait till the next day. For that matter, I did not lose anything by remaining at home. That same evening a man named Pandopipopulo, a Greek who had chanced to get stranded in O—— on his way to somewhere else, a gossip of the first magnitude, who had surpassed all others in his indignation with me because of my duel with the Prince, came to see me. He did not even give my servant time to report his arrival, but burst into my room, squeezed my hand vigorously, apologized to me a thousand times, called me a model of magnanimity and daring, described the Prince in the blackest of colors, and did not spare the old Ozhogins, whom, in his opinion, fate had justly punished; in passing he had a smack at Liza also and then ran off, after kissing me on the shoulder. Among other things, I learned from him that the Prince, *en vrai grand seigneur,*[1] on the eve of his departure, had reacted to Kirila Matveich's delicate hint with the cold reply that he did not intend to deceive anybody and had no thought of getting married, then had risen, bowed himself out, and was such a . . .

Next day I went to call on the Ozhogins. At my appearance the purpling valet jumped up from the bench with the speed of lightning. I ordered him to announce my visit; he ran off and returned at once. "Please," he said, "the master has ordered me to ask you in." I went into Kirila Matveich's private room —. Till tomorrow.

March 30. A frost.

And so I entered Kirila Matveich's room. I would have given a handsome reward to anyone, who could have shown me my own face as this worthy official, hurriedly flinging his Bokharan gown around him, came up to me with outstretched hands. I must have beamed with modest triumph, condescending sympathy, and boundless magnanimity. . . . I felt

---

[1] *en . . . seigneur:* that is, really playing the role of the great nobleman.

myself to be something after the style of Scipio Africanus. Ozhogin was obviously embarrassed and afflicted; he avoided my gaze and fidgeted where he stood. I noted also that he spoke in an unnaturally loud voice and all together expressed himself very indefinitely; he indefinitely but fervently begged my pardon, indefinitely referred to the departed guest, added a few general and indefinite remarks about the desultory and transient nature of earthly blessings, and suddenly, feeling a tear in his eyes, hurried to take a pinch of snuff, probably in order to deceive me in regard to the cause of his tearfulness. . . . He used Russian green tobacco, and it is well known that that plant makes even old men shed tears, so that the human eye looks dull and meaningless for several moments. I, of course, handled the old man very carefully, asked after the health of his wife and daughter, and at once neatly turned the conversation to the interesting question of crop rotation. I was dressed in normal attire, but the feeling of gentle decorum and mild condescension that filled me gave me a fresh and holiday feeling, as though I were wearing a white waistcoat and white tie. One thing agitated me: the thought of seeing Liza. . . . Finally Ozhogin himself offered to take me to his wife. On seeing me, that good but stupid woman was at first terribly disconcerted; but her mind was incapable of retaining one and the same impression for any length of time, and so she soon calmed down. Finally I saw Liza. She entered the room. . . .

I expected to find her a shamed and contrite sinner and had in advance given my features the most gracious and encouraging of expressions. . . . Why lie? I really did love her and was athirst for the happiness of forgiving her, of stretching out my hand to her. But, to my inexpressible amazement, in reply to my significant bow she laughed coldly, carelessly remarked: "Ah, so it's you?" and at once turned away from me. Truly, I thought her laugh seemed forced, and in any case it did not match her terribly wasted features in the least . . . but, all the same, I had not expected such a reception. . . . I stared at her in astonishment. What a transformation had been wrought in her! There was nothing in common between the former child and this woman. She seemed to have grown up, to have taken herself in hand; all the features of her face, especially the lips, seemed to have acquired definition . . . her gaze had grown deeper, firmer, and darker.

I stayed on with the Ozhogins until dinnertime; she rose, left the room, and returned, calmly answered questions, and deliberately paid no attention to me. She—I saw that—she wanted to make me feel that I was not worth even her anger, though I had all but killed her lover. At last I lost patience: a venomous innuendo burst from my lips. . . . She started, gave me a swift glance, rose, and, going over to the window, said in a voice that quivered a little: "You can all say what you like, but understand this: I love that man, and shall always love him, and I do not in the least regard him as having wronged me; on the contrary. . . ." Her voice began to break, she paused. . . . She tried to master herself, but could not; she burst into tears and left the room. . . . Her old parents were upset. . . . I squeezed their hands, sighed, turned my eyes up, and retired.

I am too weak, the time left to me is too short, I am not in a state to describe with my previous detail the new series of tormenting ideas, resolute intentions, and other fruits of so-called inward struggle that I experienced after the renewal of my acquaintance with the Ozhogins. I had no doubt that Liza still loved and would for long go on loving the Prince. . . . But as a man who has been tamed by circumstances and has tamed himself, I did not even dream of her love. I desired only her friendship; I desired to win her trust, her respect, which, so experienced people assure us, is regarded as the most reliable basis for happiness in marriage. . . . Unfortunately, I left out of calculation one rather important circumstance—namely, that ever since the day of the duel Liza had hated me. I began to visit the Ozhogins' home as in past days; Kirila Matveich showed me more affection and favor than ever before. I even have reason to think that now he would gladly have given his daughter to me, though I was not a groom to be proud of; public opinion was persecuting him and Liza, while it exalted me, on the contrary, to the very heavens. Liza's treatment of me did not change. She was silent for the most part, obeyed when she was summoned to a meal, showed no outward signs of grief whatever, but none the less she melted like a candle. I must be just to Kirila Matveich: he spared her in every way; his old wife only bristled up as she looked at her poor little child. One man Liza did not shun, though she did not talk much to him either, and that was Bizmionkov. The old Ozhogins treated him harshly, even roughly; they could not forgive him for acting as the Prince's second; but he continued to visit them, as though he did not notice their unkindness. With me he was very cold and—strange to say—I seemed to be afraid of him.

This went on for about two weeks. At last, after one sleepless night, I decided to clear up my position with Liza, to reveal my heart to her, to tell her that despite all the past, despite all the possible rumors and slanders, I would regard myself as only too happy if she would bestow her hand on me, would again give me her trust. Really, I seriously imagined that I would be displaying an incomparable example of magnanimity, as the textbooks put it, and that she would agree even if it was only in her astonishment. In any case, I wanted to clear my position with her and to free myself, finally, of uncertainty.

Behind the Ozhogins' house was quite a large garden, ending in a small, neglected, and overgrown lime grove. In the middle of this grove was an ancient arbor in Chinese style; a board fence separated the garden from a blind alley. Sometimes Liza wandered for hours in the garden. Kirila Matveich knew this and had forbidden her to be disturbed, to be watched; leave her to overcome her sorrow. When she was not to be found indoors, it was only necessary to ring a bell on the porch before dinner for her to appear at once, with the same stubborn silence on her lips and in her gaze, with a crumpled leaf in her hand. One day, observing that she was not in the house, I pretended that I was going, said good-by to Kirila Matveich, put on my hat, and went out into the yard and from the yard into the street. But I at once slipped back through the gate very quickly and made my way past the kitchen into the garden. Fortunately, no one noticed me. Not stopping to think, I went with hurried steps into the grove. Ahead of me on the path I saw Liza. My heart beat violently. I halted, sighed deeply, and was just about to go up to her when suddenly, without turning round, she raised her hand and began to listen. . . .

From beyond the trees, in the direction of the alley, came the clear sound of two blows, as though someone were knocking on the fence. Liza clapped her hands, I heard the faint creak of a wicket gate, and Bizmionkov came through the trees. I nimbly concealed myself behind a trunk. Liza silently turned to him. . . . She silently took him by the arm, and they both went quietly along the path. I gazed after them in astonishment. They halted, looked about them, vanished behind some bushes, came into sight again, and finally entered the arbor. This arbor was a little circular erection, with one door and one small window; in the middle was an old one-legged table, overgrown with delicate green moss; two old benches made of boards stood, one on either side, a little distance from the damp and darkened walls. Here on unusually hot days, and then only once a year, and then only in past days, the family had drunk tea. The door could not be closed at all; the frame had long since come away from the window and, held by one corner, hung mournfully, like the broken wing of a bird. I stole up to the arbor and cautiously peered through the window chink. Liza was sitting on one of the benches, with her head hanging; her right hand was lying on her knees, her left hand Bizmionkov was holding in both his hands. He was looking at her commiseratively.

"How do you feel today?" he asked her in an undertone.

"Just the same," she replied, "neither worse nor better. Emptiness, a terrible emptiness!" she added, raising her eyes mournfully.

He did not answer her.

"What do you think?" she continued. "Will he write to me again?"

"I don't think so, Lizaveta Kirillovna!"

She was silent. Then she said:

"And besides, what is there for him to write about? He told me everything in his first letter. I could not be his wife; but I was happy—for a brief while—I was happy...."

Bizmionkov shrank into himself.

"Ah!" she continued with animation, "if only you knew how loathsome that Chulkaturin is to me!... Whenever I see that man's hands, I still imagine I can see—his blood." (I turned cold behind my chink.) "For that matter," she added thoughtfully, "who knows? If it hadn't been for that duel, perhaps—Ah, when I saw him wounded, I at once felt that I was entirely his."

"Chulkaturin is in love with you," Bizmionkov remarked.

"And what is that to me? Do I need anyone's love?" She paused and then slowly added: "Except yours. Yes, my friend, your love is indispensable to me: without you I would perish. You have helped me to endure the terrible minutes...."

She was silent.... He began to stroke her hand with paternal tenderness.

"It can't be helped, it can't be helped, Lizaveta Kirillovna," he repeated several times in succession.

"Yes, and even now," she said thickly, "I would die without you, I think. You alone are a support to me; and besides, you remind me of him—for you knew everything. Do you remember how fine he was that day?... But forgive me: it must be painful for you—"

"Speak on! Speak on! Why do you say that? You mustn't!" he broke in.

She squeezed his hand.

"You are very good, Bizmionkov," she continued; "you are as good as an angel. It can't be helped! I feel that I shall love him even to my grave. I have forgiven him, I am grateful to him. God grant him happiness! God grant him a wife to his heart!" and her eyes filled with tears. "So long as he doesn't forget me, so long as he thinks of his Liza, if only occasionally. Let us go," she added after a brief silence.

Bizmionkov raised her hand to his lips.

"I know," she began fervently, "that everybody is reproaching me now, everybody is throwing stones at me. Let them! All the same, I would not exchange my unhappiness for their happiness.... No! No!.... He did not love me long, but he did love me! He never deceived me: he did not tell me that I would be his wife; I myself never thought of that. Only poor Papa hoped for it. And even now I am not altogether unhappy: I still have the memory, and, no matter how terrible the consequences—I am stifled here—it was here I saw him for the last time.... Let us go out."

They rose. I had hardly time to spring aside and hide behind a stout lime tree. They emerged from the arbor and, so far as I could judge by the noise of their footsteps, went into the grove. I don't know how long I remained standing there, not moving from the spot, sunk in senseless bewilderment, when suddenly I heard footsteps again. I started and cautiously peered out from my ambush, to see Bizmionkov and Liza returning along the same path. They were both deeply agitated, especially Bizmionkov. He seemed to be crying. Liza halted, looked at him, and clearly uttered the following words: "I consent, Bizmionkov. I would not consent if you wished only to save me, to get me out of a terrible situation; but you love me; you know everything—and you love me. I shall never find a more reliable, faithful friend. I will be your wife."

He kissed her hand; she smiled at him miserably and went toward the house. He rushed into the grove, and I went home. As he had probably said exactly what I had intended to say to Liza, and as she had replied with the very answer I had desired to hear from her, there was no need for me to worry my head any longer. Two weeks later she married him. The old Ozhogins were glad of any groom.

Well, tell me now, am I not a superfluous man? In all this story haven't I played the part of a man who is superfluous?

The role played by the Prince—there is no need to dilate on it. Bizmionkov's role also is comprehensible.... But I? Why was I mixed up in it all? What a stupid fifth wheel to a cart! Ah, I feel bitter, bitter!... But now just as the haulers say: "One more heave, just one more little heave"—so in another little day, or two, it will no longer be bitter for me, nor sweet.

March 31

I'm bad. I am writing these lines in bed. The weather changed suddenly yesterday evening. Today it is hot, almost a summer's day. Everything is melting, falling, running. The scent of furrowed earth is in the air: a heavy, strong, stifling scent. Everything is steaming. The sun strikes so hard, flames so fiercely. I'm in a bad way. I feel that I am disintegrating.

I thought I would keep a diary, and instead what have I done? Told just one incident from my life. I have let my pen run away with me; the faded memories awoke and carried me off. I have written unhurriedly, in detail, as though I still had years before me; but now, now I haven't time to continue. Death, death is coming. I can already hear its menacing crescendo. . . . Time . . . time!

Well, and what does it matter? Did it make any difference what I told? In face of death the last earthly anxieties disappear. I feel that I am sinking; I am growing simpler, clearer. Rather late have I clutched at sense! A strange thing! I am sinking—definitely, and at the same time I am afraid. Yes, I am afraid. Half bent over the silent, yawning abyss, I shudder, I turn away, I survey all around me with avid attention. The least article is doubly dear to me. I cannot tire of looking at my poor, cheerless room as I say farewell to every tiny spot on my walls! Satiate yourselves for the last time, eyes of mine! Life is retreating; it is quietly and steadily running away from me, like the shore from the gaze of a seafarer. My nurse's old yellow face tied up in a dark kerchief, the hissing samovar on the table, the little pot of geranium on the windowsill, and you, my poor dog Treasure, the pen with which I write these lines, my own hand, I see you now—there you are, there. . . . Is it really possible that—today, maybe—I shall never see you again? It is hard for a living creature to part from life! What are you fawning on me for, poor dog? What are you resting your breast against the bed for, convulsively tucking in your docked tail and not removing your kind, mournful eyes from me? Are you sorry for me? Or do you already feel that soon your master will be no more? Ah, if I could but pass in thought over all the other articles in my room! I know that these memories are cheerless and insignificant, but I have no others. Emptiness, a terrible emptiness! As Liza said.

Oh, my God, my God! So I am dying. . . . A heart able and ready to love will soon cease to beat. . . . And will it really grow still forever, without once having tasted happiness, without even once expanding beneath the pleasurable burden of joy? Alas! That is impossible, impossible, I know. . . . If, at the least, now, before my death—for death, after all, is a sacred thing, it does exalt any creature—if some dear, sad, friendly voice could sing a farewell song of my own sorrow over me, I might, perhaps, reconcile myself to it. But to die stupidly, stupidly. . . .

I think I am beginning to wander.

Good-by, life, good-by, my garden, and you, my limes! When summer comes, don't forget to be covered from top to foot with flowers ... and let it be good for people to lie in your perfumed shade, on the fresh grass, beneath the murmuring whisper of your leaves gently stirred by the wind. Good-by, good-by! Good-by, everything and forever!

Good-by, Liza! As I wrote those two words I all but smiled. That exclamation seems bookish to me. I would appear to be composing a moving story and ending a desperate letter. . . .

Tomorrow is the 1st of April. Surely I shall not die tomorrow? That would even be indecent, somehow. And yet it fits me. . . .

How the doctor babbled away today! . . .

April 1

Finish . . . Life is finished. I definitely shall die today. It is hot outside —almost stifling—or is it my breast that is refusing to breathe already? My little comedy is played out. The curtain falls.

In my annihilation I shall cease to be superfluous. . . .

Ah, how hot this sun is! Those mighty rays breathe of eternity. . . .

Good-by, Terentievna. . . . This morning, as she sat by the window, she burst into tears . . . over me, perhaps—but perhaps over the fact that she herself will have to die soon. I made her promise "not to hurt" Treasure.

It is difficult for me to write . . . I throw down the pen. . . . Time! Death is already approaching with a rising thunder, like a carriage along the road at night. It is here, it is fluttering round me, like that gentle wafting which caused the hair of the prophet to stand on end. . . .

I am dying. . . . Live on, the living!

> *And round the dark tomb's chilly entrance*
> *Let the young life, the children, play;*
> *And let indifferent nature's radiance*
> *With beauty infinite array.*

PUBLISHER'S NOTE. Beneath these last lines is the profile of a head with a large forelock and mustaches, with the eyes *en face* and radiating eyelashes; and under the head someone has written the following words:

> *This manuscript was read*
> *And Its Contents were not Approved*
> *by Piotr Zudoteshin*
> *M   M   M   M*

> Dear Sir
> Piotr Zudoteshin
> My dear Sir.

But as the handwriting of these lines is nothing like that in which all the rest of the book is written, the publisher feels justified in concluding that the above-mentioned lines were added later, by someone else, especially as it has come to his (the publisher's) knowledge that Mr. Chulkaturin did in fact die during the night of April 1, 18——, on his hereditary estate, Lambswater.

FOR WRITING OR DISCUSSION

1. How is Chulkaturin like Oblomov? How is he unlike him? Do you find him more or less attractive than Dobrolyubov's characterization of Oblomov? If you wish to be entirely fair in answering this question, what do you have to do to check Dobrolyubov's opinions?

2. Summarize the details of the plot in a short paragraph or brief statement. Would you say that the plot of this story concerns what happens to the hero or what does *not* happen? Explain.

3. Cite some instances of humor in the story. How is Chulkaturin funny when he thinks himself most pathetic? When is he actually most pathetic? Why?

4. Where does Turgenev satirize the "romantic" writers? Read aloud one or two passages that parody the oversentimental style of these writers.

5. How is Chulkaturin himself a caricature of the "romantic" hero? How is his story an example of the kind of romantic "realism" that represents an escape from, or attack on, life, as described in Janko Lavrin's discussion of the varieties of realism. (See the excerpt by Lavrin on page 261.)

6. What picture of provincial life is conveyed by this story? How is this life contrasted with the life of the peasants as portrayed in the stories from Turgenev's *Sportsman's Notebook?*

7. How does Turgenev show in this story his understanding of and liking for women? Contrast Liza's change from girlhood to womanhood with the narrator's continuing childishness and egocentricity.

8. Do you think Chulkaturin is similar to the "Honest Thief" in Dostoevsky's story of that name? Is his "meekness" or ineffectiveness a form of humility or an inverted form of hostility toward others? Explain.

9. Contrast the number of sentences or passages that carry the narra-

tive or plot with those that describe or reproduce dialogue (or Chulkaturin's monologues to himself). What is the purpose of this degree of balance between description and narration? How does the *actual* plot of the story unfold—as events or as memories in the hero's head?

10. What is your own reaction to Chulkaturin? Is it uniform throughout, or does it change as the story progresses? Explain your answer.

REACTING TO CRITICISM

Turgenev himself provided a clue to his own interpretation of the negative hero in a famous lecture, "Hamlet and Don Quixote," given in 1860, excerpts of which are presented below. These two characters embody, according to Turgenev, two polar clusters of human traits. Don Quixote is the idealist who accepts every challenge of his principles, tries to redress every wrong in some active, though not always carefully reasoned or even relevant way. Hamlet, on the other hand, represents the rational side of man that, if unaccompanied by sensitivity and spirituality, is carried to extremes of rationalizations and to eventual paralysis of action.

> Don Quixote is imbued with devotion toward his ideal, for which he is ready to suffer all possible privations, to sacrifice his life; life itself he values only so far as it can serve for the incarnation of the ideal, for the promotion of truth, of justice on Earth. . . . He lives for his brothers, for opposing the forces hostile to mankind: the witches, the giants—that is, the oppressors. . . . Therefore he is fearless, patient; he is satisfied with the most modest food, the poorest cloth: he has other things to think of. Humble in his heart, he is great and daring in his mind. . . . And who is Hamlet? Analysis, first of all, and egotism, and therefore no faith. He lives entirely for himself, he is an egotist; but to believe in one's self—even an egotist cannot do that: we can believe only in something which is outside us and above us. . . . As he has doubts of everything, Hamlet evidently does not spare himself; his intellect is too developed to remain satisfied with what he finds in himself: he feels his weakness, but each self-consciousness is a force wherefrom results his irony, the opposite of the enthusiasm of Don Quixote. . . . Don Quixote, a poor man, almost a beggar, without means and relations, old, isolated—undertakes to redress all the evils and to protect oppressed strangers over the whole earth. What does it matter to him that his first attempt at freeing the innocent from his oppressor falls twice as heavy upon the

head of the innocent himself? . . . What does it matter that, thinking that he has to deal with noxious giants, Don Quixote attacks useful windmills? . . . Nothing of the sort can ever happen with Hamlet: how could he, with his perspicacious, refined, skeptical mind, ever commit such a mistake! No, he will not fight with windmills, he does not believe in giants . . . but he would not have attacked them even if they did exist. . . . And yet, although Hamlet is a skeptic, although he disbelieves in good, he does not believe in evil. Evil and deceit are his inveterate enemies. His skepticism is not indifferentism. . . . But in negation, as in fire, there is a destructive power, and how to keep it in bounds, how to tell it where to stop, when that which it must destroy, and that which it must spare are often inseparably welded together? Here it is that the often-noticed tragical aspect of human life comes in: for action we require will, and for action we require thought; but thought and will have parted from each other, and separate every day more and more.

And thus the native hue of resolution
Is sicklied o'er by the pale cast of thought. . . .[1] [*Ivan Turgenev*]

1. What characteristics of Turgenev's "Hamlet" does Chulkaturin have? Is he as admirable or as likable as Shakespeare's character? Explain your answer.
2. Are any of Chulkaturin's "positive" qualities like those of Don Quixote? Are his actions as erratic? From what motivation do his actions stem?
3. In your opinion, is Chulkaturin more like Oblomov or Hamlet? Explain.
4. Did you get the impression that Turgenev intends the reader to regard Chulkaturin as a Hamlet figure, or is Chulkaturin portrayed as a man of less stature and dignity than Hamlet?
5. In what way is Chulkaturin an example of what modern Americans are used to hearing referred to as the "alienated" man? How is he alienated from himself, from others, and from society in general? How is an alienated man a negative hero?
6. Some Russian critics, contemporaries of Turgenev, resented his "art for art's sake" theories of literature as well as his leaving Russia to live in Europe. They referred to Turgenev himself as a "Hamlet." Does

---

[1] As quoted by Prince Kropotkin in *Ideals and Realities in Russian Literature*. Reprinted by permission of the publisher, Alfred A. Knopf, Inc.

what you know about Turgenev's life confirm or deny this label? Explain.

7. Compare Turgenev with Chulkaturin. Who is the more "active"? Who is *actually* "superfluous"?

THE MEMOIRS OF A MADMAN

LEO TOLSTOY

The Tolstoyan "heroes" you have met—Captain Khlopov and the young lieutenant in "The Raid," the narrator of "After the Ball," and Alyosha—are not Oblomovs in any sense of the word. Indeed, although he presents the opposing types of thinkers and doers in his great novels, Tolstoy's heroes are more "positive" than "negative"; they are often, in fact, that fortunate combination of the two that makes a hero of epic proportions. Actually, the struggle in which Tolstoy's heroes engage is less between thought and action than it is between simplicity and complexity, sham and sincerity, life and death. Tolstoy started his writing career as an observer of life and ended it as a reforming activist. As he grew older, his question—and his heroes' question—came to be not "What should I do with my life?" but "What is the nature and purpose of life, confronted as we are by the insuperable fact of our mortality?" Like all the negative heroes, Tolstoy's heroes have suffered disillusionment of some sort, but as Ernest Simmons says:

> Disillusionment with reality is not resolved in metaphysical quests as in Dostoevsky's fiction and in that of not a few novelists today. Tolstoy's alienated man does not ask himself the everlasting question: 'Who am I?', but rather: 'Why am I here and where am I going?' At least the matter of self-identity is already resolved.[1]

Evidently, the one thing that Tolstoy himself feared most was death, which is understandable in a man for whom the external world was so alive and human flesh so vital. As you have seen, some critics believe that it was Tolstoy's own tremendous sense of physical life that he guiltily expiated in his later self-denials. The story that most lengthily and expertly catalogues the process of dying and the self-examination that accompanies it is "The Death of Ivan Ilyitch." The shorter story that fol-

---

[1]From *Introduction to Russian Realism* by Ernest Simmons. Reprinted by permission of the publisher, Indiana University Press.

lows, "The Memoirs of a Madman," was written late in Tolstoy's life, and, like so many of Tolstoy's stories, is quite evidently autobiographical in origin. Like the stories of other negative heroes, it concerns the pointlessness of life and alienation from life. As you read, keep this question in mind: How does the narrator's awareness of death in this story produce an effect on his actions different from that produced on Chulkaturin by the knowledge of his imminent death?

The Memoirs of a Madman

20th October 1883–

Today I was taken to the Provincial Government Board to be certified. Opinions differed. They disputed, and finally decided that I was not insane—but they arrived at this decision only because during the examination I did my utmost to restrain myself and not give myself away. I did not speak out, because I am afraid of the madhouse, where they would prevent me from doing my mad work. So they came to the conclusion that I am subject to hallucinations and something else, but am of sound mind.

They came to that conclusion, but I myself knew that I am mad. A doctor prescribed a treatment for me, and assured me that if I would follow his instructions exactly all would be right—all that troubled me would pass. Ah, what would I not give that it might pass! The torment is too great. I will tell in due order how and from what this medical certification came about—how I went mad and how I betrayed myself.

Up to the age of thirty-five I lived just as everybody else does and nothing strange was noticed about me. Perhaps in early childhood, before the age of ten, there was at times something resembling my present condition, but only by fits, and not continually as now. Moreover in childhood it used to affect me rather differently. For instance I remember that once when going to bed, at the age of five or six, my nurse Eupraxia, a tall, thin woman who wore a brown dress and a cap and had flabby skin under her chin, was undressing me and lifting me up to put me into my cot. "I will get into bed by myself—myself!" I said, and stepped over the side of the cot.

"Well, lie down then. Lie down, Fedya! Look at Mitya. He's a good boy and is lying down already," she said, indicating my brother with a jerk of her head.

I jumped into the bed still holding her hand, and then let it go, kicked

"The Memoirs of a Madman" from *Leo Tolstoy's Short Stories,* Vol. 1, edited by Ernest Simmons. Translation by Louise and Aylmer Maude and reprinted by permission of Oxford University Press.

about under my bedclothes, and wrapped myself up. And I had such a pleasant feeling. I grew quiet and thought: "I love Nurse; Nurse loves me and Mitya; and I love Mitya, and Mitya loves me and Nurse. Nurse loves Taras, and I love Taras, and Mitya loves him. And Taras loves me and Nurse. And Mamma loves me and Nurse, and Nurse loves Mamma and me and Papa—and everybody loves everybody and everybody is happy!"

Then suddenly I heard the housekeeper run in and angrily shout something about a sugar-basin, and Nurse answering indignantly that she had not taken it. And I felt pained, frightened, and bewildered, and horror, cold horror, seized me, and I hid my head under the bedclothes but felt no better in the dark.

I also remembered how a serf boy was once beaten in my presence, how he screamed, and how dreadful Foka's face looked when he was beating the boy. "Then you won't do it any more, you won't?" he kept repeating as he went on beating. The boy cried, "I won't!" but Foka still repeated, "You won't!" and went on beating him.

And then it came upon me! I began to sob, and went on so that they could not quiet me for a long time. That sobbing and despair was the first attack of my present madness.

I remember another attack when my aunt told us about Christ. She told the story and was about to go away, but we said: "Tell us some more about Jesus Christ!"

"No, I have no time now," she said.

"Yes, do tell us!"

Mitya also asked her to, and my aunt began to repeat what she had told us. She told us how they crucified, beat, and tortured him, and how he went on praying and did not reproach them.

"Why did they torment him, Auntie?"

"They were cruel people."

"But why, when he was good?"

"There, that's enough. It's past eight! Do you hear?"

"Why did they beat him? He forgave them, then why did they hit him? Did it hurt him, Auntie? Did it hurt?"

"That will do! I'm going to have tea now."

"But perhaps it isn't true and they didn't beat him?"

"Now, now, that will do!"

"No, no! Don't go away!"

And again I was overcome by it. I sobbed and sobbed, and began knocking my head against the wall.

That was how it befell me in my childhood. But by the time I was fourteen, and from the time the instincts of sex were aroused and I yielded to vice, all that passed away and I became a boy like other boys, like all the rest of us reared on rich, overabundant food, effeminate, doing no physical work, surrounded by all possible temptations that inflamed sensuality, and among other equally spoiled children. And so, seeking enjoyments and finding them, I lived till the age of thirty-five. I was perfectly well and there were no signs of my madness.

Those twenty years of my healthy life passed for me so that I can hardly remember anything of them, and now recall them with difficulty and disgust. Like all mentally healthy boys of our circle I entered the high school and afterwards the university, where I completed the course of law studies. Then I was in the Civil Service for a short time, and then I met my present wife, married, had a post in the country and, as it is called, "brought up" our children, managed the estates, and was Justice of the Peace.

In the tenth year of my married life I again had an attack—the first since my childhood.

My wife and I had saved money—some inherited by her and some from the bonds I, like other landowners, received from the Government at the time of the emancipation of the serfs—and we decided to buy an estate. I was much interested, as was proper, in the growth of our property and in increasing it in the shrewdest way—better than other people. At that time I inquired everywhere where there were estates for sale, and read all the advertisements in the papers. I wanted to buy an estate so that the income from it, or the timber on it, should cover the whole purchase price and I should get it for nothing. I looked out for some fool who did not understand business, and thought I had found such a man.

An estate with large forests was being sold in Penza province. From all I could learn about it, it seemed that its owner was just such a fool as I wanted and the timber would cover the whole cost of the estate. So I got ready and set out.

We (my servant and I) traveled at first by rail and then by road in a post-chaise. The journey was a very pleasant one for me. My servant, a young good-natured fellow, was in just as good spirits as I. We saw new places and met new people and enjoyed ourselves. To reach our destination we had to go about a hundred and forty miles, and decided to go without stopping except to change horses. Night came and we still went on. We grew drowsy. I fell asleep, but suddenly awoke feeling that there was something terrifying. As often happens, I woke up thoroughly alert and feeling as if sleep had gone forever. "Why am I going? Where am I going to?" I suddenly asked myself. It was not that I did not like the idea of buying an estate cheaply, but it suddenly occurred to me that there was no need for me to travel all that distance, that I should die here in this strange place, and I was filled with dread. Sergey, my servant, woke up, and I availed myself of the opportunity to talk to him. I spoke about that part of the country, he replied and joked, but I felt depressed. I spoke about our folks at home, and of the business before us, and I was surprised that his answers were so cheerful. Everything seemed pleasant and amusing to him while it nauseated me. But for all that, while we were talking I felt easier. But besides everything seeming wearisome and uncanny, I began to feel tired and wished to stop. It seemed to me that I should feel better if I could enter a house, see people, drink tea, and above all have some sleep.

We were nearing the town of Arzamas.

"Shall we put up here and rest a bit?"

"Why not? Splendid!"

"Are we still far from the town?"

"About five miles from the last milepost."

The driver was a respectable man, careful and taciturn, and he drove rather slowly and wearily.

We drove on. I remained silent and felt better because I was looking forward to a rest and hoped that the discomfort would pass. We went on and on in the darkness for a terribly long time as it seemed to me. We reached the town. Everybody was already in bed. Mean little houses showed up through the darkness, and the sound of our jingling bells and the clatter of the horses' feet reechoed, especially near the houses, and all this was far from cheerful. We passed large white houses here and there. I was impatient to get to the poststation and a samovar, and to lie down and rest.

At last we came up to a small house with a post beside it. The house was white, but appeared terribly melancholy to me, so much so that it seemed uncanny and I got out of the carriage slowly.

Sergey briskly took out all that would be wanted, running clattering up the porch, and the sound of his steps depressed me. I entered a little corridor. A sleepy man with a spot on his cheek (which seemed to me terrifying) showed us into a room. It was gloomy. I entered, and the uncanny feeling grew worse.

"Haven't you got a bedroom? I should like to rest."

"Yes, we have. This is it."

It was a small square room, with whitewashed walls. I remember that it tormented me that it should be square. It had one window with a red curtain, a birchwood table, and a sofa with bentwood arms. We went in.

Sergey prepared the samovar and made tea, while I took a pillow and lay down on the sofa. I was not asleep and heard how Sergey was busy with the tea and called me to have some. But I was afraid of getting up and arousing myself completely, and I thought how frightful it would be to sit up in that room. I did not get up but began to doze. I must have fallen asleep, for when I awoke I found myself alone in the room and it was dark. I was again as wide awake as I had been in the chaise. I felt that to sleep would be quite impossible. "Why have I come here? Where am I betaking myself? Why and whither am I escaping? I am running away from something dreadful and cannot escape it. I am always with myself, and it is I who am my tormentor. Here I am, the whole of me. Neither the Penza nor any other property will add anything to or take anything from me. And it is myself I am weary of and find intolerable and a torment. I want to fall asleep and forget myself and cannot. I cannot get away from myself!"

I went out into the passage. Sergey was sleeping on a narrow bench with one arm hanging down, but he was sleeping peacefully and the man with the spot was also asleep. I had gone out into the corridor thinking to escape from what tormented me. But *it* had come out with me and cast a gloom over everything. I felt just as filled with horror or even more so.

"But what folly this is!" I said to myself. "Why am I depressed? What am I afraid of?"

"Me!" answered the voice of death, inaudibly. "I am here!"

A cold shudder ran down my back. Yes! Death! It will come—here it is—and it ought not to be. Had I been actually facing death I could not have suffered as much as I did then. Then I should have been frightened. But now I was not frightened. I saw and felt the approach of death, and at the same time I felt that such a thing ought not to exist.

My whole being was conscious of the necessity and the right to live, and yet I felt that death was being accomplished. And this inward conflict was terrible. I tried to throw off the horror. I found a brass candlestick, the candle in which had a long wick, and lighted it. The red glow of the candle and its size—little less than the candlestick itself—told me the same thing. Everything told me the same: "There is nothing in life. Death is the only real thing, and death ought not to exist."

I tried to turn my thoughts to things that had interested me—to the estate I was to buy, and to my wife—but found nothing to cheer me. I had all become nothing. Everything was hidden by the terrible consciousness that my life was ebbing away. I needed sleep. I lay down, but the next instant I jumped up again in terror. A fit of the spleen seized me

— spleen such as the feeling before one is sick, but spiritual spleen. It was uncanny and dreadful. It seems that death is terrible, but when remembering and thinking of life it is one's dying life that is terrible. Life and death somehow merged into one another. Something was tearing my soul apart and could not complete the severance. Again I went to look at the sleepers, and again I tried to go to sleep. Always the same horror: red, white, and square. Something tearing within that yet could not be torn apart. A painful, painfully dry and spiteful feeling, no atom of kindliness, but just a dull and steady spitefulness toward myself and toward that which had made me.

What created me? God, they say. God ... what about prayer? I remember. For some twenty years I had not prayed, and I did not believe in anything, though as a matter of propriety I fasted and went to Communion every year. Now I began to pray. "Lord have mercy!" "Our Father." "Holy Virgin." I began to compose new prayers, crossing myself, bowing down to the ground and glancing around me for fear that I might be seen. This seemed to divert me — the fear of being seen distracted my terror — and I lay down. But I had only to lie down and close my eyes for the same feeling of terror to knock and rouse me. I could bear it no longer. I woke the hotel servant and Sergey, gave orders to harness, and we drove off again.

The fresh air and the drive made me feel better. But I realized that something new had come into my soul and poisoned my former life.

By nightfall we reached our destination. The whole day I had been fighting my depression and had mastered it, but it had left its terrible dregs in my soul as if some misfortune had befallen me, and I could forget it only for a time. There it remained at the bottom of my soul and had me in its power.

The old steward of the estate received me well, though without any pleasure. He was sorry the estate was to be sold.

The furniture in the little rooms was upholstered. There was a new, brightly polished samovar, a large-sized tea service, and honey for tea. Everything was good. But I questioned him about the estate unwillingly, as if it were some old forgotten lesson. However, I fell asleep without any depression, and this I attributed to my having prayed again before going to bed.

After that I went on living as before, but the fear of that spleen always hung over me, I had to live without stopping to think, and above all to live in my accustomed surroundings. As a schoolboy repeats a lesson learned by heart without thinking, so I had to live to avoid falling a prey to that awful depression I had first experienced at Arzamas.

I returned home safely. I did not buy the estate—I had not enough money—and I continued to live as before, only with this difference, that I began to pray and went to church. As before—it seemed to me, but I now remember that it was not as before—I lived on what had been previously begun. I continued to go along the rails already laid by my former strength, but I did not undertake anything new. And I took less part in those things I had previously begun. Everything seemed dull to me and I became pious. My wife noticed this, and scolded and nagged me on account of it. But my spleen did not recur at home.

But once I had unexpectedly to go to Moscow. I got ready in the afternoon and left in the evening. It was in connection with a lawsuit. I arrived in Moscow cheerful. On the way I had talked with a landowner from Kharkov about estate-management and banks, and about where to put up, and about the theater. We both decided to stop at the Moscow Hotel on the Myasnitsky Street, and to go to see *Faust* that same evening.

When we arrived I was shown into a small room. The oppressive air of the corridor filled my nostrils. A porter brought in my portmanteau and a chambermaid lighted a candle. The wick was lighted and then as usual the flame went down. In the next room someone coughed, probably an old man. The maid went out, but the porter remained and asked if he could uncord my luggage. The flame of the candle burned up, revealing the blue wallpaper with yellow stripes on the partition, a shabby table, a small sofa, a looking glass, a window, and the narrow dimensions of the room. And suddenly I was seized with an attack of the same horror as in Arzamas. "My God! How can I stay here all night?" I thought.

"Yes, uncord, my good fellow," I told the porter to keep him longer in the room. "I'll dress quickly and go to the theater." When the porter had uncorded, I said: "Please go to Number Eight and tell the gentleman who came here with me that I shall be ready immediately and will come to him."

The porter went out and I dressed hurriedly, afraid to look at the walls. "What nonsense!" I thought. "What am I afraid of? Just like a child! I am not afraid of ghosts. Ghosts! Ghosts would be better than what I am afraid of. Why, what is it? Nothing. Myself.... Oh, nonsense!"

However, I put on a hard, cold, starched shirt, inserted the studs, donned my evening coat and new boots, and went to find the Kharkov landowner, who was ready. We started for the opera. He stopped on the way at a hairdresser's to have his hair curled, and I had mine cut by a French assistant and had a chat with him, and bought a pair of gloves. All was well, and I quite forgot my oblong room with its partition. In the theater, too, it was pleasant. After the opera the Kharkov landowner suggested that we should have supper. That was contrary to my habit, but just then I again remembered the partition in my room and accepted his suggestion.

We got back after one. I had had two glasses of wine, to which I was unaccustomed, but in spite of that I felt cheerful. But no sooner had we entered the corridor in which the lamp was turned low and I was surrounded by the hotel smell, than a shiver of horror ran down my spine. There was nothing to be done however, and I pressed my companion's hand and went into my room.

I spent a terrible night—worse than at Arzamas. Not till dawn, when the old man at the other side of the door was coughing again, did I fall asleep, and then not in the bed, in which I had lain down several times during the night, but on the sofa. I had suffered all night unbearably. Again my soul and body were being painfully torn asunder. "I am living, have lived, and ought to live, and suddenly—here is death to destroy everything. Then what is life for? To die? To kill myself at once? No, I am afraid. To wait for death till it comes? I fear that even more. Then I must live. But what for? In order to die?" And I could not escape from that circle. I took up a book, read, and forgot myself for a moment, but then again the same question and the same horror. I lay down in bed and closed my eyes. It was worse still!

God has so arranged it. Why? They say: "Don't ask, but pray!" Very well. I prayed, and prayed as I had done at Arzamas. Then and afterward I prayed simply, like a child. But now my prayers had a meaning. "If Thou dost exist, reveal to me why and what I am!" I bowed down, repeated all the prayers I knew, composed my own, and added: "Then reveal it!" and became silent, awaiting an answer. But no answer came. It was just as if there were no one who could give an answer. And I remained alone with myself. And in place of Him who would not reply I answered my own questions. "Why? In order to live in a future life," I said to myself. "Then why this obscurity, this torment? I cannot believe in a future life. I believed when I did not ask with my whole soul, but now I cannot, I cannot. If Thou didst exist Thou wouldst speak to me and to all men. And if Thou dost not exist there is nothing but despair. And I do not want that. I do not want that!"

I became indignant. I asked Him to reveal the truth to me, to reveal Himself to me. I did all that everybody does, but He did not reveal Himself. "Ask and it shall be given you" I remembered, and I had asked and in that asking had found not consolation but relaxation. Perhaps I did not pray to Him but repudiated Him. "You recede a span and He recedes a mile" as the proverb has it. I did not believe in Him but I asked, and He did not reveal anything to me. I was balancing accounts with Him and blaming Him. I simply did not believe.

The next day I did all in my power to get through my ordinary affairs so as to avoid another night in the hotel. Although I did not finish everything, I left for home that evening. I did not feel any spleen. That night in Moscow still further changed my life, which had begun to change from the time I was at Arzamas. I now attended still less to my affairs and became apathetic. I also grew weaker in health. My wife insisted that I should undergo a treatment. She said that my talks about faith and God arose from ill health. But I knew that my weakness and ill health were the effect of the unsolved question within me. I tried not to let that question dominate me, and tried to fill my life amid my customary surroundings. I went to church on Sundays and feast days, prepared to receive Communion, and even fasted, as I had begun to do since my visit to Penza, and I prayed, though more as a custom. I did not expect any result from this, but as it were kept the demand-note and presented it at the due date, though I knew it was impossible to secure payment. I only did it on the chance. I did not fill my life by estate-management—it repelled me by the struggle it involved (I had no energy)—but by reading magazines, newspapers, and novels, and playing cards for small stakes. I only showed energy by hunting which I did from habit. I had been fond of hunting all my life.

One winter day a neighboring huntsman came with his wolfhounds. I rode out with him. When we reached the place we put on snowshoes and went to the spot where the wolf might be found. The hunt was unsuccessful, the wolves broke through the ring of beaters.[1] I became aware of this from a distance and went through the forest following the fresh tracks of a hare. These led me far into a glade, where I spied the hare, but it jumped out so that I lost it. I went back through the thick forest. The snow was deep, my snowshoes sank in, and branches of the trees entangled me. The trees grew ever more and more dense. I began to ask myself: "Where am I?" The snow had altered the look of everything.

Suddenly I realized that I had lost my way. I was far from the house and from the hunters too, and could hear nothing, I was tired and bathed

[1] *beaters:* those who drive the game from cover out into the open.

in perspiration. If I stopped, I should freeze. If I went on, my strength would fail me. I shouted. All was still. No one answered. I turned back, but it was the same again. I looked around—nothing but trees, impossible to tell which was east or west. Again I turned back. My legs were tired. I grew frightened, stopped, and was seized with the same horror as in Arzamas and Moscow, but a hundred times worse. My heart palpitated, my arms and legs trembled. "Is this death? I won't have it! Why death? What is death?" Once again I wanted to question and reproach God, but here I suddenly felt that I dare not and must not do so, that it is impossible to present one's account to God, that He had said what is needful and I alone was to blame. I began to implore His forgiveness, and felt disgusted with myself.

The horror did not last long. I stood there for a while, came to myself, went on in one direction and soon emerged from the forest. I had not been far from its edge, and came out onto the road. My arms and legs still trembled and my heart was beating, but I felt happy. I found the hunting party and we returned home. I was cheerful, but I knew there was something joyful which I would make out when alone. And so it was. I remained by myself in my study and began to pray, asking forgiveness and remembering my sins. There seemed to me to be but few, but when I recalled them they became hateful to me.

After that I began to read the Scriptures. The Old Testament I found unintelligible though enchanting, but the Gospels moved me profoundly. But most of all I read the Lives of the Saints, and that reading consoled me, presenting examples that it seemed more and more possible to follow. From that time forth farming and family matters occupied me less and less. They even repelled me. They all seemed to me wrong. What it was that was "right" I did not know, but what had formerly constituted my life had now ceased to do so. This became plain to me when I was going to buy another estate.

Not far from us an estate was for sale on very advantageous terms. I went to see it. Everything was excellent and advantageous; especially so was the fact that the peasants there had no land of their own except their kitchen-gardens. I saw that they would have to work on the landlord's land merely for permission to use his pastures. And so it was. I grasped all this, and by old habit felt pleased about it. But on my way home I met an old woman who asked her way. I had a talk with her, during which she told me about her poverty. I got home, and when telling my wife of the advantages that estate offered, I suddenly felt ashamed and disgusted. I told her I could not buy it because the advantages we should get would be based on the peasants' destitution and sorrow. As I said this I suddenly realized the truth of what I was saying—the chief truth, that the peasants, like ourselves, want to live, that they are human beings, our brothers, and sons of the Father, as the Gospels say. Suddenly something that had long troubled me seemed to have broken away, as though it had come to birth. My wife was vexed and scolded me, but I felt glad.

That was the beginning of my madness. But my utter madness began later—about a month after that.

It began by my going to church. I stood there through the liturgy and prayed well, and listened and was touched. Then suddenly they brought me some consecrated bread: after that we went up to the Cross, and people began pushing one another. Then at the exit there were beggars. And it suddenly became clear to me that this ought not to be, and not only ought not to be but in reality was not. And if this was not, then neither was there either death or fear, and there was no longer the former tearing asunder within me and I no longer feared anything.

Then the light fully illumined me and I became what I now am. If there is nothing of all that—then it certainly does not exist within me. And there at the church door I gave away to the beggars all I had with me—some thirty-five rubles—and went home on foot talking with the peasants.

FOR WRITING OR DISCUSSION

1. Until the time of the crisis at Arzamas, in what sense did the narrator live what is usually termed a normal life?

2. What was the nature of the crisis at Arzamas? What events led up to it? What premonitions of the crisis did the narrator have?

3. What childhood "attacks" had preceded the crisis at Arzamas?

4. Why is the reader supposed to consider these attacks as incipient insanity?

5. How is the narrator like and unlike Turgenev's "superfluous" man?

6. Compare the hero's thoughts on the night at Arzamas with Chulkaturin's thoughts on his approaching death. Who is the more fearful of dying, who the more regretful?

7. How are the rectilinear shapes and the colors white and red used symbolically? How does their use as symbols help you identify the narrator's "negative" qualities?

8 How is the narrator's reaction to death different from Alyosha's?

9. How did the narrator live after the attack at Arzamas? How did the fear of another crisis affect his behavior?

10. Describe the attack at Moscow. What did the setting of this period of depression have in common with the setting at Arzamas?

11. How did the final attack in the snowstorm differ from the others? Was the fear of death in this instance psychological or actual? What elements of this setting were similar to those of the other attacks?

12. What was the unsolved question? How was it finally answered?

13. In what sense is the solution to the problem, which Tolstoy evidently considered a "positive" solution, a negation of life? Do you think Tolstoy intended the reader to interpret the story in this way?

14. How is the story ironic in its reversal of what we ordinarily regard as negative and affirmative attitudes toward life?

15. What elements of this story do you recognize as autobiographical? How is Tolstoy himself a sort of positive hero who gradually negated the very values in life that most people cleave to?

16. Which is "mad" — the narrator or the world?

REACTING TO CRITICISM

The story you have just read has been called by one critic the "key to Tolstoy's work." The passage that leads up to and explains that statement occurs in an article by the critic, Leo Shestov. Shestov summarizes the story and then goes on to say:

> If we take seriously what we are told in "The Diary [*sic* Memoirs] of a Madman," ... either we must repudiate Tolstoy and cut him off from our midst as lepers and others suffering from contagious diseases were cut off in the Middle Ages; or else, if we consider his experiences justifiable, we must be prepared for others to undergo the same, for the world "common to us all" to fall to pieces and men to begin to live in their own separate world, not in dreams but in their waking moments. Common sense, and science which derives from it, cannot hesitate for a moment before this dilemma. Tolstoy is in the wrong with his senseless anxieties, his unreasonable terror, and his mad uncertainty. It is "the world common to us all" which is right, with its solid beliefs, its eternal, satisfying truths, clear, defined, and accessible to all. If the person concerned had not been a world-famous writer, his fate would have been quickly decided: he would have been exiled from society as a dangerous and unhealthy member. ... All his life Tolstoy was aware that there was something in his soul driving him out of the world common to all. ... The pleasures, preoccupations, and all the innumerable business affairs of life

naturally distracted Tolstoy's attention from his extraordinary visions for many years. And then, as he tells us, he had an instinctive dread of the madhouse, and an even greater dread of madness, of having to live in his own individual world instead of in the common world. Therefore he made desperate efforts to live like everyone else, and to see only what is contained within everyday limits.

"The Diary of a Madman" is in a sense the key to Tolstoy's works. . . . Only death and the madness of death are able to awaken man from the nightmare of existence. This is what Tolstoy's "Diary of a Madman" tells us. . . . His "madness" lay in the fact that everything which had formerly seemed to him to be real and to have a solid existence now appeared illusory, whereas all that had seemed illusory and unreal now seemed to him the only reality.[1] [*Leo Shestov*]

1. According to this critic, what are the two alternatives open to the reader who takes the story seriously? Do you think Tolstoy meant the story to be taken seriously? Which alternative does he advocate? Which does "science" and common sense advocate?
2. Does the critic make his own position clear in this passage? Or is he trying to present the two points of view as objectively as possible? Explain.
3. Does "The Memoirs of a Madman" communicate to you the fear of madness or the fear of death?
4. How does the last paragraph of the critical excerpt reinforce the following statement by Ernest Simmons: "That reality is often so different from what men and women hope and dream, that life often disappoints them because they have confused the imagined with the real, is a central problem with Tolstoy's more reflective characters."[2]
5. According to Leo Shestov, is the "madman" necessarily a negative hero?

No doubt you were able to recognize in the story Tolstoy's own change from interest in the physical and material sides of life to a complete abnegation of his former tastes and occupations. The extent to which the story is autobiographical and, tentatively at least, the key to the kind of a "hero" Tolstoy himself was, is documented in an article by

---

[1] From "The Last Judgment: Tolstoy's Last Works" from *In Job's Balances* by Leo Shestov, translated by Coventry and Macartney. Reprinted by permission of J. M. Dent & Sons Ltd., Publishers.
[2] From *Introduction to Russian Realism*.

Fedor Stepun, "The Religious Tragedy of Tolstoy." Notice the word "tentatively," for as Stepun points out in the first paragraph of his essay, no one knows exactly what Tolstoy himself actually was like:

> Anyone undertaking a discussion of Tolstoy should bear in mind the words of his wife, who eight years after his death, said to one of his biographers: "For forty-eight years I lived by the side of Lev Nikolaevich and to this day do not know what sort of person he was." The enigmatic character of the great novelist, religious thinker, and social reformer may principally be explained through the bewildering number of contradictions in his nature and by his untoward tendency to make dogmatic generalizations about his multifarious probings into the spheres of life and the human spirit. It would be simple to extract characteristic quotations from his many writings and to group them in such a way that they could give completely different portraits—each one resembling the great man yet each mutually irreconcilable.[1] [*Fedor Stepun*]

After a discussion of Tolstoy's talents and of the happiness of his early life, Stepun relates the history of Tolstoy's intensifying spiritual anguish that actually did come to a head in a crisis at Arzamas.

> Yet, even this great initial happiness of his life was overcast periodically by fits of melancholy and dejection. He read widely in Schopenhauer and declared this philosopher of pessimism to be one of the greatest geniuses who had ever lived. An insurmountable fear of death beset him suddenly in an attack of depression. In 1863, at the time when his happiness was in full flower, he wrote: "Ever more swiftly I am cascading into the abyss of death and cannot grab hold of myself. But I refuse to die. I crave and I love immortality."
>
> Seven years after his marriage Tolstoy learned that an estate in a distant province was available at an attractive price. En route to the place he stopped over in the small town of Arzamas. Sleep was out of the question, and at two o'clock in the morning, he was seized by an inexplicable pain and fit of terror. Not being able to fathom the cause of this seizure, he wrote to his wife from the next station to find if there had been any untoward event at home.

---

[1] From "The Religious Tragedy of Tolstoy" by Fedor Stepun from *The Russian Review*, April 1960. Reprinted by permission of The Russian Review, Inc.

Tolstoy revealed this incident fifteen years later in his autobiographical story, "Sketches of a Madman," which appeared posthumously. In it we learn that it became clear to him that night in Arzamas not only that his trip was completely futile, but that nothing in his whole life had made any sense. In a manner that never had occurred before he felt himself suddenly split in two and become estranged from himself. Trying to overcome this sensation he went into the next room where his servant was soundly asleep. The feeling stayed with him, however, and he was evermore confronted with the questions, "Where am I dragging myself? What am I sad about? What am I afraid of? The voice of death appeared before me — 'I am here!' " His back was drenched in sweat. "He will come indeed," he said to himself aloud, "and is already at hand, but that cannot be!"

Tolstoy, who had been cited for bravery in battle, did not experience fear of death in Arzamas, but something entirely different — an impassioned protest against man's mortality. It was as though something strove to rip his soul into pieces and yet could not. He tried to go back to his room and fall asleep. He was tormented by a delirium, "red, white, and quadratic." (Notice the unusual expressionistic phrases that Tolstoy uses.) There was not a drop of compassion left in his soul. He only felt a calm anger at himself and at what had fashioned him. He tried praying, but that failed to help.

The "agony of Arzamas," as the incident was later called in Tolstoy's family, did not dissipate completely after his return to "Bright Meadows." While his delight in artistic creation and the joy of being father and husband remained, yet his life took on a bitter savor, aggravated by external circumstances. Four times within five years death struck at the once so happy household. Tolstoy's old governess, to whom he had been attached, his aunt, and two of his children died. A sense of the transitoriness of life increasingly troubled him. The thought of suicide was constantly with him. Contented though he appeared, he was afraid to go hunting with a firearm, and he hid away a rope, lest he hang himself in his room at night. A sharp light is focused on his preoccupation with death by the fact that of the two hundred and thirty-nine chapters of *Anna Karenina* only one has a title, and that is: "Death." As he relates in his *Confession,* turning to Christianity saved him from utter desperation.

Although Tolstoy was one of the most widely read men of his time it is almost impossible to determine which key works of world literature molded him. He possessed a singular immunity to the reading material he stored away. In reading, he was concerned chiefly with the confirmation of his own ideas, and hardly at all with ramifications and variations on them. This unproductive, egocentric path in the realm of literature led him to seek answers to the questions that haunted him not so much in books as in fellow men.

In that society to which he was born he found scarcely a person to whom he was able to speak on his own terms. They lived on, happily and frivolously as long as their accustomed life had flavor and then sank into anguish and pettiness as soon as the taste for life waned. Tolstoy found the real answers to his questions about death among the peasants: from those he knew in his village and from pilgrims he sought out on the highways with whom he engaged in long discussions over refreshment. His friend Strakhov tells of this. From these discussions there developed in him a very particular idea of the wisdom of life seen in the simple, hardworking Russian people. In *Confession* he says: "Every human being came to the world by the will of God and God has created every human being in such a way that he not only can save his soul but can also destroy it. The task of man is to save his soul. This can only succeed if he harkens to God, if he renounces what is pleasurable, if he toils and remains humble and compassionate to his neighbor." . . .

As Dostoevsky predicted after reading *Anna Karenina,* this attempt at salvation failed most tragically. The real reason for this collapse may be found in its unreality, which initially was probably not apparent to Tolstoy, but which could not long remain concealed from a man so earnestly seeking the truth.

The chief reason for this failure was that his conception of the essence of the faith of the Russian people overlooked everything vital to this faith — the triune God, Christ as the only-begotten son of God, the intercession of Mary, who was especially revered by the Russian people, and the resurrection of the body transfigured — in short, the whole mystery of Christianity.

Furthermore, the peasants through their faith lived on, unconcerned about death whilst Tolstoy embraced the faith of the peasants out of his fear of death.[1] [*Fedor Stepun*]

[1] *Ibid.*

1. How do the preceding quotations help to deepen your understanding of "The Memoirs of a Madman"?

2. What aspects of "negation" or "alienation" from life in the story become more apparent to you as a result of reading this additional information?

3. Tolstoy's own opinion of the Oblomovs of this world is summarized in the following statement from *What Is Art?:* "The third feeling transmitted by the art of the rich—that of discontent with life—appeared later in modern art. This feeling, which at the beginning of the present [nineteenth] century was expressed only by exceptional men, has latterly become fashionable and is expressed by most ordinary and empty people." How does the narrator of "The Memoirs of a Madman" exemplify the feeling of discontent about which Tolstoy speaks?

4. In what sense can it be said that what Tolstoy came to consider a "positive" approach to life was perhaps ironically a negation or denial of life?

THE DREAM OF A RIDICULOUS MAN

THEODORE DOSTOEVSKY

Turgenev's negative hero is a "superfluous man," alienated from himself and others; Tolstoy's is the self-consciously "mortal" man, fearful of death but guiltily unable to partake of the pleasures of life. Dostoevsky made famous his own particular adaptation of the negative hero as the "underground man," a phrase from the title of his famous story "Notes from the Underground." As you can anticipate from your earlier reading and discussion of Dostoevsky, the underground man dramatizes Dostoevsky's obsession with duality, intensity, and the predominance of men's irrational, subconscious impulses. "The Dream of a Ridiculous Man" is a late story that first appeared in Dostoevsky's periodical, *A Writer's Diary*. It is especially interesting because it presents not only his version of a negative hero but also the affirmation of his positive faith in man's salvation through religion and Christlike suffering and acceptance. Like Tolstoy's madman, Dostoevsky's narrator finds himself depressed and thinking about death. His solution to his problem is, however, both like and unlike that of Tolstoy's hero—as is his dream. Ask yourself as you read whether Dostoevsky's hero is afraid of death or whether he actively seeks it. What is negative about his view of life? How is his final solution to the problem of life like that of Tolstoy's character in that it is at the same time both a rejection and an acceptance of life and death?

The Dream of a Ridiculous Man

1

I am a ridiculous person. Now they call me a madman. That would be a promotion if it were not that I remain as ridiculous in their eyes as before. But now I do not resent it, they are all dear to me now, even when they laugh at me—and, indeed, it is just then that they are particularly dear to me. I could join in their laughter—not exactly at myself, but through affection for them, if I did not feel so sad as I look at them. Sad because they do not know the truth and I do know it. Oh, how hard it is to be the only one who knows the truth! But they won't understand that. No, they won't understand it.

In old days I used to be miserable at seeming ridiculous. Not seeming, but being. I have always been ridiculous, and I have known it, perhaps, from the hour I was born. Perhaps from the time I was seven years old I knew I was ridiculous. Afterward I went to school, studied at the university, and, do you know, the more I learned, the more thoroughly I understood that I was ridiculous. So that it seemed in the end as though all the sciences I studied at the university existed only to prove and make evident to me as I went more deeply into them that I was ridiculous. It was the same with life as it was with science. With every year the same consciousness of the ridiculous figure I cut in every relation grew and strengthened. Everyone always laughed at me. But not one of them knew or guessed that if there were one man on earth who knew better than anybody else that I was absurd, it was myself, and what I resented most of all was that they did not know that. But that was my own fault; I was so proud that nothing would have ever induced me to tell it to anyone. This pride grew in me with the years; and if it had happened that I allowed myself to confess to anyone that I was ridiculous, I believe that I should have blown out my brains the same evening. Oh, how I suffered in my early youth from the fear that I might give way and confess it to my schoolfellows. But since I grew to manhood, I have for some unknown reason become calmer, though I realized my awful characteristic more fully every year. I say "unknown," for to this day I cannot tell why it was. Perhaps it was owing to the terrible misery that was growing in my soul through something which was of more consequence than anything else about me: that something was the conviction that had come upon me that *nothing in the world mattered.* I had long had an ink-

"The Dream of a Ridiculous Man" from *An Honest Thief and Other Stories* by Dostoevsky, translated by Constance Garnett. Published in England by William Heinemann Ltd. and reprinted with their permission.

ling of it, but the full realization came last year almost suddenly. I suddenly felt that it was all the same to me whether the world existed or whether there had never been anything at all: I began to feel with all my being that there was *nothing existing*. At first I fancied that many things had existed in the past, but afterward I guessed that there never had been anything in the past either, but that it had only seemed so for some reason. Little by little I guessed that there would be nothing in the future either. Then I left off being angry with people and almost ceased to notice them. Indeed this showed itself even in the pettiest trifles: I used, for instance, to knock against people in the street. And not so much from being lost in thought: what had I to think about? I had almost given up thinking by that time; nothing mattered to me. If at least I had solved my problems! Oh, I had not settled one of them, and how many they were! But I gave up caring about anything, and all the problems disappeared.

And it was after that that I found out the truth. I learned the truth last November — on the third of November, to be precise — and I remember every instant since. It was a gloomy evening, one of the gloomiest possible evenings. I was going home at about eleven o'clock, and I remember that I thought that the evening could not be gloomier. Even physically. Rain had been falling all day, and it had been a cold, gloomy, almost menacing rain, with, I remember, an unmistakable spite against mankind. Suddenly between ten and eleven it had stopped, and was followed by a horrible dampness, colder and damper than the rain, and a sort of steam was rising from everything, from every stone in the street, and from every by-lane if one looked down it as far as one could. A thought suddenly occurred to me, that if all the street lamps had been put out it would have been less cheerless, that the gas made one's heart sadder because it lighted it all up. I had had scarcely any dinner that day, and had been spending the evening with an engineer, and two other friends had been there also. I sat silent — I fancy I bored them. They talked of something rousing and suddenly they got excited over it. But they did not really care, I could see that, and only made a show of being excited. I suddenly said as much to them. "My friends," I said, "you really do not care one way or the other." They were not offended, but they all laughed at me. That was because I spoke without any note of reproach, simply because it did not matter to me. They saw it did not, and it amused them.

As I was thinking about the gas lamps in the street I looked up at the sky. The sky was horribly dark, but one could distinctly see tattered clouds, and between them fathomless black patches. Suddenly I noticed in one of these patches a star, and began watching it intently. That was because that star gave me an idea: I decided to kill myself that night. I had firmly determined to do so two months before, and poor as I was, I bought a splendid revolver that very day, and loaded it. But two months had passed and it was still lying in my drawer; I was so utterly indifferent that I wanted to seize a moment when I would not be so indifferent —why, I don't know. And so for two months every night that I came home I thought I would shoot myself. I kept waiting for the right moment. And so now this star gave me a thought. I made up my mind that it should certainly be that night. And why the star gave me the thought I don't know.

And just as I was looking at the sky, this little girl took me by the elbow. The street was empty, and there was scarcely anyone to be seen. A cabman was sleeping in the distance in his cab. It was a child of eight with a kerchief on her head, wearing nothing but a wretched little dress all soaked with rain, but I noticed particularly her wet broken shoes and I recall them now. They caught my eye particularly. She suddenly pulled me by the elbow and called me. She was not weeping, but was spasmodically crying out some words which she could not utter properly, because she was shivering and shuddering all over. She was in terror about something, and kept crying, "Mummy, mummy!" I turned facing her, I did not say a word and went on; but she ran, pulling at me, and there was that note in her voice which in frightened children means despair. I know that sound. Though she did not articulate the words, I understood that her mother was dying, or that something of the sort was happening to them, and that she had run out to call someone, to find something to help her mother. I did not go with her; on the contrary, I had an impulse to drive her away. I told her first to go to a policeman. But clasping her hands, she ran beside me sobbing and gasping, and would not leave me. Then I stamped my foot, and shouted at her. She called out "Sir! sir!..." but suddenly abandoned me and rushed headlong across the road. Some other passer-by appeared there, and she evidently flew from me to him.

I mounted up to my fifth story. I have a room in a flat where there are other lodgers. My room is small and poor, with a garret window in the shape of a semicircle. I have a sofa covered with American leather, a table with books on it, two chairs and a comfortable armchair, as old as old can be, but of the good old-fashioned shape. I sat down, lighted the candle, and began thinking. In the room next to mine, through the partition wall, a perfect Bedlam was going on. It had been going on for the last three days. A retired captain lived there, and he had half a dozen visitors, gentlemen of doubtful reputation, drinking vodka and playing *stoss* with old cards. The night before there had been a fight, and I know that two of them had been for a long time engaged in dragging each other about by the hair. The landlady wanted to complain, but she was in abject terror of the captain. There was only one other lodger in the flat, a thin little regimental lady, on a visit to Petersburg, with three little children who had been taken ill since they came into the lodgings. Both she and her children were in mortal fear of the captain, and lay trembling and crossing themselves all night, and the youngest child had a sort of fit from fright. That captain, I know for a fact, sometimes stops people in the Nevsky Prospect and begs. They won't take him into the service, but strange to say (that's why I am telling this), all this month that the captain has been here his behavior has caused me no annoyance. I have, of course, tried to avoid his acquaintance from the very beginning, and he, too, was bored with me from the first; but I never care how much they shout on the other side of the partition nor how many of them there are in there: I sit up all night and forget them so completely that I do not even hear them. I stay awake till daybreak, and have been going on like that for the last year. I sit up all night in my armchair at the table, doing nothing. I only read by day. I sit — don't even think; ideas of a sort wander through my mind and I let them come and go as they will. A whole candle is burned every night. I sat down quietly at the table, took out the revolver and put it down before me. When I had put it down I asked myself, I remember, "Is that so?" and answered with complete conviction, "It is." That is, I shall shoot myself. I knew that I should shoot myself that night for certain, but how much longer I should go on sitting at the table I did not know. And no doubt I should have shot myself if it had not been for that little girl.

2

You see, though nothing mattered to me, I could feel pain, for instance. If anyone had struck me, it would have hurt me. It was the same morally: if anything very pathetic happened, I should have felt pity just as I used to do in old days when there were things in life that did matter to me. I had felt pity that evening. I should have certainly helped a child. Why, then, had I not helped the little girl? Because of an idea that occurred to me at the time: when she was calling and pulling at me, a question suddenly arose before me and I could not settle it. The question was an idle one, but I was vexed. I was vexed at the reflection that if I were going to make an end of myself that night, nothing in life ought to have mattered to me. Why was it that all at once I did not feel that nothing mattered and was sorry for the little girl? I remember that I was very sorry for her, so much so that I felt a strange pang, quite incongruous in my position. Really I do not know better how to convey my fleeting sensation at the moment, but the sensation persisted at home when I was sitting at the table, and I was very much irritated as I had not been for a long time past. One reflection followed another. I saw clearly that so long as I was still a human being and not nothingness, I was alive and so could suffer, be angry and feel shame at my actions. So be it. But if I am going to kill myself, in two hours, say, what is the little girl to me and what have I to do with shame or with anything else in the world? I shall turn into nothing, absolutely nothing. And can it really be true that the consciousness that I shall *completely* cease to exist immediately and so everything else will cease to exist, does not in the least affect my feeling of pity for the child nor the feeling of shame after a contemptible action? I stamped and shouted at the unhappy child as though to say—not only do I feel no pity, but even if I behave inhumanly and contemptibly, I am free to, for in another two hours everything will be extinguished. Do you believe that that was why I shouted that? I am almost convinced of it now. It seemed clear to me that life and the world somehow depended upon me now. I may almost say that the world now seemed created for me alone: if I shot myself, the world would cease to be at least for me. I say nothing of its being likely that nothing will exist for anyone when I am gone, and that as soon as my consciousness is extinguished the whole world will vanish too and become void like a phantom, as a mere appurtenance of my consciousness, for possibly all this world and all these people are only me myself. I remember that as I sat and reflected I turned all these new questions that swarmed one after another quite the other way, and thought of something quite new. For instance, a strange reflection suddenly occurred to me, that if I had lived before on the moon or on Mars and there had committed the most disgraceful and dishonorable action and had there been put to such shame and ignominy as one can only conceive and realize in dreams, in nightmares, and if, finding myself afterwards on earth, I was able to retain the memory of what I had done on the other planet and at the same time knew that I should never, under any circumstances, return there, then looking from the earth to the moon—*should I care or not?* Should I feel shame for that action or not? These were idle and superfluous questions for the revolver was already lying before me, and I knew in every fiber of my being that *it* would happen for certain, but they excited me and I raged. I could not die now without having first settled something. In short, the child had saved me, for I put off my pistol shot for the sake of these questions. Meanwhile the clamor had begun to subside in the captain's room: they had finished their game, were settling down to sleep, and meanwhile were grumbling and languidly winding up their quarrels. At that point I suddenly fell asleep in my chair at the table — a thing which had never happened to me before. I dropped asleep quite unawares.

Dreams, as we all know, are very queer things: some parts are presented with appalling vividness, with details worked up with the elaborate finish of jewelry, while others one gallops through, as it were, without noticing them at all, as, for instance, through space and time. Dreams seem to be spurred on not by reason but by desire, not by the head but by the heart, and yet what complicated tricks my reason has played sometimes in dreams, what utterly incomprehensible things happen to it! My brother died five years ago, for instance. I sometimes dream of him; he takes part in my affairs, we are very much interested, and yet all through my dream I quite know and remember that my brother is dead and buried. How is it that I am not surprised that, though he is dead, he is here beside me and working with me? Why is it that my reason fully accepts it? But enough. I will begin about my dream. Yes, I dreamed a dream, my dream of the third of November. They tease me now, telling me it was only a dream. But does it matter whether it was a dream or reality, if the dream made known to me the truth? If once one has recognized the truth and seen it, you know that it is the truth and that there is no other and there cannot be, whether you are asleep or awake. Let it be a dream, so be it, but that real life of which you make so much I had meant to extinguish by suicide, and my dream, my dream — oh, it revealed to me a different life, renewed, grand and full of power!

Listen.

3

I have mentioned that I dropped asleep unawares and even seemed to be still reflecting on the same subjects. I suddenly dreamed that I picked up the revolver and aimed it straight at my heart — my heart, and not my head; and I had determined beforehand to fire at my head, at my right temple. After aiming at my chest I waited a second or two, and suddenly my candle, my table, and the wall in front of me began moving and heaving. I made haste to pull the trigger.

In dreams you sometimes fall from a height, or are stabbed, or beaten, but you never feel pain unless, perhaps, you really bruise yourself against the bedstead, then you feel pain and almost always wake up from it. It was the same in my dream. I did not feel any pain, but it seemed as though with my shot everything within me was shaken and everything was suddenly dimmed, and it grew horribly black around me. I seemed to be blinded and benumbed, and I was lying on something hard, stretched on my back; I saw nothing, and could not make the slightest movement. People were walking and shouting around me, the captain bawled, the landlady shrieked—and suddenly another break and I was being carried in a closed coffin. And I felt how the coffin was shaking and reflected upon it, and for the first time the idea struck me that I was dead, utterly dead, I knew it and had no doubt of it, I could neither see nor move and yet I was feeling and reflecting. But I was soon reconciled to the position, and as one usually does in a dream, accepted the facts without disputing them.

And now I was buried in the earth. They all went away, I was left alone, utterly alone. I did not move. Whenever before I had imagined being buried the one sensation I associated with the grave was that of damp and cold. So now I felt that I was very cold, especially the tips of my toes, but I felt nothing else.

I lay still, strange to say I expected nothing, accepting without dispute that a dead man had nothing to expect. But it was damp. I don't know how long a time passed—whether an hour, or several days, or many days. But all at once a drop of water fell on my closed left eye, making its way through a coffin lid; it was followed a minute later by a second, then a minute later by a third—and so on, regularly every minute. There was a sudden glow of profound indignation in my heart, and I suddenly felt in it a pang of physical pain. "That's my wound," I thought; "that's the bullet. . . ." And drop after drop every minute kept falling on my closed eyelid. And all at once, not with my voice, but with my whole being, I called upon the power that was responsible for all that was happening to me:

"Whoever you may be, if you exist, and if anything more rational than what is happening here is possible, suffer it to be here now. But if you are revenging yourself upon me for my senseless suicide by the hideousness and absurdity of this subsequent existence, then let me tell you that no torture could ever equal the contempt which I shall go on dumbly feeling, though my martyrdom may last a million years!"

I made this appeal and held my peace. There was a full minute of unbroken silence and again another drop fell, but I knew with infinite unshakable certainty that everything would change immediately. And behold my grave suddenly was rent asunder, that is, I don't know whether it was opened or dug up, but I was caught up by some dark and unknown being and we found ourselves in space. I suddenly regained my sight. It was the dead of night, and never, never had there been such darkness. We were flying through space far away from the earth. I did not question the being who was taking me; I was proud and waited. I assured myself that I was not afraid, and was thrilled with ecstasy at the thought that I was not afraid. I do not know how long we were flying, I cannot imagine; it happened as it always does in dreams when you skip over space and time, and the laws of thought and existence, and only pause upon the points for which the heart yearns. I remember that I suddenly saw in the darkness a star. "Is that Sirius?" I asked impulsively, though I had not meant to ask any questions.

"No, that is the star you saw between the clouds when you were coming home," the being who was carrying me replied.

I knew that it had something like a human face. Strange to say, I did not like that being, in fact I felt an intense aversion for it. I had expected complete nonexistence, and that was why I had put a bullet through my heart. And here I was in the hands of a creature not human, of course, but yet living, existing. "And so there is life beyond the grave," I thought with the strange frivolity one has in dreams. But in its inmost depth my heart remained unchanged. "And if I have got to exist again," I thought, "and live once more under the control of some irresistible power, I won't be vanquished and humiliated."

"You know that I am afraid of you and you despise me for that," I said suddenly to my companion, unable to refrain from the humiliating question which implied a confession, and feeling my humiliation stab my heart as with a pin. He did not answer my question, but all at once I felt that he was not even despising me, but was laughing at me and had no compassion for me, and that our journey had an unknown and mysterious object that concerned me only. Fear was growing in my heart. Something was mutely and painfully communicated to me from my silent companion and permeated my whole being. We were flying through dark, unknown space. I had for some time lost sight of the constellations familiar to my eyes. I knew that there were stars in the heavenly spaces the light of which took thousands or millions of years to reach the earth. Perhaps we were already flying through those spaces. I expected something with a terrible anguish that tortured my heart. And suddenly I was thrilled by a familiar feeling that stirred me to the depths: I suddenly caught sight of our sun! I knew that it could not be *our* sun, that gave life to *our* earth, and that we were an infinite distance from our sun, but for some reason I knew in my whole being that it was a sun exactly like ours, a duplicate of it. A sweet, thrilling feeling resounded with ecstasy in my heart: the kindred power of the same light which had given me light stirred an echo in my heart and awakened it, and I had a sensation of life, the old life of the past for the first time since I had been in the grave.

"But if that is the sun, if that is exactly the same as our sun," I cried, "where is the earth?"

And my companion pointed to a star twinkling in the distance with an emerald light. We were flying straight toward it.

"And are such repetitions possible in the universe? Can that be the law of Nature? . . . And if that is an earth there, can it be just the same earth as ours . . . just the same, as poor, as unhappy, but precious and beloved forever, arousing in the most ungrateful of her children the same poignant love for her that we feel for our earth?" I cried out, shaken by irresistible, ecstatic love for the old familiar earth which I had left. The image of the poor child whom I had repulsed flashed through my mind.

"You shall see it all," answered my companion, and there was a note of sorrow in his voice.

But we were rapidly approaching the planet. It was growing before my eyes; I could already distinguish the ocean, the outline of Europe; and suddenly a feeling of a great and holy jealousy glowed in my heart.

"How can it be repeated and what for? I love and can love only that earth which I have left, stained with my blood, when, in my ingratitude, I quenched my life with a bullet in my heart. But I have never, never ceased to love that earth, and perhaps on the very night I parted from it I loved it more than ever. Is there suffering upon this new earth? On our earth we can only love with suffering and through suffering. We cannot love otherwise, and we know of no other sort of love. I want suffering in order to love. I long, I thirst, this very instant, to kiss with tears the earth that I have left, and I don't want, I won't accept life on any other!"

But my companion had already left me. I suddenly, quite without noticing how, found myself on this other earth, in the bright light of a sunny day, fair as paradise. I believe I was standing on one of the islands that make up on our globe the Greek archipelago, or on the coast of the mainland facing that archipelago. Oh, everything was exactly as it is with us, only everything seemed to have a festive radiance, the splendor of some great, holy triumph attained at last. The caressing sea, green as emerald, splashed softly upon the shore and kissed it with manifest, almost conscious love. The tall, lovely trees stood in all the glory of their blossom, and their innumerable leaves greeted me, I am certain, with their soft, caressing rustle and seemed to articulate words of love. The grass glowed with bright and fragrant flowers. Birds were flying in flocks in the air, and perched fearlessly on my shoulders and arms and joyfully struck me with their darling, fluttering wings. And at last I saw and knew the people of this happy land. They came to me of themselves, they surrounded me, kissed me. The children of the sun, the children of their sun —oh, how beautiful they were! Never had I seen on our own earth such beauty in mankind. Only perhaps in our children, in their earliest years, one might find some remote, faint reflection of this beauty. The eyes of these happy people shone with a clear brightness. Their faces were radiant with the light of reason and fullness of a serenity that comes of perfect understanding, but those faces were gay; in their words and voices there was a note of childlike joy. Oh, from the first moment, from the first glance at them, I understood it all! It was the earth untarnished by the Fall[1]; on it lived people who had not sinned. They lived just in such a paradise as that in which, according to all the legends of mankind, our first parents lived before they sinned; the only difference was that all this earth was the same paradise. These people, laughing joyfully, thronged round me and caressed me; they took me home with them, and each of them tried to reassure me. Oh, they asked me no questions, but they seemed, I fancied, to know everything without asking, and they wanted to make haste and smooth away the signs of suffering from my face.

4

And do you know what? Well, granted that it was only a dream, yet the sensation of the love of those innocent and beautiful people has remained with me forever, and I feel as though their love is still flowing out to me from over there. I have seen them myself, have known them and been convinced; I loved them, I suffered for them afterward. Oh, I understood at once even at the time that in many things I could not understand them at all; as an up-to-date Russian progressive and contemptible Petersburger, it struck me as inexplicable that, knowing so much, they had, for instance, no science like ours. But I soon realized that their knowledge was gained and fostered by intuitions different from those of us on earth, and that their aspirations, too, were quite different. They desired nothing and were at peace; they did not aspire to knowledge of life as we aspire to understand it, because their lives were full. But their knowledge was higher and deeper than ours; for our science seeks to explain what life is, aspires to understand it in order to teach others how to live, while they without science knew how to live; and that I understood, but I could not understand their knowledge. They showed me their trees, and I could not understand the intense love with which they

---

[1] *the Fall:* that is, the Fall of man, as described in Genesis, from a state of innocence into a state of sin.

looked at them; it was as though they were talking with creatures like themselves. And perhaps I shall not be mistaken if I say that they conversed with them. Yes, they had found their language, and I am convinced that the trees understood them. They looked at all Nature like that—at the animals who lived in peace with them and did not attack them, but loved them, conquered by their love. They pointed to the stars and told me something about them which I could not understand, but I am convinced that they were somehow in touch with the stars, not only in thought, but by some living channel. Oh, these people did not persist in trying to make me understand them, they loved me without that, but I knew that they would never understand me, and so I hardly spoke to them about our earth. I only kissed in their presence the earth on which they lived and mutely worshiped them themselves. And they saw that and let me worship them without being abashed at my adoration, for they themselves loved much. They were not unhappy on my account when at times I kissed their feet with tears, joyfully conscious of the love with which they would respond to mine. At times I asked myself with wonder how it was they were able never to offend a creature like me, and never once to arouse a feeling of jealousy or envy in me. Often I wondered how it could be that, boastful and untruthful as I was, I never talked to them of what I knew—of which, of course, they had no notion—that I was never tempted to do so by a desire to astonish or even to benefit them.

They were as gay and sportive as children. They wandered about their lovely woods and copses, they sang their lovely songs; their fare was light—the fruits of their trees, the honey from their woods, and the milk of the animals who loved them. The work they did for food and raiment was brief and not laborious. They loved and begot children, but I never noticed in them the impulse of that *cruel* sensuality which overcomes almost every man on this earth, all and each, and is the source of almost every sin of mankind on earth. They rejoiced at the arrival of children as new beings to share their happiness. There was no quarreling, no jealousy among them, and they did not even know what the words meant. Their children were the children of all, for they all made up one family. There was scarcely any illness among them, though there was death; but their old people died peacefully, as though falling asleep, giving blessings and smiles to those who surrounded them to take their last farewell with bright and loving smiles. I never saw grief or tears on those occasions, but only love, which reached the point of ecstasy, but a calm ecstasy, made perfect and contemplative. One might think that they were still in contact with the departed after death, and that their earthly union was not cut short by death. They scarcely understood me when I questioned them about immortality, but evidently they were so convinced of it without reasoning that it was not for them a question at all. They had no temples, but they had a real living and uninterrupted sense of oneness with the whole of the universe; they had no creed, but they had a certain knowledge that when their earthly joy had reached the limits of earthly nature, then there would come for them, for the living and for the dead, a still greater fullness of contact with the whole of the universe. They looked forward to that moment with joy, but without haste, not pining for it, but seeming to have a foretaste of it in their hearts, of which they talked to one another.

In the evening before going to sleep they liked singing in musical and harmonious chorus. In those songs they expressed all the sensations that the parting day had given them, sang its glories and took leave of it. They sang the praises of nature, of the sea, of the woods. They liked making songs about one another, and praised each other like children; they were the simplest songs, but they sprang from their hearts and went to one's heart. And not only in their songs but in all their lives they seemed to do nothing but admire one another. It was like being in love with each other, but an all-embracing, universal feeling.

Some of their songs, solemn and rapturous, I scarcely understood at all. Though I understood the words I would never fathom their full significance. It remained, as it were, beyond the grasp of my mind, yet my heart unconsciously absorbed it more and more. I often told them that I had had a presentiment of it long before, that this joy and glory had come to me on our earth in the form of a yearning melancholy that at times approached insufferable sorrow; that I had had a foreknowledge of them all and of their glory in the dreams of my heart and the visions of my mind; that often on our earth I could not look at the setting sun without tears ... that in my hatred for the men of our earth there was always a yearning anguish: why could I not hate them without loving them? why could I not help forgiving them? and in my love for them there was a yearning grief: why could I not love them without hating them? They listened to me, and I saw they could not conceive what I was saying, but I did not regret that I had spoken to them of it: I knew that they understood the intensity of my yearning anguish over those whom I had left. But when they looked at me with their sweet eyes full of love, when I felt that in their presence my heart, too, became as innocent and just as theirs, the feeling of the fullness of life took my breath away, and I worshiped them in silence.

Oh, everyone laughs in my face now, and assures me that one cannot dream of such details as I am telling now, that I only dreamed or felt one sensation that arose in my heart in delirium and made up the details myself when I woke up. And when I told them that perhaps it really was so, my God, how they shouted with laughter in my face, and what mirth I caused! Oh, yes, of course I was overcome by the mere sensation of my dream, and that was all that was preserved in my cruelly wounded heart; but the actual forms and images of my dream, that is, the very ones I really saw at the very time of my dream, were filled with such harmony, were so lovely and enchanting and were so actual, that on awakening I was, of course, incapable of clothing them in our poor language, so that they were bound to become blurred in my mind; and so perhaps I really was forced afterward to make up the details, and so of course to distort them in my passionate desire to convey some at least of them as quickly as I could. But on the other hand, how can I help believing that it was all true? It was perhaps a thousand times brighter, happier and more joyful than I describe it. Granted that I dreamed it, yet it must have been real. You know, I will tell you a secret: perhaps it was not a dream at all! For then something happened so awful, something so horribly true, that it could not have been imagined in a dream. My heart may have originated the dream, but would my heart alone have been capable of originating the awful event which happened to me afterward? How could I alone have invented it or imagined it in my dream? Could my petty heart and my fickle, trivial mind have risen to such a revelation of truth? Oh, judge for yourselves: hitherto I have concealed it, but now I will tell the truth. The fact is that I . . . corrupted them all!

Yes, yes, it ended in my corrupting them all! How it could come to pass I do not know, but I remember it clearly. The dream embraced thousands of years and left in me only a sense of the whole. I only know that I was the cause of their sin and downfall. Like a vile trichina, like a germ of the plague infecting whole kingdoms, so I contaminated all this earth, so happy and sinless before my coming. They learned to lie, grew fond of lying, and discovered the charm of falsehood. Oh, at first perhaps it began innocently, with a jest, coquetry, with amorous play, perhaps indeed with a germ, but that germ of falsity made its way into their hearts and pleased them. Then sensuality was soon begotten, sensuality begot jealousy, jealousy—cruelty. . . . Oh, I don't know, I don't remember; but soon, very soon the first blood was shed. They marveled and were horrified, and began to be split up and divided. They formed into unions, but it was against one another. Reproaches, upbraidings followed. They came to know shame, and shame brought them to virtue.

The conception of honor sprang up, and every union began waving its flags. They began torturing animals, and the animals withdrew from them into the forests and became hostile to them. They began to struggle for separation, for isolation, for individuality, for mine and thine. They began to talk in different languages. They became acquainted with sorrow and loved sorrow; they thirsted for suffering, and said that truth could only be attained through suffering. Then science appeared. As they became wicked they began talking of brotherhood and humanitarianism, and understood those ideas. As they became criminal, they invented justice and drew up whole legal codes in order to observe it, and to ensure their being kept, set up a guillotine. They hardly remembered what they had lost, in fact refused to believe that they had ever been happy and innocent. They even laughed at the possibility of this happiness in the past, and called it a dream. They could not even imagine it in definite form and shape, but, strange and wonderful to relate, though they lost all faith in their past happiness and called it a legend, they so longed to be happy and innocent once more that they succumbed to this desire like children, made an idol of it, set up temples and worshiped their own idea, their own desire; though at the same time they fully believed that it was unattainable and could not be realized, yet they bowed down to it and adored it with tears! Nevertheless, if it could have happened that they had returned to the innocent and happy condition which they had lost, and if someone had shown it to them again and had asked them whether they wanted to go back to it, they would certainly have refused. They answered me:

"We may be deceitful, wicked and unjust, we *know* it and weep over it, we grieve over it; we torment and punish ourselves more perhaps than that merciful Judge who will judge us and whose name we know not. But we have science, and by means of it we shall find the truth and we shall arrive at it consciously. Knowledge is higher than feeling, the consciousness of life is higher than life. Science will give us wisdom, wisdom will reveal the laws, and the knowledge of the laws of happiness is higher than happiness."

That is what they said, and after saying such things everyone began to love himself better than anyone else, and indeed they could not do otherwise. All became so jealous of the rights of their own personality that they did their very utmost to curtail and destroy them in others, and made that the chief thing in their lives. Slavery followed, even voluntary slavery; the weak eagerly submitted to the strong, on condition that the latter aided them to subdue the still weaker. Then there were saints who came to these people, weeping, and talked to them of their pride, of their loss of harmony and due proportion, of their loss of shame. They were laughed at or pelted with stones. Holy blood was shed on the threshold of the temples. Then there arose men who began to think how to bring all people together again, so that everybody, while still loving himself best of all, might not interfere with others, and all might live together in something like a harmonious society. Regular wars sprang up over this idea. All the combatants at the same time firmly believed that science, wisdom and the instinct of self-preservation would force men at last to unite into a harmonious and rational society; and so, meanwhile, to hasten matters, "the wise" endeavored to exterminate as rapidly as possible all who were "not wise" and did not understand their idea, that the latter might not hinder its triumph. But the instinct of self-preservation grew rapidly weaker; there arose men, haughty and sensual, who demanded all or nothing. In order to obtain everything they resorted to crime, and if they did not succeed—to suicide. There arose religions with a cult of nonexistence and self-destruction for the sake of the everlasting peace of annihilation. At last these people grew weary of their meaningless toil, and signs of suffering came into their faces, and then they proclaimed that suffering was a beauty, for in suffering alone was there meaning. They glorified suffering in their songs. I moved about among them, wringing my hands and weeping over them, but I loved them perhaps more than in old days when there was no suffering in their faces and when they were innocent and so lovely. I loved the earth they had polluted even more than when it had been a paradise, if only because sorrow had come to it. Alas! I always loved sorrow and tribulation, but only for myself, for myself; but I wept over them, pitying them. I stretched out my hands to them in despair, blaming, cursing and despising myself. I told them that all this was my doing, mine alone; that it was I who had brought them corruption, contamination, and falsity. I besought them to crucify me, I taught them how to make a cross. I could not kill myself, I had not the strength, but I wanted to suffer at their hands. I yearned for suffering, I longed that my blood should be drained to the last drop in these agonies. But they only laughed at me, and began at last to look upon me as crazy. They justified me, they declared that they had only got what they wanted themselves, and that all that now was could not have been otherwise. At last they declared to me that I was becoming dangerous and that they should lock me up in a madhouse if I did not hold my tongue. Then such grief took possession of my soul that my heart was wrung, and I felt as though I were dying; and then . . . then I awoke.

It was morning, that is, it was not yet daylight, but about six o'clock. I woke up in the same armchair; my candle had burned out; everyone was asleep in the captain's room, and there was a stillness all round, rare in our flat. First of all I leaped up in great amazement: nothing like this had ever happened to me before, not even in the most trivial detail; I had never, for instance, fallen asleep like this in my armchair. While I was standing and coming to myself I suddenly caught sight of my revolver lying loaded, ready—but instantly I thrust it away! Oh, now, life, life! I lifted up my hands and called upon eternal truth, not with words but with tears; ecstasy, immeasurable ecstasy flooded my soul. Yes, life and spreading the good tidings! Oh, I at that moment resolved to spread the tidings, and resolved it, of course, for my whole life. I go to spread the tidings, I want to spread the tidings—of what? Of the truth, for I have seen it, have seen it with my own eyes, have seen it in all its glory.

And since then I have been preaching! Moreover I love all those who laugh at me more than any of the rest. Why that is so I do not know and cannot explain, but so be it. I am told that I am vague and confused, and if I am vague and confused now, what shall I be later on? It is true indeed: I am vague and confused, and perhaps as time goes on I shall be more so. And of course I shall make many blunders before I find out how to preach, that is, find out what words to say, what things to do, for it is a very difficult task. I see all that as clear as daylight, but, listen, who does not make mistakes? And yet, you know, all are making for the same goal, all are striving in the same direction anyway, from the sage to the lowest robber, only by different roads. It is an old truth, but this is what is new: I cannot go far wrong. For I have seen the truth; I have seen and I know that people can be beautiful and happy without losing the power of living on earth. I will not and cannot believe that evil is the normal condition of mankind. And it is just this faith of mine that they laugh at. But how can I help believing it? I have seen the truth—it is not as though I had invented it with my mind, I have seen it, seen it, and *the living image* of it has filled my soul forever. I have seen it in such full perfection that I cannot believe that it is impossible for people to have it. And so how can I go wrong? I shall make some slips no doubt, and shall perhaps talk in secondhand language, but not for long: the living image of what I saw will always be with me and will always correct and guide me. Oh, I am full of courage and freshness, and I will go on and on if it were for a thousand years! Do you know, at first I meant to conceal the fact that I corrupted them, but that was a mistake—that was my first mistake! But truth whispered to me that I was *lying,* and preserved me and corrected me. But how establish paradise—I don't know, because I do not know how to put it into words. After my dream I lost command of words. All the chief words, anyway, the most necessary ones. But never mind, I shall go and I shall keep talking, I won't leave off, for anyway I have seen it with my own eyes, though I cannot describe what I saw. But the scoffers do not understand that. It was a dream, they say, delirium, hallucination. Oh! As though that meant so much! And they are so proud! A dream! What is a dream? And is not our life a dream? I will say more. Suppose that this paradise will never come to pass (that I understand), yet I shall go on preaching it. And yet how simple it is: in one day, *in one hour* everything could be arranged at once! The chief thing is to love others like yourself, that's the great thing, and that's everything; nothing else is wanted—you will find out at once how to arrange it all. And yet it's an old truth which has been told and retold a billion times—but it has not formed part of our lives! The consciousness of life is higher than life, the knowledge of the laws of happiness is higher than happiness—that is what one must contend against. And I shall. If only everyone wants it, it can all be arranged at once.

And I tracked out that little girl . . . and I shall go on and on!

FOR WRITING OR DISCUSSION

1. Compare the beginning of this story with the first part of Tolstoy's "Memoirs of a Madman." Which transmits a sense of actual madness? What details of content and style convey this impression?
2. What is the purpose and the effect of Dostoevsky's repetition of the word "ridiculous"?
3. What was the narrator's growing conviction about life? What effect did this conviction have upon his disposition and behavior?
4. Summarize the events of the evening leading up to the narrator's encounter with the little girl. Describe the encounter. How did it alter his plans?
5. Why was the narrator disturbed by his inability to commit suicide? What questions did he raise with himself?
6. Describe the dream. How is it different from Tolstoy's account of his hero's nightmares?
7. Ernest Simmons says that the island the "ridiculous man" finds in his dream is a picture of the earth before the Fall of man. What characteristics of the setting and the inhabitants described by Dostoevsky would bear out this interpretation?

8. What *is* the truth that the narrator finally learns? How does it represent both negative and positive points of view?

9. Like Tolstoy, Dostoevsky's character ends his life "preaching." How is his message both like and unlike Tolstoy's? Which is more "negative" in regard to the acceptance of life?

10. One of Dostoevsky's concerns was the limit of human freedom of choice. Does this story have anything to say about this question? If so, what?

11. You have met an example of one of Dostoevsky's "meek" types in "An Honest Thief," but a more characteristic hero is the "double," the man with dual impulses toward good and evil, pleasure and pain, humility and pride. What characteristics of duality does the "ridiculous man" have?

12. André Gide has pointed out that "most of Dostoevsky's characters are seized at certain moments — and almost, in invariably unexpected and ill-advised fashion — with the urgent desire to make confession, to ask pardon of some fellow creature who often has not a notion what it is all about, the desire to place themselves in a posture of inferiority to the person addressed." Apply this statement to the story you have just read. Then project an occasion on which the hero actually meets the girl he failed to help and makes his confession to her. Would this occasion be similar to or different from the story, which is a "confession" to the reader? Explain.

13. Do you think Dostoevsky would have agreed with Tolstoy's statement that "There is no Evil. Life is good. Evil, the absence of good, is only a sign of confusion, of error"? Explain your answer.

REACTING TO CRITICISM

If Tolstoy's main question became "What is the purpose of life, if we are to die?" Dostoevsky's questions are "Who am I? What is the nature of my freedom to choose between good and evil? What is human nature really like?" Most critics examine Dostoevsky's answers to these questions from a psychological point of view exclusively, but one of the foremost Dostoevsky scholars, Nicholas Berdyaev, considers the double and the underground man examples of the duality of human spiritual freedoms — the freedom to choose death or life, evil or good, negation or affirmation.

> In the *Letters from the Underworld* Dostoevsky made many things clear about human nature. It is extreme and irrational; man is overwhelmingly attracted toward unreasonableness, toward a

lawless freedom, toward suffering. He is not necessarily acquisitive, and at any moment may capriciously choose suffering rather than profit. He does not adapt himself to a rational organization of life and he puts freedom before happiness. But this freedom is not the primacy of reason over the psychic element; rather is it irrational and senseless to the highest degree, enticing him beyond his proper limits. This unlimited liberty is a torment and ruination to man, but its pain and disaster are dear to him. . . .

. . . Human nature cannot be brought within the operations of reason: there is always "something over," an irrational something which is the very wellspring of life. And human society can never be "rationalized," because there is an irrational principle in it; it is not a nest of ants, but to deny freedom which urges every man to "live in his own silly way" is to treat it as such.

. . . Was Dostoevsky himself among the underworld men?[1]
[*Nicholas Berdyaev*]

Let another critic answer the last question before you read Berdyaev's own answer.

Dostoevsky's psychology was part and parcel of his own spiritual quest. And as for his intuitive clairvoyance, he owed it to the wide range of his inner life. He owed it also to such extraordinary experiences as the death sentence in the Semyonovsky Square, or the Siberian katorga. His very self-division was a proof of his chaotic inner wealth which he tried to organize through his art. And contrary to the preachers of healthy normality, he saw in such a state not only a danger, but also the promise of a fuller life —provided our "duality" and chaos are duly faced and overcome.

In 1880, only a few months before his death, Dostoevsky wrote the following letter to one of his correspondents: "But now, to what you have told me of your inward duality. That trait is indeed common to all . . . that is, to all who are not wholly commonplace. Nay, it is common to human nature, though it does not evince itself so strongly in all as it does in you. It is precisely on this ground that I cannot but regard you as a twin soul, for your inward duality corresponds most exactly with my own. Such duality means that you have a strong sense of yourself, much aptness of self-criticism, and an innate feeling for your moral duty to your-

---

[1] From *Dostoevsky* by Nicholas Berdyaev, translated by Donald Attwater, published by Sheed & Ward, Inc., New York. Reprinted by permission of the publisher.

self and mankind. If your intelligence were less developed, if you were more limited, you would be less sensitive, and would not possess that duality. Rather the reverse: in its stead would have appeared great arrogance. Yet such duality is a great torment."

Dostoevsky accepted this torment. Most of his efforts to master it, to arrive through the tragedy of self-division at a new unity and integration of his own self, are recorded in his works. It is here that he comes very close to another modern psychologist, C. G. Jung. He would be the first to endorse Jung's statement (in the latter's essay about the differences between Freud and himself): "We moderns are faced with the necessity of rediscovering the life of the spirit; we must experience it anew for ourselves. It is the only way in which we can break the spell that binds us to the cycle of biological events."[1] [*Janko Lavrin*]

And now let Berdyaev give his less psychological, more religious or philosophical answer:

> Was Dostoevsky himself among the underworld men? . . . The underground man's conception of the world is not the positive religious conception that Dostoevsky had, the conception in which he made plain the dangerousness of the arbitrary ways and rebellion in which underworld men are engaged because they were heading for the destruction of human freedom and the decomposition of personality. But underworld man and his astounding dialectic of irrational liberty represent a moment on the tragic road whereon mankind tries out and experiences freedom; for freedom is the supreme good: man cannot renounce it without renouncing himself and ceasing to be a man. So Dostoevsky in his conception of the world rejected what underworld man rejected in his dialectic. To the very end he refused to rationalize human society and repudiated all attempts to exalt happiness, reason, and well-being above liberty. . . . Instead he wanted to take men along the ways of wildest self-will and revolt in order to show them that they lead to the extinction of liberty and self-annihilation. This road of liberty can only end either in the deification of man or in the discovery of God; in the one case, he is lost and done for; in the other, he finds salvation and the definitive confirmation of himself as God's earthly image.

[1]From *Dostoevsky: A Study* by Janko Lavrin (1943); New York: Russell & Russell, 1968. Reprinted by permission of Janko Lavrin and Russell & Russell.

... But one point is already clear: in Dostoevsky's view, man cannot return to that idea of an obligatory and imposed reason against which underworld man has risen; he must pass through the test of freedom. And Dostoevsky shows, as we have seen, that if man is forced into rational molds and his life fenced about with formulae he "will go insane on purpose so as to have no judgment and behave as he likes." According to him, a certain "fantasticalness" or eccentricity is an essential element in human nature...."[1] [*Nicholas Berdyaev*]

1. Relate these critical explanations of the "double" and the "underground" man to "The Dream of a Ridiculous Man." In what sense is the hero at the beginning of the story a negative hero and, at the end, a positive one? How are these two positions typical of the Dostoevsky double?

2. How does the end of the story bear out Berdyaev's statement that Dostoevsky himself did not accept the point of view of the underground man, though he did accept man's "doubleness"?

3. How does man's freedom to choose good or evil, life or death, result in both negative and positive heroes? Is the negative hero always the one who *thinks* overmuch (as Turgenev's "superfluous" man), *fears* overmuch (as Tolstoy's "moral" man), or follows self-will overmuch (as in Dostoevsky's "proud" characters and his "underground men")? Or is the negative hero simply one who is unable to accept the world as it is and consequently rejects it or is rejected by it? Explain.

4. Was Dostoevsky interested primarily in political or spiritual freedom?

5. Does Dostoevsky's negative hero have, in your opinion, more or less dignity and tragic stature than Turgenev's "superfluous man" and Tolstoy's "madman"?

6. D. H. Lawrence filed a "minority report" on Dostoevsky's characters:

> Of these self-divided, *gamin*-religious Russians, who are so absorbingly concerned with their own dirty linen and their own piebald souls we have had a little more than enough. The contradictions in them are not so very mysterious, or edifying, after all. They have a spurting, *gamin* hatred of civilization, of Europe, of Christianity, of governments, and of everything else, in their moments of energy; and in their inevitable relapses into weak-

[1] From *Dostoevsky*.

ness, they make the inevitable recantation; they whine, they humiliate themselves, they seek unspeakable humiliation for themselves, and call it Christlike, and then with the left hand commit some dirty little crime or meanness, and call it the mysterious complexity of the human soul.[1] [*D. H. Lawrence*]

Would you say that Lawrence has given a fair picture of Dostoevsky's heroes? Of course, you have not read Dostoevsky's major works, so you can respond only in light of the few selections you have read. What might lead you to believe that Lawrence perhaps was overreacting?

SUMMARY DISCUSSION

1. In all three stories you have read, the negative hero suffers from paralysis of will, but the inability of each of these heroes to come to terms with life stems from fears and personality traits of differing kinds. Which of the three seems to wish to enjoy life but is unable to learn how? Which character finds his own life and the lives of people in his own class empty and unproductive? Which character finds life absolutely meaningless?

2. How is the negative attitude toward life held by all three characters related to their feelings about death?

3. How does the negative hero react toward other people? Why?

4. What answers to questions regarding the nature of human life do all three characters find? Do you think these answers are the same as those the authors of each of these stories would give? Explain.

5. All three stories are written in the form of a monologue. Which do you find the most dramatic? Why?

6. Which of the three heroes is most nearly "Everyman," a typical, quite average human being? Which is most tragic?

7. Which of the three authors do you think would be best able to understand and accept the violence in today's world? Why?

8. Reread the excerpts from *Oblomov* at the beginning of this section. What elements of Oblomov's "disease" do all three characters share?

FOR COMPOSITION

Write an extended definition of a negative hero, using examples from the three stories you have read as illustrative details.

[1]From *Phoenix: The Posthumous Papers of D. H. Lawrence,* edited by Edward D. McDonald. Copyright 1936 by Frieda Lawrence, renewed 1964 by the Estate of the late Frieda Lawrence Ravagli. All rights reserved. Reprinted by permission of The Viking Press, Inc.

A MOSCOW HAMLET
ANTON CHEKHOV

That the Russian negative hero was not simply a creation of the nineteenth century, but a universalized Russian type, is evident in the works of Anton Chekhov, a writer closely associated with the three authors whose stories you have considered but more nearly a twentieth-century, "modern," Russian author than they. Chekhov, who started professional life as a doctor but who won lasting fame as a writer of plays and stories, lived from 1860 to 1904; and although, technically, he lived most of his life during the nineteenth century, his view of life and art places him more clearly in our own times.

Chekhov, unlike Tolstoy and Turgenev, was not a member of the aristocratic landed classes. He was, like Dostoevsky, poor and urban, but unlike him, he faced life objectively, reserving his intensity for his work and his art. Chekhov's antiheroes are alienated from themselves, from society, and even from a sense of destiny or of the future toward which his predecessors' major characters ultimately looked. Yet Chekhov's characters share most of the traits of the negative heroes you have met.

The following story, "A Moscow Hamlet," appeared in a literary magazine in 1891. As you read it, compare the narrator's character and problems with those of his counterparts in the three stories you have just discussed and with the definition of a negative hero that you were asked to write.

A Moscow Hamlet

I am a Moscow Hamlet. Yes. I go to houses, theaters, restaurants and editorial offices in Moscow, and everywhere I say the same thing:

"God, how boring it is, how ghastly boring!"

And the sympathetic reply comes:

"Yes, indeed, it is terribly boring."

This goes on through the day and the evening; and at night when I come home and lie down in bed and ask myself in the dark why I am so tormented with boredom, I have a restless, heavy feeling in my chest, and remember how in one house a week ago, when I began to ask what to do for my boredom, an unknown gentleman, obviously not a Moscow man, suddenly turned to me and said, with irritation:

"A Moscow Hamlet" by Chekhov from *Chekov, Literary and Theatrical Reminiscences*, translated by S. S. Koteliansky. Published in England by Routledge & Kegan Paul Ltd. and reprinted with their permission.

"Oh, you take a piece of telephone cord and hang yourself on the nearest telegraph pole! That's all that's left for you!"

Yes, and all the while at night it seems to me that I am beginning to understand why I am so bored. Why? Why? This, I believe, is the reason. . . .

To begin with, I know absolutely nothing. I studied something once, but damn it, is it because I have forgotten everything, or because my knowledge is good for nothing, that it turns out that I am discovering America every minute? For instance, when I am told that Moscow needs main drainage, or that whortleberries don't grow on trees, I ask in astonishment: "Is that so, really?"

I have lived in Moscow since I was born, but, heavens above, I don't know the origin of Moscow, what it exists for, why, what's the good of it or what it needs. At the meetings of the City Council I discuss the management of the town with the others, but I don't know how many square miles there are in Moscow, how many people, the number of births and deaths, the income and expenditure, how much trade we do, or with whom. . . . Which city is richer, Moscow or London? If it's London, then why? God only knows. And when a question is raised on the Council, I tremble and am the first to shout: "Hand it over to a committee! A committee!"

I murmur to businessmen that it is time Moscow opened up trading relations with China and Persia, but we don't know where China and Persia are, or whether they need anything beside damped and worm-eaten raw silk. From morning till evening I gobble at Tiestov's restaurant and don't know what I'm gobbling for. Sometimes I get a part in a play, and I don't know what's in the play. I go to the opera to hear *The Queen of Spades*[1] and only when the curtain goes up do I remember that I haven't read Pushkin's tale, or I've forgotten it. I write a play and get it produced, and only after it has come a smash do I realize that a play exactly like it was written by V. Alexandrov, and by Fedotov before him, and by Shpazhinsky before him. I cannot speak, or argue, or keep up a conversation. When a conversation arises in company about something I do not know, I simply begin bluffing. I give my face a rather sad, sneering expression, and take my interlocutor by the buttonhole, and say:

"This is *vieux jeu*,[2] dear fellow," or "My dear man, you are contra-

---

[1] *The Queen of Spades:* an opera by Peter Ilich Tchaikovsky, (1840–1893), based on a story by Alexander Pushkin (1799–1837).
[2] *vieux jeu:* old stuff; literally, old play.

dicting yourself. . . . We'll settle this interesting question some other time, and come to some agreement; but now, for Heaven's sake, tell me: have you seen *Imogen*?" . . . In this matter I have learned something from the Moscow critics: When I'm present at a conversation about the theater or the modern drama, I understand nothing about it, but I find no difficulty in replying, if I am asked my opinion: "Well, yes, gentlemen. Suppose it is. . . . But where's the idea, the ideals?" Or, after a sigh, I exclaim: "Oh, immortal Molière, where art thou?" and, gloomily waving my hand, I go into the next room. There's a certain Lope de Vega,[1] a Danish playwright, I fancy. I sometimes stun the audience with him. "I'll tell you a secret," I whisper to my neighbor, "Calderon stole this phrase from Lope de Vega. . . ." And they believe me. . . . Well, let them verify! . . .

On account of my utter lack of knowledge I am quite uncultured. True, I dress according to the fashion, I have my hair cut at Théodore's and my establishment is chic, yet I am an Asiatic and *mauvais ton*.[2] With a writing desk, of inlaid work, which costs about four hundred rubles, velvet upholstery, pictures, carpets, busts, tiger skins—lo, the flue in the fireplace is stopped up with a lady's blouse, or there's no spittoon, and I and my friends spit on the carpet. From the staircase comes a smell of roast goose, the butler's face is heavy eyed, there's dirt and filth in the kitchen, and under the beds and behind the wardrobes there are dust, cobwebs, old boots covered with green mold, and papers smelling of cats. There's always something wrong in the house; the chimneys smoke or the lavatory is drafty, or the ventilator does not shut, and in order that the snow should not come flying from the street into my study, I hasten to stop up the ventilator with a cushion. At times I go to live in furnished apartments. I lie down on the sofa in my room, thinking on the subject of boredom and in the next room to the right the German woman lodger fries cutlets on a kerosene stove; and in the room to the left—little ladies drum with beer bottles on the table. From my room I am studying "life," I am looking at everything from the point of view of furnished apartments, and I write solely about the German woman, the little ladies, dirty serviettes; or I play the part exclusively of drunkards and fallen idealists; and the most important problem I consider the question of doss houses[3] and of the intellectual proletariat. Yet I feel nothing and observe nothing. I quite readily reconcile myself to the low ceilings,

[1] *Lope de Vega:* Spanish dramatist and poet (1562–1635).
[2] *mauvais ton:* undistinguished; literally, "bad tone."
[3] *doss houses:* cheap lodging houses.

black beetles, the dampness, drunken friends who settle themselves on my bed with their dirty boots on. Neither the pavements, covered with a yellow-brown slime, nor the dust heaps, nor the filthy gates, nor the illiterate signboards, nor the ragged beggars—nothing offends my aesthetic sense. I sit, shriveled up like a hobgoblin on a narrow sledge, the wind gets at me from all sides, the driver blindly whips me with his whip, the scabby horse hardly trots—but I take no heed of it all. It's all of no consequence! They say that the Moscow architects have erected soapboxes for houses and have thereby spoiled the city. But I don't think that those soapboxes are bad. They say that our museums are beggarly, unscientific, and useless. But I do not go to museums. They complain that there used to be one decent picture gallery, and even that one has been closed by Tretyakov. Well, let him close it if he pleases. . . .

The second cause of my boredom is that I believe I am very clever and extraordinarily important. Whether I enter a house, or speak, or keep silent, or recite at a literary soirée, or gobble at Tiestov's, I do it with the greatest aplomb. There is no discussion I would not intervene in. It's true, I can't speak, but I can smile ironically, shrug my shoulders, interject. I, an ignorant, and uncultured Asiatic, at bottom, I'm satisfied with everything; but I assume an air of being discontented with everything, and I manage this so subtly that sometimes I believe it myself. When there's a funny play on at the theater, I long to laugh, but I hasten to give myself a serious, concentrated air. God forbid I should smile! What will my neighbors say? Someone behind me is laughing. I look round sternly. A wretched lieutenant, a Hamlet like myself, is put out, and says, apologizing for his fit of laughter:

"How cheap! Mere Punch and Judy show!"

And during the interval I say aloud at the bar: "Hang it all, what a play! It's disgusting."

"Yes, a regular Punch and Judy show," someone answers, "but it's got an idea. . . ."

"Well, the motive was worked out ages ago by Lope de Vega, and, of course, there can be no comparison! But how boring, how incredibly boring!"

At *Imogen* my jaws ache with suppressed yawns my eyes sink into my forehead for boredom, my mouth is parched. . . . But on my face is a blissful smile.

"This is a whiff of the real thing," I say in an undertone; "it's a long while since I had such real pleasure."

At times I have a desire to play the fool, to take part in a farce, and would do it gladly, and I know it would be the very thing for these gloomy times; but — what will they say in the offices of *The Artist*?

No, God forbid!

At picture exhibitions I usually screw up my eyes, shake my head knowingly and say aloud:

"Everything seems to be here, atmosphere, expression, tones. But where's the essential? . . . Where's the idea? I ask you, where is the idea?"

From the reviews I demand honest principles, and above all, that the articles should be signed by professors, or by men who have been exiled to Siberia. No one who isn't a professor or an exile can have real talent. I demand that Mme Yermolov shall play only idealistic girls, never more than twenty-one. I insist that classical plays must absolutely be staged by professors — absolutely. I insist that the most minor actors, before taking a part, should be acquainted with the literature on Shakespeare, so that when an actor says for instance, "Good night, Bernado," the whole audience shall feel that he has read eight volumes of criticism.

I get into print very often indeed. Only yesterday I went to the editor of a fat monthly to ask whether he was going to publish my novel of 900 pages.

"I really don't know what to do," the editor said in embarrassment. "You see it's so long . . . and so tedious."

"Yes," I say, "but it's honest."

"Yes, you're right," the editor agrees in still greater embarrassment. "Of course, I'll publish it."

My girl and women friends are also unusually clever and important. They are all alike; they dress alike, they speak alike, they walk alike. There's only this difference, that the lips of one of them curve in a heart shape, while the mouth of another opens as wide as an eel trap when she smiles.

"Have you read Protopopov's last article?" the heart-shaped lips ask me. "It is a revelation."

"You must agree," says the eel trap, "that Ivan Ivanovich Ivanov's passionate convictions remind one of Belinsky. He's my only hope."

I confess there was a *she*. I remember our declaration of love so well. She sat on the divan. Lips heart shaped. Badly dressed, "no pretensions"; her hair was stupidly done. I take her by the waist; her corset scrunches. I kiss her cheek — it tastes salty. She is confused, stunned, bewildered. "Good heavens, how can one combine honest principles with such a trivial thing as love? What would Protopopov say if he saw us? No, never! Let me go! You shall be my friend." I say that friendship is not enough for me. . . . Then she shakes her finger at me archly and says:

"Well, I'll love you on condition that you keep your flag flying."

And when I hold her in my arms, she murmurs:

"Let us fight together. . . ."

Then, when I live with her, I get to know that the flue of the fireplace is stopped up with her blouse, that the papers under her bed smell of cats, that she also bluffs in arguments and picture exhibitions, and jabbers like a parrot about atmosphere and expression. And she too must have an idea! She drinks vodka on the quiet, and when she goes to bed she smears her face with sour cream in order to look younger. In her kitchen there are beetles, dirty dish-clouts,[1] filth; and when the cook bakes a pie, she takes the comb out of her hair and makes a pattern on the crust before putting it into the oven; and when she makes pastry she licks the currants to make them stick on the paste. And I run! run! My romance flies to the devil, and *she,* important, clever, contemptuous, goes everywhere and squeaks about me: "He betrayed his convictions."

The third cause of my boredom is my furious, boundless envy. When I am told that so-and-so has written a very interesting article, and so-and-so's play is a success, that X won two hundred thousand rubles in a lottery, and that N's speech made a profound impression, my eyes begin to squint. They close right up, and I say:

"I'm awfully glad for his sake; of course, you know he was tried for theft in '74."

My soul turns into a lump of lead. I hate the successful man with all my being, and I go on:

"He treats his wife very badly. He has three mistresses. He always squares the reviewers by dining them. Altogether, he's an utter rogue. . . . His novel isn't bad, but he's certainly lifted it from somewhere. He's a blatant incompetent. . . . And, to tell the truth, I don't find anything particular in this novel even. . . ."

But if someone's play is a failure, I'm very happy and hasten to take the writer's side.

"No, my dear fellows, no!" I shout. "In this play, there's *something.* It is literature, at all events."

Do you know that all the mean, spiteful, dirty things that are being said about people of any reputation in Moscow were started by me? Let the Mayor know that if he managed to give us good roads, I should begin to hate him, and I'd spread the rumor that he's a highway robber. . . . If I am told a certain newspaper already has fifty thousand subscribers,

[1]*dish-clouts* (archaic): dishcloths.

I'll tell everyone that the editor is kept by a woman. The success of another is a disgrace, a humiliation, a stab in the heart for me. ... What question can there be of a social or political consciousness? If I ever had one, envy devoured it long ago.

And so, knowing nothing, uncultured, very clever and excessively important, squinting with envy, with a huge liver, yellow, gray, bald, I wander from house to house all over Moscow, discoloring life, and bringing with me into every house something yellow, gray, bald. ...

"God, how boring!" I say with despair in my voice. "How ghastly boring!"

I'm catching, like the influenza. I complain of boredom, look important, and slander my friends and acquaintances from envy, and lo, a young student has already taken in what I say. He passes his hand over his hair solemnly, throws away his book, and says:

"Words, words, words ... God, how boring!"

He squints, his eyes begin to close, like mine, and he says:

"The professors are lecturing for the famine fund now. I'm afraid half the money will go into their own pockets."

I wander about like a shadow, doing nothing; my liver is growing, growing. ... Time passes, passes. Meanwhile, I'm getting old, weak. One day I'll catch the influenza and be taken off to the Vagankov cemetery. My friends will remember me for a couple of days and then forget, and my name will no longer be even a sound. ... Life does not come again; if you have not lived during the days that were given you, once only, then write it down as lost. ... Yes, lost, lost.

And yet I could have learned anything. If I could have got the Asiatic out of myself, I could have studied and loved European culture, trade, crafts, agriculture, literature, music, painting, architecture, hygiene. I could have had superb roads in Moscow, begun trade with China and Persia, brought down the death rate, fought ignorance, corruption and all the abominations which hold us back from living. I could have been modest, courteous, jolly, cordial; I could have rejoiced sincerely at other people's success, for even the least success is a step towards happiness and truth.

Yes, I could have! I could have! But I am a rotten rag, useless rubbish. I am a Moscow Hamlet. Take me off to the Vagankov cemetery!

I toss about under my blanket, turning from side to side. I cannot sleep. All the while I think why I am so tortured with boredom, and these words echo in my ears until the dawn:

"You take a piece of telephone cord and hang yourself on the nearest telegraph pole. That's all that's left for you."

FOR WRITING OR DISCUSSION

1. What characteristics does the narrator of this story share with the negative heroes of the tales by Turgenev, Tolstoy, and Dostoevsky? Cite examples and illustrations from the story to support your statements.

2. What word, repeated throughout the story, summarizes the central problem of the narrator? How is this problem similar to and different from the kind of indifference or apathy suffered by the other three antiheroes?

3. What, according to the narrator, are the three reasons for his condition? Do you accept the narrator's self-diagnosis? Or do you reach a different conclusion?

4. Do you feel that the narrator in this story is "small" himself, or do you think that the context of his life is limited by external conditions? Explain.

5. At what points in the story does the narrator contemplate suicide? Compare your reaction to the sincerity of the narrator's death wish with the motivations and honesty of the other three heroes.

6. Relate this story to the "Hamlet–Don Quixote" theme as described by Turgenev (see page 330). Is Chekhov's narrator either a true Hamlet or a true Don Quixote? Or is he a fake?

7. What elements of social satire in the story remind you of similar elements in "The Crocodile"?

8. The narrator calls himself an "Asiatic" Russian. Is he truly an "Eastern" Russian in the Dostoevskyan sense, or is he more Westernized? Explain.

9. Point out the touches of humor in this story. Do they increase or decrease the reader's empathy with the main character?

10. It has been said that Chekhov's view of life as a tragedy stems from his conviction that what does *not* happen to one is more tragic than what happens—that emptiness of life is the tragedy that must be faced by modern man. How does "A Moscow Hamlet" illustrate this statement? Do you agree or disagree with this point of view about life? Explain your answer.

11. Complete your discussion of the negative hero in Russian fiction by using this story as an example of the "composite" type and comparing the characteristics of the hero of "A Moscow Hamlet" with those of all the preceding negative heroes about whom you have read.

PART SIX
On Translation

ON TRANSLATION

That you have been discussing stories by three great *Russian* writers seems too obvious to mention. That you have been reading them in translation may not be so immediately apparent. Unless you are a speaker or reader of Russian, you actually have no way of recognizing the subtle, but often significant differences between the original and the English versions. You have probably, in fact, been reading these "translated" Russian stories as if they were, indeed, "English" originally. "But of what importance is this to me?" you will say. "If I were compelled to read Russian writers in Russian, German poets in German, Greek playwrights in Greek, and so on—I would never become acquainted with some of the greatest writers in the world." And you would be right. According to some educators and scholars, unless you read a masterwork in the language from which it springs, you have not actually understood or appreciated it in the same way that a native speaker has read and enjoyed it. However true this may be, most of us, certainly, are completely dependent on translations for the only acquaintance we will ever have with the great amount of literature not written in English. How many of us can read the Bible in the original? or, for that matter, understand one of our own English classics, *Beowulf,* in its original Anglo-Saxon form? How many Russians can understand *Hamlet* in English, although they may have seen excellent versions performed all over Russia in Russian translation?

The purposes of this section are to make you aware of some of the reasons that reading a work in translation is not the same as reading it in the original, and to help you understand the importance and difficulty of the translator's task in introducing us to world literature.

The Impossibilities of Translation

Werner Winter, a professor of linguistics with a solid training in Slavic languages, has this to say about the "impossibilities of translation":

> It seems to me that we may compare the work of a translator with that of an artist who is asked to create an exact replica of a marble statue, but who cannot secure any marble. He may find some other stone or some wood, or he may have to model in clay or work in bronze, or he may have to use a brush or a pencil and a sheet of paper. Whatever his material, if he is a good craftsman,

his work may be good or even great; it may indeed surpass the original, but it will never be what he set out to produce, an exact replica of the original.

In a nutshell, we seem to have here all the challenge and all the frustration that goes with our endeavors to do the ultimately impossible. We know from the outset that we are doomed to fail; but we have the chance, the great opportunity to fail in a manner that has its own splendor and its own promise. . . .

There is no completely exact translation. There are only approximations, and the degree of similarity possible between original and translation depends on the degree of similarity between the systems of form and meaning in the two languages involved. The more serious the deviations from one language to the other, the less of the original can be salvaged in the process of transfer.

To be sure, there are partial exceptions to this. One-to-one correspondences are possible as long as one confines oneself to utterances of limited size outside a larger context (the rendering of an English cry *Fire!* by German *Feuer!* would be a fairly good example), but this observation does not invalidate the overall statement.

However, it may be asked: Is it not possible to convey in a second language completely, without omission or addition, the *content* of a statement in the original language — even if one has to grant that the formal properties of the two utterances have to be different? Isn't it the same thing whether we express a certain semantic unit by *father* or *Vater* or *père*? . . .

. . . The natural logic of such a term and such a notion strikes us as inevitable. A living being has to have a father, the relationship father : mother : child is provided for in nature. Nonetheless, if one goes out to western Arizona and asks speakers of Mohave for their equivalent of English *father,* one will get not one term, but two — not stylistic variants of the type of *father* and *dad,* but mutually exclusive, contrasting terms. One of them can be paraphrased "father of male referent," the other, "father of female referent." Clearly, there is no difference between the biological facts of the father-child relationship in Parker, Arizona, and in Austin, Texas; yet the linquistic interpretation of this relationship is totally different, and a translation without loss or addition is not possible.

Thus not even "basic notions," central points in a human sphere of experience, stand outside the area of arbitrary segmentation and arrangement and subsequent conventionalization; and the extent to which semantic boundaries as determined by linguistic form and linguistic usage coincide with absolute boundaries in the world around us is negligible. . . .

For instance, the spectrum of colors is not divided up in any "natural," consistent way by speakers of different languages. *We would never hesitate to affirm the importance of the difference between "green" and "blue"* — whereas the Yuman languages (of which Mohave is one), although otherwise employing a set of basic color terms very similar in application to our own, do not have separate forms to indicate these two colors, and consequently do not have separate meanings "blue" and "green" (though speakers of these languages will note the physical difference between a dark blue and a light green without hesitation).

For us, "gray" is a unified meaning field, whether the word is applied to the color of a wall or a person's hair; Russian has two different terms and therefore two meanings correspond to our one. For us, "high" and "low" are "natural" categories; *mons altus* and *mare altum* indicate that we cannot say the same for the Romans. "Round" we apply to a ball or a hoop without further differentiation; in Yuman languages, the two terms used in this connection have nothing in common with each other except possibly a feature of reduplication.

And these examples could be multiplied, but the point is clear already. Even the simplest, most basic requirement we make of translation cannot be met without difficulty: one cannot always match the content of a message in language A by an expression with exactly the same content in language B, because what can be expressed and what must be expressed is a property of a specific language in much the same way as *how* it can be expressed. It is only so that the area of agreement in the analysis of the world around us is usually very much greater than the area of agreement in the formal expression of this analysis. As a result, we get the impression only too easily that the content of the original message can always be transmitted in the second language.[1] [*Werner Winter*]

---

[1]From "Impossibilities of Translation" by Werner Winter from *Craft and Context of Translation: A Critical Symposium*, edited by William Arrowsmith and Roger Shattuck. (Published by University of Texas Press and Doubleday Anchor Editions.) Reprinted by permission of the author and editors.

Dostoevsky would not have agreed with Werner Winter that translations from another language *into* Russian are impossible. He felt, in fact, that Russians have a special talent for translation:

> We . . . understand Dickens, when rendered into Russian, almost as well as the English—perhaps, even all nuances. Moreover, we love him—perhaps, not less than his own countrymen. And yet, how typical, original and national is Dickens! What can be derived from this? Is such an understanding of alien nationalities a special gift of the Russians, as compared with Europeans? Perhaps such a special gift actually exists; and if it exists (as well as the gift of speaking foreign languages which, indeed, is more pronounced among us than among other Europeans), it is a very significant gift, carrying a great promise for the future—one that predestines the Russians to many a thing, although I do not know whether this is a good gift or whether there is something bad in it.[1] [*Theodore Dostoevsky*]

His opinion of translations of Russian writers into other tongues was not, however, so flattering:

> I recall, in my youthful days, I became greatly interested in the fact that Mr. Viardot, a Frenchman (the husband of the famous singer who, at the time, had been singing in our Italian opera), not knowing a word of Russian, had been translating our Gogol under the guidance of Mr. Turgenev. . . . At the same time, it goes without saying that Mr. Turgenev understood Gogol in every minute detail, enthusiastically loved him, I take it—much as everybody else in those days—and, on top of that, was himself a poet, although then he had hardly begun his poetic pursuits. Thus, something could have come of it. I may note that Mr. Turgenev, probably, knows the French language to perfection. . . . But what was the result?—Such a strange thing was produced by this translation that, even though I had anticipated that Gogol cannot be rendered into French, nevertheless I had not expected such an outcome. This translation is available at present—look what it amounts to. Gogol has literally vanished. All the humor; all that is comical; all individual details and the principal phases of the denouements which if suddenly recalled in solitude (and oftentimes in the least literary moments of one's life) will set one breaking

---

[1] From *The Diary of a Writer*, F. M. Dostoevsky. translated by Boris Brasol: copyright 1949 Charles Scribner's Sons. Reprinted by permission of Charles Scribner's Sons.

into irresistible laughter to oneself—all this has vanished, as if it had never been there.

I cannot imagine what opinion the French could have formed at the time about Gogol, judging by that translation.

Briefly, in my opinion, everything characteristic—everything that is ours, preeminently national (and therefore, everything genuinely artistic)—is unintelligible to Europe. Translate Turgenev's novel *Rudin*—(I speak of Mr. Turgenev because he has been translated more than other Russian authors, and of the novel *Rudin*, for the reason that among all of Mr. Turgenev's works it conforms the most to something German)—into any European language, and even then it will not be understood. The real gist of the matter will even remain unsuspected. *A Hunter's Sketches* will be as little understood as Pushkin and Gogol. So that—it would seem to me—all our outstanding talents are, perhaps, destined, for many years to come, to remain utterly unknown to Europe; and even: the greater, the more original, the talent—the more unintelligible he will be.[1] [*Theodore Dostoevsky*]

The Russian Language

Among those who attributed the excellence of Russian translations to the Russian tongue itself was Turgenev, who pleaded with his contemporaries to honor it:

> As for my request, it is as follows: guard our Russian tongue, our beautiful Russian tongue, that treasure, that trust handed down to you by your predecessors, headed again by Pushkin! Treat this powerful instrument with respect; it may work miracles in the hands of those who know how to use it! Even those who dislike "philosophic abstractions" and "poetic sentimentalities," even to practical people, for whom language is merely a means for expressing thoughts, a means to an end, just like an ordinary lever, even to them I will say: respect at least the laws of mechanics and extract every possible use from everything![2] [*Ivan Turgenev*]

Some of the intricacies and richness of the Russian language were described years later by a Russian aristocrat turned scholar-critic, Prince

---

[1] *Ibid.*
[2] From *Turgenev's Literary Reminiscences*, edited by David Magarshack, copyright © 1958 by Farrar, Straus & Cudahy, Inc. Reprinted by permission of Farrar, Straus & Giroux, Inc.

Kropotkin, who began a series of lectures on Russian literature with a reference to Turgenev's statement, which he used to introduce his remarks on the Russian language:

> The richness of the Russian language in words is astounding: many a word which stands alone for the expression of a given idea in the languages of Western Europe has in Russian three or four equivalents for the rendering of the various shades of the same idea. It is especially rich for rendering various shades of human feeling—tenderness and love, sadness and merriment—as also various degrees of the same action. Its pliability for translation is such that in no other language do we find an equal number of most beautiful, correct, and truly poetical renderings of foreign authors. Poets of the most diverse character, such as Heine and Béranger, Longfellow and Schiller, Shelley and Goethe—to say nothing of that favorite with Russian translators, Shakespeare—are equally well turned into Russian. . . . The desperate vagueness of German metaphysics is quite as much at home in Russian as the matter-of-fact style of the eighteenth-century philosophers; and the short, concrete and expressive, terse sentences of the best English writers offer no difficulty for the Russian translator.
>
> Together with Czech and Polish, Moravian, Serbian and Bulgarian, as also several minor tongues, the Russian belongs to the great Slavonian family of languages which, in its turn—together with the Scandinavo-Saxon and the Latin families, as also the Lithuanian, the Persian, the Armenian, the Georgian—belongs to the great Indo-European, or Aryan, branch. . . .
>
> Like all other languages, the Russian has adopted many foreign words: Scandinavian, Turkish, Mongolian and, lately, Greek and Latin. But notwithstanding the assimilation of many nations and stems of the Ural-Altayan or Turanian stock which has been accomplished in the course of ages by the Russian nation, her language has remained remarkably pure. It is striking indeed to see how the translation of the Bible which was made in the ninth century into the language currently spoken by the Moravians and the South Slavonians remains comprehensible, down to the present time, to the average Russian. Grammatical forms and the construction of sentences are indeed quite different now. But the roots, as well as a very considerable number of words, remain the same as those which were used in current talk a thousand years ago. . . .

At the present time, the Russian language (the Great-Russian) is remarkably free from *patois*. Little-Russian, or Ukrainian, which is spoken by nearly 15,000,000 people,[1] and has its own literature—folklore and modern—is undoubtedly a separate language, in the same sense as Norwegian and Danish are separate from Swedish, or as Portuguese and Catalonian are separate from Castilian or Spanish. White-Russian, which is spoken in some provinces of western Russia, has also the characteristics of a separate branch of the Russian, rather than those of a local dialect. As to Great-Russian, or Russian, it is spoken by a compact body of nearly eighty million people in northern, central, eastern, and southern Russia, as also in northern Caucasia and Siberia. Its pronunciation slightly varies in different parts of this large territory; nevertheless the literary language of Pushkin, Gogol, Turgenev, and Tolstoy is understood by all this enormous mass of people. The Russian classics circulate in the villages by millions of copies, and when, a few years ago, the literary property in Pushkin's works came to an end (fifty years after his death), complete editions of his works—some of them in ten volumes—were circulated by the hundred-thousand, at the almost incredibly low price of three shillings (75 cents) the ten volumes; while millions of copies of his separate poems and tales are sold now by thousands of ambulant booksellers in the villages, at the price of from one to three farthings each. Even the complete works of Gogol, Turgenev, and Goncharov, in twelve-volume editions, have sometimes sold to the number of 200,000 sets each, in the course of a single year. The advantages of this intellectual unity of the nation are self-evident.[2] [*Prince Kropotkin*]

Some more specific attributes of the Russian language that contribute to the difficulty of a translation from Russian into another language (rather than from that language into Russian—which, according to Kropotkin and Dostoevsky, is less arduous) are pointed out in an article by Sidney Monas, a scholar to whom we are indebted for many translations from the Russian.

Most nouns in English are neuter in gender. A few exceptions remain in which the feminine or masculine gender adheres to a common noun. We

---

[1]Prince Kropotkin delivered his lectures in 1915. Since that time the population and reading public in Russia has more than quadrupled.
[2]From *Ideals and Realities of Russian Literature*, by Prince Kropotkin. Reprinted by permission of the publisher, Alfred A. Knopf, Inc.

refer, for example, to a ship or to the moon as *she*. In general, however, the English noun is genderless. Not so with the Russian noun.

Russian like many European languages retains a strong feeling for the gender of nouns. The days of the week are personified according to their endings; Friday is feminine and Thursday masculine, and a whole iconography depends on these attributes. In Russian families, the dropping of a fork at dinner presages the arrival of a female guest, and of a knife a male; because *fork* is feminine and *knife* masculine. This presents a simple, but often not easily soluble, problem for translators. Pasternak's first well-known book of poems, for example, is called *My Sister Life* (*life* is feminine in Russian—and *death,* too) which does not jar in English, though perhaps it loses some of its dash. But in German *life* is neuter, and in Czech, which, like Russian, retains a vivid animism, the translator goes wild because *life* is masculine. That Russian is an agglutinative[1] language invests it with further "magical" possibilities that often pose a problem of tone or intensity, if not of meaning, for the translator. *Snow* for example (*sneg,* masculine) can be turned into a *snow-maiden* (*snegurochka,* feminine) by the addition of a few simple suffixes (including a diminutive and a feminine ending) without any joints awkwardly perceptible to the ear or eye.[2] [*Sidney Monas*]

EXERCISE: A number of English words can be made into masculine and feminine nouns by adding the suffixes *–ess* for feminine nouns and *–or* or *–er* for masculine nouns (as in *act, actress,* and *actor*). Compile a list of such words. Then compile a list of English nouns whose gender is indicated only when the personal pronoun *he* or *she* is substituted for the noun.

Monas goes on to discuss the peculiarities of the Russian verb, which— like verbs in many languages—is very difficult to translate.

The Russian verb is not very good at expressing *relationships* in time. For example, the English sentence: "By the time I shall have been there, he will not yet have arrived," would be very

---

[1]*agglutinative:* characterized by a process of word formation described in the following sentence of the extract.

[2]From "Boian and Iaroslavna: Some Lyrical Assumptions in Russian Literature" by Sidney Monas from *Craft and Context of Translation: A Critical Symposium,* edited by William Arrowsmith and Roger Shattuck. (Published by University of Texas Press and Doubleday Anchor Editions.) Reprinted by permission of the author and editors.

difficult to translate accurately into Russian. On the other hand, Russian verb forms possess unmatched resources for rendering the precise nature of a movement, its frequency and duration, in a compressed way. A Russian friend of mine, as a joke, once composed a participle, a single word, which has to be rendered in English as "He who makes a practice of making fresh starts on projects involving a limited amount of beating." This practically unpronounceable word is a monster, granted—*perezapobivyvyvushchii*—but there it is.

It has been said of Tolstoy that he could endow even animals with individuality. Perhaps the most memorable example of this is the scene of the hunt in *War and Peace* in which not only the rabbit, but each of the hounds pursuing it, has a distinct character. The artistic means used to accomplish this is the precise use of verbs and verb forms which say a great deal in little space, permitting accuracy of perception without slowing down the pace of the story. Aylmer Maude's rendering of this scene into English is a kind of *tour de force* of translation. Nothing quite like it had ever been done in English; it is a touchstone of his merit as a translator.[1]
[*Sidney Monas*]

EXERCISE: Linguists tell us that there are only two tenses in English verb forms—past and nonpast. Yet Sidney Monas says that the English verb expresses very fine time differences. It does this by using a number of auxiliaries with the main verb form. Think of several other examples in addition to Mr. Monas's example of the fine divisions of time made possible by the addition of auxiliaries to a main verb form. What difficulty do you suppose this flexibility of English auxiliaries would present to a translator trying to render English into Russian?

Kinds of Translations

With all their pitfalls, however, translations are here to stay. Translators, in attempting to establish for readers channels of communication between two different languages, have several choices open to them. Jean Paris, a teacher of French literature particularly interested in the problems of translating French and English poetry, describes the two polar positions—that of rendering a slavishly "literal" transcription of the text and that of making an extremely free translation, one more true to the language of the reader than to the actual words used by the writer:

[1]*Ibid.*

In one of his remarkable fictions, Jorge Luis Borges tells of a certain Pierre Ménard whom we could regard as the ideal translator. Not only is he mad enough to devote his whole life to a single book—namely *Don Quixote*—but this work he painfully tries to rewrite in Spanish, with the very same words, sentences and order as in Cervantes. No one will ever go further. And we may well wonder if Borges has not the right to call him the [author of the *Quixote*]. In the same way, with his odd kind of wit, the Argentinian writer relates the drama of a geographer obsessed by an ever-increasing need for precision, who draws larger and larger maps until finally they become as great as the country itself and cover it entirely.

These stories are meant to point out the traditional limit of translation, that is, the original. How close we can get to it is a problem which torments, or should torment, all translators. But it is a naive question, for we may choose various ways of reproducing the work, according to its elements. The most common, and also the most unaesthetic, is the mere transcription of the "meaning." The rationalist translator is satisfied when he has expressed what he believes to be "the ideas of the author," with a minimum of misinterpretations. Furthermore, he may be tempted to repeat the sounds or rhythm of the text, regardless of its precise signification. . . .

The problem is this: does not the transforming of a written work from one language to another utterly alter its character? And, in performing this metamorphosis, does not the translator commit, if not a sacrilege, at least an offense against art and spirit?

Until now, translation has fluctuated between two limits, which are also its negations: extreme freedom and extreme slavery. The former is to literature what parody is to theater—and the best, or rather the worst example of it is certainly Ducis's versions of Shakespeare's plays. Not only did this "honnête homme" take the liberty to add or cut some lines or to alter whole scenes, to change the names of the characters and rebaptize them according to the allegoric tradition, but he also forced the most subtle rhythms of blank verse into the stiff corset of the alexandrine.[1] Naturally, the result was anything but Shakespearean, and it is surprising that such piracy could have flourished on French stages until the first World War. But should we call it a piracy? Transla-

---

[1] *alexandrine:* a poetic line consisting of six iambic feet.

tion had not yet discovered the notion of "alterity," and the copy remains so far from the original that we may rather think Ducis made use of Shakespeare as Shakespeare himself made use of Bandello or Belleforest.

Perhaps an interesting parallel could be drawn here between literature and painting. It does not seem that painters were ever obsessed by our problems with translation, although copying the old masters was for a long time an essential part of their apprenticeship. But the fact that a painter has to be a copyist before becoming an artist encourages him to see only in the original an opportunity of discovering his own genius. So we may be struck by the liberties he allows himself. We may be struck for instance, by Degas's copy of Mantegna's *Crucifixion,* where the expression is definitely sacrificed to composition; or by Van Gogh's version of Delacroix's *Le Bon Samaritain,* which is certainly more concerned with problems of color and movement than with the psychological tone of the scene....

... But it is also true that some other painters, and great painters, sometimes approached the problem of imitation in an almost scholarly spirit. Rubens is certainly the best example of this fidelity; his copies of Van Scondrel's *Portrait of Paracelsus* and Titian's *Rape of Europa* show how much he tried to forget his personal genius and to render the original as accurately as possible—a fact which we may well regret.

Now, when the translator imitates Rubens and keeps too closely to the text, we reach the other pole of translation, mere mechanical reproduction, a genre which is to real translation what a photograph is to a portrait. It belongs to the positivist tradition, which still prevails in many universities, and provides us with those incredible bilingual books, where beside the verse of Milton or Coleridge we find the stalest, flattest, and most unprofitable *ersatz.* To be sure, these translations are accurate to a degree, but this accuracy concerns only the meaning and practically never the spirit of the work. The reader feels only too grateful when he is allowed, here and there, to catch a glimpse of the author's genius....

... It is difficult enough in this perspective for a novel to keep its aesthetic value, but for poetry, such interpretation results in complete nonsense, as it tends to reduce a poem to a logical arrangement of words, and a clear meaning, which is precisely what the poet wants to keep obscure.

What, then, should be done? If we turn our back on the original, we may produce monstrous fantasies à la Ducis, but if we are overwhelmed with respect, we can also betray the beauty, the nuance.[1] [*Jean Paris*]

The solution Jean Paris offers is that the translator become an artist in his own right and that the act of translation become an act of creation rather than mere imitation.

> The most current error which has impaired the spirit of translation is the belief that one must necessarily imitate the written text....
>
> ... The translator has to work in his own language exactly as the poet did in his, putting forth the same effort to organize the same images and to shape similar rhythms. The result may sometimes prove disappointing, but in this regard translation ceases to be a minor genre and becomes an equivalent of a genuine creation.
>
> I would go even further. Thus understood, translation may sometimes be more difficult than poetry itself. The translator must retrace the initial intuition, the root of the work; he must devote his whole intelligence and sensitivity to the research of what may have been, for the poet, a mere illumination, a gift from the gods. Then, having worked out the core of the poem, having rebuilt the spiritual process according to its numerous elements, he has, finally, to go to more trouble than the artist himself; he must pass from this construction to the concrete, written expression, and with no freedom whatsoever, try desperately to adjust every word, every line, every single cadence to the transcendental model. When this effort is carried out satisfactorily, the translation may be considered as an equivalent of the original, and becomes in its turn another facet of the form, another facet which may even be able to modify, sharpen, and deepen the first one.[2] [*Jean Paris*]

In sharp contrast to Paris's position, which favors the creativity of the translator, his freedom as an artist in his own right, Vladimir Nabokov — a well-known novelist who is also a translator of Russian into English — takes the floor in favor of very literal translation. The following excerpt is taken from Nabokov's foreword to his own translation of one of the first great Russian novels, Lermontov's *A Hero of Our Time*.

[1]From "Translation and Creation" by Jean Paris from *Craft and Context of Translation: A Critical Symposium,* edited by William Arrowsmith and Roger Shattuck. (Published by University of Texas Press and Doubleday Anchor Editions.) Reprinted by permission of the author and editors.

[2]*Ibid.*

The experienced hack may find it quite easy to turn Lermontov's Russian into slick English clichés by means of judicious omission, amplification, and levigation[1]; and he will tone down everything that might seem unfamiliar to the meek and imbecile reader visualized by his publisher. But the honest translator is faced with a different task.

In the first place, we must dismiss, once and for all, the conventional notion that a translation "should read smoothly," and "should not sound like a translation" (to quote the would-be compliments, addressed to vague versions, by genteel reviewers who never have and never will read the original texts). In point of fact, any translation that does *not* sound like a translation is bound to be inexact upon inspection; while, on the other hand, the only virtue of a good translation is faithfulness and completeness. Whether it reads smoothly or not depends on the model, not on the mimic.

In attempting to translate Lermontov, I have gladly sacrificed to the requirements of exactness a number of important things — good taste, neat diction, and even grammar (when some characteristic solecism[2] occurs in the Russian text). The English reader should be aware that Lermontov's prose style in Russian is inelegant; it is dry and drab; it is the tool of an energetic, incredibly gifted, bitterly honest, but definitely inexperienced young man. His Russian is, at times, almost as crude as Stendhal's French; his similes and metaphors are utterly commonplace; his hackneyed epithets are only redeemed by occasionally being incorrectly used. Repetition of words in descriptive sentences irritates the purist. And all this, the translator should faithfully render, no matter how much he may be tempted to fill out the lapse and delete the redundancy.

When Lermontov started to write, Russian prose had already evolved that predilection for certain terms that became typical of the Russian novel. Every translator becomes aware, in the course of his task, that, apart from idiomatic locutions, the "From" language has a certain number of constantly iterated words which, though readily translatable, occur in the "Into" language far less frequently and less colloquially. Through long use, these words have become mere pegs or signs, the meeting places of mental associations, the reunions of related notions. They are tokens of

---

[1] *levigation:* making smooth, polished.
[2] *solecism:* violation of grammatical rules.

sense, rather than particularizations of sense. Of the hundred or so peg words familiar to any student of Russian literature, the following may be listed as being especial favorites with Lermontov:

zadúmat'sya	To become pensive; to lapse into thought; to be lost in thought.
podoytí	To approach; to go up to.
prinyát' vid	To assume an air (serious, gay, etc.). Fr. *prendre un air*.
molchát'	To be silent. Fr. *se taire*.
mel'kát'	To flick; to flicker; to dart; to be glimpsed.
neiz'yasnímïy	Ineffable (a Gallicism).
gíbkiy	Supple; flexible. Too often said of human bodies.
mráchnïy	Gloomy.
prístal'no	Intently; fixed; steadily; steadfastly (said of looking, gazing, peering, etc.).
nevól'no	Involuntarily. Fr. *malgré soi*.
on nevól'no zadúmalsya	He could not help growing thoughtful.
vdrug	Suddenly.
uzhé	Already; by now.

It is the translator's duty to have, as far as possible, these words recur in English as often, and as irritatingly, as they do in the Russian text; I say, as far as possible, because in some cases the word has two or more shades of meaning, depending on the context. "A slight pause," or "a moment of silence," for instance, may render the recurrent *minuta molchan'ya* better than "a minute of silence" would.

Another thing that has to be kept in mind is that in one language great care is taken by novelists to tabulate certin facial expressions, gestures, or motions that writers in another language will take for granted and mention seldom, or not at all. The nineteenth-century Russian writer's indifference to exact shades of visual color leads to an acceptance of rather droll epithets condoned by literary usage (a surprising thing in the case of Lermontov, who was not only a painter in the literal sense, but saw colors and was able to name them); thus in the course of *A Hero* the faces of various people turn purple, red, rosy, orange, yellow, green and blue. A romantic epithet of Gallic origin that occurs four times in the course of the novel is *tuslaya blednost', paleur mate,* dull (or lusterless) pallor. In "Taman," the delinquent girl's face is covered with "a dull pallor betraying inner agitation." In "Princess Mary," this phenomenon occurs three times: a dull pallor is spread over Mary's face when she accuses Pechorin of disrespect; a dull pallor is spread over Pechorin's face revealing "the traces of painful insomnia"; and just before the duel, a dull pallor is spread over Grushnitski's cheeks as his conscience struggles with his pride.[1] [*Vladimir Nabokov*]

Although Nabokov was speaking of Lermontov's writing, what he has said about color shadings also applies to Turgenev. Note, for instance, examples in any of the stories by Turgenev of the repetitive and finely differentiated descriptions of colors.

An editor who has worked on several translated masterpieces believes that the question of literal, or free, translation is relative to the nearness in time and linguistic similarity of the original language to the language and culture of the translation.

> The question of literal accuracy has been long and fruitlessly debated. It is essentially meaningless. The translator, if only for his own convenience, will try for as much literal accuracy as is consistent with his purpose of transmitting his author's meaning as accurately as possible in a style that corresponds as closely as possible to the original....
>
> ... A translator's most essential business, and his most exciting activity, is a traffic in meaning. A moment comes in the translation of any important passage in any significant book when the author's intent hangs naked in the translator's mind. It has shed its original clothes and has not yet found new ones. The translator, a little like Edna St. Vincent Millay's Euclid, looks on meaning bare....
>
> Communication—that is the purpose and the delight of translation. "This is something I admire so much," says the translator, "something I find so profound, so beautiful, so piercing that I must make you understand and admire it too, even though you,

---

[1] From the Foreword from *A Hero of Our Time* by Mikhail Lermontov, copyright © 1958 by Vladimir and Dmitri Nabokov. Reprinted by permission of Doubleday & Company, Inc.

through some inadvertence, have neglected to learn the language in which it is written. Let me show you how it goes."

This is a healthy impulse, very similar, on a different level, to the urge to share a good story. It is healthier, for instance, than the solipsistic belief that you alone fully understand Shakespeare and that therefore *you* must be the author of his plays. But it is harder to carry out than the telling of an anecdote. The difficulty increases in proportion to the literary excellence of the work, the degree to which its form and content are forever wedded. At the top of the scale, all authorities agree, translation becomes impossible. (Translators are the first to assent to this proposition, if they have not already signed an affidavit that *all* translation is impossible.) Moritz Haupt put the matter quite clearly: "Do not translate: translation is the death of understanding. The first stage is to learn to translate; the second to see that translation is impossible."[1] [*Denver Lindley*]

And now that you understand what the problems of translations are, try your hand at translations from the Russian into English.

Putting Yourself in the Translator's Place

How, you ask, translate from Russian into English if Russian is unfamiliar to you? You can't, of course, but you *can* participate in a little experiment or two that may help give you the feel of being a translator. Here is a descriptive passage from Turgenev's "Bezhin Lea," as it appears in the Cyrillic alphabet.

БЕЖИН ЛУГ

Был прекрасный июльский день, один из тех дней, которые случаются только тогда, когда погода установилась надолго. С самого раннего утра небо ясно; утренняя заря не пылает пожаром: она разливается кротким румянцем. Солнце—не огнистое, не раскаленное, как во время знойной засухи, не тускло-багровое, как перед бурей, но светлое и приветно

---

[1]From "The Editor's Problem" by Denver Lindley from *Craft and Context of Translation: A Critical Symposium,* edited by William Arrowsmith and Roger Shattuck. (Published by University of Texas Press and Doubleday Anchor Editions.) Reprinted by permission of the author and editors.

лучезарное—мирно всплывает под узкой и длинной тучкой, свежо просияет и погрузится в лиловый ее туман. Верхний, тонкий край растянутого облачка засверкает змейками; блеск их подобен блеску кованого серебра.... Но вот опять хлынули играющие лучи,—и весело, и величаво, словно взлетая, поднимается могучее светило. Около полудня обыкновенно появляется множество круглых высоких облаков, золотисто-серых, с нежными белыми краями. Подобно островам, разбросанным по бесконечно разлившейся реке, обтекающей их глубоко прозрачными рукавами ровной синевы, они почти не трогаются с места; далее, к небосклону, они сдвигаются, теснятся, синевы между ними уже не видать; но сами они так же лазурны, как небо: они все насквозь проникнуты светом и теплотой. Цвет небосклона, легкий, бледнолиловый, не изменяется во весь день и кругом одинаков; нигде не темнеет, не густеет гроза; разве кое-где протянутся сверху вниз голубоватые полосы: то сеется едва заметный дождь. К вечеру эти облака исчезают; последние из них, черноватые и неопределенные, как дым, ложатся розовыми клубами напротив заходящего солнца; на месте, где оно закатилось, так же спокойно, как спокойно взошло на небо, алое сиянье стоит недолгое время над потемневшей землей, и, тихо мигая, как бережно несомая свечка, затеплится на нем вечерняя звезда. В такие дни краски все смягчены; светлы, но не ярки; на всем лежит печать какой-то трогательной кротости. В такие дни жар бывает иногда весьма силен, иногда даже «па́рит» по скатам полей; но ветер разгоняет, раздвигает накопившийся зной, и вихри-круговороты—несомненный признак постоянной погоды—высокими белыми столбами гуляют по дорогам через пашню. В сухом и чистом воздухе пахнет полынью, сжатой рожью, гречихой; даже за час до ночи вы не чувствуете сырости. Подобной погоды желает земледелец для уборки хлеба.

A literal translation of this paragraph, as faithful to the original as possible, goes something like this:

> It was a beautiful July day, one of those days which happen only then, when the weather has been unchanged for a long time. From the very earliest morning the sky is clear; the morning sunrise does not blaze like a fire, it spreads out in a gentle pinkness. The sun—not burning, not molten, as it is during a period of torrid

drought, not murkily crimson, as it is before a storm, but bright and invitingly radiant—peacefully swims up from under a thin and long cloud, freshly shines out and is plunged in its lilac haze. The upper thin edge of the elongated little cloud sparkles like snakes; their gleam resembles the gleam of beaten silver. . . . But here again gushed the playful rays—and gaily, and grandly, as if flying, rises the mighty luminary. About midday usually appears a mass of round, high clouds, golden-gray, with tender white edges. Like islands, scattered over an endless flooding river, flowing around their deep translucent sleeves of an even blue, they almost don't move from their place; further off, toward the horizon, they move, crowd together, the blueness between them is already not to be seen; but they themselves are as azure as the sky: they are penetrated through with light and warmth. The color of the heavens, light, pale-lilac, doesn't change all day and is everywhere the same; nowhere does it darken, does it thicken as for a storm; though here and there stretch from above downward bluish stripes, sowing hardly noticeable rain. Toward evening these clouds disappear; the last of them, blackish and indefinite, as smoke, lie down in rosy puffs opposite the setting sun; at the place, where it has just disappeared just as calmly as it rose in the sky, a scarlet radiance stands for a short time over the darkening earth, and softly twinkling, as a carefully carried candle, begins to burn on it the evening star. On such days all the colors are softened; clear, but not brilliant; on everything lies the stamp of a kind of a touching meekness. On such days the heat is sometimes very strong, sometimes even "steams" over the slopes of the fields; but the wind drives away, disperses the accumulated heat, and whirlwinds—a sure sign of settled weather—in tall white columns travel along the roads through the plowland. In the dry and clean air smelling of wormwood, harvested rye and buckwheat; even an hour before nightfall you don't feel the dampness. Similar weather wishes the farmer for harvesting grain. [*Translated by Joseph Glus*]

Now try your hand at writing a smoother, freer version—one that seems more "English" while at the same time maintaining the accuracy of the descriptive details. Compare your version with that of another student in your class. At what points do differences occur? Can you explain why these particular words or expressions cause difficulty?

Next, read these three versions of the same passage—all written by professional translators, the first being the version that appears in this book.

BEZHIN LEA

It was a beautiful July day; one of those days which occur only when the weather has been unchanged for a long time. From early morning the sky is clear and the sunrise does not so much flare up like a fire as spread like a mild pinkness. The sun—not fiery, not molten, as it is during a period of torrid drought, not murkily crimson as it is before a storm, but bright and invitingly radiant—peacefully drifts up beneath a long, thin cloud, sends fresh gleams through it and is immersed in its lilac haze. The delicate upper edge of the long line of cloud erupts in snaky glints of light: their gleam resembles the gleam of beaten silver. But then again the playful rays break out—and as if taking wing the mighty sun rises gaily and magnificently. About midday a mass of high round clouds appear, golden-gray, with soft white edges. They move hardly at all, like islands cast down on the infinite expanses of a flooding river which flows around them in deeply pellucid streams of level blue; away toward the horizon they cluster together and merge so that there is no blue sky to be seen between them; but they have themselves become as azure colored as the sky and are pervaded through and through with light and warmth. The light, pale-lilac color of the heavens remains the same throughout the day and in all parts of the sky; there is no darkening anywhere, no thickening as for a storm, though here and there pale-blue columns may stretch downward, bringing a hardly noticeable sprinkling of rain. Toward evening these clouds disappear. The last of them, darkling and vague as smoke, lie down in rosy mistiness before the sinking sun. At the point where the sun has set just as calmly as it rose into the sky, a crimson glow lingers for a short time over the darkened earth, and, softly winking, the evening star burns upon the glow like a carefully carried candle. On such days all the colors are softened; they are bright without being gaudy; everything bears the mark of some poignant timidity. On such days the heat is sometimes very strong and occasionally even "simmers" along the slopes of the fields. But the wind drives away and disperses the accumulated heat, and whirling dust storms—a sure sign of settled weather—travel in tall white columns along roads through the plowland. The dry pure air is scented with wormwood, harvested rye, and buckwheat. Even an hour before nightfall you can feel no dampness. It is just such weather that the farmer wants for harvesting his grain.[1]

And next, a translation by Charles and Natasha Hepburn:

BEZHIN MEADOW

It was a beautiful July day, one of those days which come only after long spells of settled weather. From the earliest morning the sky is clear; the dawn does not blaze and flame, but spreads out in a gentle blush. Instead of the flaming incandescence that goes with sultriness and drought, or the dark crimson that precedes the storm, the sun has a bright and friendly radiance, as it swims peacefully up from behind a long, narrow cloud, shines out briskly, and then veils itself in the lilac-colored mist. The tenuous upper edge of the spreading cloud sparkles with a serpentine brilliance, like that of beaten silver. But now the dancing beams come shooting out again—and gaily, grandly, as if on wings, the mighty luminary emerges. About midday there usually appears a multitude of high, round clouds, golden-gray, with edges of tender white. Like islands, scattered across a boundless and brimming river, which surrounds them with deep, translucent expanses of an even blueness, they scarcely stir; farther off, toward the horizon, they concentrate, crowd together, there is no more blueness to be seen between them; but the clouds themselves are of the same azure as the heaven, they are penetrated through and through with light and warmth. The color of the horizon, a pale and floating lilac color, remains unchanged the whole day, and uniform all around; there is no darkening or deepening to foretell a storm; sometimes, here and there, there are bluish shafts falling down, betokening the passage of a hardly perceptible shower. Toward evening, these clouds vanish; the last of them, blackish and vague as smoke, lie with a pink curling face turned to the setting sun; over the place where it disappears, as quietly as it rose into the heavens, a scarlet radiance stands for a while over the darkening earth, and, trembling gently, like a carefully carried taper, the evening star begins to burn. On such days, all colors are softened; they are clear, but not brilliant; they are tinged with a

---

[1] From "Bezhin Lea" from *Sketches From a Hunter's Album* by Ivan Turgenev, translated by Richard Freeborn. Published in England by Penguin Books Ltd. and reprinted with their permission.

gentleness that is somehow touching. Such days may be scorching-hot, and the steam may rise from the sloping fields; but the wind disperses and breaks up the accumulated sultriness, and whirlwinds—sure sign of settled weather—march in tall white pillars along the tracks across the plowland. In the dry, clean air there is a smell of wormwood, of rye-harvest, and of buckwheat; even an hour before nightfall you feel no dampness. This is the weather that the husbandman needs to gather in his crop.[1]

And finally, a translation by Bernard Guerney:

BEZHIN MEADOW

It was a splendid day in July, one of those days which occur only during a long spell of good weather. Since earliest morning the sky is clear; the dawn glow does not flare like a conflagration —it diffuses itself like a gentle blush. The sun is not fire, is not incandescent, as it is during a sultry drought, nor is it a dull purple, as before a storm, but bright and affably radiant; it floats upward peacefully from under a narrow and lengthy cloud, sends its fresh radiance through it, and then plunges into its lilac haze. The thin upper rim of the distended cloudlet begins to coruscate with little snakes of light: their gleam is like the gleam of wrought silver. But now the playful beams have again gushed forth—and blithely and majestically, as if it were winging upward, the mighty luminary comes up.

About noontime a host of round, lofty clouds appears, aureately gray, rimmed with soft whiteness. Like islands scattered over a river in infinite flood that runs around them in deeply transparent channels, they hardly budge; farther on, toward the sky's rim, they move near to one another, they huddle; there is no longer any blue to be seen between them, but they themselves are of the same azure as the sky; all of them are shot through and through with light and warmth. The hue of the horizon, ethereal, pale lilac, does not change throughout the day and is uniform all around; nowhere is there a thunderstorm darkling, gathering, save that here and there streaks of pale blue may extend downward: a barely noticeable drizzle, this, being sown upon the earth. Toward evening these clouds vanish; the last of them, rather black and of indeterminate form, like smoke, lie down in roseate swirls against

---

[1] From "Bezhin Meadow" from *A Sportsman's Notebook* by Ivan Turgenev, translated by Charles and Natasha Hepburn. Reprinted by permission of The Viking Press, Inc.

the setting sun; at the spot where it has set, as calmly as it had risen in the sky, a ruby-red aura lingers for the brief while over the darkened earth and, gently flickering, like a candle solicitously borne along, the evening star will come to a soft glow against it.

On such days all pigments are softened, they are bright yet not vivid; an impress of some touching mildness lies upon all things. On such days the heat can, at times, be quite intense — occasionally it even steams along the slopes of the fields; but the wind scatters, sunders the accumulated sultriness, and whirlwinds (an indubitable sign of a long spell of good weather) wander in towering white pillars on their rounds over the roads, across plowed land. The dry and pure air is filled with the odors of wormwood, of reaped rye, of buckwheat; even at the hour before nightfall you feel no dampness. It is weather such as this that the husbandman longs for to gather in his grain.[1]

Which of the three translations seems the most literal? Which is the freest? Support your answers by referring to specific passages and expressions in each of the versions.

To make a more exact comparison of the three with your own "translation" and with the extremely literal translation by Joseph Glus, list for each of the following expressions from the literal rendering, the equivalent from any of the three translations that seems closest to the literal version; then list the freest, most "English" translation. Indicate by an initial (F, H, or G) which translator wrote each version. Compare your own version with the others for closeness to the most literal or to the smoothest and freest.

LITERAL TRANSLATION

1. "one of those days which happen only then, when the weather has been unchanged"
2. "the morning sunrise does not blaze like a fire"
3. "—not burning, not molten . . . but bright and invitingly radiant"
4. "The upper thin edge of the elongated little cloud sparkles like snakes"
5. "rises the mighty luminary"
6. "islands . . . flowing around their deep translucent sleeves of an even blue, they almost don't move from their place"

[1]From "Bezhin Meadow" from *The Hunting Sketches* by Ivan Turgenev, translated by Bernard Guilbert Guerney, copyright © 1962 by Bernard Guilbert Guerney. Reprinted by permission of The New American Library, Inc., New York.

7. "the blueness between them is already not to be seen"
8. "here and there stretch from above downward, bluish stripes"
9. "the last of them, blackish and indefinite, as smoke, lie down in rosy puffs"
10. "a scarlet radiance"
11. "and softly twinkling, as a carefully carried candle, begins to burn on it the evening star"
12. "Similar weather wishes the farmer for harvesting grain."

Which of the words in the title—*lea* or *meadow*—seems more natural to you?

Reproducing Speech in Writing

Translating straight prose is difficult, but trying to reproduce speech is even harder because of the dialectal nature of all speech. Dialect, as you probably know, refers not only to geographical differences in speech but also to the personal idiosyncrasies of speech that we all exhibit, as well as to cultural and familial and other "group" language variations. In speaking, syntactical patterns are not as deliberately chosen as they are in writing, nor does the speaker censor his word choice so deliberately. The speaker, however, has other means of conveying his message, means often more informative than words. Gestures, changes in tone, pitch, or stress, and other such "paralinguistic" means are all methods of communicating. If the speaker observes that his audience is not following him, he immediately attempts to backtrack and find other ways to get his message across. The writer who imitates speech tries to capture the flavor of a character's speech without actually duplicating it word for word. He attempts to indicate by a word or two the level of a language or the particular dialect of the speaker, and he includes a few interruptions or asides, some reversals and hesitations, to convey the manner of the speaker.

The following passages of dialogue are taken from the same story as the preceding descriptive prose excerpts. Read them, compare them, and make specific comparisons as indicated in the list of expressions (see page 412) that follows the final excerpt.

The Russian version:

—Ну, и что ж ты, так и видел домового?

—Нет, я его не видал, да его и видеть нельзя,—отвечал Ильюша сиплым и слабым голосом, звук которого как нельзя более соответствовал выражению его лица,—а слышал... Да и не я один.

—А он у вас где водится?—спросил Павлуша.

—В старой рольне.

—А разве вы на фабрику ходите?

—Как же, ходим. Мы с братом с Авдюшкой в лисовщиках состоим.

—Вишь ты—фабричные!...

—Ну, так как же ты его слышал?—спросил Федя.

—А вот как. Пришлось нам с братом Авдюшкой, да с Федором Михеевским, да с Ивашкой Косым, да с другим Ивашкой, что с Красных Холмов, да еще с Ивашкой Сухоруковым, да еще были там другие ребятишки; всех было нас ребяток человек десять—как есть вся смена; но а пришлось нам в рольне заночевать, то есть не то чтобы этак пришлось, а Назаров, надсмотрщик, запретил, говорит: «Что, мол, вам, ребяткам, домой таскаться; завтра работы много, так вы, ребятки, домой не ходите». Вот мы остались и лежим все вместе, и зачал Авдюшка говорить, что, мол, ребята, ну, как домовой придет?... И не успел он, Авдей-от, проговорить, как вдруг кто-то над головами у нас и заходил; но а лежали-то мы внизу, а заходил он наверху, у колеса. Слышим мы: ходит, доски под ним так и гнутся, так и трещат; вот прошел он через наши головы; вода вдруг по колесу как зашумит, зашумит; застучит, застучит колесо, завертится; но а заставки у дворца-то спущены. Дивимся мы: кто ж это их поднял, что вода пошла; однако, колесо повертелось, повертелось да и стало. Пошел тот опять к двери наверху, да по лестнице спускаться стал, и этак спускается, словно не торопится; ступеньки под ним так даже и стонут.... Ну, подошел тот к нашей двери, подождал, подождал—дверь вдруг вся так и распахнулась. Всполохнулись мы, смотрим—ничего.... Вдруг, глядь, у одного чана форма зашевелилась, поднялась, окунулась, походила, походила этак по воздуху, словно кто ею полоскал, да и опять на место. Потом у другого чана крюк снялся с гвоздя да опять на гвоздь; потом будто кто-то к двери пошел, да вдруг как закашляет, как заперхает, словно овца какая, да зычно так.... Мы все так ворохом и свалились, друг под дружку полезли.... Уж как же мы напужались о ту пору!

—Вишь как!—промолвил Павел.—Чего ж он раскашлялся?

—Не знаю; может, от сырости.

Все помолчали.

The literal translation:

"Well, and what (emphatic particle), so you saw a (little person, ghost, brownie, elf, goblin)?"

"No, I didn't see him, and to see him is impossible," answered Ilyusha in a hoarse and weak voice, the sound of which was impossible to be more suited to the expression on his face. "I heard ... and I wasn't the only one."

"And where at your place does he stay?" asked Pavlusha.

"In the old rolling-room."

"And can it be you go to the factory?"

"How (emphatic particle), we do. We with my brother Avdyushka work as glazers."

"So you—are factory workers! ..."

"Well, so how (emphatic word) did you hear him?" asked Fedya.

"Like this. It happened to us with my brother Avdyushka, and with Fyodor from Mikheyev and Squinting Ivashka and the other Ivashka from the Red Hills, and yet Ivashka from Sukhorukov, and still there were other boys; altogether there were about ten of us—so was the whole shift; so it happened to us to spend the night in the rolling-room, that is, it wasn't that it happened, but Nazarov, the overseer, forbid: 'Why, I say, to you, to you boys, homeward traipsing; tomorrow there is work aplenty, so you, boys, homeward don't go." So we stayed and all lay down together, and started Avdyushka to speak, what, I say, boys, well, if the (little person, ghost, etc.) comes? ... And he didn't succeed, Avdey, to finish speaking, when suddenly somebody over our heads started walking; so we were lying below, and he started walking above, by the wheel. We listened, the floorboards under him bend so, and creak so, here he passes over our heads; the water suddenly beside the wheel starts to ripple so, ripple; the wheel starts to knock and knock, starts turning, but the gates of the Keep are lowered. We wonder: who (emphatic particle) raised them that the water started; anyway, the wheel turned, turned and then stopped. He started again towards the door above, and down the stairway he began, and so descends, as if not hurrying; the steps under him even groan. ... Well, he came up to our door, waited, waited—the door suddenly burst open. We started, look—nothing. ... Suddenly, look, at one of the tubs a net began to rustle, arose, dropped and went back and forth in the air, as if someone were stirring it, and then again to its place. Then by another vat a hook came off its nail and back on the nail; and then as if someone toward the door started, and suddenly started coughing so, bleating so, just like some sort of sheep, and so loud. . . . We all so in a heap fell together, one under another we crawled. . . . Already so (emphatic particle) we were terrified at that time!

"So how!" said Pavel, "Why (emphatic particle) he started coughing?"

"I don't know; possibly from the dampness."

All were silent for a while. [*Translated by Joseph Glus*]

Now try your hand at writing an idiomatic "Americanized" translation of this passage that would represent the speech of unschooled teenagers today.

Next, compare the Freeborn, Hepburn, and Guerney translations:

"So you actually did see one of them little people, did you?"

"No, I didn't see him, and you can't really see him at all," answered Ilyusha in a weak, croaky voice which exactly suited the expression on his face, "but I heard him, I did. And I wasn't the only one."

"Then where does he live around your parts?" asked Pavlusha.

"In the old rolling-room."

"D'you mean you work in the factory?"

"Of course we do. Me and Avdyushka, my brother, we work as glazers."

"Cor! So you're factory workers!"

"Well, so how did you hear him?" asked Fedya.

"It was this way. My brother, see, Avdyushka, and Fyodor Mikheyevsky, and Ivashka Kosoy, and the other Ivashka from Redwold, and Ivashka Sukhorukov as well, and there were some other kids as well, about ten of us in all, the whole shift, see — well, so we had to spend the whole night in the rolling-room, or it wasn't that we had to, but that Nazarov, the overseer, he wouldn't let us off, he said: 'Seeing as you've got a lot of work here tomorrow, my lads, you'd best stay here; there's no point in the lot o'you traipsing off home." Well, so we stayed and all lay down together, and then Avdyushka started up saying something about 'Well, boys, suppose that goblin comes?' and he didn't have a chance, Avdey didn't, to go on saying anything when all of a sudden over our heads someone comes in, but we were lying down below, see, and he was up there, by the wheel. We listen, and there he goes walking about, and the floorboards really bending under him and really creaking. Then he walked right over our heads and the water all of a sudden starts rushing, rushing through the wheel, and the wheel goes clatter, clatter and starts turning, but them gates of the Keep are all lowered. So we start wondering who'd raised them so as to let the water through. Yet the wheel turned and turned, and then stopped. Whoever he was, he went back to the door upstairs and began coming down the stairway, and down he came, taking his time about it, and the stairs under him really groaning from his weight.... Well, so he came right up to our door, and then waited, and then waited a bit more—and then that door suddenly burst open, it did. Our eyes were poppin' out of our heads, and we watch—and there's nothing there.... And suddenly at one of the tubs the form started moving, rose, dipped itself and went to and fro just like that in the air like someone was using it for swilling, and then back again it went to its place. Then at another tub the hook was lifted from its nail and put back on the nail again. Then it was as if someone moved to the door and started to cough all suddenlike, like he'd got a tickle, and it sounded just like a sheep bleating.... We all fell flat on the floor at that and tried to climb under each other—bloody terrified we were at that moment!"

"Cor!" said Pavlusha. "And why did he cough like that?"

"Search me. Maybe it was the damp."

They all fell silent.[1] [*Richard Freeborn*]

* * *

"Well, so you really did see the ghost?"

"No, I never saw him; you can't see him," answered Ilyusha, in a low, hoarse voice, the sound of which went to perfection with the expression on his face. "But I heard him, and I wasn't the only one, either."

"But where does he walk?" asked Pavel.

"In the old paper mill."

"Do you really work in a paper mill?"

"Certainly we do. My brother Avdyushka and I work in the pulping-rooms."

[1] From "Bezhin Lea" from *Sketches From a Hunter's Album,* Penguin Books.

"I say!—factory workers! . . ."

"Well, how was it that you heard him?" asked Fedya.

"It was like this. It happened to me and my brother Avdyushka and Fyodor from Mikheyev and Squinting Ivashka and the other Ivashka, the one from Red Hills, and Ivashka from Sukhorukov, too—and other boys were there as well; there were about ten of us boys altogether—the whole shift, all complete. Well, it happened that we spent the night in the paper mill, that is, it didn't happen just like that, but Nazarov, the foreman, kept us in: 'What's the use,' he says, 'of you traipsing all the way home, my lads? There's plenty of work tomorrow, so you'd better not go home.' So we stayed and all lay down together, and Avdyushka started off and said: 'Well, boys,' he says: 'suppose the ghost comes? . . .' and he didn't finish saying it, Avdyushka didn't, when suddenly somebody started walking, over our heads; we were lying downstairs, and he was walking up aloft by the wheel. We listen: he walks, the planks fairly bend and creak beneath him; he passes over our heads; suddenly the water beside the wheel begins to ripple and ripple and knock and knock against the wheel and the wheel begins to turn; and yet the flanges of the water-inlet were closed. We were amazed—who could have lifted them and let the water through? Anyway the wheel turned and turned and then stopped. Then *he* walked again, to the door up aloft, and started coming downstairs, down he came, as if there was no hurry about it; the treads fairly groaned beneath him, too; well, he came up to our door, and waited and waited—then suddenly the door flew wide open. We started up, and stared—there was nothing there. Suddenly, look, the net on one of the tubs began to move, came up, dropped and floated and floated about in the air as if someone was stirring with it, then went back to its place. Then the hook of another tub came off its nail, then went back on the nail again. Then someone seemed to go to the door and suddenly started coughing and sort of bleating, like a sheep, and quite loud, too. . . . We had all fallen into a heap together and each of us was trying to get underneath the others. . . . Goodness, how scared we were!"

"Just fancy!" said Pavel. "Why did he start coughing, though?"

"I don't know; perhaps because of the damp."

They were all silent for a while.[1] [*Translated by Charles Hepburn and Natasha Hepburn*]

[1] From "Bezhin Meadow" from *A Sportsman's Notebook,* Viking Press.

* * *

"Well, now, and did you see the hobgoblin for fair?"

"No, see him I didn't, and besides you can't see him," Ilyusha answered in a hoarse and weak voice, the sound of which could not possibly have been more in keeping with the expression on his face. "But I did hear him. And I weren't the only one that did."

"And whereabouts in your place does he keep himself?" asked Pavlusha.

"In the old rolling-room."

"Why, do you people go to the paper mill?"

"Sure, why not? My brother Avdiushka and me work there as glossers."

"So that's how. You're factory hands!"

"Well, how come you to hear him?" asked Fedya.

"Why, this is how. It so happened that my brother Avdiushka and me, and Fedor Mihievsky, and Ivashka Kossoi, and also another Ivashka, the one from Red Knolls, and still another Ivashka, by the name of Suhorukii, and there was other lads there, too — there must have been ten boys of us altogether — the whole shift, for the matter of that — well, it so happened we had to pass the night in that rolling-room; that is, we didn't really have to, only Nazarov, the overseer, forbade us to go home: 'What's the use of you boys traipsing home,' says he, 'there's a lot of work tomorrow, so don't you go home, lads.' So we stayed on there, and we was lying together, all of us, and Avdiushka he gets to talking: 'Well, now, lads, what if the hobgoblin was to come?' And hardly had he done saying this — Avdei, I mean — when all of a sudden somebody starts walking around over our heads; we was lying down below, see, but he starts walking around up there, near the wheel. We hear him walking around, the boards simply bending, simply cracking under him; there, he'd passed right over our heads — when all of a sudden the water starts making a noise, and what a noise! going over the wheel; the wheel begins knocking, knocking, and turning — and yet the gates to the castle, now, was all lowered. So we wondered who could ever have raised them, so that the water had started flowing. However, that wheel turned and turned a while, and then stopped.

"Then he began walking about again, making for the door upstairs, and then he started down the stairs, and he was coming down them stairs like he weren't in no hurry at all; the steps was just simply groaning under him. Well, he walked right up to our door, hung around and hung around there for a bit—and then all of a sudden that door pops right open. All startled, we was; then we look—and there's nothing there. Suddenly, when we give another look, there was the form at one of the vats moving, rising, dipping; it kept going like that for a while through the air, as if someone was rinsing it, and then got back to its place again. Then at another vat the hook took off of its nail and fell back on the nail again; after that it seemed like somebody had walked over toward the door, and all of a sudden he got such a coughing spell, such a sneezing fit, like a sheep or something, and that so loud and all. We just tumbled down in a heap, all of us, trying to crawl under one another. Lord, but we was plenty scared that time!"

"So that's how it was!" Pavel commented. "But what made him go off in a coughing spell like that?"

"Don't know; maybe it was the damp."

They were all silent for a space.[1] [*Bernard Guerney*]

Compare the way the following expressions from the literal translation are rendered in the three different versions. How did you translate them in your idiomatic Americanized version? How do you account for the differences?

1. "little person . . . elf"
2. "the sound of which was impossible to be more suited to the expression on his face"
3. "And where at your place does he stay?"
4. "And can it be you go to the factory?"
5. " 'Why, I say, to you, to you boys, homeward traipsing; tomorrow there is work aplenty, so you, boys, homeward don't go.' "
6. "We all so in a heap fell together, one under another we crawled."

How is the "emphatic particle" (that is, the particle used for emphasis) translated in each version? Judging from the varying translations, what definition can you give of an emphatic particle? Do you know of any such construction in English?

What is your reaction to the following comment from Denver Lindley's article "The Editor's Problem"?

> Slang or colloquialisms of all kinds are a recurrent problem. It would be a great convenience to follow George Moore's counsel and use a neutral language. Unfortunately, this often entails too

[1] From "Bezhin Meadow" from *The Hunting Sketches*, New American Library.

great a loss, especially in the modern novel where dialogue is so extensively used for purposes of characterization. . . .

. . . Some middle way is needed—and can usually be found in the use of hints and light touches rather than the heavy hand. This, like so many problems of translation, is in theory insoluble and in practice a subject for compromise, depending upon the ingenuity, taste, and, above, all, the ear of the translator.[1] [*Denver Lindley*]

What examples from the translation you have just read support Denver Lindley's statements? Which of the translations seem to be least "tasteful"? Why?

How are the proper names of the boys translated in each version? What effect would the Anglicizing of the names (as, for example, "Paulie" or "little Paul" for "Pavlusha") have on the foreign flavor that the retention of the Russian proper names suggests?

As a final exercise in evaluating your skill in detecting awkward translations, skim the various stories and critical materials you have read to locate at least five examples of translations that are obviously awkward or too literal.

[1]From *Craft and Context of Translation: A Critical Symposium.*